EXPRESSIONS OF

MW00860868

How did Ancient Greek express the fact that an event occurred at a particular time, for a certain duration, or within a given time frame? The answer to these questions depends on a variety of conditions – the nature of the time noun, the tense and aspect of the verb, the particular historical period of Greek during which the author lived – that existing studies of the language do not take sufficiently into account. This book accordingly examines the circumstances that govern the use of the genitive, dative, and accusative of time, as well as the relevant prepositional constructions, primarily in Greek prose of the fifth century BC through the second century AD, but also in Homer. While the focus is on developments in Greek, translations of the examples, as well as a fully glossed summary chapter, make it accessible to linguists interested in the expression of time generally.

COULTER H. GEORGE is Associate Professor of Classics at the University of Virginia. The author of *Expressions of Agency in Ancient Greek* (Cambridge University Press, 2005), he has also taught at Rice University and was a Junior Research Fellow at Trinity College, Cambridge. His research interests include the syntax of the Greek verb, particles and prepositions, and contact phenomena between Greek and the other languages of the ancient Mediterranean.

CAMBRIDGE CLASSICAL STUDIES

General editors

R. L. HUNTER, R. G. OSBORNE, M. MILLETT, D. N. SEDLEY,
G. C. HORROCKS, S. P. OAKLEY, W. M. BEARD

EXPRESSIONS OF TIME IN ANCIENT GREEK

COULTER H. GEORGE
University of Virginia

CAMBRIDGE
UNIVERSITY PRESS

CAMBRIDGE
UNIVERSITY PRESS

University Printing House, Cambridge CB2 8BS, United Kingdom

One Liberty Plaza, 20th Floor, New York, NY 10006, USA

477 Williamstown Road, Port Melbourne, VIC 3207, Australia

314-321, 3rd Floor, Plot 3, Splendor Forum, Jasola District Centre, New Delhi - 110025, India

79 Anson Road, #06-04/06, Singapore 079906

Cambridge University Press is part of the University of Cambridge.

It furthers the University's mission by disseminating knowledge in the pursuit of education, learning and research at the highest international levels of excellence.

www.cambridge.org
Information on this title: www.cambridge.org/9781108820257

© Faculty of Classics, University of Cambridge 2014

This publication is in copyright. Subject to statutory exception and to the provisions of relevant collective licensing agreements, no reproduction of any part may take place without the written permission of Cambridge University Press.

First published 2014
First paperback edition 2020

A catalogue record for this publication is available from the British Library

Library of Congress Cataloging in Publication data
George, Coulter H., 1976–
Expressions of time in ancient Greek / Coulter H. George.
pages cm. – (Cambridge classical studies)
Includes bibliographical references and indexes.
ISBN 978-1-107-00394-1 (hardback)
1. Greek language – Grammar. 2. Greek language – Tense. 3. Space and time in language. 4. Greek language – Syntax. I. Title.
PA369.G46 2014
485–dc23
2013043958

ISBN 978-1-107-00394-1 Hardback
ISBN 978-1-108-82025-7 Paperback

Cambridge University Press has no responsibility for the persistence or accuracy of URLs for external or third-party internet websites referred to in this publication, and does not guarantee that any content on such websites is, or will remain, accurate or appropriate.

CONTENTS

Acknowledgments   *page* vi
List of abbreviations and other conventions   viii

1 Expressions of time: an introduction   1

2 Expressions of time in Thucydides   60

3 Expressions of time: style, genre, and diachrony   118

4 Expressions of time in Biblical Greek   245

5 A retrospective: going back in time   283

6 Summary   304

Bibliography   316
General index   323
Index of Greek words   325
Index of passages discussed   327

ACKNOWLEDGMENTS

As the final task in writing a book on Ancient Greek expressions of time, it seems fitting to take a diachronic look at its genesis. After all – if I may indulge in Vendlerian language – writing it was certainly a (durative) Accomplishment rather than an (instantaneous) Achievement; in any case, I'm very much relieved it didn't remain an (atelic) Activity! Work on it began during 2006–07, my last year as a Junior Research Fellow at Trinity College, Cambridge, and I remain extremely grateful to the Master and Fellows for providing an environment so conducive to research. In particular, I should like to record my lasting gratitude to Eric Handley, who, ever since my very first supervision at Cambridge (Greek prose composition, October 1995), had nothing but the kindest words of encouragement and advice. As always, the camaraderie of the E Caucus of the Faculty of Classics meant that there was ample opportunity for lively discussion of sundry linguistic issues.

The academic year 2010–11 was also fruitful, when, thanks to a Sabbatical Fellowship from the American Philosophical Society as well as Sesqui Leave and a summer stipend from the University of Virginia, I was able to give the project my undivided attention. During the first two months, I enjoyed a delightful stay at the Vrije Universiteit Amsterdam, and it is a true pleasure to thank the classicists there, especially my academic host, Rutger Allan, for their warm hospitality. The rest of the year, equally idyllic, was spent in Cologne, where José Luis García Ramón was tremendously welcoming and helpful. It was a great pleasure to have the chance to bounce ideas off Daniel Kölligan, and I am also very grateful to Lena Wolberg for helping me navigate bureaucratic matters.

Throughout all of this, I have enjoyed the unceasing support of the University of Virginia's Department of Classics, under the outstanding leadership of our chair John F. Miller. The remarkable collegiality of the entire department, faculty and graduate student alike, makes it impossible to single out individuals for thanks, but it would be remiss of me not to note a special debt of gratitude to the Wednesday Night Bachelors for their unstinting bonhomie. Eleanor Dickey read substantial sections of the book in draft, and both Rutger Allan and James Clackson read it in its entirety. Their kind attentions have saved me from numerous errors and infelicities; those that remain are to be attributed, of course, to my own intransigence. Once again, it has been a pleasure to work with Michael Sharp and Cambridge University Press on the book's production; Miranda Bethell's attentive work was invaluable in ensuring consistent style throughout and I am very grateful for Annette Copping's sharp-eyed scrutiny of the proofs. Finally, there is the matter of the peripatetic existence that went hand-in-hand with writing the book: work on it took place in four countries – or even five, counting the Christmas vacation I spent in my grandfather-in-law's study in Uberlândia combing the New Testament for temporal expressions. My wife Daphne deserves praise and thanks for being a constant, loyal companion throughout it all.

Charlottesville

ABBREVIATIONS AND OTHER CONVENTIONS

The abbreviations of Greek authors and works are those found in LSJ, except for names of the books of the Bible, which are abbreviated as in *The New Oxford Annotated Bible: New Revised Standard Version* (1991), p. xxvii. Papyri are abbreviated as in the Duke Databank of Documentary Papyri (http://www.papyri. info/browse/ddbdp/). An ellipsis within round brackets indicates that words may or may not occur between the words on either side.

BDAG	F. W. Danker (2000) *A Greek–English Lexicon of the New Testament and Other Early Christian Literature*, 3rd edn. Chicago.
BDB	F. Brown, S. Driver, and C. Briggs (1906) *Hebrew and English Lexicon*. Boston, MA.
BDR	F. Blass and A. Debrunner (2001) *Grammatik des neutestamentlichen Griechisch*, 18th edn., rev. F. Rehkopf. Göttingen.
BHS	K. Elliger and W. Rudolph (1987) *Biblia Hebraica Stuttgartensia*. Stuttgart.
Classen–Steup	J. Steup (ed.) (1963) *Thukydides, erklärt von Johannes Classen*, 8 vols., 6th edn. (Vols. 1–2); 4th edn. (Vols. 3–8). Berlin.
DMic.	F. Aura Jorro (ed.) (1985–93) *Diccionario micénico*, 2 vols. Madrid.
Hansen–Quinn	H. Hansen and G. M. Quinn (1992) *Greek: An Intensive Course*, 2nd rev. edn. New York.
Joüon–Muraoka	P. Joüon (1993) *A Grammar of Biblical Hebrew*, repr. with corrections, tr. and rev. T. Muraoka. Rome.

Kühner–Gerth	R. Kühner and B. Gerth (1898) *Ausführliche Grammatik der griechischen Sprache*, Part II, Vol. 1. Hanover and Leipzig.
LSJ	Liddell, H. G., and R. Scott (1940) *Greek–English Lexicon*, rev. H. S. Jones, 9th edn. Oxford, 1996.
MT	Masoretic Text
Rahlfs	A. Rahlfs and R. Hanhart (2006) *Septuaginta*, 2nd edn. Stuttgart.
Schwyzer–Debrunner	E. Schwyzer and A. Debrunner (1950) *Griechische Grammatik*, Vol. 2. Munich.
TLG	*Thesaurus Linguae Graecae* (Irvine, CA, 1972–)

I

EXPRESSIONS OF TIME: AN INTRODUCTION

When students are taught how the genitive and dative are used in temporal expressions in Greek, they are traditionally told that the genitive, on the one hand, is used when the noun in question indicates the time *within which* the event described by the verb takes place. The dative, on the other, is used when the noun expresses the time *at which* the event occurs.[1] I have never found this a satisfactory distinction. Although it makes sense in diachronic terms, if we view the genitive of time as partitive in origin, it is far from evident that it accounts for the synchronic reality. If we want to translate into Greek the sentence 'The next day, he held an assembly', are we supposed to use the genitive or the dative? On the basis of the English glosses, one could argue for either: we could imagine the assembly taking place either on the day or during some period within the day. But Xenophon uses τῇ ὑστεραίᾳ eighty-nine times, whereas τῆς ὑστεραίας occurs not a single time in his work:

(1) ταύτην μὲν οὖν τὴν ἡμέραν αὐτοῦ ἔμειναν, **τῇ δὲ ὑστεραίᾳ** Ἀλκιβιάδης ἐκκλησίαν ποιήσας παρεκελεύετο αὐτοῖς ὅτι ἀνάγκη εἴη καὶ ναυμαχεῖν καὶ πεζομαχεῖν καὶ τειχομαχεῖν

They remained there that day, and the next day Alcibiades summoned an assembly and advised them that it was necessary to fight sea-battles, land-battles, and sieges (X. *HG* 1.1.14)

However, if an event takes place at night, Xenophon is far more likely to use the genitive than the dative of νύξ. For instance, if we consider only examples where the verb modified by the temporal expression is an aorist that describes a punctual event, there are thirty-four examples of the genitive of time, but only one of the

---

[1] See e.g. Smyth (1920: §1444–7, §1539–43), Hansen–Quinn: 147, Mastronarde (1993: 73, 220).

dative of time.² Nor, in this instance, is the genitive of time limited to a single fossilized form of the individual lexeme, νυκτός, although this does account for fourteen of the examples: another seventeen times it occurs as τῆς νυκτός, twice as τῆς ἐπιούσης νυκτός, and once as ταύτης τῆς νυκτός. Thus, with example (1) contrast:

(2) τῇ δ' αὐτῇ ἡμέρᾳ ἔτυχον καὶ οἱ Ἀθηναῖοι δειπνοποιούμενοι ἐν ταῖς Ἀργινούσαις … τῆς δὲ νυκτὸς ἰδὼν τὰ πυρά, καί τινων αὐτῷ ἐξαγγειλάντων ὅτι οἱ Ἀθηναῖοι εἶεν, ἀνήγετο περὶ μέσας νυκτός

And on the same day, the Athenians happened to be having dinner at Arginusae … And at night, when he (Callicratidas) saw the fires, and some people told him that it was the Athenians, he was going to put to sea around midnight (X. *HG* 1.6.27)

As in the first example, the temporal expression in question, together with δέ, introduces a new clause which contains first an aorist participle, then a main verb in the imperfect. Both expressions thus describe remarkably similar temporal configurations, yet the dative is chosen in one passage, the genitive in the other. That the standard grammars fail to account for such differences in distribution is the basic inadequacy that underlies their explanations of the genitive and dative of time.

Adding to the confusion is the uncertainty as to how to handle related prepositional uses like ἐν with the dative (henceforth ἐν⁺ᴰ). For example, in Kühner–Gerth it is remarked in the section on the genitive of time that the use of ἐν⁺ᴰ resembles that of the genitive (1898: 387), while in the section on the dative of time, the use of ἐν⁺ᴰ is described as, in effect, a modification of the simple dative (446). Nor is there any clarification in Schwyzer–Debrunner, where the account of ἐν⁺ᴰ simply follows that of Kühner–Gerth: "Einer Präposition bedarf [der Dativ Temporalis] auch in Prosa gewöhnlich nicht; ἐν wird in Prosa regelmäßig nur

---

² In all that follows, figures of this sort must be approached with some caution. There will be many times that it is impossible to assign, say, punctual as opposed to durative value to a particular passage, as such categories inevitably have imprecise boundaries. That said, in my discussion below of the criteria that I have used for classifying them, I will argue that, despite the fuzziness at the edges, the number of core examples that lie firmly in one category or another is sufficiently large that the overall impression given by such statistics should be reliable.

beigefügt, wenn betont werden soll, daß etwas *innerhalb* eines bestimmten Zeitraums stattfindet" (1950: 158–9). Yet while there certainly are passages where ἐν⁺ᴰ can resemble the genitive or dative of time, they are by no means interchangeable. If we look at the twelve examples of ἐν (τῇ) νυκτί in Xenophon, we might expect it to have approximately the same function as the genitive of time, for the comparison of (1) and (2) has already suggested that, with νύξ, there might be a lexical preference for the genitive of time. Yet only once is the construction with ἐν⁺ᴰ found with an aorist indicative describing what might be considered a punctual event, a use that accounts for over a third of the examples of the genitive of time. And even this one example is rather different from the prototypical uses of the genitive of time to mark aorist-tense punctual events:

(3) Οὐκοῦν καὶ ἐπειδὴ ὁ μὲν ἥλιος φωτεινὸς ὢν τάς τε ὥρας τῆς ἡμέρας ἡμῖν καὶ τἄλλα πάντα σαφηνίζει, ἡ δὲ νὺξ διὰ τὸ σκοτεινὴ εἶναι ἀσαφεστέρα ἐστίν, ἄστρα **ἐν τῇ νυκτὶ** ἀνέφηναν, ἃ ἡμῖν τῆς νυκτὸς τὰς ὥρας ἐμφανίζει . . . ;

Since the sun, being bright, distinguishes for us the hours of the day as well as everything else, but the night, because it is dark, is less clear, did they not cause the stars to shine at night, which show us the hours of the night?

(X. *Mem.* 4.3.4)

On the one hand, ἐν τῇ νυκτί, strictly speaking, modifies the aorist ἀνέφηναν, which can be understood as referring to the gods' creation of the stars, viewed as a single act of beneficence. On the other, two factors distinguish this example from the majority of comparable genitives of time. First, there is a difference in register: this passage comes from the conversational *Memorabilia*, whereas most of the punctual genitives of time are found in the more monological *Hellenica* and *Anabasis*. Second, there is a subtle difference in the event type described. While the action described by the verb is punctual in a narrow parsing of the construction, there remains a strong impression that the surrounding habitual presents – ὢν, σαφηνίζει, εἶναι, ἐστίν, ἐμφανίζει – have colored this clause as well, as if it were closer to τὰ ἄστρα τὰ ἐν τῇ νυκτὶ ὄντα ἀνέφηναν. The view that an event-type context of this kind might have encouraged the use of ἐν⁺ᴰ is supported by the nature of the other examples in Xenophon of ἐν (τῇ) νυκτί. The construction is

3

most often used in generalizing expressions of time that typically have a habitual element:[3]

(4) καὶ τὸ ταραχθῆναι δὲ **ἐν τῇ νυκτὶ** πολὺ μεῖζόν ἐστι πρᾶγμα ἢ ἐν τῇ ἡμέρᾳ καὶ δυσκαταστατώτερον

And confusion is a much greater problem at night than in daytime and also more difficult to put right (X. *Cyr.* 5.3.43)

This is not to say that ἐν⁺ᴰ and the genitive of time should at this point be definitively characterized as habitual and punctual respectively.

Not only is this tendency based solely on evidence from constructions with a single lexeme in a single author, but even here it is only a tendency, not an absolute. While we can say that ἐν (τῇ) νυκτί in Xenophon is never used in aorist constructions of the type 'in the night, X did Y', such as one comes across in historical writings, we must also concede that the genitive of time can intrude on the domain of the habitual constructions provisionally argued to be prototypical of ἐν⁺ᴰ:

(5) πονηρὸν γὰρ **νυκτός** ἐστι στράτευμα Περσικόν

For a Persian army is ineffective at night (X. *An.* 3.4.35)

Indeed, such passages are common enough that it is better not to view them as intrusions, but rather as yet another perfectly natural use of the genitive of time.[4]

From this brief survey[5] it should be clear that we are far from having a complete understanding of the subtle differences between the various Greek expressions of time. The chief aim of the following study is to refine our knowledge of these constructions, above all in Classical Attic prose, but also looking at post-Classical developments as well. For the most part, poetry has been excluded from consideration: after all, teasing out the nuances of the

---

[3] Other clear examples include *Smp.* 1.9 and *Cyr.* 5.3.37, in both of which a habitual reading is supported by the presence of ὅταν 'whenever', *Cyr.* 3.3.26, and *Cyn.* 11.4.

[4] That said, if we look closer, we can still find criteria to differentiate further between habitual constructions with the genitive of time and those with ἐν⁺ᴰ. Those with the genitive of time are likelier to occur in conjunction with ἡμέρας as a parallel expression, those with ἐν⁺ᴰ likelier to be used independently of ἡμέρα. But that even this difference is not absolute can be seen immediately by comparing examples (4) and (5).

[5] For a fuller discussion of the behavior of νύξ in Xenophon, including revisitation of these examples, see Chapter 3.

numerous individual temporal expressions requires a large number of diagnostic examples, in which like can be compared with like, making a relatively extensive and homogeneous prose corpus far more useful than that of Attic drama, let alone epic or lyric poetry. To put it in more concrete terms, we can come to more definite conclusions about the use of a word form like νυκτός in Xenophon, where it occurs 103 times, than in Homer, where it only occurs ten times, half of which are in the formulaic line-end νυκτὸς ἀμολγῷ. A further emphasis on the Hellenistic and early imperial periods also seemed important, as so much recent linguistic work on Greek has been concerned with the effect of bilingualism on the development of the language. In particular, there has been interest in the extent to which Latin has influenced Greek temporal expressions in Polybius and Appian on the one hand, and that to which Semitic has influenced Judeo-Christian Greek on the other.[6]

Accordingly, I have chosen eleven authors (or, in two cases, collections of texts) and, with *Thesaurus Linguae Graecae* (*TLG*) searches, gathered all the expressions of time that occur with a select number of lexemes in them. It has proven essential to study each author individually, as different idiosyncrasies come to the fore in examining a linguistic question as rooted in stylistics as this one. The texts fall into three groups: first, Classical authors (Thucydides, Xenophon, Plato, and Demosthenes, as well as Herodotus); second, post-Classical authors who should be free of Semitic influence[7] (Polybius, Diodorus, Plutarch, and Epictetus, together with a survey of the documentary papyri up to AD 150); third, Biblical texts (parts of the Septuagint and the whole of the New Testament). The first group

---

[6] For Latin influence on Greek prose in general, see Dubuisson (1979), De Rosalia (1991), and Rochette (2010: 291–3); for expressions of time in particular, see Langslow (2002: 43–4), Adams (2003: 507–8); for Appian, see Hering (1935: 34–41); for Josephus, see Ward (2007: 640–1); and for Polybius, see Dubuisson (1985: 238–9). For Semitic influence on the presence or absence of ἐν with datives, see Maloney (1981: 179–82); for Koine in general, see García Domingo (1979: 152–7).

[7] They may, of course, show interference from Latin (see Ch. 1 n. 6), but with the expansion of the Greek world in the Hellenistic period, not to mention the spread of Roman rule, it becomes increasingly difficult to find Greek texts that would *not* be subject to some sort of outside influence. In any case, it is profitable to examine which features occur only in this group, which occur only in the Judeo-Christian group, and which in both.

provides us with a starting point for understanding temporal constructions; the second group clarifies their diachronic development; and the last group reveals the extent to which they were affected by contact with Hebrew and Aramaic. Once this diachronic arc has been traced out, a better background is in place to consider the scanty evidence from Homer in a concluding chapter. For most of the authors,[8] the individual temporal lexemes whose constructions I have collected are, from the smallest to the largest unit, ὥρα, ἡμέρα, νύξ, μήν, θέρος, χειμών, ἔαρ, μετόπωρον and φθινόπωρον, ἔτος, ἐνιαυτός, and χρόνος. This is a wide enough range of words that the results of the study should not be skewed by the peculiarities of any one lexeme, but narrow enough that one can undertake a comprehensive investigation of every temporal expression in which they occur in the relatively extensive corpus outlined above.

But lest the findings that would result from such a study drown in a sea of data, there must first be a framework into which the various constructions can be sorted. Several different linguistic factors affect the author's choice of temporal expression, and in order to give intelligent answers to questions about the relative importance of these factors, it is necessary first to categorize them and, where appropriate, to define the technical terms that prove useful in sifting through them. There are three broad classes of factors that, within the work of a single author, trigger the use of one construction rather than another, one of which needs little explanation; the other two merit fuller comment.

First, the choice of temporal expression can be affected lexically by the noun that is at the heart of the construction (henceforth, 'time noun'). As examples of this we have the difference in treatment of τῇ ὑστεραίᾳ and τῆς νυκτός seen in (1) and (2) or the existence of a phrase like νύκτωρ τε καὶ μεθ᾽ ἡμέραν ('by night and by day'), where both nouns occur in parallel, but the two constructions are not only different from each other but also unlike the constructions found with any other noun: νύκτωρ is *sui generis*, and while μετά$^{+A}$ can occur in temporal expressions with other nouns, it denotes posteriority

---

[8] For some of the texts, discussion is restricted to the time nouns that have proven to be the most informative in distinguishing between the temporal uses of the genitive, dative, and ἐν: ἡμέρα, νύξ, μήν, θέρος, χειμών, ἔτος, ἐνιαυτός.

elsewhere. But while lexical factors are certainly one component in determining the choice of construction, they do not provide the whole answer, as a particular lexeme can occur in different constructions, which often have functions that can be clearly distinguished. While the textbook rules about the difference between the genitive and dative of time are confused, they are perfectly correct in characterizing the accusative of time as marking extent or duration.

Indeed, the most promising way of trying to explain the use of different constructions with a single time noun is to start with constructions that *do* seem to be understood, such as the accusative of time or the regular use of κατά$^{+A}$ in distributive expressions. In line with this, the second factor that will be considered in evaluating temporal expressions is the event type of the verb modified by the temporal expression, be it punctual, durative, or habitual, to name the three types that come up most often. There is of course great danger of terminological muddle here, and so much of the remainder of this first chapter aims both to clarify what exactly I understand these three terms to mean and to introduce the other parallel classifications that will be necessary to explain the data.

But while such considerations account for many of the differences between temporal constructions, there remains one more factor. In a detailed study of expressions of time in Thucydides, Jiménez has shown that there is a correlation between the modifiers of the time noun and the construction that is chosen. For example, the genitive of time is associated with the pronominal adjective αὐτός and modifiers that indicate posteriority, as in τοῦ ἐπιγιγνομένου θέρους (1998: 95). Accordingly, there will also be discussion of factors connected with the composition of the noun phrase before we come to the bulk of the data.

Event type

In assessing the motivation for the selection of a particular temporal construction, it will nearly always be necessary to assess the nature of the event whose temporal location is specified by the construction in question. This, as already mentioned, is the basis of what is probably the most indisputably correct observation on the behavior of these phrases: that the accusative of time is associated

7

with extent of time, or, in other words, with durative events. In this section, I will set forth a taxonomy of such event types that will be used to classify the actual examples of temporal expressions found in the corpus under investigation.

The ideal approach to identifying different event types should combine, first, the top-down and deductive, setting up criteria for various categories at the start and noting the differences in temporal expression to which they correspond, and, second, the bottom-up and inductive, gathering together the types of events that occur with a given temporal expression and determining what they have in common. The best starting point for the first task lies in the work of Vendler and his successors, setting up distinctions between durative and instantaneous actions, and between telic and atelic ones.[9] For the second task, we may most profitably begin with Xenophon: with the diversity of material in his works, from history to philosophical conversation, from treatises on hunting and horsemanship to the *Cyropaedia*, he has ample opportunity to use temporal expressions in a wider range of contexts than one would find in Thucydides or in Plato taken separately.

In practice, it will be seen that the Vendlerian terminology is not particularly helpful in its original conception. Instead it is necessary to modify it and add to it in order to have it serve the purpose of classifying expressions of time. On the whole, the modification is such that the terms shift from expressing philosophical categories of time and action to describing the author's functional-pragmatic aims. Thus, instead of speaking of an instantaneous event in purely objective terms, we can explain the data better by setting up a punctual category to label any event that the author wishes to present as a single point in the narrative without calling attention to the length of time during which the event took place. The reason

---

[9] See Vendler (1957), Comrie (1976: 41–51), Smith (1997: esp. 17–37). Telic actions are those that have an intrinsic endpoint, e.g. *arrive at a place*; atelic actions are those that can continue indefinitely, e.g. *walk slowly*. It is often noted that durative temporal expressions of the sort *for X days* can only occur with atelic predicates, limitative expressions of the sort *in X days* with telic ones; see e.g. Fanning (1990: 141–2), Napoli (2006: 33–4), Basset (2009: 205–7). Because of this interaction with aspect, Bhat, with examples from Kannada, goes so far as to call these adverbials aspectual, rather than temporal (1999: 60–1). For further general linguistic discussion of these adverbials, see also Binnick (1991: 300–10) and Wierzbicka (1993).

for this is simple. Greek speakers did not feel the need to use different temporal expressions for an objectively instantaneous event on the one hand (*That night he died*), and one that lasts for a period of time on the other (*That night they sailed to Corcyra*). Rather, difference in temporal expression depends more on whether the author aims to locate the event in a particular temporal framework (i.e. answer the question 'When?') or whether he aims to speak of the duration of the event (i.e. answer the question 'For how long?'). Often the durative expression (frequently found with μέν) will thus act as a sort of pause button, keeping the narrative suspended until a punctual expression (typically with δέ) sets the action in motion again: see example (1).

At this point, it will be convenient to list in a table the terms I will be introducing, together with brief descriptions of their distinguishing characteristics and a prototypical example of each (see Table 1); a more detailed discussion will follow.[10]

First, we must establish the scope of these terms. It would be incorrect to understand them solely with the verb because, under different circumstances, the same verb could be construed with two different types of temporal expressions: *That summer they sailed to Corcyra* (punctual), but *They sailed to Corcyra in three days* (limitative). Similarly, applying them exclusively to the adverbial

---

[10] As I have not included in this work any detailed consideration of terms that denote anteriority or posteriority to the time noun (such as μέχρι[+G], πρό[+G], or ἀπό[+G]), I have limited the following taxonomical discussion to event types in which the action of the verb takes place at some point or points during the time indicated by the time noun. To some extent, these labels correspond to those given in Binnick (1991: 307), but I prefer punctual to 'frame adverb', as the latter is too likely to conjure up the image of the genitive of time within which; and I prefer limitative to *Frist* adverbials, so as to use Latin roots consistently. While I recognize that 'punctual' may misleadingly suggest objectively instantaneous events, this is in my view a small price to pay in order to have a term that matches the basic role of these expressions in assigning events to a particular point in time, even when that point is comparatively protracted. One may compare the Greek aorist, which can be described as reducing the action of the verb, even a durative one, to a single point, insofar as that action is viewed from outside the event, rather than from inside it; see e.g. Fanning 1990: 97–8. Now, as Comrie notes of the perfective aspect, it is more accurate to say that it "reduces a situation to a blob," insofar as 'point' suggests an object without internal complexity (1976: 18) – but it is difficult to coin a suitable adjective from the limited derivational possibilities offered by 'blob'. Cf. also Klein's classification (1994: 149–50), which is not fine-grained enough for our purposes. The recent work of Devine and Stephens (2013: 22–6), which appeared too late to be incorporated into this discussion, uses "positional" and "container" for my punctual and limitative categories.

Table 1. *Event types*

Type	Description
punctual	single event; length of time not important *That night they sailed to Corcyra*
durative	single event; length of time important; event coextensive with length of time; can also be used with repeated events[a] *They stayed there for three days*
limitative	single (often, composite) event; length of time important; event restricted to point or points within the length of time *In three days, they captured two cities*
habitual	repeated events; unmarked (i.e. not distributive); often also **modal**, especially when paired with a contrastive phrase (*by day and by night*) *They go hunting at night*
distributive	repeated events; one-to-one correspondence between temporal expression and occurrence of event *They earn three obols a day*

Note: [a] See the discussion of example (1) in Chapter 3.

temporal expressions themselves is conceptually awkward, as their use is so closely connected with the nature of the relationship between the verb and the adverbial element: note for example the contrast between the durative and the limitative types, where the difference between *for three days* and *in three days* can best be understood as arising not from the three-day period as such, but rather from the correspondence between that period and the action of the verb. These terms should thus be seen as describing the combination of the temporal expression and the verb rather than either of the two constituents on its own.[11] That said, some verbs do gravitate to particular event types, as do some temporal expressions: as an example of the former, μένειν is almost exclusively found in durative constructions; as for the latter, κατά[+A] is, with a few notable

[11] Note that the Vendlerian categories also correspond more closely to the constellation of a verb with its predicates than to the verb in isolation: *they ran in the rain* is atelic, while *they ran to the store* is telic. Cf. Verkuyl (1972: 40–97), Comrie (1976: 45–6), and several of the chs. in Verkuyl et al. (2005).

exceptions, strongly associated with the distributive type. This being so, it will occasionally be convenient to refer to either a verb or an adverbial element as belonging to one of the event types: it should not cause undue confusion to say, for instance, that ἐν⁺ᴰ is typically limitative in a given author as terminological shorthand for spelling out that ἐν⁺ᴰ is typically used with verbs to form constructions that are of the limitative type.

The five event types divide into two main categories. First, there are three that refer to constructions in which a single particular event is expressed: punctual, limitative, and durative. Second, there are two that refer to constructions where a general observation is made about a recurring pattern: habitual and distributive. The former three are naturally more common in history, where the author's aim is frequently to give the chronology in which particular historical events occurred, the latter two more common in philosophy and didactic texts, which deal not so much in specific events as in ideas that are true under any circumstances. When Xenophon writes the following sentence, he is referring to a single factual historical event, and thus the construction falls into one of the first three event types, in this case the punctual:

(6) Θράσυλλος δὲ ἑβδόμῃ καὶ δεκάτῃ ἡμέρᾳ μετὰ τὴν εἰσβολὴν εἰς Ἔφεσον
ἀπέπλευσε

And on the seventeenth day after the attack, Thrasyllus sailed off to Ephesus
(X. HG 1.2.7)

When, however, of mothers generally he writes the following, he does not have any particular day and night in mind, but rather a sequence thereof, and the construction is a habitual one:

(7) καὶ τρέφει πολὺν χρόνον καὶ ἡμέρας καὶ νυκτὸς ὑπομένουσα πονεῖν

And she raises her child for a long time, enduring hard work both day and night (X. Mem. 2.2.5)

Note also that, while the difference frequently corresponds to a dichotomy between the historical and the philosophical, this is by no means always the case. While the punctual type is indeed rare in philosophy, there are plenty of occasions when a philosophical writer might wish to specify the extent of time a general action will take – hence πολὺν χρόνον in (7). Nor is the habitual type foreign to historical works:

(8) τὰς μὲν ἡμέρας ἐχίλου τοὺς ἵππους, τὰς δὲ νύκτας ἐγκεχαλινωμένοις ἐφυλάττετο

> By day he had the horses feed, by night he stood guard with them ready to ride (X. *An.* 7.2.21)

Let us now consider the distinguishing characteristics of the three single-event types. The easiest to understand are the **punctual** and the **durative**: as already noted, the former answers the question 'When did X take place?', while the latter answers the question 'For how long did X take place?' They can be illustrated with examples (9) and (10) respectively:

(9) καὶ ταύτῃ τῇ ἡμέρᾳ ... ἀπῆλθον οἱ βάρβαροι

> And that day the barbarians left (X. *An.* 3.4.18)

(10) ἐνταῦθα ἔμειναν ἡμέρας τρεῖς

> They remained there three days (X. *An.* 3.4.31)

In (9), the temporal expression simply tells when the action of the main verb took place, as is suggested by the presence of the demonstrative pronoun ταύτῃ; the length of time that the action took is not important. In (10), by contrast, the length of time *is* important, as can be seen from the modifier in the temporal expression, the cardinal number τρεῖς.

More elusive is the **limitative** category, as it shares features with both the punctual and the durative. Like the punctual type, it locates the event in time, and that event is often telic and expressed by an aorist verb; but like the durative type, the time expression is one of extent of time (often the noun of time is plural), rather than a pinpoint. The end result is that the limitative expression of time sets a temporal boundary and confines the action to a narrower point or set of points that lies within that boundary. Some concrete examples will be useful:

(11) ὁ μὲν δὴ Δερκυλίδας ταῦτα διαπραξάμενος καὶ λαβὼν **ἐν ὀκτὼ ἡμέραις** ἐννέα πόλεις, ἐβουλεύετο

> After accomplishing this and capturing nine cities in eight days, Dercylidas deliberated (X. *HG* 3.2.1)

Example (11) is a prototypical limitative expression. On the one hand, the verb is the aorist λαβών, and the action is telic: both common characteristics of punctual expressions.[12] On the other, there is an emphasis on the extent of the time during which the action took place that is more like a durative expression: note that, as in (10), the noun in the expression is modified by a cardinal number. The end result is a construction like (11) in which the extent of time demarcated in the temporal expression simply gives the endpoints between which the event or events described by the verb take place – unlike the durative expression, in which the action of the verb is continuous for the entire extent of time expressed by the temporal phrase. Often, as in (11), limitative constructions involve a verb that expresses a multiplicity of events (in this case the capture of nine different cities).[13] Another common limitative subtype is that in which only a single event is described, but the idea that the time frame provided by the temporal expression is a *limit* comes to the fore:

(12) οὐκ ἂν δύναιο μεῖον ἢ **ἐν ἓξ ἢ ἑπτὰ ἡμέραις** ἐλθεῖν πρὸς τὴν ἐμὴν οἰκίαν

You could not get to my house in less than six or seven days
(X. *Cyr.* 5.3.28)

Here the comparative μεῖον ἤ strongly suggests a limitative reading. Another feature that points to such a reading is the presence not just of a plural cardinal number, but also of εἷς:

(13) τοῦτ' οὖν, ἔφη, λέγεις ὡς καὶ ὁ σὸς πατὴρ **ἐν τῇδε τῇ μιᾷ ἡμέρᾳ** ἐξ ἄφρονος σώφρων γεγένηται;

Are you saying that, just so, your father has gone from being foolish to sensible over the course of this one day? (X. *Cyr.* 3.1.17)

In the chapters leading up to this passage, the king of Armenia has rebelled against the Medes, who at this point are ruled by Cyrus's uncle Cyaxares. Cyrus has trapped and caught the traitorous king,

---

[12] Cf. this punctual example (Th. 4.101.1): τοῦ δὲ Δηλίου ἑπτακαιδεκάτῃ ἡμέρᾳ ληφθέντος μετὰ τὴν μάχην ("And when Delium was captured on the seventeenth day after the battle").

[13] Note that the multiplicity of events one often finds in limitative expressions is different from that in habitual expressions in that it is a bounded multiplicity. Thus, in this case the capture of nine cities is viewed as a single whole that does not form part of a repeated pattern, as opposed to, say, a regular custom of having a meal at a particular time each day.

13

but, as it happens, the king's son Tigranes is an old friend of Cyrus's and begs him to spare his father's life. In particular, he has just argued that the extent to which subjects are sensible is of paramount importance in how they should be assessed by a ruler. In passage (13) Cyrus replies, questioning whether a single day would be sufficient for the king to learn such a lesson. The temporal expression, then, is limitative: a durative expression would imply an open-ended process that the king had been undertaking all day, whereas here there is the clear idea of a transition from one state to another; a punctual expression, though a grammatical alternative in this context, would have a different force to it – 'Did your father become sensible today?' – and would be unlikely to co-occur with μιᾷ.

Because both the punctual type and the limitative type generally occur with telic verbs (unlike the durative type[14]), there is the potential for overlap between the two when it is unclear whether the temporal expression is chiefly locating the action in time or providing the frame in some subset of which the action is to be considered to have taken place. Consider the following passage:

(14) καὶ πάντες δὲ οἱ στρατιῶται **ἐν ταύτη τῆ ἡμέρᾳ** πολλὰ τὰ ἐπιτήδεια ἐκ τῶν χωρίων ἐλάμβανον

And also all the soldiers were taking a lot of provisions from the countryside that day (X. *HG* 4.5.5)

The reader will perhaps have noticed that all the examples of limitative passages I have given so far have been constructions with ἐν[+D], and so here too it would be attractive to assign a limitative reading to the temporal expression. However, the noun phrase in the expression, consisting as it does solely of the definite noun with a demonstrative pronoun, is instead the sort of phrase we would expect in a punctual construction. The numbers are not large enough to be definitive, but it is nevertheless telling that the other

---

[14] That is to say, the verbs that occur with durative expressions are atelic if taken on their own: *They stayed there* is open-ended. The moment they occur with a temporal modifier (*They stayed there for three days*), the construction as a whole becomes telic as the adverb phrase sets a limit on the action of the verb.

five times one has the phrase ταύτῃ τῇ ἡμέρᾳ in an affirmative clause, it is in a punctual construction without the preposition.[15] That said, I believe one can salvage the limitative reading here by calling attention to the fact that the verb is an imperfect. Because the aspect of the verb does not present the action as a single unit that took place that day, but rather throws emphasis on the many different constituent acts that together make up the action as a whole, it is not implausible to see this example as limitative for the same reason as example (11), namely, that it depicts a multiplicity of events occurring within a given time frame. But while I think that a limitative reading can be upheld for (14), the more important point to take from it is that, at the boundaries between these categories, there are examples that could go either way. One is, to be sure, in danger of circular reasoning here: using the fact that a passage has a particular construction as evidence for classifying it as a particular event type, then using that classification as support for arguing that that construction has that event type as its primary function. Fortunately, this worry does not, in practice, present significant problems. On the whole, there are enough temporal expressions that fall clearly into one event type or another that one can provisionally assign functional values to the different constructions on the basis of this solid ground before investigating the passages that lie on the less secure borderlines.

The next task of definition lies in distinguishing between the two primary event types that refer to repeated events, the **habitual** and the **distributive**. The easiest way to understand the difference is to take the habitual as the unmarked member of the pair, and the distributive as an offshoot thereof. Contrast the following two examples, which I consider to be habitual and distributive respectively:

(15) κύκλῳ μὲν **νυκτὸς καὶ ἡμέρας** ἐφύλαττον περὶ τὰ βασίλεια ὁπότε ἐπὶ χώρας εἴη

> They stood guard in a circle around the palace night and day whenever he was in the area (X. *Cyr.* 7.5.68)

---

[15] These occur at *HG* 3.1.19, 5.3.1, *An.* 1.7.14, 3.4.18 (ex. (9)), 7.8.6. There are two more examples of ἐν ταύτῃ τῇ ἡμέρᾳ in negative clauses, but negative clauses have their own idiosyncrasies and will be treated separately below.

(16) κόπτων συνεχῶς τὴν χώραν οὐ προσῄει πλέον **τῆς ἡμέρας** ἢ δέκα ἢ δώδεκα σταδίων

> As he was constantly laying waste to the country, he did not advance more than ten or twelve stadia each day (X. *HG* 4.6.5)

In (15), the temporal expression simply describes an event as occurring regularly during the time in question: that is, ἡμέρας means approximately 'repeatedly during the day'. The same is also true of the expression in (16): once again, an event occurs repeatedly during the stated time. The difference is that (16) also conveys the idea that there is a one-to-one correspondence between the occurrence of the time noun and the action of the verb. This nuance can be rendered in English with phrases like *each day*, *every day*, *per day*, and in Greek is often emphasized with the use of the preposition κατά$^{+A}$, the pronominal adjective ἕκαστος, or both:[16]

(17) ἐπεὶ οὐκ ὀλίγα ἔστι **καθ᾽ ἑκάστην ἡμέραν** τοιαῦτα ὁρᾶν τε καὶ ἀκούειν

> For there's no small number of such things to see and hear every day (X. *Mem.* 4.2.12)

In turn, this one-to-one correspondence can be connected to a difference in the semantics of the time noun. In the habitual constructions, 'day' is understood as a generic concept whose chief semantic feature is its opposition with 'night'. Accordingly, as in (15), it often occurs contrasted or combined with that opposite, in which case the construction can additionally be labeled as **modal**, with the expression not so much specifying a time as a general circumstance: *by night* and *by day* are treated in effect as parallel options to, for example, *by land* or *by sea*.[17] In the distributive constructions, however, the time noun refers to particular 24-hour periods. Furthermore, as in (16), the distributive type often explicitly links a particular numerical amount with each occurrence of the relevant time noun. This arithmetical subtype of the distributive construction is especially common with the expression of monetary disbursements:

---

[16] For a useful introduction to distributive expressions in Herodotus and Attic prose, see Biraud (1994).

[17] For more on this term, see the discussion following examples (34) through (36) in Ch. 2. While the modal contrast of categories like 'night' and 'day' is most frequent with repeated events, those examples show that it can also occur with single events as well.

(18) ἣν ὀβολὸν ἕκαστος ἀτελῆ **τῆς ἡμέρας** προσφέρῃ

If each one yields a net of one obol per day (X. *Vect.* 4.23)

Again, there should be scope for overlap between the two categories, insofar as it might not always be clear whether or not the author intends to emphasize that, for every single unit of time, no more and no less than the action of the verb takes place. In practice, however, such borderline examples are even rarer here than at the boundary between the punctual and the limitative (cf. (14) above) because the distributive type is almost invariably marked by a clear grammatical marker like κατά$^{+A}$ or ἕκαστος, by the content of the clause, or by both.

A further complication in the classification of event types arises in clauses with negatives.[18] In a sentence of the type *They did not obtain favorable omens that day*, is one to treat the temporal expression as punctual, as one would in the corresponding affirmative sentence? Or should one consider it durative, as the introduction of the negative shifts the event from being something that took place at a particular point on the day (namely, the obtaining of favorable omens) to a state that lasted for the entire day (namely, that of failure to obtain favorable omens)? Or should it be labeled limitative, since it states a time frame during which the event did not come to pass? Again, this question is best answered by examining the constructions which Greek uses in such contexts. Consider the thirteen examples where Xenophon uses ἡμέρα in a negated temporal construction.[19] They fall into three groups. First, there are five examples with ἡμέρας, all conjoined with νυκτός, all of which are naturally considered habitual expressions, just as the analogous affirmative sentences would be:[20]

(19) εἰσὶ δὲ καὶ φίλαι μοι, αἳ **οὔτε ἡμέρας οὔτε νυκτὸς** ἀφ᾽ αὐτῶν ἐάσουσί με ἀπιέναι

And I too have some girlfriends, who don't let me leave them either by day or by night (X. *Mem.* 3.11.16)

---

[18] For other examples of the effect negatives can have on aspectual questions in Greek, see Fanning (1990: 174–8), Allan (2003: 190, esp. n. 333), Rijksbaron (2006a: 15–16) and Napoli (2006: 19). For the particular effect of negatives on temporal expressions, see Fillmore (1969: 112).

[19] I omit *Cyr.* 4.5.14 with πρὸ ἡμέρας, as I am not considering expressions with the idea of anteriority or posteriority.

[20] The other examples are at *HG* 7.5.19, *Smp.* 4.48, *Ap.* 31, and *Cyr.* 8.1.45.

17

When Xenophon's Socrates – quite the ladies' man – remarks that he has female friends who never let him go, the action of the verb, though negated, falls into the category of the repeated-event type. Accordingly, the temporal expression οὔτε ἡμέρας οὔτε νυκτός is a clear negative counterpart to the καὶ ἡμέρας καὶ νυκτός of (7), and there is no reason to classify this as anything other than a negative habitual construction.

Next, there are four examples with the dative of time, of which the most representative is the following:[21]

(20) καὶ ὁ Ξενοφῶν, ἐπεὶ οὐκ ἐγεγένητο τὰ ἱερὰ **ταύτη τῇ ἡμέρᾳ**, λαβὼν βοῦν ὑπὸ ἁμάξης

> And Xenophon, since the sacrifices had not turned out well that day, after taking an ox from a wagon (X. *An.* 6.4.25)

Here too it seems likely that the negative construction should be viewed as nothing other than the negative equivalent of the numerous punctual expressions using the dative of time with ἡμέρᾳ. Indeed, the fact that Greek does not treat such expressions as durative (even, as above, when modifying a pluperfect) can be seen rather neatly from the next example:

(21) ὁ δὲ Κοιρατάδας **τῇ μὲν πρώτῃ ἡμέρᾳ** οὐκ ἐκαλλιέρει οὐδὲ διεμέτρησεν οὐδὲν τοῖς στρατιώταις· **τῇ δὲ ὑστεραίᾳ** τὰ μὲν ἱερεῖα εἱστήκει παρὰ τὸν βωμὸν καὶ Κοιρατάδας ἐστεφανωμένος ὡς θύσων

> And, on the first day, Coeratadas did not obtain favorable sacrifices and did not apportion out any food to the soldiers. But on the next day, the sacrificial victims were standing by the altar, as was Coeratadas, garlanded in preparation for the sacrifice (X. *An.* 7.1.40)

The opposition between τῇ μὲν πρώτῃ ἡμέρᾳ and τῇ δὲ ὑστεραίᾳ is reminiscent of example (1), which also contains both a τῇ δὲ ὑστεραίᾳ clause as well as a preparatory μέν clause that refers to the previous day: ταύτην μὲν οὖν τὴν ἡμέραν αὐτοῦ ἔμειναν, τῇ δὲ ὑστεραίᾳ Ἀλκιβιάδης ἐκκλησίαν ποιήσας παρεκελεύετο αὐτοῖς. But the contrast between the durative accusative of time in (1) and the punctual dative of time in (21) provides further evidence that despite the potential for understanding the state of non-accomplishment of

---

[21] The other examples are at *HG* 4.8.36 (οὐδὲ τῶν ἱερῶν γεγενημένων αὐτῷ ἐκείνῃ τῇ ἡμέρᾳ), *An.* 1.7.17 (ταύτῃ μὲν οὖν τῇ ἡμέρᾳ οὐκ ἐμαχέσατο βασιλεύς) and 7.1.40 (ex. (21)).

the verbal action as lasting for the entire day, Greek instead treats such constructions in the same way as the corresponding affirmative statements and reduces that state to a single point at which the verbal action is considered to have failed to take place.

The final four examples of ἡμέρα in negative temporal expressions include three examples with ἐν^{+D} and one with the genitive of time (here plural, in contrast to the habitual expressions like (19) discussed above). All of these can be understood as negative examples of the limitative type, but as they are not as unified in nature as the negative habitual or negative punctual types, they are best considered individually. Take first the two examples from the *Anabasis*, which both come from the same section:

(22) ὅτι τῇ ἑνδεκάτῃ ἀπ' ἐκείνης ἡμέρᾳ πρότερον θυόμενος εἶπεν αὐτῷ ὅτι βασιλεὺς οὐ μαχεῖται **δέκα ἡμερῶν**, Κῦρος δ' εἶπεν· Οὐκ ἄρα ἔτι μαχεῖται, εἰ **ἐν ταύταις** οὐ μαχεῖται **ταῖς ἡμέραις**

Because eleven days earlier, when he (Silanus) had offered sacrifice, he told him (Cyrus) that the king would not fight during the next ten days, and Cyrus said, "Then he will not fight any more, if he won't fight during these days" (X. *An.* 1.7.18)

Again, we might expect durative constructions to be used in the two temporal expressions that I have translated with 'during', as the extent of the period of the absence of fighting is highlighted in both instances. The first example in particular could easily be rendered 'would not fight *for* the next ten days', that is, with the English construction most often associated with the accusative of extent of time. But instead of the accusative, we have in the first instance a genitive of time, δέκα ἡμερῶν, and in the second the prepositional construction ἐν ταύταις ταῖς ἡμέραις. Now consider how one would classify the affirmative counterparts to these clauses: a sentence such as *He will fight in the next ten days* contains a limitative expression – it sets up a time frame that has the extent of time one would associate with a durative expression, but then limits the action to a particular point within that time frame. As the genitive of time and ἐν^{+D} are both associated with limitative expressions, example (22) provides good evidence that a negative limitative expression should be classified no

19

differently from the corresponding positive. Consider now the final two examples:

(23) Ἀθηναίων γὰρ οὐδεὶς **ἐν ταύτη τῆ ἡμέρᾳ** οὐδενὸς σπουδαίου ἔργου τολμῆσαι ἂν ἅψασθαι

For none of the Athenians would dare to undertake any serious work on this day (X. *HG* 1.4.12)

(24) ὡς δὲ δῆλον ἐγένετο ὅτι οὐκ ἐξίοιεν οἱ πολέμιοι ἐκ τοῦ ἐρύματος οὐδὲ μάχην ποιήσοιντο **ἐν ταύτη τῆ ἡμέρᾳ**

But when it became clear that the enemy would not leave their stronghold and would not fight on this day (X. *Cyr.* 3.3.29)

Here, as with the discussion of (14), we approach the boundary between the limitative and punctual constructions. Just as in that affirmative example, here too there is little at first sight to differentiate punctual examples like (20) and (21) from (23) and (24), which we would like, on the basis of the use of ἐν^{+D}, to consider limitative: in all four passages, after all, an event is described as not taking place on a particular day. Nevertheless, one can detect a shade of difference that accounts for the use of ἐν in the latter two, and there are two ways of approaching it. First, there is the semantic observation that in the latter two examples, one could expand the clauses with an emphatic phrase such as 'None would dare to do this *at any point* on this day'. A similar expansion of (20) and (21) does not seem possible, as it would emphasize that there had been repeated attempts to obtain favorable sacrifices, which is not a reading supported by the context.[22] Second, there is a syntactic difference in that (20) and (21) are past-tense constructions (as are the other passages mentioned in note 21), while the phrases in (23) and (24) both modify verbs (the dynamic infinitive ἅψασθαι and the future optative ποιήσοιντο) that describe not something that had already failed to occur, but rather something that was going to fail to occur. The two observations fit together rather neatly: because they have not already taken place, potential

---

[22] The imperfect ἐκαλλιέρει in (21) can be taken to imply multiple sacrifices, but since the actual act of sacrifice is described in the preceding paragraphs with only the single verb ἐθύετο at the end of section 37, it is unlikely that Xenophon here wishes to stress repeated attempts to obtain favorable sacrifices.

events of the sort described in (23) and (24) cannot be pinned down as precisely as the actual events of (20) and (21), and thus a phrase like 'at any point' can be added to them without significantly changing the sense. And the ability to add such a phrase, together with the fact that the construction points forward to the future, coincides with the conditions for choosing a limitative expression rather than a punctual one. Indeed, over the course of this book, it will become clear that this constellation of features is a common one, with limitative constructions often triggered by futurity, negativity, or the combination of the two.

Of the four most common event types, the durative is left as the only one which does not occur in negative temporal expressions with ἡμέρα in Xenophon. This does not mean, however, that the category does not exist:

(25) ὁ δὲ Κῦρος **πολὺν μὲν χρόνον** οὐκ ἐσχόλαζε τοῖς τοιούτοις ὑπακούειν· ἐπεὶ δὲ ἀκούσειεν αὐτῶν, πολὺν χρόνον ἀνεβάλλετο τὴν διαδικασίαν

And Cyrus did not have leisure to listen to such men for a long time, and when he did hear them, he would defer the trial for a long time

(X. Cyr. 8.1.18)

In this example we see πολὺν χρόνον, a durative expression, used twice in quick succession, once in a negative clause, once in an affirmative clause.[23] As the negative has no apparent effect on the choice of temporal construction, it seems best to classify this passage simply as having two durative expressions, one of which happens to be negative, rather than as setting up a distinct category for the negative construction.

At this point, it might seem that it is simply battling a straw man to question whether negative constructions should be treated in the same way as their affirmative counterparts, as in all these passages, Xenophon's Greek has given us no reason to suspect that this is anything other than a purely theoretical problem. But the next example shows otherwise:

(26) ἐπὶ δὲ τὰ ὅπλα πολλοὶ οὐκ ἦλθον **ταύτην τὴν νύκτα**

But many did not go to their weapons that night (X. An. 3.1.3)

---

[23] As it happens, these imperfects are iterative and thus show the compatibility of the durative type with recurring events; see the discussion of example (1) in Ch. 3.

On the basis of the discussion above, one could argue that this should be classified as a punctual construction: if we had the corresponding positive *That night they went to their weapons*, it would certainly be considered punctual rather than durative. But the accusative of time is so strongly associated with durative expressions that there is some reason to consider this example durative as well, with the durativity resulting from the negative: here the temporal expression seems to modify the negative state of not-going (durative) rather than a positive action of going (punctual) that happens to be negated. But despite this consideration, it seems best in practice to adhere to the taxonomy proposed above and continue to classify examples like (26) in the first instance as punctual. First, as the passages with ἡμέρα showed, while constructions like that found in (26) certainly occur, more often the negative does not affect temporal expression. Taking this distribution into account, we should base our classification on the more common, unmarked variety. Second, and more important, the taxonomy can be more consistent if negative examples are classified merely according to how the corresponding positive expression would be treated. If we attempt to distinguish between labeling examples like (20) and (21) as punctual and (26) as durative, there is a real danger of succumbing to circular reasoning in attempting to understand the rationale for the different temporal constructions, as the only immediately obvious difference setting apart (26) is the temporal expression itself. If, however, we simply label all such examples as punctual in an initial classification, even the apparent disadvantage of not calling an example like (26) durative in the first instance can still be rectified at a later stage when looking at anomalies in punctual constructions. In other words, if we classify (26) together with (25) at the start, we obscure the difference in event type between the verbs of the two passages; if, however, we classify it with (20) and (21), then the event type of the construction is held constant, and we can use patterns in the temporal expressions themselves to work out the conditions under which a negative such as that in (26) inverts the construction from having a punctual marker to having a durative one.

   There is one other small subset of negative expressions that calls for special comment:

(27) οἱ μέντοι πολέμιοι οὐδὲν ἐπαύσαντο **δι' ὅλης τῆς νυκτὸς** κυλίνδοντες τοὺς λίθους

However, throughout the whole night, the enemy did not cease to roll down stones (X. *An.* 4.2.4)

The temporal expression in (27), δι' ὅλης τῆς νυκτός, is indisputably one that ought to be classified as durative: both διά$^{+G}$ and the modifier ὅλος are closely associated with this event type. Now there are two ways that one might analyze this construction: one can take the temporal expression either with οὐδὲν ἐπαύσαντο or with κυλίνδοντες. If we assume the latter, then this example, at least, appears to be an unproblematic durative expression with the imperfective κυλίνδοντες. This solution might work for (27), but consider now the following:

(28) οἱ μέντοι Ἀρκάδες καὶ οἱ μετ' αὐτῶν οὕτως ἐπεφόβηντο τὴν ἐπιοῦσαν ἡμέραν ὥστε οὐδ' ἀνεπαύσαντο **τῆς νυκτός**, ἐκκόπτοντες τὰ διαπεπονημένα σκηνώματα καὶ ἀποσταυροῦντες

However, the Arcadians and their allies were so afraid of the next day that they did not rest during the night, taking down the housing they had labored over and setting up a palisade (X. *HG* 7.4.32)

Now it is possible that one could re-punctuate here and again take the participles ἐκκόπτοντες and ἀποσταυροῦντες as completing the construction of ἀνεπαύσαντο and this latter verb as synonymous with ἐπαύσαντο. If so, one could still interpret the temporal expression τῆς νυκτός as modifying the imperfective participles. But ἀναπαύομαι does not appear to take this construction, and the sense certainly calls for construing τῆς νυκτός with ἀνεπαύσαντο rather than the following participles: there is a balance between οὕτως ἐπεφόβηντο τὴν ἐπιοῦσαν ἡμέραν and οὐδ' ἀνεπαύσαντο τῆς νυκτός that is upset if we take the temporal expression with the participles. Indeed, a similar semantic consideration is also applicable to (27), in which the emphatic negative οὐδέν seems if anything to reinforce the similarly emphatic δι' ὅλης τῆς νυκτός. In both examples, then, the temporal expression is more likely to be modifying the negative main verb than the following participles. In that case, the classification of these temporal expressions becomes more problematic. As with the other negative constructions, it would be best to be able to classify them in the same way as their corresponding positives, that is, as limitatives. But while that is an unobjectionable approach to (28), it is very much at odds with how one would like to classify a passage with δι' ὅλης τῆς νυκτός. In an example like this, therefore, where the presence of the adjective ὅλης really does suggest that the phrase answers the question 'How long?', it seems safe to label the construction as durative from the start. It seems justifiable to admit this exception to the general rule of classifying negatives as one would the corresponding affirmatives given the fact that οὐ παύω serves essentially as a litotes for 'to continue to'.

As a coda to this discussion of the classification of temporal expressions, I should note that, even though it has been based solely on Xenophon and primarily on expressions with ἡμέρα, this lack of exhaustiveness does not invalidate the conclusions that have been reached, at least for the purposes of the task at hand: setting up the labels that I will attach to the temporal expressions under investigation and illustrating why I have chosen to classify them the way that I have. At this point, cynics might point out that the terms punctual, durative, and limitative correspond suspiciously closely to the labels traditionally applied to the dative, accusative, and genitive of time respectively: Time When, Extent of Time, and Time Within Which. While I would not deny the similarity, I believe that these terms represent a valuable improvement in two respects – beyond the fact that one-word terms generally enable a more elegant discussion than two- and three-word phrases. First, they are defined more carefully: as alluded to at the start of the chapter, the standard accounts that use the phrase Time Within Which never, it seems, set out clearly the characteristics that distinguish it from Time When. The potential for confusion between the genitive and dative of time, not to mention ἐν^{+D}, becomes clearer once the limitative type has been described in terms of its composition, sharing the expression of a time frame with the durative type, and the telic verb with the punctual type. Second, these new labels do not have the strong association with particular constructions that the older terms do. If I were to go on to write that the genitive is used in limitative constructions, the dative in punctual ones, and the accusative in durative ones, I would accept the charge of merely having introduced cosmetic changes.

But, as we shall see, the genitive in particular is hardly restricted to limitative constructions and often competes with the dative in expressing punctual events; something similar happens with ἐν^{+D} as well. Discussing such linguistic phenomena intelligently requires terminological clarification of the sort detailed above.

Aspect

A second objection might be that I have failed thus far to deal with the elephant in the room: aspect.[24] The interaction between aspect and temporal expressions is indeed intricate and worthy of considerable attention. But it is in fact too intricate an interaction for aspect to serve as a sound basis for classifying temporal expressions.[25] Initially, one might expect a tendency for the imperfect to occur with durative, the aorist with punctual expressions. Even Wackernagel thought that the ability to add a modifier such as 'for the whole day' was characteristic of imperfective aspect.[26] But this is not in fact the case: Comrie noted the grammaticality in Greek of ἐβασίλευσε δέκα ἔτη, with the perfective aorist (1976: 17),[27] and if we look for examples of durative temporal expressions with supposedly punctual aorists and examples of punctual temporal

---

[24] The most recent book-length study of aspect in Greek is Napoli (2006). The reader may also consult Ruipérez (1982), Fanning (1990), Binnick (1991: 158–69), Duhoux (1992), Jacquinod (2000), Lorente Fernández (2003), Kölligan (2007), and the chs. by Allan, Buijs, and Lallot in Allan & Buijs (2007); of the relevant chs. in Bakker & Wakker (2009), Basset's contribution is particularly informative in considering the interaction between aspect and temporal phrases. Note also George (2008: *passim*, but esp. n. 7) and (2011: 239–40).

[25] One may compare Muchnová's observation that all four possible combinations of imperfect and aorist are found in preposed ἐπεί-clauses and the main clauses they introduce (2011: 42). As broadly important as aspect is, it simply does not always align straightforwardly with other linguistic variables.

[26] "Als Beispiel für den imperfektiven Ausdruck führt Leskien hier an: 'Sie jagten den Hirsch den ganzen Tag.' Da wird nicht daran gedacht, ob das Jagen zum Abschluss gekommen ist oder nicht, sondern es wird nur ausgesagt, dass die Handlung als fortlaufend ins Auge gefasst wird. Und nun mache ich darauf aufmerksam, dass absichtlich gesagt ist: 'den ganzen Tag.' Darin, ob man eine Bezeichnung der Dauer beifügen kann oder nicht, ist ein sicheres Merkmal gegeben. Sobald dies der Fall ist, haben wir eine imperfektive Verbalform; das ist für die Aktionsarten nicht bloss des Slavischen massgebend" (1920: 154). For translation and further notes, see Langslow (2009: 198).

[27] The use of durative expressions with the aorist of verbs of ruling is esp. common in Herodotus; see the discussion in Ch. 3 of examples (121) through (129).

25

expressions with supposedly durative imperfects, they are not hard to find:

(29) ἐνταῦθα ἔμεινεν ἡμέρας ἑπτά

He remained there seven days (X. *An.* 1.2.6)

(30) ταύτῃ μὲν οὖν τῇ ἡμέρᾳ οἱ Θηβαῖοι ἠθύμουν

On this day, the Thebans were discouraged (X. *HG* 3.5.21)

Example (29) shows a construction that occurs twenty-three times in Xenophon (of which twenty-one are in the *Anabasis*): the aorist of μένω together with an accusative of time consisting of the plural of ἡμέρα modified by a cardinal number. The imperfect, by contrast, never occurs in this construction. Thus, even Comrie does not go far enough in dissociating durative temporal expressions from imperfective aspect, insofar as he maintains that Greek could use the imperfect as an alternative to the aorist in the phrase ἐβασίλευσε δέκα ἔτη. Indeed, we rather expect the aorist in such constructions, because the presence of the temporal phrase in effect turns what would otherwise be atelic into a telic predicate. To stay somewhere is atelic; to stay somewhere for a certain number of days is telic.[28] Conversely, in example (30) we see a punctual expression modifying an imperfect verb. To be sure, examples of this sort, in which an imperfect is modified by a punctual temporal expression, are considerably rarer than those like (29), in which an aorist is modified by a durative expression.[29] But the fact remains that a simple attempt to explain temporal constructions with reference to aspect will not get very far: it is far more productive to explain them with reference to the event type of the construction – in these two examples, the accusative and dative of time unproblematically occur in the durative and punctual constructions respectively – and then, as a second stage of examination, see what the apparent mismatches between event type and aspect can tell us about the workings of aspect in Greek.

---

[28] See n. 14.

[29] Many of the examples one does find are with verbs whose aorists are rare or non-existent, e.g. ἥκω, the imperfect of which is modified by a dative of time at *HG* 1.1.13 and *Ages.* 1.29. In such cases, the range of the imperfect may extend into what otherwise would be the territory of the aorist; for the possibility of the neutralization of aspectual differences in such verbs, cf. Ruipérez's discussion of φημί and εἰμί (1982: 133–6).

In slightly more practical terms, we can thus learn a lot about aspect by holding the event type constant, ideally by studying all the examples with a given temporal expression in connection with each other, and seeing what conditions correlate to variation in aspect. As an initial step in this direction, I have elsewhere examined Thucydides' use of aspect in clauses with the temporal expressions τοῦ αὐτοῦ/ἐπιγιγνομένου θέρους/χειμῶνος.[30] These four expressions are ideal for such a study because they are used by Thucydides so regularly and frequently – in total, sixty-nine times – in punctual constructions that set the temporal stage for what follows. The chief finding relevant to the issues at hand is that, after the aorist (44×), it is the historical present (HP) that is the most common tense (15×) to be modified by these temporal phrases, while the imperfect only occurs eight times. This distribution makes sense given the role that the HP plays in highlighting the peaks of a narrative. Viewed in terms of its temporal properties, it in effect reduces the verbal event to an even smaller point than the aorist does: an aorist verb can collocate quite readily with an accusative of extent of time (see example (29)), while Thucydides never uses the HP with durative verbs like μένω.[31] In Homer, as shown by Napoli (2006), the behavior of the present tense is that of a verb form with imperfective aspect. That this is decidedly not the case in Thucydides is made all the clearer when the tense distribution of his verbs is studied in relationship with the temporal expressions that modify them.

The role of modifiers in temporal expressions

So far, my discussion of the proper classification of temporal expressions has revolved around the role of the verb and the extent to which a full understanding of the differences between these expressions requires determining the event type to which the verb (or, to be more accurate, the verb–time phrase complex) belongs.

---

[30] See George (2011).

[31] Other authors occasionally allow the use of the HP with durative, atelic verbs, but none of the Classical prose authors in my corpus (Herodotus, Thucydides, Xenophon, Plato, Demosthenes) use it with the accusative of time (at least with the time nouns studied here).

That this is a reasonable approach can be seen, as already mentioned, in the success with which the accusative of time can be explained along these lines. But it is not the only way of addressing the issue. Indeed, in the most recent study to look at Greek temporal expressions in any detail, M. Dolores Jiménez emphasizes the role of the modifiers that occur in the temporal noun phrase in determining what construction is used – though not, of course, without also taking what I call event type into consideration as well. I cite her conclusion in full:

> Los casos acusativo, genitivo y dativo, como marcas gramaticales de función Tiempo, están sujetos a una distribución precisa, de manera que son muy pocos los contextos en que realmente dos casos pueden utilizarse indistintamente: además de las diferencias de sentido que puedan existir entre ellos, hay dos factores de distribución fundamentales que condicionan también la presencia de un caso u otro: el lexema específico de que se trate, por un lado; y, por otro, el tipo de determinante que acompaña a ese lexema. En términos generales se constata, además, que el dativo, a diferencia del acusativo y el genitivo, tiene una productividad mínima (1998: 99).[32]

In essence, Jiménez states the same three criteria for understanding the distribution of temporal phrases that I listed above on pp. 6–7: event type ("las diferencias de sentido"), lexical restrictions on the time noun itself, and the determiners that occur with that time noun. But while she is certainly correct to include the first two criteria, I am reluctant to assign too much importance to the role of the modifiers of the time noun in determining the choice of construction. On the one hand, there is undoubtedly a correlation between these modifiers and the choice of case; on the other, this correlation is better explained as resulting from affinities between particular event types and time-noun modifiers than as evidence that the modifiers themselves motivated the use of particular constructions. In other words, a combination of rules related to event types and to lexical

---

[32] "The accusative, genitive, and dative cases, as grammatical markers of the function Time, are subject to a precise distribution, such that there are very few contexts in which two cases can really be used indiscriminately; in addition to the differences of meaning which can exist between them, there are two fundamental factors of distribution that also condition the presence of one case or another: on the one hand, the specific lexeme in question; on the other, the type of determiner that accompanies that lexeme. In general terms, it has been found, moreover, that the dative, in contrast to the accusative and the genitive, has minimal productivity."

restrictions is sufficient to explain nearly all of the distinctions in temporal expression in a given author: patterns relating to the modifier are epiphenomenal.

The best way to illustrate this point is to go through the examples Jiménez gives of correlations between modifiers of the time noun and the construction chosen. We must see whether there is ever an example in which the only explanation for the use of a particular construction lies in the nature of the modifier of the time noun and not in a combination of lexical restrictions and the event type. I do not believe that there are any such examples, at least in Thucydides, the text to which Jiménez restricts this part of her study. First, I give the particular examples of correlations between time-noun modifiers and temporal constructions that Jiménez sees: (i) the accusative occurs with quantifying adjectives like πολύς, ὀλίγος, and, above all, cardinal numbers; (ii) the genitive occurs with the adjective αὐτός and adjectives and participles that express the idea of the future; (iii) the dative is associated with time nouns modified by an ordinal number (1998: 95). Let us consider each of these types of modifiers in turn.

First, as Jiménez notes, quantifying adjectives and cardinal numbers are all associated with the accusative of time, rather than the genitive or the dative (prepositional uses being excluded from consideration in this section of her article). There is no need, however, to say that it is the modifier that determines this directly: quantifying adjectives and cardinal numbers cannot but state a duration. Accordingly, the use of the accusative of time, as against a punctual construction like the dative of time, is already pre-determined by the event type of the construction. Now, as the nature of these modifiers is also compatible with the limitative event type, which also involves the stating of a duration, we might conclude that it is not the event type, but rather the modifiers that trigger the use of the accusative of time if they only occur with the accusative, but not with limitative constructions like the genitive or ἐν^{+D}. Now the genitive is, admittedly, not particularly common – as I will argue in Chapter 2, it is primarily a punctual rather than a limitative construction in Thucydides – but there are still several examples of the limitative genitive used with time nouns with quantifying modifiers:[33]

---

[33] See also 5.14.3 (with ὀλίγος), and 2.97.2 and 4.105.2 (with cardinals).

(31) οὓς ᾤοντο ἡμερῶν ὀλίγων ἐκπολιορκήσειν ἐν νήσῳ τε ἐρήμῃ καὶ ὕδατι ἁλμυρῷ χρωμένους

Whom they expected to force to surrender in a few days as they were on a desert island with only salt water (Th. 4.26.4)

(32) εἰ βούλονται ἐξιέναι ἐκ τῆς Σικελίας πέντε ἡμερῶν

If they were willing to leave Sicily within five days (Th. 7.3.1)

Moreover, there are also several examples of these modifiers occurring with ἐν[+D], a more common limitative construction in Thucydides:[34]

(33) τειχίσαντες δὲ οἱ Ἀθηναῖοι τοῦ χωρίου τὰ πρὸς ἤπειρον καὶ ἃ μάλιστα ἔδει ἐν ἡμέραις ἕξ

And the Athenians, having fortified in six days those parts of the area that faced the mainland and which needed it the most (Th. 4.5.2)

In short, the evidence of temporal constructions with quantifying adjectives and cardinal numbers, for their part, gives us no reason to set up the modifier of the time noun as a third criterion in determining the temporal construction. The fact that they occur most often with the accusative is explained by the fact that these modifiers usually occur in durative constructions; the fact that they also occur with the genitive of time and ἐν[+D] can only be explained by giving event type precedence over the modifier as the more significant factor in determining the construction used.

Second, there is the observation that the genitive of time is frequent with the adjective αὐτός and adjectives and participles that express the idea of posteriority,[35] such as λοιπός and ἐπιγιγνόμενος. Here too, there is a better explanation for the correlation between the use of a particular construction and that of particular modifiers than that it is the modifier that triggers the construction. However, in contrast to the proclivities of the accusative of time, the compatibility of the genitive of time with these modifiers results more from the lexical restrictions arising from the

---

[34] See also 1.93.1 and 3.51.4 (with ὀλίγος), 1.12.4, 2.49.3, and 2.102.3 (with πολύς), and 1.118.2, 2.58.3, and 5.112.2 (with cardinals).

[35] Jiménez refers to these as expressions "con idea de 'futuro'" (1998: 95), but it is more convenient to refer to them as expressions of posteriority as that captures better the fact that they are generally only future relative to a past-time reference point.

time nouns with which they typically occur than from their association with a particular event type. That said, the event type is still important insofar as most of the relevant constructions are punctual, and the lexical restrictions in question are those that affect the punctual constructions favored by particular time nouns. Consider first the constructions with αὐτός. While it is again undeniable that αὐτός occurs mostly in expressions with the genitive of time, it is also the case that most of the constructions with αὐτός are either τοῦ αὐτοῦ θέρους (23 examples) or τοῦ αὐτοῦ χειμῶνος (16 examples). Now, as we will see in Chapter 2, θέρος and χειμών are both nouns that in Thucydides exhibit a lexical preference for using the genitive of time to express the punctual event-type, so it is not surprising that they should occur with τοῦ αὐτοῦ a combined total of thirty-nine times, but in the dative with τῷ αὐτῷ only once.[36] This distribution may be contrasted with that of αὐτός with ἡμέρα. Thucydides never writes τῆς αὐτῆς ἡμέρας, as we would expect if this modifier did indeed trigger the genitive of time; instead, he writes τῇ αὐτῇ ἡμέρᾳ. Now it is true that there are only four examples of this, as opposed to the much larger number of examples of the genitive of time with θέρος and χειμών. But this imbalance no doubt arises from the simple fact that, days being shorter than seasons, Thucydides has less occasion to say that something happened on the same day than in the same summer or winter. Essentially, as will again be shown in Chapter 2, ἡμέρα is a noun that, unlike θέρος and χειμών, has a lexical preference for the dative as the preferred construction for the punctual event type. Thus, the reason that αὐτός occurs more frequently with the genitive of time is not that αὐτός itself triggers the genitive of time, but rather that Thucydides uses this modifier more often with time nouns that favor the genitive of time than those that favor the dative.

The same reasoning explains why the genitive of time is more common with the adjectives denoting posteriority. Consider the

---

[36] This dative occurs at 2.27.1 and is extremely anomalous. The only other dative of time in Thucydides with either θέρος or χειμών, at 1.30.3, is another matter altogether, as it occurs in the phrase περιιόντι τῷ θέρει. One is tempted to assume that an ἐν has dropped out of the text at 2.27.1, as there are eleven examples of ἐν τῷ αὐτῷ θέρει, two of which, like 2.27.1, have an additional demonstrative (7.27.1, 8.99.1).

Table 2. *Time nouns with modifiers of posteriority in selected temporal constructions in Thucydides*

Lexeme	G	D	A
θέρος	10	1	1
χειμών	15	–	–
χρόνος	2	1	1
ἔτος	1	–	–
ἡμέρα	–	3	1
νύξ	1	1	1
Total	29	6	4
Total without θέρος and χειμών	4	5	3

Source: Jiménez (1998: Table 4).

figures in Table 2, taken from Jiménez's Table 4, which state the number of times the given time noun occurs with a modifier of posteriority in a given temporal construction (1998: 106–7).

If one considers only the simple totals, then it certainly appears that there is a strong connection between the use of modifiers of posteriority and the genitive of time. But if one excludes the figures for θέρος and χειμών, which in both instances consist exclusively of the collocation τοῦ ἐπιγιγνομένου θέρους/χειμῶνος, then the distribution of temporal phrases with these modifiers among the three cases is essentially completely even. A comparison of the three examples with νύξ is instructive:

(34) καὶ ταύτην μὲν τὴν ἡμέραν καὶ **τὴν ἐπιοῦσαν νύκτα** ἐν φυλακῇ εἶχον αὐτούς

And they held them under guard for this day and the following night (Th. 4.38.4)

(35) οἱ δὲ τριακόσιοι τῶν Σκιωναίων **τῆς ἐπιούσης νυκτὸς** ἀπεχώρησαν ἐπ᾽ οἴκου

And the three hundred Scionaeans left the following night for home (Th. 4.130.1)

(36) καὶ **τῇ ἐπιούσῃ νυκτὶ** ἔφθασαν παροικοδομήσαντες καὶ παρελθόντες τὴν τῶν Ἀθηναίων οἰκοδομίαν

And the following night they finished first in building a wall alongside and extending past that of the Athenians (Th. 7.6.4)

I would argue that the accusative is chosen in (34) because the construction is durative, and the genitive in (35) because the construction is punctual, the genitive being the usual case for punctual constructions with νύξ. The dative in (36) is admittedly more difficult to explain, but it is likely that both it and the other two examples of the dative of time with νύξ (4.103.4 and 6.27.1) result from the influence of ἡμέρα, with which the dative is the usual punctual construction. At any rate, it is clear that, as with τοῦ αὐτοῦ, the overwhelming predominance of the genitive when time nouns are construed with modifiers of posteriority is due to these modifiers' equally overwhelming tendency to occur in punctual constructions with θέρος and χειμών, which lexically favor the genitive in this context.

There remains the third association: that of the dative of time with time nouns modified by ordinal numbers. The situation here is essentially the inverse of that with the genitive of time. Like temporal expressions with αὐτός and modifiers of posteriority, those with ordinal numbers are, by the nature of ordinal numbers, likely to occur in punctual expressions. But the exclusive occurrence of the dative, rather than the genitive, with ordinals is explained by the fact that, whereas αὐτός and ἐπιγιγνόμενος occur mostly with θέρος and χειμών, nouns that favor the genitive in punctual constructions, ordinals occur almost exclusively with ἔτος (14 times) and ἡμέρα (15 times), nouns that favor the dative. Indeed, they never occur with θέρος, χειμών, or νύξ, the three time nouns that favor the genitive. Accordingly, as we do not have either *τοῦ πρώτου θέρους or *τῷ πρώτῳ θέρει, we cannot say with the same degree of certainty that it is the time noun, rather than the modifier, triggering the use of a particular case, as we can with the αὐτός and modifiers of posteriority (where the fact that the examples with ἡμέρα take the dative shows conclusively that the time noun trumps the modifier in determining the case used). Nevertheless, it would be uneconomical to suggest that it is anything other than the lexical preference of ἡμέρα and ἔτος that motivates the use of the dative rather than the genitive in these ordinal constructions. In short, taking together the distribution of all three cases, we see that, since Thucydides' choice

33

of temporal construction can be explained sufficiently with recourse solely to event types and lexical preferences of the time noun, it is best to downplay the idea that the modifiers of the time noun are a major factor in affecting the construction. Still, Jiménez is absolutely right to have drawn attention to these correlations, as they show the close connection between the modifier and the event type, and there will be the occasional construction where the nature of the modifier may have played a role in shunting the expression from one event type to another.[37]

Syntactic ambiguities

One final set of problems must be addressed in this chapter before we can proceed to look at the actual data: how can we tell that a given temporal phrase is in fact a genitive, dative, or accusative of time? The prepositional usages are rarely problematic: a phrase like ἐν τῇ νυκτί usually has a clear syntactic location in its host clause and can be included in a compilation of temporal expressions without further ado. But those temporal expressions that consist only of the use of case marking to show their grammatical relation in the sentence can be more difficult to classify: genitives of time can be confused with adnominal genitives and with genitive absolutes, datives of time with datives of reference or of degree of difference, and accusatives of time with direct objects. There is no avoiding the fact that many constructions straddle the line, and no objective criterion is available by which one may include or exclude them in the inventory of temporal phrases: in such instances, I have usually included them. For, even if one could posit an alternative syntactic interpretation for a given phrase, if it looks syntactically parallel to one that *is* indisputably temporal, then it is temporal enough that it could affect and be affected by more unequivocally temporal constructions. I shall now consider these constructions in more detail, case by case.

[37] See the discussion of examples (43) in Ch. 2 and (78) in Ch. 3.

The genitive

Depending on how one subdivides, there are, in addition to the genitive of time, approximately six types of genitive phrase in which time nouns can occur. Three of these – genitives of comparison, genitives of measure, and genitives that are verbal objects – are easy to eliminate from consideration as temporal genitives. I give examples of each in turn:

(37) παρέμεινε δὲ τὸ μὲν ὕστερον οὐκ ἔλασσον **ἐνιαυτοῦ**

And it stayed in the latter instance no less than a year (Th. 3.87.2)

(38) ὅτε δὲ ἀπέθνῃσκεν ἦν **ἐτῶν ὡς τριάκοντα**

And when he died, he was about thirty years old (X. *An.* 2.6.20)

(39) ἀλλὰ **πολλοῦ χρόνου** δέονται εἰς τὴν ἐξόπλισιν

But they need a lot of time to arm themselves (X. *Cyr.* 8.5.9)

In (37), ἐνιαυτοῦ is in the genitive because it is the object of the comparative ἔλασσον, and it is not a genitive of time. The example does, of course, still contain a temporal construction, which happens to be durative (note the verb παρέμεινε). But the time noun is here ἔλασσον, in the expected accusative, not ἐνιαυτοῦ. In (38), we see a construction of limited productivity that exhibits what is best considered a genitive of measure: εἶναι CARDINAL NUMBER ἐτῶν 'to be CARDINAL years old'.[38] The phrase with ἐτῶν should not be classified together with the temporal phrases examined in this study because it does not so much tell at what time or for how long the event of the verb took place, but rather describes a characteristic of the subject, which only looks adverbial because it happens to be expressed predicatively.[39] In other words,

---

[38] See Smyth 1920: 318. All the examples of time nouns that I have found used with this type of genitive in Thucydides, Xenophon, and Plato are of precisely the same construction (εἶναι / γίγνεσθαι CARDINAL ἐτῶν). There is occasional conflation of the genitive of comparison and the genitive of measure, e.g. μὴ ἔλαττον πεντήκοντα γεγονότα ἐτῶν (Pl. *Lg.* 946a). Note also γεγονὼς ἔστω πλειόνων ἐτῶν ἢ πεντήκοντα (*Lg.* 951c), which can only be a genitive of measure because the comparative adjective itself is in the genitive. None of these constructions have much bearing on the genitive of time, although they occur in the same contexts as accusatives of time (see n. 39).

[39] Contrast the use of the accusative of time in a phrase like οὐδέπω εἴκοσιν ἔτη γεγονώς, "not yet having lived for twenty years" (X. *Mem.* 3.6.1).

the syntax of the genitive in (38) is closer to that of ἀνὴρ τριάκοντα ἐτῶν ('a man of thirty years') than to τριάκοντα ἔτη ἔζη ('he lived thirty years'). Finally, in (39) the syntactic function of πολλοῦ χρόνου is to complete the sense of the verb δέονται by stating what is needed. It would be impossible to take the genitive as a temporal adverb phrase and δέονται as used absolutely: 'But for a long time they are in need, with a view towards arming themselves'.

Three other types of genitive, however, can be less easy to dismiss as potential genitives of time: genitive absolutes, adnominal genitives adjacent to time nouns, and partitive genitives adjacent to temporal adverbs. Consider first the genitive absolute. It is not always clear where the boundary lies between this construction and the genitive of time, for there is a continuum from the use of the noun on its own, to the use of the noun with a participle in the attributive position, to the use of the noun with a participle in the predicative position:[40]

(40) τοῦ ἦρος → τοῦ ἐπιγιγνομένου ἦρος → τοῦ ἦρος ἀρχομένου

    during the spring→ the following spring→ at the beginning of spring

If one considers both the placement of the participle with respect to the definite article, as well as the semantic and syntactic function of the participle (i.e. τοῦ ἦρος ἀρχομένου can be expanded to ἐπεὶ τὸ ἔαρ ἤρχετο, whereas τοῦ ἐπιγιγνομένου ἦρος cannot be expanded to ἐπεὶ τὸ ἔαρ ἐπεγίγνετο), the assignment of a particular phrase into one class or the other should generally be straightforward. We can thus distinguish between the following two examples, one a genitive of time, the other a genitive absolute:

(41) **τοῦ δ' αὐτοῦ θέρους** οἱ Ἀθηναῖοι τριάκοντα μὲν ναῦς ἔστειλαν περὶ Πελοπόννησον

    And the same summer the Athenians sent thirty ships around the Peloponnesus (Th. 3.91.1)

(42) **τοῦ δ' αὐτοῦ θέρους τελευτῶντος** Ἀθηναῖοι εἴκοσι ναῦς ἔστειλαν ἐς Σικελίαν

    And as the same summer was coming to an end, the Athenians sent twenty ships to Sicily (Th. 3.86.1)

---

[40] Wackernagel sees the Greek genitive absolute as having originated in the genitive of time (1920: 293), Langslow (2009: 368).

But although it is *possible* to draw a syntactic line between these two constructions, it is not clear that it is *desirable* to do so. For, as these two examples show, while the syntactic difference between the genitive absolute and the genitive of time may be easy to detect, functionally they are often virtually equivalent to one another. Thus, despite the formal distinction between the two constructions, it would have been quite possible for one to have influenced the behavior of the other, and there is evidence that this has indeed happened. Perhaps the best way to illustrate this is to start from the opposite hypothesis, namely that there was no interaction between the genitive absolute and the other temporal expressions. If this were the case, then we might expect genitive absolutes to correspond in roughly equal measure to genitives, datives, and accusatives of time in constructions that do not have a predicative participle. In other words, incorporating the conclusions of the following chapter and taking Thucydides and Xenophon together as our corpus, we would expect to find distributed fairly evenly among our genitive absolutes not just punctual expressions with θέρος, χειμών, and νύξ (which we would expect to take the genitive, even when not in an absolute construction), but also punctual expressions with ἔτος and ἡμέρα (which we otherwise expect to take the dative) and durative expressions (which would otherwise be in the accusative).[41] As it happens, the distribution is not even, but very much skewed in favor of the first group. In Thucydides, for example, as can be seen in Table 3, the genitive absolutes with time nouns break down as follows, in descending order of frequency.[42]

Right from the start, the raw figures in the left-hand column reveal that the genitive absolute is more common with time nouns that favor the genitive than those that favor the dative: ἔτος and ἡμέρα, even taken together, do not occur in as many genitive absolutes as do χειμών, θέρος, or νύξ taken separately. But the

---

[41] The five time nouns mentioned here are five of the six most common. I have left out the sixth, χρόνος, because it very rarely occurs in punctual expressions without a preposition, and so does not fall into the same category as either θέρος, χειμών, and νύξ on the one hand, or ἡμέρα and ἔτος on the other.

[42] For explanation of the causal category, see the following discussion; for more detailed information on the numerous punctual constructions with χειμών, θέρος, and νύξ, see n. 43.

Table 3. *Genitive absolutes with time nouns in Thucydides*

Time noun	Description of genitive absolutes
χειμών (15×)	11× punctual τελευτῶντος ἤδη τοῦ χειμῶνος Ὠρωπὸν εἷλον The winter already near its end, they took Oropus (8.60.1)
	3× causal (see also 2.102.2 and 3.22.5) ἅμα δὲ καὶ χειμῶνος ὄντος καὶ ἀπροσδοκήτοις προσπεσών, διέβη τὴν γέφυραν As it was stormy and he was attacking unexpected, he crossed the bridge (4.103.5)
	1× limitative πρὸς ἔαρ ἤδη ταῦτα ἦν τοῦ χειμῶνος λήγοντος All this happened towards spring, as winter was already drawing to a close (5.81.2)
θέρος (13×)	13× punctual τοῦ θέρους εὐθὺς ἀρχομένου ... ἐσέβαλον ἐς τὴν Ἀττικήν When the summer was just beginning, they invaded Attica (2.47.2)
νύξ (8×)	4× punctual νυκτὸς ἐπελθούσης ἐς τὴν πόλιν ἀπῆλθον When night came, they went back to the city (4.129.5)
	4× causal (see also 3.22.5, 4.96.8, 4.134.2) οὐ καθορωμένους ... νυκτὸς ἔτι οὔσης Not visible, as it was still night (3.112.4)
ἔτος (4×)	3× plural + δια- (see also 1.82.2, 5.20.1) ὕστερον δὲ διαλιπόντων ἐτῶν τριῶν σπονδαὶ γίγνονται And later, after three years, a treaty was made (1.112.1)
	1× habitual οἷα τοῦ ἔτους πρὸς μετόπωρον ἤδη ὄντος φιλεῖ γίγνεσθαι Such as often happens when the year is close to autumn (7.79.3)
ἡμέρα (3×)	1× punctual γεγενημένης δὲ ἡμέρας ἤδη καὶ βεβαίως τῆς πόλεως ἐχομένης ... κήρυγμα ἐποιήσατο When it was day already and the city was held securely, he made a proclamation (4.114.1)
	1× δια- διαλιπούσης δ' ἡμέρας μάχη αὖθις γίγνεται A day having passed, fighting broke out again (3.74.1)

Table 3. (cont.)

Time noun	Description of genitive absolutes
	1× plural + δια-[a] αὐτόδεκα ἐτῶν διελθόντων καὶ ἡμερῶν ὀλίγων παρενεγκουσῶν Ten full years and a few extra days having passed (5.20.1)

Note: [a] See n. 47.

difference in behavior between the two sets of time nouns becomes even more pronounced if we examine the characteristics of the genitive absolutes detailed in the right-hand column. Of the thirty-six genitive absolutes with χειμών, θέρος, and νύξ, twenty-eight occur in punctual constructions of the sort which we would expect to take the genitive of time anyway. One could replace the participle with a demonstrative, and the sentence would still be grammatical. With χειμών and θέρος, the participle is, with only one exception, a verb specifying a particular point in the broader frame of the time noun: either the beginning (ἀρχομένου), the middle or peak (μεσοῦντος or ἀκμάζοντος), or the end (τελευτῶντος or λήγοντος).[43] This being the case, the genitive absolute construction is, in effect, simply a variant of the genitive of time with the participle adding more specificity to the temporal location of the event.[44] Only once is the participle in the genitive absolutes of these nouns a verb prefixed with δια-, the class of verb that occurs most often in the genitive absolutes with ἔτος and ἡμέρα – and one which changes the sense of the construction from

---

[43] The distribution and location of the punctual (and limitative) expressions is as follows: χειμών occurs with ἀρχομένου at 2.93.1, 2.95.1, 4.89.1, 5.76.1, with τελευτῶντος at 3.25.1, 3.115.6, 5.20.1, 5.39.3, 5.56.5, 8.60.1, with λήγοντος at 5.81.2, and with διελθόντος at 4.116.3; θέρος occurs with ἀρχομένου at 2.47.2, 5.52.1, with ἀκμάζοντος at 2.19.1, with μεσοῦντος at 5.57.1, 6.30.1, with τελευτῶντος at 2.32.1, 2.67.1, 2.68.1, 3.86.1, 4.49.1, 4.133.4, 5.12.1, 8.25.1.

[44] A particularly nice example of the way in which the genitive absolute can be analyzed as a genitive of time to which a participle has been appended is the following: ἀπεπείρασε δὲ τοῦ αὐτοῦ χειμῶνος καὶ ὁ Βρασίδας τελευτῶντος καὶ πρὸς ἔαρ ἤδη Ποτειδαίας "And the same winter Brasidas – while it was ending and already close to spring – tried to take Potidaea" (4.135.1). I have not included it in my list of genitive absolutes because of the discontinuous word order.

'during (a specific point in) the TIME NOUN' to 'after the TIME NOUN had passed'. With νύξ, the participle is always one denoting the arrival of the night: ἐπιγενομένης at 3.112.1 and 4.125.1, ἐπελθούσης at 4.129.5, and ἀφικομένης at 3.72.3. Again, the participle could be omitted, and νυκτός would still stand on its own as a genitive of time.[45] It is also worth noting that even the modifiers that occur with the time noun in the punctual genitive absolutes broadly match those that occur with the time noun when it occurs in the simple genitive of time: χειμών and θέρος are usually definite (11 of 11, and 11 of 13 examples respectively) and often further modified by a demonstrative, αὐτοῦ, or ἐπιγιγνομένου (3 of the 11 constructions with χειμών, 6 of the 13 with θέρος), while νύξ is indefinite all four times, just as, in the simple genitive of time, νυκτός occurs seventeen times without an article (although admittedly it also occurs eighteen times with an article). As for the non-punctual examples, of the four with χειμών, the limitative construction here is not far removed from the punctual examples, and the other three constructions have a causal nuance that sets them apart: while this is most evident from the general sense of the passages, that they belong together is also suggested by the fact that the verb is the simple ὄντος all three times, and, in two of the three passages, χειμών means 'storm' rather than 'winter'.[46] The causal constructions with νύξ also form a group: two, like those with χειμών, have εἰμί as the verb – indeed, at 3.22.5 the absolute construction conjoins νύξ with χειμών – and two, at 4.96.8 and 4.134.2, like the punctual absolutes, involve the onset of night, but the participle is in both cases a transitive one, the night being viewed as putting a stop to works in progress (ἐπιλαβούσης τὸ ἔργον and ἀφελομένης τὸ

---

[45] Because the participles in these examples are aorists, the event of the absolute construction is anterior to that of the main verb; however, it is still reasonable to classify them as punctual here since they share with the constructions with θέρος and χειμών the fact that, if the participle is taken away, the resulting genitive of time would be a grammatical punctual expression. Moreover, in all of these constructions, the participle serves to specify a particular subset of time within the wider period designated by the time noun.

[46] One may disagree about the exact amount of temporal or causal force in the individual examples, but there remains a distinction – as seen perhaps most objectively in the semantics of the participles found in the two groups – between those genitive absolutes whose role is simply to specify a particular subset of the time noun and those which provide additional information that takes them beyond being neutral expressions of time.

ἔργον respectively). In short, the genitive absolutes with θέρος, χειμών, and νύξ all fall into one of two categories: twenty-nine are punctual (or limitative) and very similar to the constructions these nouns take with the genitive of time, while the other seven are more causal than temporal.

Consider now the genitive absolutes with ἔτος and ἡμέρα. In five of the seven, the verb is a compound of δια- meaning 'to pass by' (3× διελθεῖν, 2× διαλιπεῖν).[47] Thus, as the construction places the action not *during*, but *after* the time noun, it is semantically more distant from the simple genitive of time than was the case with the genitive absolutes with χειμών, θέρος, and νύξ. This difference is further increased by the fact that in four of these five passages, the time noun is plural, whereas punctual constructions typically have singular time nouns. As for the other two absolutes, the one with ἔτος is in a habitual construction (note φιλεῖ), precisely the sort of construction where even these dative-favoring nouns still appear in the genitive,[48] while the one with ἡμέρα, though in a punctual construction, is also conjoined with a second genitive absolute that could have attracted the expression away from the more usual τῇ δ' ὑστεραίᾳ (26× in Thucydides). In short, the data from Thucydides show clearly that the nature of the genitive absolutes in which time nouns occur is affected by the type of punctual temporal construction favored by those nouns. Nouns that take a punctual genitive of time are far more likely to occur in a genitive absolute – and, what is more, a genitive absolute that closely resembles the genitive of time – than are nouns whose chief punctual construction is the dative.

This finding may to some extent be checked against Xenophon (see Table 4). The figures here are lower and therefore less

---

[47] Following Classen–Steup (as well as Gomme (1956b) and Hornblower (1996)) ad loc., I take both ἐτῶν and ἡμερῶν as notional subjects of διελθόντων, with παρενεγκουσῶν (from intransitive παραφέρω 'be different, be in excess') as an attributive modifier of ἡμερῶν – rather than taking ἡμερῶν παρενεγκουσῶν as an independent genitive absolute parallel to ἐτῶν διελθόντων. This interpretation is suggested by the coordination of τοσαῦτα ἔτη and ἡμέρας οὐ πολλὰς παρενεγκούσας a few chapters later (5.26.3).

[48] While ἔτος does not occur in any habitual constructions in Thucydides, ἐνιαυτός occurs twice in the genitive in (closely related) distributive constructions (1.138.5, 3.50.2); ἡμέρα occurs four times in the genitive in distributive constructions and once in a habitual construction (4.23.2).

41

Table 4. *Genitive absolutes with time nouns in Xenophon*

Time noun	Description of genitive absolutes
χειμών (5×)	4× punctual (*HG* 1.1.2, 5.4.14, *An.* 5.8.3, *Ages.* 2.31) 1× with παρελθεῖν (*HG* 4.7.1)
θέρος (3×)	2× punctual (*HG* 1.2.1, 2.3.9) 1× causal (*HG* 5.2.29)
νύξ (2×)	2× punctual (*HG* 5.1.8, *An.* 2.2.19)
ἔτος*ᵃ* (2×)	1× with παρελθεῖν (*HG* 1.3.1) 1× causal (*HG* 7.4.28)
ἡμέρα (0×)	–

Note: ᵃ See n. 49.

conclusive than those for Thucydides, largely because Xenophon does not use summers and winters as a means of tracking when events occurred nearly as much as his predecessor. Still, they are consistent with what was observed above.

Once again, it is the nouns that favor the genitive over the dative of time – χειμών, θέρος, and νύξ – that are found in more genitive absolute constructions. Indeed, ἡμέρα is not found in any at all. Furthermore, while there are two genitive absolutes with ἔτος, neither one is a straightforward punctual construction.[49] By contrast, the eight genitive absolutes of χειμών, θέρος, and νύξ in punctual constructions all belong to broadly the same type that was found in Thucydides. Apart from that with χειμών at *An.* 5.8.3 (which is also unusual because it occurs in direct speech), they all specify a narrower point within the time noun in question, although the specific verbs used are often different: ἀρχομένου, μάλα ὄντος, and μέσου ὄντος with χειμῶνος; ἀρχομένου and τελευτῶντος with θέρους; ἐπιγενομένης and προϊούσης with νυκτός.

To summarize these data as follows: out of fifty-five genitive absolutes with time nouns in Thucydides and Xenophon, thirty-eight (69%) occur in punctual (or, once, limitative) expressions

---

[49] I omit the two genitive absolutes at *HG* 1.6.1 and 2.1.7, both in square brackets in Marchant's Oxford Classical Text (OCT). Were they to be included, they would both fall into the category of constructions with παρελθεῖν.

with θέρος, χειμών, and νύξ, or in a habitual expression with ἔτος, and so the genitive is the case that would be expected if the time noun were stripped of its participle and used adverbially; another nine (16%) are causal, and another seven (13%) have verbs with δια- or παρα-, and so would not be equivalent in sense to the temporal construction that would result if the participle were removed; this leaves Th. 4.114.1 as the sole example of a genitive absolute used where another case, the dative, would be expected if the time noun occurred on its own, and even this is not a clear-cut example, insofar as the temporal construction is conjoined with a second genitive absolute. Moreover, this interaction between constructions with and without predicative participles is not just a peculiarity of the genitive. An analogous syntactic ambiguity occurs with ἅμα⁺ᴰ as well:

(43) ἅμα δὲ τῷ ἦρι ἀποπορευόμενος ὁ Δερκυλίδας ἐκ τῶν Βιθυνῶν ἀφικνεῖται εἰς Λάμψακον

And, at the start of spring, Dercylidas set off from Bithynia and arrived at Lampsacus (X. *HG* 3.2.6)

(44) ἅμα δὲ τῷ ἦρι ὑποφαινομένῳ οἱ μὲν Ὀλύνθιοι ἱππεῖς ὄντες ὡς ἑξακόσιοι κατεδεδραμήκεσαν εἰς τὴν Ἀπολλωνίαν ἅμα μεσημβρίᾳ

And, when spring was just beginning, the Olynthian cavalry, numbering about 600, went down to Apollonia at midday (X. *HG* 5.3.1)

But the fact that there was interaction between genitive absolutes and the genitive of time, paralleled by the similarity between these two types of construction with ἅμα, does not mean that it would be right to treat them as undifferentiated from one another in this study. Because there exists a syntactic criterion – the presence or absence of a predicative participle – whereby the constructions can be distinguished, it would be ill-advised not to take advantage of this rare clarity in assessing the nature of temporal expressions generally. However much the predominance of the genitive absolute with particular time nouns is a phenomenon connected with the simple genitive of time, there are many genitive absolutes, notably causal constructions and those with verbs like διελθεῖν, that do not share this connection and so should be excluded from consideration in this respect. In short, it is far better to omit genitive absolutes from the initial study of the genitive of time, then assess separately the extent to which they are related to it, than to muddy the waters by including them from the start.

A second type of ambiguous genitive consists of those that could be considered either adverbial temporal constructions of the sort this study is examining or adnominal genitives dependent on neighboring time nouns. That there can be adnominal genitives of this sort, which should be excluded from consideration here, is not in question. We have already seen one subset of this type in the genitives of measure with εἶναι discussed above (see example (38)). The other subsets that must now be considered are as follows: other types of genitive of material, objective genitives, distributive genitives, and partitive genitives. Generally, genitives of the first two categories are unmistakably adnominal, while the syntactic structures of the second two are more ambiguous. First, consider the genitive of material. The vast majority of adnominal genitives in Thucydides and Xenophon fall into this category, a typical example being the following:

(45) διὰ τῆς ἀλλοτρίας **πολλῶν ἡμερῶν** ὁδὸν ἰόντες

    going on a march of many days through a foreign land (Th. 4.85.4)

In addition to ὁδός, the head nouns for genitives of this category are other words for journeys (πλοῦς and περίπλους), words for payment (μισθός), and words for food and provisions (τροφή, σῖτος and σιτία, and ἐπιτήδεια). They form such a coherent set that they can easily be omitted from consideration as adverbial temporal constructions. Second, there are time nouns that are, loosely speaking, objective genitives. On the one hand, these constructions make up a more disparate group: in Thucydides and Xenophon, the head nouns for these genitives are λογισμός ('a calculation of the days'), διαμαρτία ('an error as to the day to arrive'), ὑποφορά ('the pretext of the sacred months'), and δίκη ('a judicial inquiry into the time that had passed'). On the other, as the genitives are clearly necessary for completing the sense of the head noun, it should again pose no problems to discard these genitives from the subsequent study. A third structure in which a time noun in the genitive might be considered either adnominal or adverbial occurs in distributive constructions. Consider the following examples:

(46) δαρεικὸς ἑκάστῳ ἔσται μισθὸς **τοῦ μηνός**

Each man will have as wages a daric every month (X. *An.* 7.6.1)

(47) καὶ μισθὸν ἑκάστῳ **μηνὸς** διέδωκε

And he gave out a month's wages to each man (X. *HG* 2.1.5)

(48) δαρεικὸν ἕκαστος οἴσει **τοῦ μηνὸς** ὑμῶν

Each one of you will get a daric every month (X. *An.* 7.6.7)

Possibly, one could construe the genitive τοῦ μηνός in (46) as dependent on μισθός rather than on the verbal syntagm ἑκάστῳ ἔσται, taking the sentence as roughly equivalent to 'Each man will have a daric as wages for the month'. Indeed, in example (47) we see these two nouns found together in an adnominal construction of precisely this sort, for the context makes clear that this is a one-time disbursal of wages rather than a repeated, distributive construction.[50] Nevertheless, there is a good reason not to group (46) in the same category as (47): the presence of the article in τοῦ μηνός. In all the examples where the time noun is clearly adnominal, it does not have the definite article, whereas the article *is* characteristic of constructions – like (48) – where the genitive must be adverbial because there is no head noun like μισθός on which it could be dependent.[51] Constructions like (46) will thus be considered adverbial and included in the study.

The fourth type of genitive that can lie at the boundary of the adnominal and the adverbial is the partitive genitive. Again, most of the adnominal examples are easily categorized as such because the potential head noun requires the dependent genitive in order to complete its sense:

(49) (in a treaty) Ἐλαφηβολιῶνος **μηνὸς** ἕκτῃ φθίνοντος

On the twenty-fifth day of the month Elaphebolion (Th. 5.19.1)

---

[50] Other examples similar to (47) occur at *HG* 5.1.24 and 5.4.37 (and also Th. 6.8.2); the construction is also found with μηνῶν modified by a cardinal number at *HG* 5.3.25, *An.* 1.1.10 (2×), 1.2.11, 1.2.12, 7.5.10.

[51] There are, to be sure, time nouns with the article that are adnominal genitives, but, unlike those of the μηνὸς μισθός type, they are not likely to be confused with distributive genitives: τοῦ μηνὸς τὰ μέρη φανερὰ ἡμῖν ποιεῖ "It makes clear to us the divisions of the month" (X. *Mem.* 4.3.4).

45

(50) καὶ τὸ λοιπὸν **τῆς ἡμέρας** οἱ μὲν ἐπορεύοντο, οἱ δ᾽ εἵποντο

And for the rest of the day, they marched, while the others followed

(X. An. 3.4.16)

Nearly all the examples of the class are either like (49), where the time noun in the genitive unambiguously specifies which month the day in question belongs to, or like (50), where the head noun is a neuter noun of quantity – apart from λοιπόν, one also finds μέσον, ἥμισυ, μέρος, μόριον, τέλος, ἀκμή, πολύ, πλέον, πλεῖστον in this slot – which again needs the genitive as a complement. The matter becomes more complicated, however, when what might be the head noun could be seen as an independent temporal construction in its own right:

(51) περὶ δὲ τὸ φθινόπωρον **τοῦ θέρους τούτου** Ἀθηναῖοι ... ἐσέβαλον ἐς τὴν Μεγαρίδα

And in the autumn of this summer or during this summer, the Athenians invaded the Megarid (Th. 2.31.1)

Thucydides in particular uses this construction in a subtle gradation of variants that ranges from the more adnominal to the more adverbial. Consider first the endpoints, with (52) and (53) representing the adnominal end of the cline, (54) and (55) the adverbial end:

(52) οἱ δὲ Ἀθηναῖοι **ταύτης τῆς νυκτὸς** τῇ ἐπιγιγνομένῃ ἡμέρᾳ ἐξητάζοντο

And the Athenians, the next day after this night, held a review of their troops

(Th. 6.97.1)

(53) καὶ τὸ θέρος ἦρχε **τοῦ ἐνδεκάτου ἔτους**

And the summer of the eleventh year began (Th. 5.24.2)

(54) **τοῦ δ᾽ ἐπιγιγνομένου θέρους** Πελοποννήσιοι καὶ οἱ ξύμμαχοι ἅμα τῷ σίτῳ ἀκμάζοντι ἐστράτευσαν ἐς τὴν Ἀττικήν

And the next summer, the Peloponnesians and their allies invaded Attica when the grain was ripe (Th. 3.1.1)

(55) **τοῦ δ᾽ αὐτοῦ θέρους**, καὶ περὶ τὸν αὐτὸν χρόνον ὃν ἐν τῇ Μήλῳ οἱ Ἀθηναῖοι κατεῖχον, καὶ οἱ ἀπὸ τῶν τριάκοντα νεῶν Ἀθηναῖοι περὶ Πελοπόννησον ὄντες πρῶτον ἐν Ἑλλομενῷ τῆς Λευκαδίας φρουρούς τινας λοχήσαντες διέφθειραν

And the same summer, and about the time that the Athenians were detained in Melos, the other Athenians on the thirty ships sailing around the

46

Peloponnesus first ambushed some garrisons in Leucadian Ellomenus and killed them (Th. 3.94.1)

In (52), the genitive must be dependent on the noun phrase τῇ ἐπιγιγνομένῃ ἡμέρᾳ rather than on the verb ἐξητάζοντο as the action of the verb takes place *after* the night, not *on* it; in (53), the genitive τοῦ ἑνδεκάτου ἔτους is again far better understood as dependent on the noun τὸ θέρος, specifying which θέρος was beginning – in effect, paralleling the construction of (49). At the other end of the spectrum, it would strain the word order in (54) considerably to take τοῦ ἐπιγιγνομένου θέρους as dependent on σίτῳ ('when the grain of the following summer was ripe'); τοῦ αὐτοῦ θέρους in (55) is unquestionably adverbial, and the passage is useful as evidence that a genitive of time can be a constituent parallel to and conjoined with a prepositional phrase of the περὶ τὸν αὐτὸν χρόνον type. To turn now to the more ambiguous examples, we find that they mostly resemble either (54), where a genitive (usually τοῦ ἐπιγιγνομένου θέρους) could be dependent on a designation of a specific season within the summer half-year (usually ἅμα (τῷ) ἦρι), or (55) – but without the καί between the θέρους phrase and the περί phrase, such that the genitive (usually τοῦ θέρους τούτου) could be dependent on a phrase with χρόνος (usually ὑπὸ τοὺς αὐτοὺς χρόνους).[52] For the most part, examples of the first set look relatively adverbial (at least compared to those of the second):[53]

(56) **τοῦ δ' ἐπιγιγνομένου θέρους** ἅμα ἦρι οἱ τῶν Ἀθηναίων πρέσβεις ἧκον ἐκ τῆς Σικελίας

And the following summer, when it was spring, the Athenians' ambassadors arrived from Sicily (Th. 6.8.1)

(57) ἅμα δὲ τῷ ἦρι εὐθὺς ἀρχομένῳ **τοῦ ἐπιγιγνομένου θέρους** οἱ ἐν τῇ Σικελίᾳ Ἀθηναῖοι ... παρέπλευσαν ἐπὶ Μεγάρων τῶν ἐν τῇ Σικελίᾳ

---

52 The association of the ἅμα (τῷ) ἦρι construction with τοῦ ἐπιγιγνομένου θέρους and that of the ὑπὸ τοὺς αὐτοὺς χρόνους construction with τοῦ θέρους τούτου follows naturally from the narratological consequences of their semantics: in the former case, as spring is the first part of summer, it is not surprising that it should occur in statements relating events of the transition from one winter to the next summer and thus collocate with ἐπιγιγνόμενον; in the latter case, an event that happens at the same time as another is going to be in the same season and thus collocate with τοῦτο.

53 Other examples which I assign to this set occur at 2.28.1 (with τοῦ αὐτοῦ θέρους), 2.31.1 (with τοῦ θέρους τούτου; probably the most adnominal of the set), and 4.1.1, 4.117.1, 5.40.1, and 8.61.1 (all with τοῦ ἐπιγιγνομένου θέρους).

And at the very start of spring the next summer, the Athenians in Sicily ... sailed around to Sicilian Megara (Th. 6.94.1)

(58) ἅμα δὲ τῷ ἦρι **τοῦ ἐπιγιγνομένου θέρους** εὐθὺς ἐπειγομένων τῶν Χίων ἀποστεῖλαι τὰς ναῦς καὶ δεδιότων μὴ οἱ Ἀθηναῖοι τὰ πρασσόμενα αἴσθωνται ... ἀποπέμπουσιν οἱ Λακεδαιμόνιοι ἐς Κόρινθον ἄνδρας Σπαρτιάτας τρεῖς

And when spring of the following summer came, as the Chians were immediately pressing them to send the ships and were afraid that the Athenians would learn what was going on ... the Lacedaemonians sent to Corinth three Spartan men (Th. 8.7.1)

The word order of (56) strongly suggests an adverbial reading for the genitive; in (57), with the genitive following the ἅμα phrase, the genitive starts to look more adnominal, but the intrusion of the εὐθὺς ἀρχομένῳ phrase again inclines one towards considering it adverbial. Finally, in (58), with the genitive directly following the ἅμα phrase, and a long genitive absolute intervening between the two temporal expressions and the main verb, an adnominal interpretation has certainly become more likely, if not certain. The second set, on the other hand, is on the whole rather more adnominal:[54]

(59) ὑπὸ δὲ τοὺς αὐτοὺς χρόνους **τοῦ θέρους τούτου** καὶ οἱ Πλαταιῆς ... ξυνέβησαν τοῖς Πελοποννησίοις τοιῷδε τρόπῳ

And at the same time of or during this summer the Plataeans came to terms with the Peloponnesians in the following way (Th. 3.52.1)

(60) Βρασίδας δὲ κατὰ τὸν αὐτὸν χρόνον **τοῦ θέρους** πορευόμενος ἑπτακοσίοις καὶ χιλίοις ὁπλίταις ἐς τὰ ἐπὶ Θράκης

And Brasidas, traveling at the same time of the summer with 1700 hoplites in the direction of Thrace (Th. 4.78.1)

(61) ὑπὸ δὲ τοὺς αὐτοὺς χρόνους **τοῦ ἦρος**, πρὶν τὸν σῖτον ἐν ἀκμῇ εἶναι, Πελοποννήσιοι καὶ οἱ ξύμμαχοι ἐσέβαλον ἐς τὴν Ἀττικήν

And at the same time of or during the spring, before the crops had ripened, the Peloponnesians and their allies invaded Attica (Th. 4.2.1)

---

[54] Other examples which I assign to this set (all, like linguistic snowflakes, slightly different from one another) occur at 3.7.1 (κατὰ τὸν αὐτὸν χρόνον τοῦ θέρους τούτου), 5.32.1 (περὶ τοὺς αὐτοὺς χρόνους τοῦ θέρους τούτου), 6.105.1 (κατὰ τοὺς αὐτοὺς χρόνους τούτου τοῦ θέρους), 7.21.1 (ὑπὸ τοὺς αὐτοὺς χρόνους τούτου τοῦ ἦρος), and 8.99.1 (ὑπὸ τοὺς αὐτοὺς χρόνους τοῦ θέρους τούτου).

48

In (59), the most representative example of this subtype, one could argue for either an adnominal or an adverbial interpretation: on the one hand, the inclusion of τοὺς αὐτοὺς in the first phrase suggests taking the genitive as completing the sense of the ὑπό phrase; on the other, both ὑπό τοὺς αὐτοὺς χρόνους and τοῦ θέρους τούτου occur independently as adverbial phrases – the former at 1.100.3, 8.20.1, and 8.108.1 (and recall also example (55)), the latter at 5.49.1 – so there is no reason why the second phrase has to be understood as dependent on the first. That said, the parallels just cited are remarkably rare, considering the proliferation of τοῦ θέρους with other modifiers (particularly τοῦ αὐτοῦ and τοῦ ἐπιγιγνομένου), and the number of times that ὑπό τοὺς αὐτοὺς χρόνους occurs followed by genitives of this type (in addition to (59) and (61), see also 2.95.1, 5.12.1, 7.21.1, 8.99.1).[55] This leaning towards an adnominal view is further supported by example (60), where the following genitive is the simple τοῦ θέρους, which, unlike τοῦ αὐτοῦ θέρους or even τοῦ θέρους τούτου, never occurs on its own as a genitive of time in Thucydides; the strength of this argument, however, is lessened by example (61), for, unlike τοῦ θέρους, τοῦ ἦρος *is* used as a straightforward genitive of time (at 7.50.1).

Another potential argument in favor of describing these as genitives of time is that, as with the genitive absolutes, the time nouns that occur in the genitive after τοὺς αὐτοὺς χρόνους are precisely those that also favor the genitive of time outside of this context. But this fact is still not decisive, for one could argue either (a) these are like the genitive absolutes in that just because this construction happens to occur with nouns that regularly prefer a genitive of time does not mean that the genitive must also be a genitive of time in this construction as well, or (b) unlike the genitive absolutes, the reason that this genitive construction only has those time nouns that take the genitive of time

---

[55] At first glance, these counter-parallels might seem to be of dubious value: in two of them (2.95.1, 5.12.1), the genitive that follows is a genitive absolute. But the genitive absolute with time nouns, as seen in the discussion above, is apparently not all that syntactically different from the non-absolute genitives of these lexemes, so the counter-parallels are probably worthwhile after all as an indication that ὑπό τοὺς αὐτοὺς χρόνους really does strongly prefer a following, adnominal genitive.

is that they are, in fact, genitives of time. In the end, then, it seems impossible to determine for certain whether or not these genitives count as adnominal or adverbial. The bulk of the evidence – notably, the regularity with which ὑπὸ/περὶ/κατὰ τοὺς αὐτοὺς χρόνους is followed by a genitive (and the rarity of the reverse order) – should probably incline us towards treating them as adnominal. But because the adverbial reading cannot be excluded, such passages will be included in the figures for adverbial genitives throughout this study, as will those of the ἅμα (τῷ) ἦρι type.

The third and final problematic genitive resembles the previous adnominal genitives in that the ambiguity of the construction lies in the uncertainty about which constituent the genitive is syntactically dependent on. But, whereas above the genitive could be considered dependent either on an adjacent noun or directly on the verb, here the alternative to construing the genitive with the verb is to take it as a partitive genitive dependent on a neighboring adverb:

(62) καὶ τῆς ἡμέρας ὀψὲ ἦν

And it was late in the day (X. HG 2.1.23)

Fortunately, the semantics of these constructions almost always make it clear that they are partitive rather temporal genitives. The occasional examples where the borderline is not as sharply defined can be dealt with individually.

The dative

In contrast to the genitive, it is generally much easier to determine whether a time noun in the dative is a dative of time or some other type of dative because most of these datives are simply too semantically different from the temporal construction for there to be any potential for confusion. Accordingly, the exclusion of the following types of dative from the database on which this study is based should require no further comment: (i) datives that are verbal objects, either indirect (e.g. Th. 5.16.1) or instrumental, like objects of χρῆσθαι (e.g. X. HG 6.1.15); (ii) other instrumental datives, for

example, καταφέρεται χειμῶνι⁵⁶ (Th. 1.137.2), including datives of
cause, for example, ἐν καλύβαις πνιγηραῖς ὥρᾳ ἔτους "in huts that
were stifling because of the season of year"⁵⁷ (Th. 2.52.2); (iii)
datives of respect, for example, τῷ μὲν χρόνῳ ἰσήλικος τοῖς
ἀειγενέσι θεοῖς "equal in age to the eternal gods" (X. Smp. 8.1).
Two other types of dative are slightly more problematic. First,
there are what are probably best considered datives of reference
that could perhaps also be taken as temporal:⁵⁸

(63) ταύτῃ μὲν τῇ ἡμέρᾳ τοῦτο τὸ τέλος ἐγένετο

Such was the end of that day (X. An. 5.6.1)

The general construction of (63), with a punctual dative of ἡμέρα at
the start of a μέν clause followed by an aorist describing an event
that occurs on the day in question, is not so far removed from
indisputable temporal datives such as the following:

(64) καὶ ταύτῃ μὲν τῇ ἡμέρᾳ, ἐπεὶ κατεστρατοπεδεύοντο οἱ Ἕλληνες κώμαις
ἐπιτύχοντες, ἀπῆλθον οἱ βάρβαροι

And on this day, when the Greeks had come upon some villages and set up
their camps, the barbarians went away (X. An. 3.4.18)

Nevertheless, ταύτῃ τῇ ἡμέρᾳ in (63) should not be considered a
temporal dative because its function in the clause is too different
from that of the canonical dative of time: it does not specify when
the end happened, but rather what was ending. In other words, the
dative phrase is not a loosely connected adjunct that, inasmuch as it
only gives incidental temporal information, could be omitted without disrupting the sense of the clause. It is instead a complement
without which the phrase τοῦτο τὸ τέλος is insufficiently determined. Significantly, both here and in the only other parallel I have
found (X. An. 6.1.13), the verb in question is ἐγένετο. That this is

---

⁵⁶ This example is also distinguished from the typical temporal constructions in that χειμών
here means 'storm' rather than 'winter'. In fact, this is the only sense in which
Thucydides ever uses this time noun in the preposition-less dative, and it is always an
instrumental dative with the passive of καταφέρω (see also 4.120.1 and 6.2.3). One might
conceivably argue that these are in fact temporal datives meaning 'in the storm', but the
limitation of the dative of this time noun to this one passive verb strongly suggests that the
instrumental interpretation is the better one.
⁵⁷ See Rusten (1989) ad loc.   ⁵⁸ See also X. An. 6.1.13.

51

the verb renders the construction that much closer to a dative of possession than to the dative of time. The other dative that requires a little more attention is the dative of degree of difference. Most of the time, these datives occur in conjunction with a word or phrase – most often the comparative ὕστερον, but also verbs with the prefix προ- and prepositional phrases with μετά and πρό – that make it clear that the dative is not specifying when an event happened, but rather the relation between the event of the verb and another temporal landmark. As such, the function of such a dative is different enough that it can be separated into a category distinct from that of the ordinary dative of time:

(65) δύο γὰρ ἡμέραις ὕστερον ἀπέστησαν οἱ Σκιωναῖοι

For two days later, the people of Scione revolted (Th. 4.122.6)

(66) ἔτεσι δὲ ἐγγύτατα ὀκτὼ καὶ ἑκατὸν μετὰ τὴν σφετέραν οἴκισιν Γελῷοι Ἀκράγαντα ᾤκισαν

And close to 108 years after their own founding, the people of Gela founded Acragas (Th. 6.4.4)

From these examples it is clear that the action of the verb does not take place during the time period expressed by δύο ἡμέραις and ἔτεσι ὀκτὼ καὶ ἑκατόν respectively, but rather after it. Accordingly, these constructions are not included in this study. But the distinction is not always as clear-cut as in (65) and (66), particularly when the time noun in question is χρόνῳ. Consider the following two passages:

(67) χρόνῳ δὲ ὕστερον ξυνέβη Θασίους αὐτῶν ἀποστῆναι

And some time later, it happened that the Thasians revolted from them
(Th. 1.100.2)

(68) καὶ χρόνῳ ξυνέβησαν καθ᾽ ὁμολογίαν

And in time they reached an agreement to surrender (Th. 1.98.3)

While (67) has the same sort of dative of degree of difference as (65) and (66), it is less obvious how one should classify the dative χρόνῳ in (68). A superficial glance at the English translation would suggest that χρόνῳ should be a simple punctual dative, as in TIME NOUN is one common way of translating this construction into

English. Indeed, one may compare a phrase that comes only a few chapters later:

(69) δεκάτῳ ἔτει ... ξυνέβησαν πρὸς τοὺς Λακεδαιμονίους

In the tenth year, they surrendered to the Lacedaemonians (Th. 1.103.1)

Here the combination of a time noun in the dative, rendered with *in* in English, together with an aorist verb (in fact, the very same one, ξυνέβησαν) results in a perfectly ordinary punctual dative of time. But the apparent similarity is actually only an illusion created by the translation. The function of a punctual temporal expression (as I have set up the category for this study) is to locate an event as occurring at some point during the period of time specified by the time noun, not a point before or after it.[59] And while one cannot completely exclude the possibility that the agreement in (68) is viewed as taking place *during* the time period delimited by χρόνῳ, it still seems better to see it as taking place *after* this period. The most fundamental reason for preferring the latter view is semantic and pragmatic. In a construction like (68), χρόνῳ simply does not mean 'at an (unspecified) time'. First, this is a relatively empty function for a word or phrase to exercise, at least in an affirmative clause. Second, and more important, Greek does have a word for this, ποτε, which, as one would expect, is more at home in questions, conditionals, and interrogatives than in a sentence like (68); nor, for that matter, would (68) mean the same thing if ποτε were substituted for χρόνῳ.[60] Instead, since these χρόνῳ clauses always mark the passage of time between one event and the next, it is far

---

[59] To review a potentially confusing distinction, the limitative construction also locates the event as occurring at some point during the period of time specified by the time noun. The difference is that, in the limitative construction, the author is drawing attention to the gap between the amount of time the event takes and the frame provided by the time noun, whereas in the punctual construction, this gap is not highlighted.

[60] To illustrate the difference between ποτε and χρόνῳ, we may consider their respective relationships with the word ὕστερον. Of the ninety examples of ποτε in Thucydides, only twice does it collocate with ὕστερον (as opposed to nine of the fifteen examples of χρόνῳ). Once, at 4.18.5, it occurs in the phrase μή ποτε ὕστερον – that is, in one of the contexts where it would be most expected – and so does not provide a real contrast with the examples of χρόνῳ ὕστερον. But the other time, at 4.40.2, is in fact in an affirmative clause: καί τινος ἐρομένου ποτὲ ὕστερον "And when someone asked later at some point." Here we see what χρόνῳ would have to be doing in (68) for it to be considered a punctual expression. Fränkel, in discussing χρόνῳ, also notes its relationship with ποτε (1960: 10–11).

more pragmatically natural to take them as meaning 'after an (unspecified) time'. Another reason for taking (68) as meaning 'after some time' is the parallel with (67). Initially, there might appear to be a fairly large syntactic gap between these two, with the presence of ὕστερον instrumental in creating a syntactic environment in which χρόνῳ can be understood as a dative of degree of difference. But, limiting ourselves to Thucydides, there are two potential examples of intermediate constructions, in which hyperbaton (albeit limited) separates the ὕστερον from the χρόνῳ:

(70) ὕστερον δὲ αὖθις **χρόνῳ** ἐπίτιμοι ἐγένοντο

And later, after some time, they regained their rights (Th. 5.34.2)

(71) ἀναστάτων δὲ Καμαριναίων γενομένων . . . **χρόνῳ** Ἱπποκράτης ὕστερον Γέλας τύραννος . . . αὐτὸς οἰκιστὴς γενόμενος κατῴκισε Καμάριναν

And when the people of Camarina were expelled, some time later Hippocrates, tyrant of Gela, himself became a founder and re-established Camarina (Th. 6.5.3)

Now, there is no denying that, in both examples, the hyperbaton is a very gentle one, and the dative is still easily construed as dependent on the comparative element in ὕστερον. But the fact remains that, since χρόνῳ need not be immediately adjacent to ὕστερον for it to mean 'after some time', it is that much more reasonable to view constructions like (68) as datives of degrees of difference that have, in effect, been turned loose. A final reason for not taking χρόνῳ as a punctual expression is the behavior of χρόνος in constructions with διά⁺ᴳ. Consider the following three passages, which, as it happens, are the only temporal constructions with διά⁺ᴳ in Thucydides:[61]

---

[61] I cite the examples from Thucydides here to be consistent with the examples used in the preceding material. While there are only three, they are in fact an accurate microcosm of what happens in authors like Xenophon who use διά⁺ᴳ more often. He uses this preposition 12× in total with ἡμέρα, νύξ, χειμών, ἐνιαυτός, and ἔτος. All but twice, the expression is durative, and the two counter-examples (at *Cyn.* 6.3 and *Ath.* 3.5 – the latter not real Xenophon anyway) are clearly marked as distributive rather than durative by the presence of an ordinal number modifying the time noun. As for expressions with χρόνος, Xenophon once has διὰ παντὸς ἀεὶ τοῦ χρόνου in a durative construction, but the other examples are all διὰ χρόνου, without any modifiers, and they mostly mean 'after some time', apart from one example (*Ath.* 3.5 – again, not real Xenophon) where the verb is frequentative and so a distributive reading ('every now and then') is forced.

(72) **δι' ἡμέρας** βάλλοντες πανταχόθεν τοὺς Ἀθηναίους καὶ ξυμμάχους

Throughout the day striking the Athenians and their allies from all sides
(Th. 7.82.1)

(73) καὶ ὑετοῦ ἅμα **διὰ νυκτὸς** πολλοῦ ἐπιγενομένου

And as there was also a lot of rain throughout the night (Th. 2.4.2)

(74) ἔστι γὰρ ὅτι καὶ αἱ νῆες αὐτοὺς **διὰ χρόνου** καθελκυσθεῖσαι καὶ οὐδὲν στέγουσαι ἐφόβουν

For it is the case that even the ships frightened them, as they were being launched after some time and did not keep out the water (Th. 2.94.3)

In the first two examples, διά⁺ᴳ has its usual function, that of marking a durative construction and roughly equivalent to English *throughout*. In the third, however, we see that it takes on a different meaning when used with χρόνου and comes closer to English *after*.⁶²
It is also worth noting that the non-temporal function of διά⁺ᴳ as marking the instrument is very close to that of the instrumental dative. While one might be skeptical that a dative of degree of difference in the strict sense can break free from a comparative or similar word and be used on its own, if we bear in mind the similarity between this dative and the instrumental dative – which can, of course, be used independently of a trigger word like ὕστερον – there should be no objections to seeing χρόνῳ in (68) or, even more so, in the following example as belonging in this category, rather than with the more locatival datives like τῇ ὑστεραίᾳ:⁶³

(75) πολλὰ δὲ καὶ ἄλλα ἔτι καὶ νῦν ὄντα καὶ οὐ **χρόνῳ** ἀμνηστούμενα καὶ οἱ ἄλλοι Ἕλληνες οὐκ ὀρθῶς οἴονται

And the other Greeks as well have erroneous ideas about many other things, which are still in existence now and are not forgotten through the passage of time (Th. 1.20.3)

In short, as a result of the greater similarity of the χρόνῳ constructions to instrumental datives and datives of degree of difference than to the usual punctual datives of time, they will not be included as temporal constructions in the rest of the study.

⁶² For this translation, see also Rusten (1989: 239).
⁶³ That said, there are of course other circumstances in which the locatival and instrumental dative are harder to distinguish from each other; see Bers (1984: 87–90).

The accusative

The final case for which we must set boundaries on what will be considered temporal constructions is the accusative. Again, the difficulties here are not as great as they are with the genitive. Nearly all the accusatives of time nouns can be labeled unambiguously as (a) temporal accusatives, (b) accusatives that are the objects of verbs, or (c) accusatives that are either the subject or copular predicate of an embedded infinitive or participial clause. As examples of (b) and (c), see the following:

(76) ἡμέραν ξυνθέμενοι ᾗ παρέσονται

Setting a day on which they would be there (Th. 6.65.1)

(77) οὐκ ἀνέμεινεν ἡμέραν γενέσθαι

He did not wait for it to be day (Th. 4.135.1)

Not infrequently, however, there is ambiguity between categories (a) and (b), as there is a class of verbs, such as διάγω, that refer to the spending or passing of time, for which it is often difficult to tell whether the verb is intransitive, taking a neighboring time noun in the accusative as a temporal construction, or whether the verb is transitive, taking the accusative as its object:[64]

(78) ταύτην μὲν δὴ τὴν ἡμέραν οὕτω διαγαγόντες

So they spent this day in this way (X. Cyr. 6.1.1)

In this example, one's first instinct – perhaps based on the English translation – might be to take ταύτην τὴν ἡμέραν as the direct object of διάγω. After all, διάγω is, by virtue of being a compound of ἄγω, likely to be transitive. Furthermore, the semantics of διάγω, like those of English *spend*, seem too empty for it to exist comfortably as an intransitive verb: it seems to require the object in order to

---

[64] For discussion of a similar problem, namely where to draw the line between direct objects and the accusative of place to which, see Bers (1984: 63–7). Brixhe (1994) looks more broadly at the interrelationships between the various uses conveyed by the accusative; see esp. p. 42 for the fuzziness of the boundary between direct objects and the accusatives of extent of space or time.

have any sense at all. But this line of argumentation is refuted by passages like the following:[65]

(79) ἀνιαρὸς δὲ καὶ σκυθρωπὸς ὢν σιωπῇ διῆγεν

Annoyed and frowning, he remained silent (X. *Cyr.* 1.4.14)

Apparently, διάγω is in fact unlike English *spend* in that it does not require a direct object, leaving the accusative in (78) free to be construed as an adverbial accusative of time. Another angle by which to approach (78) is to compare it with the following example:

(80) ἡμέρας γὰρ τεσσαράκοντα μάλιστα ἐν τῇ γῇ τῇ Ἀττικῇ ἐγένοντο

For they spent about forty days in Attica (Th. 2.57.2)

Example (80) is close enough in sense to (78) that the same English construction can be used to translate the verb-accusative complex. But in (80), as the verb is the intransitive γίγνομαι, the accusative is unquestionably an accusative of time rather than a direct object. Given, then, that διάγω can be intransitive, so an accusative construed with it need not be a direct object, and that a close parallel to the διάγω+accusative construction exists in which the accusative is certainly an accusative of time, it seems impossible to exclude the accusative of (78) from consideration as an accusative of time. On the other hand, the fact that διάγω can take accusative objects that are at least relatively unlikely to be accusatives of time means that we also cannot reject the possibility that ταύτην τὴν ἡμέραν is a direct object.[66]

---

[65] Cf. also the other examples that LSJ cites for intransitve διάγω used with an adverbial complement, Th. 7.71.3 and X. *Mem.* 4.4.15. In (79), one could perhaps take ὢν as a complement of διῆγεν, but this option is not possible with the passage from the *Memorabilia*; also, the examples of participial complements cited in LSJ (s.v. II.2.d) suggest that these tend to be from more agentive verbs than εἰμί.

[66] The evidence in LSJ is unclear. On the one hand, syntagms like τὸν βίον διάγειν (Pl.) or, esp., τὴν ἑορτὴν διάγειν (admittedly only in Ath.) are in my view unlikely to contain accusatives of time because the nouns in question are too far removed from prototypical time nouns for the temporal interpretation to prevail over the direct object reading with an ambiguous verb like διάγω. This supports the position that ταύτην τὴν ἡμέραν in (78) is a direct object. On the other hand, it is also noticeable that διάγω (unlike, say, διατρίβω) is not used of spending money or of exhausting or wearing out an object. This suggests that διάγω is not particularly transitive, and so ταύτην τὴν ἡμέραν is better seen as an accusative of time after all. As further evidence of the relative intransitivity of compounds of ἄγω, it is worth noting that ὑπάγω is already common in Koine as an intransitive verb – the first step in its development into modern πηγαίνω ('go').

57

The following example, with two potential accusatives of time, offers slightly different interpretative problems, although in this case the syntax is somewhat easier to resolve:

(81) οἱ δὲ πρὸς τὸ ἄγγελμα ἐπέσχον **τὴν νύκτα**, νομίσαντες οὐκ ἀπάτην εἶναι. καὶ ἐπειδὴ καὶ ὡς οὐκ εὐθὺς ὥρμησαν, ἔδοξεν αὐτοῖς καὶ **τὴν ἐπιοῦσαν ἡμέραν** περιμεῖναι, ὅπως ξυσκευάσαιντο ὡς ἐκ τῶν δυνατῶν οἱ στρατιῶται ὅτι χρησιμώτατα

And, in response to the report, they stayed in place for the night in the belief that there was no trickery involved. And since, that being so, they did not set off immediately, they decided to wait for the following day as well, so that the soldiers could pack up the most useful supplies as far as was possible

(Th. 7.74.1)

Taking first the phrase ἐπέσχον τὴν νύκτα, we see a relatively clear example of an accusative of time with an intransitive verb. While ἐπέχω can potentially take an accusative object, the various senses of the transitive construction of ἐπέχω ('hold (out), offer; hold back, check; have power over, occupy') are too different from the sense required here ('stay in place') for this to be a possible interpretation of the syntax of this construction. Turning next to τὴν ἐπιοῦσαν ἡμέραν περιμεῖναι, we find in the case of μένω and its compounds a smaller, but still noticeable, semantic difference between the accusative of time and the accusative of the direct object, a difference neatly paralleled in the English translation as well. In the construction 'wait for the following day', the verb *wait* can be taken as intransitive, and the prepositional phrase as equivalent to an accusative of extent of time. In other words, the construction could be equivalent to *stay waiting throughout the following day*. Alternatively, *wait for* could be understood as a phrasal verb taking an accusative object, such that the construction is instead roughly equivalent to *await the following day* (e.g. as their cue to leave). Fortunately, the context of the Greek allows us to conclude that in (81) it is the former construction that Thucydides is using. In particular, the use of καί before τὴν ἐπιοῦσαν ἡμέραν aligns this accusative with the τὴν νύκτα that came earlier: *they stayed in place during the night and decided to remain there for the following day as well* is far more coherent than *they stayed in place during the night and decided to await the following day as well.* As further evidence of the difference between the two constructions of περιμένω, we may compare the following construction from Xenophon, which combines both types of accusative:[67]

(82) μετὰ ταῦτα περιέμενον Τισσαφέρνην οἵ τε "Ελληνες καὶ ὁ Ἀριαῖος ἐγγὺς ἀλλήλων ἐστρατοπεδευμένοι **ἡμέρας πλείους ἢ εἴκοσιν**

Afterwards, the Greeks and Ariaeus, camped close to one another, waited for Tissaphernes for more than twenty days (X. *An.* 2.4.1)

Taken together, these examples reveal that there is no easy way, in constructing a database of temporal expressions in Greek, to deal with the occasional ambiguity between the accusative of time and the direct object. On the one hand, an example like (82) shows that there can be a contrastive difference between the two types of accusative, even with a verb, like περιμένω, that falls into the broad category of verbs of passing time. On the other hand, even though this difference is far more meaningful with περιμένω than it is with διάγω, one is still forced to rely on contextual clues – some obvious, as in (82), some less so, as in (81) – to work out which construction is intended. Furthermore, with verbs like διάγω, as shown by examples (78) and (79), the two constructions are too similar for any syntactic or semantic test to isolate one from the other. In the end, the best practical solution to the methodological problem posed by these constructions is to include examples like (78) in the data on which the following chapters are based. If one decides to try to exclude those which might be direct objects, it is impossible to be completely consistent about where one draws the line between the two constructions, but if one's guideline is to include all those accusatives that could be accusatives of time, there is a reasonable chance of setting up a uniform collection of examples.

---

[67] See also X. *An.* 2.1.3.

2

EXPRESSIONS OF TIME IN THUCYDIDES

In this chapter, I will examine the expressions of time used by Thucydides, before turning in the next chapter to the usage of other Classical prose writers, especially Xenophon, Plato, and Demosthenes. I have chosen Thucydides as a starting point for two reasons: first, as history is the genre that offers the greatest density of expressions of time, it makes sense to begin with a historian;[1] second, Thucydides offers a better standard for comparison than Xenophon given the latter's reputation as the 'naughty boy of Attic syntax' (Gildersleeve 1903: 406).[2] In order to prevent the material from becoming unwieldy, I have divided it into five sections, each of which addresses a particular problem: (i) the distribution of the accusative of time and prepositional constructions to indicate extent of time; (ii) the distribution of the genitive and dative of time with the words for day, month, and year, all of which have a lexical preference for the dative; (iii) as the previous heading, but with the words for night and the seasons, which prefer the genitive; (iv) limitative expressions with χρόνος; (v) the other prepositional constructions occurring with χρόνος, especially κατά, ὑπό, and περὶ τοὺς αὐτοὺς χρόνους.

Durative expressions in Thucydides

The accusative of time is the easiest of the temporal expressions to understand, in Thucydides as in other authors. The traditional view that it expresses extent of time is, for all practical purposes, correct. In other words, it is associated with the durative event type:

---

[1] In addition to Jiménez's 1998 study, there is also useful discussion of Thucydides' chronological reckoning in Gomme (1956b: 699–721), Gomme et al. (1981: 445–53), Dewald (2005: *passim*, but esp. 35–47), and Rood (2007: 137–9).

[2] This is particularly true in the – here relevant – sphere of prepositions: see Gautier (1911: 48–50).

(1) καὶ ἡμέρας μὲν πέντε ἡσύχαζον

And they stayed quiet for five days (Th. 3.107.3)

This does not mean, however, that the verbs with which the accusative of time occurs must necessarily be imperfective in aspect. There are several verbs, notably μένω, which, even in the aorist, describe an action that extends over a period of time and has no inherent endpoint:

(2) ἡμέρας γὰρ πέντε καὶ δέκα ἔμειναν ἐν τῇ Ἀττικῇ

For they remained in Attica for fifteen days (Th. 4.6.2)

That the aorist should be found in such constructions is not in fact surprising: while a verb like μένω is atelic when considered in its own right, the addition of a phrase such as ἡμέρας πέντε καὶ δέκα in effect sets a time limit on the action of the verb, thus making the entire predicate telic, in which case the aorist is the appropriate aspectual choice. That durativity and atelicity are key features of the accusative of time can also be seen in the nature of the modifiers that Jiménez found to be associated with the accusative of time: quantifying adjectives like πολύς and ὀλίγος and cardinal numbers (1998: 95).

There are very few examples of accusatives of time that do not seem to mark durative and atelic events: in other words, accusatives of time that seem to answer the question 'at what time?' rather than 'for how long?' This can best be seen by examining the characteristics taken on by the accusative of time with each of the time nouns in turn.

(a) ἡμέρα occurs forty-two times in accusative of time constructions. Of these, nineteen have the plural of ἡμέρα, thus making the extent of time reading plausible from the start. Furthermore, of these nineteen, ἡμέρα is modified by ὀλίγας, τινας, πολλάς, or a cardinal number in all but two, and the verb in the construction is atelic (most often μένω). As for the two examples that do not have such a modifier, one provides the time frame in which a limitative event, indicated by ἐν^{+D}, can take place:

(3) ὁ δὲ ἡμέρας τε ἐσπείσατο ἐν αἷς εἰκὸς ἦν κομισθῆναι

And he made a treaty for a number of days in which it was reasonable to return
(Th. 2.73.1)

61

In the other, the durative nature of the construction is clearly indicated by the following clause with ὅσαι:

(4) τὰς οὖν ναῦς ἐπλήρουν καὶ ἀνεπειρῶντο **ἡμέρας** ὅσαι αὐτοῖς ἐδόκουν ἱκαναὶ εἶναι

So they manned the ships and led them in exercises for as many days as seemed to them to be sufficient (Th. 7.51.2)

In constructions with the singular, the situation is similar. Of the twenty-three examples, six have μίαν, ὅλην, or ἅπασαν as a modifier in clear durative constructions.[3] More numerous is the construction with ταύτην, which occurs eight times. One might expect expressions with demonstratives to favor the punctual construction with the dative of time, insofar as the demonstrative specifies *which* day an event occurred. But in fact the emphasis in such expressions can still lie on the duration of time, and so they split fairly evenly between the accusative and dative (Jiménez 1998: 98). Of those in the accusative with ἡμέρα, six are unproblematic durative constructions, which can be seen in the nature of the verb modified, the presence of a following δέ-clause with a punctual dative that is set up by the accusative of time, or both:[4]

(5) καὶ **ταύτην μὲν τὴν ἡμέραν** καὶ **τὴν ἐπιοῦσαν νύκτα** ἐν φυλακῇ εἶχον αὐτοὺς οἱ Ἀθηναῖοι· **τῇ δ᾽ ὑστεραίᾳ** οἱ μὲν Ἀθηναῖοι τροπαῖον στήσαντες

And for this day and the following night, the Athenians held them under guard; and on the next day, the Athenians, after setting up a trophy (Th. 4.38.4)

The remaining two constructions, however, occur where one might expect the temporal dative instead, as the context does not exclude the possibility that the phrase is specifying the day on which the event occurred, rather than the duration of the event:

(6) ἔτυχε γὰρ αὐτοῖς Ἡρακλεῖ **ταύτην τὴν ἡμέραν** θυσία οὖσα

For they happened to have a festival for Heracles on this day (Th. 7.73.2)

---

[3] With μίαν, 4.31.1, 4.115.2, 6.7.2, 8.28.1; with ὅλην, 7.38.3 (see also 4.39.3, which I have considered together with the constructions with ταύτην); with ἅπασαν, 4.130.1.
[4] See also 3.91.5, 4.13.1, 4.69.3, 5.54.3, 5.65.5.

(7) μετὰ δὲ τοῦτο ταῖς τε ἐξ Ἀβύδου ξυμμιγείσαις καὶ ταῖς ἄλλαις ξυμπάσαις ἓξ καὶ ὀγδοήκοντα πολιορκήσαντες Ἐλαιοῦντα **ταύτην τὴν ἡμέραν**, ὡς οὐ προσεχώρει, ἀπέπλευσαν ἐς Ἄβυδον

And after this they blockaded Elaeus this day both with the ships that met them from Abydos and with the others, eighty-six in all, but, as it did not surrender, they sailed back to Abydus (Th. 8.103.1)

But in both examples, it remains fully possible to construe the temporal expression as durative: in (6), the festival in question, along with elation at their recent victory, has already led the men of Syracuse to drinking that will prevent them from setting up road-blocks against the Athenians for the duration of the day; in (7), the emphasis is almost certainly not on pinpointing the particular day on which the blockade took place, but rather on the fact that it lasted for the entire day without achieving its end. Stepping back for a moment, we can also see how the examples presented so far illustrate that, while there is danger of circular reasoning in theory, it is not too great a worry in practice: the twenty-five accusatives of time that may be safely ascribed to the durative category even without much attention to the surrounding passage,[5] together with the six examples of ταύτην τὴν ἡμέραν where the context clearly indicates that durativity is intended, when set against the thirty-one examples of the dative used with the punctual event-type (to be discussed in the next section), provide a solid enough foundation to justify assigning more dubious examples, such as (6) and (7), to the durative category.

There remain nine examples of ἡμέραν as an accusative of time with various other modifiers. None of them is very problematic. It occurs three times without even an article, twice in durative constructions (1.137.2, 4.114.2), once in a habitual construction, where, as often in such constructions, it is parallel with νύκτα:

(8) σπουδῇ δὲ ὁμοίως **καὶ νύκτα καὶ ἡμέραν** ἔσται τῆς ὁδοῦ

And we will hurry on our way both by night and by day (Th. 7.77.6)

The exact distribution of the different habitual expressions will be dealt with later in the chapter; for the time being, it suffices to

---

[5] I refer to the nineteen with the plural ἡμέρας as well as the six with the singular ἡμέραν modified by μίαν, ὅλην, and ἅπασαν.

63

observe that the use of the accusative in a habitual construction as in (8) is consistent with its use to mark duration: Nicias tells his men that they will hurry for the entire extent of both night and day. Another three times, the temporal expression is τὴν ἡμέραν, of which two (3.88.3, 7.28.2) resemble example (8) in that they are habitual constructions, with νύκτα in parallel both times; the third (2.81.8) is a standard durative construction with ἡσυχάζω (cf. example (1)). The final three temporal accusatives of ἡμέραν include one each with ἐπιοῦσαν, τήνδε, and τρίτην; of these, the first (7.74.1) is a durative construction with περιμεῖναι,[6] and the second is also likely to be durative:

(9) τὴν <δ’> ἐκεχειρίαν εἶναι ἐνιαυτόν, ἄρχειν δὲ **τήνδε τὴν ἡμέραν**

And the truce will last a year, and it begins on this day (Th. 4.118.12)

While we might at first glance expect a punctual dative in this context, the temporal modifiers of treaties very often emphasize the length of time the treaty is to last,[7] so an accusative of extent of time is natural. The last construction looks anomalous at first, but is in fact illustrative of a pattern seen elsewhere in Greek too:

(10) καὶ **τρίτην ἡμέραν** αὐτοῦ ἥκοντος αἱ Ἀττικαὶ νῆες πέντε καὶ εἴκοσιν ἔπλεον ἐς Λέσβον, ὧν ἦρχε Λέων καὶ Διομέδων . . . ἀναγαγόμενος δὲ καὶ ὁ Ἀστύοχος **τῇ αὐτῇ ἡμέρᾳ** ἐς ὀψὲ καὶ προσλαβὼν Χίαν ναῦν μίαν ἔπλει ἐς τὴν Λέσβον

And [Astyochus] having arrived [at Chios] two days ago, the twenty-five Athenian ships sailed to Lesbos; they were commanded by Leon and Diomedon . . . and Astyochus too, putting to sea on the same day towards evening and taking a single Chian ship, sailed to Lesbos (Th. 8.23.1–2)

The general sense seems clear, the details of the construction rather less so. From a strictly syntactic perspective, what does the phrase modify? Classen–Steup ad loc. takes it with ἥκοντος, translating "da er den dritten Tag (d. i. seit zwei Tagen) da war," which makes it easier to explain the accusative of time, but it is less than ideal to translate ἥκω in so static a way.[8] Hornblower (2008) offers "on the

---

[6] See example (81) in Chapter 1.

[7] See 3.114.3, 5.47.1, 5.60.1, and example (3), as well as the discussion in George (2011: 232 n. 19).

[8] The fact that it construes with place-to-which prepositions (chiefly εἰς, but also πρός⁺ᴬ and παρά⁺ᴬ, according to LSJ) suggests that translation as a dynamic verb of motion is more appropriate.

third day after his arrival," which, at least in English, requires it to modify ἔπλεον. But for this sort of punctual construction in which a particular day is specified by an ordinal number, we expect a dative of time (τρίτῃ ἡμέρᾳ), as Thucydides writes at 7.75.1 and 8.24.1. The solution cannot lie with the verb ἔπλεον. Although the imperfect might suggest durativity, this particular verb has a lexical predilection for the imperfect, even in telic constructions with the goal explicitly reached: in passage (10), ἐς (τὴν) Λέσβον occurs twice with the imperfect, and the second time the verb is modified by the regular punctual construction with the dative of time, τῇ αὐτῇ ἡμέρᾳ. Instead, the best parallels for τρίτην ἡμέραν are found outside of Thucydides, a couple of examples each in Xenophon, Plato, and Demosthenes, all of which attest to the fact that Greek could express the idea 'x days ago' by using the accusative of time modified by the ordinal number, not the cardinal as in English.[9] In this light, it is best to take the phrase with ἥκοντος, with the durative accusative possible because, in this idiom, the extent of time in question is not that of the (instantaneous) verbal event itself, but rather that between the verbal event and a reference point, here that of the verb ἔπλεον. As it happens, this use of the accusative also matches a common pattern: an accusative of time is placed in a μέν-clause to set the stage for an action; then, in the corresponding δέ-clause, the dative of time pinpoints the action. In addition to example (5), one may compare, for example, 3.107.3 and 4.69.3. While passage (10) does not match these parallels exactly, since the extent of time in question is that between two verbs, rather than that conveyed by a single verb, the same organizational principle appears to be at work.

In short, as can be seen in Table 5, when ἡμέραν or ἡμέρας is used as an accusative of time, it is overwhelmingly in durative constructions.

Now it is, to be sure, hardly surprising to learn that the accusative of time is used in durative constructions. Nevertheless, it is important to go through the data at length in these first few sections for two related reasons. First, the reader can thus understand the practical principles according to which I am classifying temporal

---

[9] See examples (104), (105), (108), (109), and (110) in Ch. 3.

65

Table 5. *Accusative of time constructions with* ἡμέρα *in Thucydides*

class of examples	event-type of examples
plural	19× clearly durative
with μίαν, ὅλην, ἅπασαν	6× clearly durative
with ταύτην	6× clearly durative
	2× probably durative
used absolutely, or with	3× durative
article	3× habitual
with ἐπιοῦσαν	1× durative
with τήνδε	1× durative (in description of a truce)
with τρίτην	1× probably durative in an 'ago' construction

constructions into the various event-types, in particular those which I consider to be relatively straightforward, so that these can serve as a baseline for dealing with the more problematic examples throughout the rest of the book. Second, even in the case of a well-understood construction, there are already examples like (9) or (10) where the Greek does not behave as one might at first expect. Only by having a clear idea of prototypical examples is it possible to assess just how far the borderline cases deviate therefrom. The further importance of this is most easily explained with a concrete example: if – as will turn out to be the case – the accusative of time is used for ordinary punctual constructions on occasion in the Septuagint, we can only appreciate how much of a shift from Attic this represents if we have examined just how punctual the accusative of time can be in an author like Thucydides. We turn now, less exhaustively, to the other time nouns.

(b) νύξ occurs fifteen times in accusative of time constructions. Four of these are habitual expressions (3.21.4, 3.88.3, 7.28.2, 7.77.6), and the other eleven are durative (1.137.2, 2.75.3, 3.74.3, 4.38.4, 4.45.1, 4.67.2, 4.68.5, 4.103.1, 6.61.2, 7.29.3, 7.74.1). Of these, the only passage where the accusative is not completely predictable is the following:

(11) καὶ ᾔσθετο οὐδεὶς εἰ μὴ οἱ ἄνδρες οἷς ἐπιμελὲς ἦν εἰδέναι **τὴν νύκτα ταύτην**. καὶ ἐπειδὴ ἕως ἔμελλε γίγνεσθαι, οἱ προδιδόντες τῶν Μεγαρέων οὗτοι τοιόνδε ἐποίησαν

And, that night, no one noticed except for the men whose business it was to know. And when dawn was about to break, those of the Megarians who were betraying the city did as follows (Th. 4.67.2–3)

This is the only example where the accusative of time νύκτα is modified by a demonstrative pronoun, and where we might therefore expect a punctual construction. The accusative of time that is found instead can be explained in two ways. First, if, as seems likely, the temporal expression modifies the main verb ᾔσθετο, the clause is negative, rendering a durative reading easier: for the entire length of the night, no one notices what is going on. Second, even if it should be taken more closely with εἰδέναι, the structure is similar to that of example (10): the accusative of time in the first sentence sets the stage for the punctual ἐπειδή-clause in the second.

(c) μήν occurs four times in accusative of time constructions (1.109.4, 2.2.1, 2.65.6, 5.60.1). Each time it is modified by a cardinal number in an unambiguous durative construction.

(d) θέρος and χειμών occur four and three times respectively in accusative of time constructions. They are slightly more problematic than most of the other temporal accusatives because, with one exception they are all modified by a demonstrative or ἐπιών.[10] Still, it does not require special pleading to see them as durative. Take the four constructions with θέρος. There are three with τὸ θέρος τοῦτο, of which one is clearly durative because of the additional modifier πᾶν (5.35.2), and the other two also modify predicates of the sort that frequently elicit a durative expression (ἀντικαθεζόμενοι (1.30.4) and ἡσυχία ἦν (5.35.8)); the fourth example also belongs in this category:

(12) ὡς **τό γ' ἐπιὸν θέρος** οἷοί τ' ἔσονται περιγενέσθαι

that [the Athenians] would be able to survive for the following summer at least (Th. 8.2.2)

The idea of survival conveyed by περιγενέσθαι naturally calls for a durative expression: the Athenians' subjects do not expect them to

---

[10] Like the demonstratives, ἐπιών usually serves to locate an event at a particular time, rather than to indicate how long it lasted.

last longer than the extent of the summer. As for the three examples of χειμών, the two of τὸν χειμῶνα τοῦτον are straightforward durative constructions (5.17.2, 5.56.4). Only the third is slightly awkward:

(13) **τόν τε χειμῶνα** μεθορμισάμενοι ἐκ τῆς Νάξου ἐς τὴν Κατάνην καὶ τὸ στρατόπεδον ὃ κατεκαύθη ὑπὸ τῶν Συρακοσίων αὖθις ἀνορθώσαντες διεχείμαζον

During the winter, after moving their ships from Naxos to Catana and rebuilding the camp which had been burned by the Syracusans, they spent the winter there (Th. 6.88.5)

Despite the strained word order and the tautology, the accusative of time must go with the atelic imperfect διεχείμαζον, not with the participles that intervene, as there are no good parallels for its use with telic verbs like μεθορμίσασθαι or ἀνορθῶσαι. That τὸν χειμῶνα could modify διεχείμαζον at such distance is rendered easier not only by the shared root χειμ- but also by the fact that both participial phrases are closely connected in sense with the main verb: they set the stage for it.

(e) ἔτος occurs twenty-three times in accusative of time constructions, always in the plural.[11] Twenty-one times it is modified by a cardinal number, and once each by πολλά and τοσαῦτα. The verbs with which it occurs are those typical of durative constructions, for example, εἰμί, compounds of μένω, and σπονδὰς ποιεῖσθαι. The uniformity of usage extends even to a treaty quoted in Doric:

(14) "**καττάδε** ἔδοξε τοῖς Λακεδαιμονίοις καὶ Ἀργείοις σπονδὰς καὶ ξυμμαχίαν ἦμεν **πεντήκοντα ἔτη**"

"The Lacedaemonians and Argives have resolved that there should be a treaty and an alliance for fifty years on these terms" (Th. 5.79.1)

(f) ἐνιαυτός occurs nine times in accusative of time constructions, always in the singular.[12] The difference between ἐνιαυτός and

---

[11] 1.11.1, 1.24.4, 1.110.1, 2.2.1 (2×), 2.65.6, 2.65.12, 3.87.2, 3.114.3, 5.18.3, 5.23.1, 5.24.2, 5.26.4, 5.26.5, 5.41.2, 5.47.1, 5.47.3, 5.79.1, 5.112.2, 6.2.5, 6.4.2, 6.10.5, 6.59.4.
[12] 1.31.1, 1.109.4, 1.137.4, 3.68.3, 4.118.10, 4.118.12, 4.118.14, 7.28.3, 7.48.5.

ἔτος with respect to number arises naturally from their contrastive semantics;[13] the following sentence shows the distinction well:

(15) οἱ μὲν ἐνιαυτόν, οἱ δὲ δύο, οἱ δὲ τριῶν γε ἐτῶν οὐδεὶς πλείω χρόνον ἐνόμιζον περιοίσειν αὐτούς

Some thought they would survive for a year, others for two, others for three, but none for more than that (Th. 7.28.3)[14]

Six times, as in (15), the accusative of time ἐνιαυτόν occurs without a modifier; once it occurs with τινα, once with the definite article, and once with πάντα. In all, it is clearly durative.

(g) χρόνος occurs forty-four times in accusative of time constructions, all but once (7.87.1) in the singular. Nearly all of these examples are clearly durative: they commonly modify ἀντέχω or μένω and its compounds, and χρόνον in turn is typically modified by ὀλίγον, πολύν, τινα, and similar expressions of extent:[15]

(16) καὶ ὀλίγον μὲν χρόνον ξυνέμεινεν ἡ ὁμαιχμία

And the alliance lasted for a short time (Th. 1.18.3)

Only twice might one expect a punctual construction instead:

(17) καὶ οὐχ ἥκιστα δὴ τὸν πρῶτον χρόνον ἐπί γε ἐμοῦ Ἀθηναῖοι φαίνονται εὖ πολιτεύσαντες

And during this first period, in my time at least, the Athenians clearly conducted their government the very best (Th. 8.97.2)

(18) ἐς φιλονικίαν τε καθέστασαν τὸν χρόνον τοῦτον οἱ μὲν τὴν πόλιν ἀναγκάζοντες δημοκρατεῖσθαι, οἱ δὲ τὸ στρατόπεδον ὀλιγαρχεῖσθαι

During this time they started to contend with each other, some [the army] pushing for the city to be ruled by the people, others [the Four Hundred] for the army to be ruled by an oligarchy (Th. 8.76.1)

In (17), the ordinal modifier πρῶτον is more typical of punctual than of durative constructions. Still, Thucydides' emphasis appears to lie more on the extent of time that the period of good government lasted than on the point at which it began.[16] So too in (18), the

---

[13] Chantraine 1999 s.v. ἔτος: "'année en cours' en principe distinct de ἐνιαυτός 'année révolue'."

[14] For the elliptical syntax, see Gomme et al. (1970) ad loc.   [15] See also example (15).

[16] This sentence is one of the most hotly debated in Thucydides (in Gomme et al. (1981), discussion runs to eight full pages), and opinions divide as to whether τὸν πρῶτον χρόνον

demonstrative τοῦτον is relatively uncommon as a modifier in durative expressions. But the durative construction is nevertheless appropriate given that Thucydides goes on to describe a lasting state of affairs that obtained during this period of φιλονικία (note the present participle ἀναγκάζοντες that follows), rather than pinpointing any single incident that acted as a trigger to initiate it. Curiously, both of these examples as well as (10), the most problematic example with ἡμέρα, come from Book Eight. It is tempting to see this gentle extension of the accusative of time as a slighly loose construction that Thucydides might have edited away, had he had more time to tidy up the final book.[17]

In short, Thucydides' use of the accusative of time is essentially unproblematic. It is very seldom indeed that he uses it where we might expect a punctual construction instead, and the preceding paragraphs are more important as a baseline for understanding other authors' usage than as an exciting discovery in their own right. The more interesting question about Thucydides' durative expressions is what factors motivate the use of prepositional constructions with διά$^{+G}$ or ἐπί$^{+A}$ rather than the simple accusative. For with the prepositional temporal expressions, the lack of uniformity from author to author comes to the fore: for example, Thucydides uses διά$^{+G}$ three times and ἐπί$^{+A}$ ten times, while Xenophon uses διά$^{+G}$ twenty-one times and ἐπί$^{+A}$ only four times.

We begin with διά$^{+G}$, which does not have the prominence in Thucydides it does in other authors. Of the three examples, one is not even a durative expression:

refers narrowly to the first period of the rule of the 5000 ('in the first phase') or more broadly to Thucydides' entire life ('for the first time'). Gomme et al. prefer the first view (the combination of two superlatives, 'for the first time' and 'best' (οὐχ ἥκιστα), is awkward; for 'for the first time', we expect simply τὸ πρῶτον, as χρόνον does not mean 'time' in the sense of French *fois*; cf. Rijksbaron (2006b) on τὸ πρότερον, noting esp. p. 445 and, incidentally to his main argument, the force of τοῦτόν γε τὸν χρόνον in his ex. 25 (Pl. *Phd.* 91b). Hornblower (2008) prefers the latter view (on the grounds that ἐπί γε ἐμοῦ 'in my life' most naturally qualifies a phrase meaning 'for the first time'). I am myself inclined to the former position: it seems easier to posit some elasticity in the sense of ἐπί γε ἐμοῦ (might it be not so much temporal as rather something like 'at least to judge from my personal experience'? cf. LSJ *s.v.* ἐπί A.I.2.e, Kühner–Gerth 1898: 497–8) than to take χρόνος as equivalent to *fois*. But either way, the accusative of time emphasizes the duration of the period of good government.

[17] For the relatively unpolished appearance of Book 8 (it has no speeches and cites treaties verbatim), see the discussion in Gomme et al. (1981: 113–16 and 361–83); Hornblower is more skeptical (2008: 1–4).

(19) ἔστι γὰρ ὅτι καὶ αἱ νῆες αὐτοὺς **διὰ χρόνου** καθελκυσθεῖσαι καὶ οὐδὲν στέγουσαι ἐφόβουν

For it is the case that even the ships frightened them, as they were being launched after some time and did not keep out the water (Th. 2.94.3)

A construction found also in Xenophon, διὰ χρόνου stands apart from other expressions with διά$^{+G}$. It is regularly used, as here, to mean 'after some time' (rather than 'for a time').[18] Like μεθ' ἡμέραν, it thus provides a good example of how temporal expressions can take on specialized meanings in constructions with particular time nouns. The other two examples, by contrast, are good durative constructions:

(20) ἐπειδὴ δ' οὖν **δι' ἡμέρας** βάλλοντες πανταχόθεν τοὺς Ἀθηναίους καὶ ξυμμάχους ἑώρων ...

But, after firing on the Athenians and their allies from all sides throughout the day, when they saw ... (Th. 7.82.1)

(21) ὑετοῦ ἅμα **διὰ νυκτὸς** πολλοῦ ἐπιγενομένου

At the same time, since a lot of rain fell throughout the night (Th. 2.4.2)

Both (20) and (21) consist only of the preposition and the time noun. Not even the article is present, although we might expect it because, in both passages, the reference is to a particular day or night.[19] That being so, could Thucydides have written simply τὴν ἡμέραν and τὴν νύκτα with the same force? Perhaps, but probably not, as there are two differences between these two constructions and the seven examples of durative τὴν ἡμέραν and τὴν νύκτα.[20]

First, the verbs modified by the durative accusative of time are different from those modified by διά$^{+G}$: the former are verbs of staying and remaining (ἡσυχάζω (2×), αὐλίζομαι (2×), ἐπέχω) and of traveling (πορεύομαι, χωρέω) – that is, verbs that form the routine temporal framework of the narrative, and which frequently occur with other accusative of time expressions – whereas the latter

[18] See the discussion of ex. (74) in Ch. 1.
[19] That said, it is not uncommon for articles to be omitted in prepositional phrases, esp. those referring to time (Kühner–Gerth 1898: 605–6, Gildersleeve 1911: 259–60).
[20] They are also found twice in habitual expressions, both of which contain both time nouns: 3.88.3 and 7.28.2. The durative example with τὴν ἡμέραν occurs at 2.81.8, those with τὴν νύκτα at 3.74.3, 4.45.1, 4.68.5, 4.103.1, 7.29.3, 7.74.1.

two verbs, βάλλω and ἐπιγίγνομαι, describe events that represent comparatively prominent points in the narrative. Second, the relationship between the temporal expression and the wider context is different when διά⁺ᴳ is used. In five of the seven passages with durative τὴν ἡμέραν and τὴν νύκτα, the accusative of time is picked up in a closely following sentence with a temporal expression referring to the next unit of time. For example, ἡσύχαζον αὐτοῦ τὴν ἡμέραν (2.81.8) is followed by ἐπειδὴ δὲ νὺξ ἐγένετο (2.82.1), and ἡσυχάσαντες τὴν νύκτα ἐν φυλακῇ ἦσαν (3.74.3) by τῇ δὲ ἐπιγιγνομένῃ ἡμέρᾳ (3.75.1).²¹ By contrast, the two examples with διά⁺ᴳ do not orient themselves to the broader temporal framework in the same way; instead, they relate more to constituents in their own clause. For both (20) and (21) contain emphatic words (πανταχόθεν and πολλοῦ respectively) whose significance is underscored by the διά⁺ᴳ phrase: they fired *throughout* the day from *all* sides; there was a *lot* of rain *throughout* the night.²² Finally, we may ask what it is about these two conditions – modified verbs that are both more salient and less naturally suited to a durative expression, and the primary function of emphasizing a clause-internal constituent rather than integrating the clause into the surrounding temporal framework – that would elicit the prepositional use rather than the simple accusative. The obvious answer is probably the correct one: as a preposition whose chief role is to denote the path along which an object travels, διά⁺ᴳ would stress the idea of extent of time more than the accusative on its own. The latter is a weaker expression of path, both because of the wider range of meanings it conveys (it can also occur in habitual expressions) and because of the iconic principle, which leads us to expect that an expression that

---

²¹ See too 4.45.1 (τὴν νύκτα ηὐλίσαντο is immediately followed by τῇ δ' ὑστεραίᾳ), 7.29.3 (τὴν μὲν νύκτα ... ηὐλίσατο is followed by ἅμα δὲ τῇ ἡμέρᾳ), and 7.74.1 (ἐπέσχον τὴν νύκτα is followed by ἔδοξεν αὐτοῖς καὶ τὴν ἐπιοῦσαν ἡμέραν περιμεῖναι) (= ex. (81) in Ch. 1).
²² In between these two groups lie the two examples of the accusative of time that are *not* followed by another temporal expression (4.68.5, 4.103.1). As they lack the orientation towards the broader temporal framework, we might expect Thucydides to use διά⁺ᴳ here, esp. as the temporal phrase is somewhat emphatic (i.e. 'they marched through the *whole* night'). Perhaps the accusative is favored because the acts of marching described in both are still not as striking or salient as the events described in the two passages where διά⁺ᴳ is used.

72

contains only the noun should have less weight than one that contains a clarifying preposition as well.[23]

The durative constructions with ἐπί[+A] are more numerous than those with διά[+G], but still rare compared to the accusative of time.[24] Their usage is also closer to the simple accusative than that of the expressions with διά[+G]: nearly all of them could probably be replaced with the accusative, although the reverse is not true. Apart from one anomalous distributive expression (ἐφ' ἡμέραν γὰρ ἐκ τῆς ἄνω πόλεως ἐχρῶντο "for every day they used to get provisions from the upper city" (4.69.3)),[25] they fall into two classes: (a) five expressions with ἡμέρα, μήν, and ἔτος, in all of which the time noun is modified by a cardinal number; (b) four expressions with χρόνος, all modified by either πλεῖστος or πολύς.

(a) The two expressions with ἡμέρα are both of the sort in which we might expect the accusative of time, for example:[26]

(22) ἐπὶ μὲν ἓξ ἢ ἑπτὰ ἡμέρας ἀνθώρμουν ἀλλήλοις

For six or seven days they were stationed opposite each other (Th. 2.86.5)

While this μέν-clause is not followed up by a δέ-clause with a punctual expression, an accusative of time would still not be out of place here, as the narrative is simply put on hold (note the relatively static verb ἀνθώρμουν): there is none of the sense of 'for six or seven *entire* days' that διά[+G] would convey. The same is also true of a passage that includes both μήν and ἔτος:[27]

---

[23] For διά[+G] as a marker of path, see Luraghi (2003: 168–70, 176–7); for the iconic connection between the length and (what I call here) the weight of an expression, see Givón (1985: 196–8).

[24] For an overview of how the figurative uses of ἐπί with different cases correspond to the local uses, see Ruijgh 1994. Note esp. pp. 140–3, which include mention of temporal ἐπί[+G] (not covered here because it occurs with personal objects rather than time nouns) and ἐπί[+D] (an archaic use found at e.g. *Il.* 19.110). For temporal ἐπί[+D], cf. de la Villa 1994a: 201.

[25] Probably ἐπί[+A] here has some of the sense of purpose seen in (24) below. Cf. also X. *Cyr.* 6.2.34 (= ex. (4) in Ch. 3), along with n. 8 in that chapter.

[26] See also 2.25.3 (ἐπὶ δύο ἡμέρας).

[27] See also 7.87.2 (ἐπὶ ὀκτὼ μῆνας). Both here and in the passage mentioned in n. 26, the verbs (ἐδῄουν and ἐδίδοσαν respectively) are admittedly less static than those in the examples in the main text. But ἐπί[+A] still does not throw the emphasis on the fact that the verbal event lasted throughout the period of the time noun in the same way that διά[+G] would.

(23) καὶ ἐπὶ ἓξ ἔτη μὲν καὶ δέκα μῆνας ἀπέσχοντο μὴ ἐπὶ τὴν ἑκατέρων γῆν στρατεῦσαι

> And for six years and ten months they kept themselves from marching against the others' lands (Th. 5.25.3)

Again, ἐπί$^{+A}$ does not highlight the temporal phrase in the way that διά$^{+G}$ would. True, there is not an explicit expression of time in the following δέ- and ἔπειτα-clauses as would be most prototypical for the accusative of time, but the static verb ἀπέσχοντο still pauses the action, and the cessation of the peace *is* referred to in what follows. Slightly different is a final example with ἔτος:

(24) τὴν δὲ γῆν δημοσιώσαντες ἀπεμίσθωσαν **ἐπὶ δέκα ἔτη**, καὶ ἐνέμοντο Θηβαῖοι

> And they confiscated the land and hired it off for ten years, and Thebans occupied it (Th. 3.68.3)

Here, the prepositional phrase looks forward: the extent of time in question lies after the main chronological thread of the episode rather than during it. That is, the story does not pick up again after the ten-year period, as is the case with most other durative expressions. Indeed, ἐπί$^{+A}$ here comes close to expressing purpose, as it clearly does elsewhere in Thucydides.[28]

These temporal expressions with ἐπί$^{+A}$ clearly do not work the same way as those with διά$^{+G}$. But is there some other respect in which they differ from the default durative constructions with the accusative of time? What seems to link at least the examples already presented is the invariable use of a cardinal number as a modifier: this gives them the appearance of a precision that is absent from many (though certainly not all) of the accusatives of time. In example (23) in particular, it looks as if some arithmetic might have gone into working out the length of time that the peace lasted. There are also, to be sure, a couple of accusatives of time which combine both years and months (1.109.4, 2.65.6), but in both of these expressions, it is a *six*-month period added to a stretch of a year or two, giving the impression that Thucydides is adding καὶ ἓξ μῆνας simply because it is the shortest way to say 'and a half'. An additional sign that the specific number of units is important in selecting for ἐπί$^{+A}$ lies in the word order of these phrases: in all five

---

[28] For example, ἀνήγοντο ὡς ἐπὶ ναυμαχίαν "they sailed out for a sea-battle" (1.48.1).

expressions, the numeral precedes the time noun, which suggests it is particularly salient.[29] By contrast, in temporal expressions where it is the simple accusative of ἡμέρα or ἔτος that is modified by a cardinal number, the numeral-first order is preferred by a count of only twenty to sixteen.[30]

(b) The second class of temporal expressions with ἐπί$^{+A}$ has χρόνος as the time noun, three times modified by πολύς (1.17.1, 4.1.3, 6.32.3), once by πλεῖστος (1.18.1). Thus, as when governed by διά$^{+G}$ (see example (19)), χρόνος behaves differently from the other time nouns. Here too we may wonder what prompts the use of the prepositional construction rather than the simple accusative. Compare the following:

(25) **χρόνον μὲν οὖν πολὺν** ἀντεῖχον οὐκ ἐνδιδόντες ἀλλήλοις

They held out for a long time, neither side yielding to the other (Th. 4.44.1)

(26) τὸ γὰρ Ῥήγιον **ἐπὶ πολὺν χρόνον** ἐστασίαζε καὶ ἀδύνατα ἦν ἐν τῷ παρόντι τοὺς Λοκροὺς ἀμύνεσθαι

For Rhegium had been torn by faction for a long time, and it was impossible at present for them to defend themselves against the Locrians (Th. 4.1.3)

One suspects that the accusative of time would be perfectly grammatical in (26) as well. But despite the apparent similarity between the above two examples, and despite the superficial difference between (26) and the examples with ἡμέρα, μήν, and ἔτος, one of the same factors is at work: after ἐπί$^{+A}$, πολύς and πλεῖστος always precede the noun; in constructions with the accusative of time, these modifiers precede the noun three times, but follow it six times. The modifiers in the prepositional construction are thus likely to be more salient than those with the simple accusative of time. Note too that the semantics of πολύς and πλεῖστος are particularly compatible with receiving emphasis.[31] Even though the expressions with ἐπί$^{+A}$ are not greatly more emphatic than those

[29] See Dik (1997, 2007: 84–122), Bakker (2007, 2009: 38–52).
[30] I exclude expressions with εἷς, as it is inherently more emphatic than the other cardinals.
[31] This is borne out by patterns of word order: Dover includes πολύς and πλεῖστος in his list of 'preferential words' that gravitate towards the beginning of their clause (1960: 20–1); Dik's figures show that πολύς is preposed 82% of the time in Sophocles (2007: 90).

with just the accusative,[32] it remains probable that the temporal expression in (26) bears more weight than that in (25). This
emphasis is close in nature to what in (20) and (21) is
expressed by διά⁺ᴳ: both 'for a *long* time' and 'throughout
the *whole* time' are emphatic in the sense that the extent of
time is greater than might be expected by the reader. But διά⁺ᴳ
is of course excluded from carrying this meaning with χρόνος
because it takes on the lexically conditioned sense 'after' with
this time noun.

Summary

1. The **accusative of time** is the default durative construction
(e.g. (1), (2)), but it is also used in habitual expressions (e.g. (8)).
There are only a handful of passages where it even begins to show
any overlap with punctual constructions like the dative of time
(e.g. (6), (7), (10)).

2. Apart from the phrase διά χρόνου 'after some time' (see (19)),
διά⁺ᴳ is also used in durative constructions (see (20), (21)). It
differs from the accusative of time in emphasizing that the event
expressed by the verb lasts throughout the entire unit of time. The
accusative of time, by contrast, simply fits the verbal event into the
broader temporal framework.

3. Temporal phrases with **ἐπί⁺ᴬ** are also durative; they resemble the accusative of time more closely than those with διά⁺ᴳ.
They fall into two broad categories: with ἡμέρα, μήν, and ἔτος,
ἐπί⁺ᴬ only governs time nouns modified by cardinal numbers,
thus giving the impression that the exact length of time is
more important than is the case in constructions with the
simple accusative (see (23)); with χρόνος, ἐπί⁺ᴬ only occurs
when the noun is modified by πολύς or πλεῖστος. The modifier
is always preposed in these constructions, suggesting that they
are preferentially used when the great length of time denoted
by the phrase is unusually salient.

---

[32] 1.17.1 is probably the most emphatic of the lot: as in (20), the verb is also modified by
πανταχόθεν.

Table 6. *Genitives and datives of time with selected time nouns in Thucydides*

Time noun	Genitives of time	Datives of time
ἡμέρα	14	31
μήν	2	3
ἔτος	2	16
νύξ	35	3
θέρος	48	2
χειμών	35	none

Punctual and limitative expressions in Thucydides: day, month, and year

The need mentioned in the last section to treat χρόνος differently from other time nouns introduces a theme that will run throughout this book: not all time nouns behave alike. Nowhere is this more evident than in the distribution of the genitive and dative of time in punctual and limitative expressions, the aspect of Greek temporal expressions that has till now received the most confused treatment. Accordingly, the following two sections deal separately with the two major classes of time noun. First, there are the words for day, month, and year, which behave the way they are supposed to: the dative is the preferred punctual construction. Second, there are the words for night and the seasons, which take a *genitive* of time when. In both classes, we will also consider the rather less clear-cut distribution of the genitive and ἐν⁺ᴰ in limitative constructions. As a starting point, see Table 6, which gives the number of genitives and datives of time in Thucydides with the relevant time nouns.

While by no means conclusive, this table should provide enough preliminary evidence of the genitive-friendly behavior of night and the seasons to justify the decision to treat the two classes separately – and to show why the overall question about their distribution needs to be asked in the first place.

We begin with ἡμέρα, as it is the time noun which shows the greatest freedom to use either the genitive or the dative of time.[33]

---

[33] Strictly speaking, μήν has similar freedom, but being rare it should be examined in light of the more frequent time nouns.

The thirty-one constructions with the dative of time are the easiest to understand because they are the most uniform: all have the singular of ἡμέρα, all are definite, and they are essentially all punctual expressions.

Typical is the following:

(27) τῇ δὲ ἐπιγιγνομένῃ ἡμέρᾳ Νικόστρατος ὁ Διειτρέφους Ἀθηναίων στρατηγὸς παραγίγνεται βοηθῶν ἐκ Ναυπάκτου

And on the next day Nicostratus son of Diitrephes, the general of the Athenians, arrived with help from Naupactus (Th. 3.75.1)

Ἡμέρα is modified fourteen times by an ordinal number (in which case the definite article is dropped, except in τῇ πρώτῃ), nine times by a demonstrative pronoun, four times by τῇ αὐτῇ, three times by ἐπιγιγνομένῃ, and once by προτέρᾳ. These are all modifiers that we would expect to occur in punctual expressions as they specify which day the event took place (unlike cardinal numbers, which indicate an extent of time). Fifteen times the verb is an aorist, and five times it is a historical present, again conforming to the typical punctual expression. The other eleven verbs (two present participles, two generalizing presents, and one true present in a speech; five imperfects; and one perfect), while perhaps less prototypical, are certainly not incompatible with a true punctual expression, as can be seen in the following example:

(28) καὶ ἡ ἀνάστασις ἤδη τοῦ στρατεύματος τρίτῃ ἡμέρᾳ ἀπὸ τῆς ναυμαχίας ἐγίγνετο

And the removal of the army took place already on the third day after the sea-battle (Th. 7.75.1)

The use of the imperfect instead of the aorist does not mean a punctual expression is out of place: the presence of the ordinal τρίτη makes clear that the phrase is meant to specify which day it took place, not how long it took.

The examples of the genitive of time, by contrast, are much more diverse, even though there are only fourteen of them. Six of them, including the four constructions with the plural and the only one with the dual, belong in the limitative category:[34]

---

[34] The other examples are found at 2.97.2, 4.105.2, 7.3.1, 8.101.1.

(29) οὓς ᾤοντο **ἡμερῶν ὀλίγων** ἐκπολιορκήσειν ἐν νήσῳ τε ἐρήμῃ καὶ ὕδατι ἁλμυρῷ χρωμένους

Whom they thought they would force to surrender in a few days, as they were on a deserted island and had brackish water (Th. 4.26.4)

(30) τά τε ἄλλα διεπράσσοντο καὶ τὰ ἀμφὶ τὸ ἄριστον ὡς **τῆς γε ἡμέρας ταύτης** οὐκέτι οἰόμενοι ἂν ναυμαχῆσαι

They attended to everything, including breakfast, in the belief that they would not fight any more that day (at least) (Th. 7.40.2)

Example (29) is particularly characteristic of the limitative type. As in durative constructions, the temporal expression (ἡμερῶν ὀλίγων) refers to an extent of time; but as in punctual constructions, the verbal event described (ἐκπολιορκήσειν) is telic. With an atelic verb, one would expect the accusative of time instead, as happens here:

(31) τοὺς δ' ἐπελθόντας **ὀλίγας τινὰς ἡμέρας** ἐν τῇ γῇ μείναντας ἀπέπεμψεν ἐπ' οἴκου

And when they had stayed in the country for a few days after their arrival, he sent them home (Th. 8.71.3)

In (30), the temporal expression τῆς γε ἡμέρας ταύτης is less clearly limitative, since the demonstrative phrase could equally well be pinpointing a particular time rather than a stretch of time. But the limitative reading is still the best option here because of the future time reference. When an event has not yet taken place, its temporal location is not yet absolutely certain; as a result, the narrow precision of the punctual construction gives way to the more expansive boundaries established by the limitative. In (29) as well, the verb is a morphological future, which is true of none of the forty-seven datives of time with ἡμέρα or ἔτος.[35]

The next four examples of ἡμέρας as a genitive of time form an even closer-knit group. They are all distributive constructions of the following sort:[36]

(32) δραχμὴν γὰρ **τῆς ἡμέρας** ἕκαστος ἐλάμβανεν

For each received a drachma per day (Th. 7.27.2)

---

[35] See also the genitive πέντε ἡμερῶν in 4.105.2 and 7.3.1, which both times specifies the length of time people have to carry out particular orders.
[36] See also 3.17.4 (obelized in the OCT), 5.47.6, 6.31.3.

In three of the four, the presence of ἕκαστος makes the distributive reading particularly likely. This is, we will see, a very standard use of the genitive of time. Closely related is the following habitual construction:

(33) καὶ τὰ περὶ Πύλον ὑπ' ἀμφοτέρων κατὰ κράτος ἐπολεμεῖτο, Ἀθηναῖοι μὲν δυοῖν νεοῖν ἐναντίαιν αἰεὶ τὴν νῆσον περιπλέοντες **τῆς ἡμέρας** (τῆς δὲ νυκτὸς καὶ ἅπασαι περιώρμουν . . .)

And the war at Pylos was fought forcefully by both sides, the Athenians constantly sailing about the island with two ships in opposite directions by day (and by night all the ships blockaded it . . .) (Th. 4.23.2)

The temporal phrase does not state that the sailing happened on a particular day, nor for the extent of a day, nor that it occurred precisely once per day: rather it indicates that it was a regular, repeated event. This too is a common use of the genitive of time, although – for reasons that will become clear shortly – in this particular example we must also be alert to the (almost) parallel use of τῆς νυκτός directly afterwards.

There remain three more genitives of time with ἡμέρα. All of them are punctual in broad terms, but also deviate noticeably from the prototypical examples of this event type, which otherwise calls for the dative of time:

(34) ἐκέλευον φράζειν Νικίᾳ μὴ ἀπάγειν **τῆς νυκτὸς** τὸ στράτευμα ὡς Συρακοσίων τὰς ὁδοὺς φυλασσόντων, ἀλλὰ καθ' ἡσυχίαν **τῆς ἡμέρας** παρασκευασάμενον ἀποχωρεῖν

And they asked them to tell Nicias not to lead off the army by night, as the Syracusans were watching the roads, but, taking his time, to get ready and leave by day (Th. 7.73.3)

(35) καὶ **ἡμέρας** μὲν ἀδύνατα ἐδόκει εἶναι λαθεῖν προσελθόντας τε καὶ ἀναβάντας

And it did not seem possible that they could approach and ascend by day without being seen [so they made preparations for a night assault] (Th. 7.43.2)

(36) οἱ δὲ Ἀργεῖοι γνόντες ἐβοήθουν **ἡμέρας ἤδη** ἐκ τῆς Νεμέας

And when the Argives realized this, they went to the rescue from Nemea when it was already day (Th. 5.59.1)

In (34), we see the confluence of several factors leading to the selection of the genitive of time τῆς ἡμέρας. First, the event still lies in the future, so the passage has some affinity to the limitative type.[37] Second, τῆς ἡμέρας is parallel with τῆς νυκτός, a noun that, as we will see, favors the genitive of time even in contexts where ἡμέρα takes the dative. Third, the opposition of night and day in the passage gives the temporal expressions an importance beyond the simple establishing of a chronological framework: they go so far as to indicate two different modalities under which alternative verbal events would take place.[38] Put differently, both temporal phrases in (34) are more critical to the meaning of the sentence than the limitative genitives of time in (29) and (30). If the latter are omitted, their host clauses still make sense, but if the former are omitted, the sentence becomes meaningless. Such temporal phrases can also carry a causal nuance; here too the genitive is frequently used. This is the case with (35), where, even without an explicit parallelism with τῆς νυκτός, there is an implied contrast with a night-time approach. Again, ἡμέρας is essential to the proper under-standing of the sentence. In the last example, (36), the situation is somewhat different: with ἤδη following ἡμέρας, the construction almost looks like a genitive absolute that has lost its participle οὔσης. But there is a factor that ties this construction more closely to (34) and (35) than to (29) and (30): in all three of these last examples ἡμέρα means essentially 'daylight, not-night'; by contrast, in the limitative constructions (and in the true punctual constructions with the dative), it means '12- or 24-hour span of time'. This dis-tinction will remain important.

Clearly, it does not do justice to these examples to call them simply punctual or limitative. What they chiefly have in common is that days are seen in opposition to nights, rather than as units in a calendrical sequence used to keep track of time. As this throws more emphasis on daytime and night-time as general – rather than specifically temporal – circumstances under which the event is carried out, it seems best to label such passages as

---

[37] Despite this affinity, I group it separately from the prototypical limitative examples because the temporal phrase functions not so much on its own to mark a specific day (the Athenians do not in fact leave that day, as seen in 7.75.1 (= ex. (28)) – although that this would be the case was admittedly not yet clear), as in connection with τῆς νυκτός to set up a general contrast between leaving by night or by day.

[38] That a temporal phrase could have this modal nuance can also be seen in the English translation, where the preposition *by* has similar overtones. This usage can be as easily spatial as temporal: *one if by land, two if by sea*.

modal.[39] While not particularly prominent in Thucydides, such expressions will turn out to be much more widespread in other authors, like Xenophon and Plato, whose works contain more passages that make general statements of the sort conducive to modal constructions.

A further problem is the relationship between the modal construction and the habitual: example (33), like the modal expressions, uses ἡμέρα in opposition to νύξ, so why not call it modal and scrap the habitual category? Chiefly because the modal category apparently operates on a different level from the other event types introduced: whether an event occurs (or is to occur) only once (as in (34) through (36)) or multiple times (as in (33)), it can still be colored by this nuance – a nuance that, on the whole, causes what might otherwise be expressed with a punctual marker to be expressed with a habitual one instead.[40] Finally, before passing on to constructions with ἐν[+D], a brief recapitulation is in order: six genitives of time with ἡμέρα (including all the examples with the dual or plural) are limitative; four are distributive; one is habitual; three are modal.

With the nouns included in this study, ἐν[+D] is the most common preposition to be found in temporal expressions in Thucydides. Indeed, with eighty examples, it is more common even than the dative of time (found seventy-two times). It occurs eleven times with ἡμέρα, and its range of functions is very close to that of the genitive of time. Six times, it occurs in limitative contexts, always in the plural:[41]

(37) ὡς δὲ τοῦτο ἐξειργάσαντο **ἐν ἡμέραις ὀλίγαις**

And as they finished this in a few days (Th. 3.51.4)

---

[39] It is not obvious in every example, of course, whether a particular phrase places more emphasis on when the event occurred or on the general circumstances under which it occurred: as Muchnová has noted is the case with ἐπεί-clauses, there is a continuum from the more temporal to the more circumstantial (2011: 57). But even if this is, consequently, less an objectively discrete category, like those delimited in Ch. 1, and more an additional semantic factor to consider in assessing adverbial phrases with time nouns, the prototypical examples, in which two types of time noun are explicitly contrasted, are identifiable enough to justify setting it up as a category.

[40] It should be borne in mind throughout the book that, for the sake of clarity in tabulating the data, I count as habitual many constructions that could also be considered modal. This should not cause any problems, since (i) the task at hand is not to assign every single temporal expression into one and only one category, but rather to explain the distribution of the various constructions; (ii) as the modal label captures a feature that causes what would otherwise be a punctual or limitative construction to be expressed more like habitual one, it would be particularly nonsensical to insist on a sharp division between the modal and habitual types.

[41] The other examples: ἐν τεσσαράκοντα μάλιστα ἡμέραις (2.58.3), ἐν ἴσαις ἡμέραις (3.113.6), ἐν ἡμέραις ἕξ (4.5.2), ἐν ταῖς ἡμέραις ταύταις (4.91.1), ἐν ἡμέραις ῥηταῖς (6.29.3).

While none of them have the future time reference that character-izes most of the limitative expressions with the genitive of time, they still have the telltale combination of a telic predicate with a time span of multiple days. On a further three occasions, the temporal phrase is the fixed collocation ἐν ἡμέρᾳ ῥητῇ:[42]

(38) ἐς τὸν Πειραιᾶ καταβάντες **ἐν ἡμέρᾳ ῥητῇ** ἅμα ἕῳ ἐπλήρουν τὰς ναῦς ὡς ἀναξόμενοι

They went down to the Piraeus on the appointed day at dawn and were manning the ships with the intention of sailing off (Th. 6.30.1)

It is a curious expression: not only is the article absent (for the same reason that it is dropped with ordinal numbers?[43]), but one also might expect the dative of time rather than ἐν: (38) at least looks more punctual than limitative. It gives the impression of being a technical legal term, but it is not found in other Classical authors.[44] Perhaps the collocation has its origin in the contexts in which one is most likely to speak of an appointed day: rather than simply mentioning that an event occurred on a day, one will often be specifying that the appointed event should occur at some point during the day in question. The day is thus treated more like a bounded timespan than as a simple point. This, at any rate, is the nuance thrown on the phrase by virtue of its not being simply τῇ ῥητῇ ἡμέρᾳ.

Two more passages with ἐν remain, neither of which fits clearly into the two categories already mentioned:

(39) περιέμενον δὲ Παναθήναια τὰ μεγάλα, **ἐν ᾗ μόνον ἡμέρᾳ** οὐχ ὕποπτον ἐγίγνετο ἐν ὅπλοις τῶν πολιτῶν τοὺς τὴν πομπὴν πέμψοντας ἀθρόους γενέσθαι

And they awaited the Great Panathenaea, on which day alone it was not suspicious for those of the citizens who would escort the procession to be gathered together and armed (Th. 6.56.2)

---

[42] See also 4.76.4, 6.64.3, both referring to events that have not yet come to pass.

[43] See Kühner–Gerth: 639, and Gildersleeve 1911: 261.

[44] Plutarch, for one, did pick up on it (*Nic.* 16.2, *Caes.* 30.4). There is future time reference in both, making ἐν rather than the simple dative more understandable. The passage from the *Life of Nicias* is in fact from the exact same episode as the Thucydidean example at 6.64.3. That Plutarch adopted turns of phrase from Thucydides in this *Life* is noted by Trédé in reference to κατὰ τοῦτο τοῦ καιροῦ (Th. 7.2.5), borrowed as ἐν τούτῳ δὲ καιροῦ (*Nic.* 19.1) (1992: 212–13, esp. n. 76).

(40) ἐν μὲν γὰρ ἡμέρᾳ σαφέστερα μέν, ὅμως δὲ οὐδὲ ταῦτα οἱ παραγενόμενοι πάντα πλὴν τὸ καθ' ἑαυτὸν ἕκαστος μόλις οἶδεν· ἐν δὲ νυκτομαχίᾳ

For during the day, it is easier to see what's going on, but even so those who are there still do not see it all – except that each one has a vague idea of what is happening around him; but in night-battles (Th. 7.44.1)

Example (39) probably goes most closely with the ἐν ἡμέρᾳ ῥητῇ phrases just discussed: ἐν ᾗ μόνον ἡμέρᾳ does after all look forward to the appointed day for Harmodius and Aristogiton's plan. Still, one cannot rule out a habitual reading, if the relative clause is emphasizing not so much the particular Panathenaea for which the attack is planned as the fact that it was regularly a day on which such a plot could be carried out. As for (40), it is a good modal construction, but it is not clear how it differs from the modal phrases with the genitive of time ((34) through (36)), unless it is significant that the example at hand has less reference to a particular day and night than is the case with the earlier examples. Another possible motivation for ἐν might be that the passage is explicitly contrasting the difficulty of determining what is going on at night as opposed to during the day. There might thus be some trace of an almost local sense to the preposition here: 'in the light of day'. At any rate, whatever the exact classification for these two examples ought to be, it is clear that, on the whole, the use of ἐν is much closer to that of the genitive of time (6× certainly limitative, 1× modal, and the rest with some limitative overtones) than it is to the dative.

Having looked at ἡμέρα with some detail, we can move more quickly through the examples with μήν and ἔτος, all the more so since these nouns have fewer of the problematic constructions with the genitive and ἐν[+D] to sort through. First, consider μήν, which is relatively uncommon, occurring three times in the dative of time, twice in the genitive of time, and once after ἐν. As with ἡμέρα, the dative is used exclusively in punctual expressions; it is always modified by an ordinal number.[45] Of the two genitive examples, one is distributive (8.29.2), and the other, while slightly less easy to pigeonhole, still belongs in the limitative category:

---

(41) ἐς ἀλλοτρίαν πᾶσαν ἀπαρτήσοντες, ἐξ ἧς **μηνῶν οὐδὲ τεσσάρων τῶν χειμερινῶν** ἄγγελον ῥᾴδιον ἐλθεῖν

About to depart for a completely foreign land, from which it is not even easy for a messenger to leave during the four winter months (Th. 6.21.2)

Probably the negative (strangely placed though it is) is the decisive factor in triggering the limitative construction: at no point in the given stretch of time can the telic action in question take place.[46] There remains the single example with ἐν:

(42) τὸ <τοῦ> ἐν Λίμναις Διονύσου, ᾧ τὰ ἀρχαιότερα Διονύσια [τῇ δωδεκάτῃ] ποιεῖται **ἐν μηνὶ Ἀνθεστηριῶνι**

the temple of Dionysus in Limnae, for whom the older Dionysia are held [on the twelfth day] in the month Anthesterion (Th. 2.15.4)

Despite the textual corruption in this passage, it seems safe to assume that Thucydides did write ἐν μηνὶ Ἀνθεστηριῶνι.[47] Here ἐν marks the habitual relationship: the festival is held every year in Anthesterion. While ἐν does not carry this force with ἡμέρα, it is not surprising that it should do so here. It should already be clear that, while the dative of time is used in a very circumscribed way, the genitive of time is far more heterogeneous, with a network of meanings extending from limitative to habitual to modal. Given that constructions with ἐν resemble those with the genitive in that they are found in limitative and modal expressions with ἡμέρα, the extension to the habitual construction with μήν is only to be expected. All in all, as far as can be determined from the smaller number of examples, μήν behaves the same way that ἡμέρα does.

---

[46] In passing, it should be noted that the fact that 'during' works as a translation does not mean that the construction is durative. Indeed, in the most prototypical durative constructions (e.g. *he reigned for ten years, he stayed there for three days*), 'during' would be extremely awkward.

[47] Opinions divide on whether τῇ δωδεκάτῃ belongs in the text. Stuart Jones's OCT excludes it (one generally expects μηνός, not ἐν μηνί, with the specification of a date); Classen–Steup (strongly) and Gomme 1956a (more cautiously) defend it (it is in a papyrus, and there are inscriptional parallels for the date together with ἐν μηνί). If it is genuine, then it is a typical punctual dative of time. This of course raises the question: why would the month take a habitual construction, the date a punctual one? There are probably two contributory causes: (a) the scope of the habitual construction only extends to the expression with the month, not that with the day (the festival happens every Anthesterion, but not every twelfth day of every month); (b) ordinals are common enough in punctual expressions with the dative of time that it would be difficult to displace the dative as the means of marking which day in the month an event occurred.

85

So too the words for year, ἐνιαυτός and ἔτος. The former can be dealt with very easily: it never occurs in the dative of time or with ἐν, and there are only two examples of the genitive of time. Both are good distributive constructions, with the noun modified only by the definite article (1.138.5, 3.50.2). Nor does ἔτος cause many problems. The sixteen passages where it is found in the dative of time are remarkably uniform: it always modifies a verb in the aorist, and it is itself always modified by an ordinal number.[48] As for the genitive of time with ἔτος, one example is a straightforward limitative construction (ᾤοντο ὀλίγων ἐτῶν καθαιρήσειν τὴν τῶν Ἀθηναίων δύναμιν, 5.14.3), but the other is more difficult to understand:

(43) Συρακούσας δὲ **τοῦ ἐχομένου ἔτους** Ἀρχίας τῶν Ἡρακλειδῶν ἐκ Κορίνθου ᾤκισε

And the next year, Archias of the Heraclids from Corinth founded Syracuse

(Th. 6.3.2)

We expect the punctual construction with the dative of time here. The genitive is probably triggered by the modifier ἐχόμενος, insofar as the best comparandum is the use of ἐν rather than the simple dative in the expression ἐν ἡμέρᾳ ῥητῇ (see (38)). In this case, the sense 'following' might have given ἐχόμενος a propensity for occurring with future-time reference, where the limitative genitive of time would be the expected construction. If that happened often enough, it might lead to the regular use of the genitive of time even in a past-time construction, as here.

Similarly, of the two examples of ἔτος with ἐν, one is a simple limitative construction, but the other looks as if it ought to have a punctual dative of time:

(44) ταῦτα δὲ ξύμπαντα . . . ἐγένετο **ἐν ἔτεσι πεντήκοντα μάλιστα**

And all of this happened in about fifty years (Th. 1.118.2)

(45) ἡ δὲ διαγνώμη αὕτη τῆς ἐκκλησίας, τοῦ τὰς σπονδὰς λελύσθαι, ἐγένετο **ἐν τῷ τετάρτῳ καὶ δεκάτῳ ἔτει τῶν τριακοντουτίδων σπονδῶν**

And this decision of the assembly, that the truce was over, took place in the fourteenth year of the thirty-year truce (Th. 1.87.6)

---

[48] See 1.12.3 (2×), 1.18.2, 1.101.3, 1.103.1, 1.115.2, 2.2.1, 3.68.5, 3.116.2, 4.102.3, 5.16.3, 6.3.3, 6.4.3, 6.59.4, 7.28.3, 8.58.1.

While the verb is the same in both passages, the time expression itself is significantly different: in (44), it designates a stretch of time during which a telic event (or, in this case, as often in limitative constructions, a set of discrete events) took place; in (45), however, it indicates the particular year in which a single decision took place. The latter example resembles the sixteen examples of the dative of time with ἔτει all the more in that it is modified by an ordinal number. One may compare 2.2.1, 3.68.5, and 6.4.3, all of which share with (45) the additional similarity of a compound ordinal.[49] Perhaps the most likely motivation for the use of ἐν lies in the combination of the demonstrative αὕτη and the verb ἐγένετο. Looking forward to the next section, we will find that, with θέρος and χειμών, one context in which the limitative occurs when one might expect the punctual is in summary statements at the end of a narrative section, for example, ταῦτα μὲν οὖν ἐν τῷ θέρει τούτῳ ἐγένετο (4.88.2); indeed, (44) belongs to the same family. Something similar is probably at work in (45).

At this point, the broad outlines of the constructions should be clear (see Table 7): with the words for day, month, and year, the dative is used in punctual constructions, the genitive and ἐν in pretty much everything else: limitative, above all, but also distributive, habitual, and modal. In a couple of examples, ἐν even encroaches on the punctual territory of the dative. More difficult to assess is the difference between the genitive of time and temporal ἐν. The clearest distinction is that only the genitive expresses the distributive event-type. The limitative can be expressed equally well by either construction: of the twelve limitative expressions with ἡμέρα (omitting the uncertain example in (39)), six have the genitive, six have ἐν; both are also used with similar modifiers (cardinal numbers, ὀλίγαι). Still, there is a subtle difference in the verbs they modify. The genitive has a preference for future-time reference (not, it must be emphasized, the same as morphological future verbs), ἐν for past-time reference. Of the six genitives of time, only one refers to a specific event in the past (8.101.1); the

---

[49] The construction at 8.58.1 is even closer in that the verbal phrase modified is ξυνθῆκαι ἐγένοντο, but it occurs in the quoted text of a treaty so is not a very useful parallel.

other five all look forward to events still to come in the narrative thread (2.97.2, 4.26.4 = (29), 4.105.2, 7.3.1, 7.40.2 = (30)). It is the exact opposite with the phrases governed by ἐν: five refer to past-time events (2.58.3, 3.51.4 = (37), 3.113.6, 4.5.2, 4.91.1), and only one looks forward (6.29.3). This distribution helps explain why temporal constructions with ἐν have been so hard to pin down, with past grammars associating them sometimes with the genitive, sometimes with the dative.[50] While their wider usage is closest to that of the genitive, the type of limitative expression they gravitate towards is precisely that subclass of the limitative which comes closest to the punctual.

Summary

Table 7. *Punctual and limitative expressions in Thucydides: Day, month, and year*

	ἡμέρα	μήν	ἐνιαυτός	ἔτος
genitive	4× distrib.	1× distrib.	2× distrib.	
	6× limitative	1× limitative		2× limitative[a]
	3× modal			
	1× habitual			
ἐν[+D]	7× limitative[b]			1× limitative
	1× modal	1× habitual		
	3× punctual (w. ῥητῇ)			1× punctual
dative	31× punctual	3× punctual		16× punctual

Note:

[a] This counts (43) as limitative.
[b] This counts (39) as limitative.

With the words for day, month, and year:

1. The dative of time is used only in punctual constructions.
2. Both the genitive of time and phrases with ἐν are most often limitative, but the habitual and modal uses are also common. In

---

[50] Kühner–Gerth sees ἐν[+D] as similar to the genitive of time on p. 387, but on p. 446 speaks of it as being added to datives of time (as well as again noting its similarity to the genitive). The account in Schwyzer–Debrunner follows the same lines, pp. 158–9.

limitative constructions, the genitive is preferred when the verbal event has not yet taken place, ἐν when it has.

3. The genitive of time is also common in distributive constructions.

4. At times, ἐν is found in punctual constructions that resemble those with the dative, but they always have some slight limitative nuance. That this should happen with ἐν rather than the genitive of time results from the preference for ἐν in past-time limitative constructions.

Punctual and limitative expressions in Thucydides: night and the seasons

The summary just given is only valid for the time nouns covered in that section. The cursory glance we have already had at the temporal expressions with νύξ, θέρος, and χειμών is enough to suggest that they follow different rules. In particular, the genitive is used at the expense of the dative. It is possible that this could simply reflect a tendency for these time nouns to occur in limitative and habitual constructions rather than punctual ones. But in fact we will see that the genitive predominates even in punctual constructions.

First, consider νύξ. It occurs only three times in the dative of time. Two of these are standard punctual constructions, but the third is rather different:

(46) καὶ ἀποστάντες τῶν Ἀθηναίων **ἐκείνη τῇ νυκτὶ** κατέστησαν τὸν στρατὸν πρὸ ἕω ἐπὶ τὴν γέφυραν τοῦ ποταμοῦ

And they revolted from the Athenians that night and set up their army before dawn on the bridge over the river (Th. 4.103.4)

(47) καὶ **τῇ ἐπιούσῃ νυκτὶ** ἔφθασαν παροικοδομήσαντες καὶ παρελθόντες τὴν τῶν Ἀθηναίων οἰκοδομίαν

And the following night they finished first in building a wall alongside and extending past that of the Athenians (Th. 7.6.4)

(48) ἐν δὲ τούτῳ, ὅσοι Ἑρμαῖ ἦσαν λίθινοι ἐν τῇ πόλει τῇ Ἀθηναίων (εἰσὶ δὲ κατὰ τὸ ἐπιχώριον, ἡ τετράγωνος ἐργασία, πολλοὶ καὶ ἐν ἰδίοις προθύροις καὶ ἐν ἱεροῖς), **μιᾷ νυκτὶ** οἱ πλεῖστοι περιεκόπησαν τὰ πρόσωπα

89

And meanwhile, all the stone Herms in the city of the Athenians – and there are many of them according to local custom, these square-cut objects, both in front of private houses and in temples – most of them had their faces mutilated on one night (Th. 6.27.1)

In (46) and (47), we have aorist indicatives describing past-time events, modified by temporal expressions that specify the night on which the event took place; both the demonstrative ἐκείνη and the adjective ἐπιούσῃ are consistent with a punctual reading. But (48) should be considered a limitative expression for two reasons. Broadly speaking, it is limitative because it refers to multiple events, all of which have occurred inside a single bracketing time period. More narrowly, the limitative interpretation is suggested by the fact that νυκτί is modified by μιᾷ. This modifier is very typical of limitative expressions, because one does not usually say that something happened on a single night unless it is an event one would not expect to fit into so short a period – often, as here, precisely because it is a composite event of the sort that typifies the limitative event-type. Now εἷς is by no means a common modifier of time nouns. In Thucydides and Xenophon, it never occurs with the genitive of time, and occurs with the dative of time only here. However, it does occur four times with ἐν: once in Thucydides we have ἐν ἑνὶ θέρει (3.17.2), twice in Xenophon we have ἐν μιᾷ ἡμέρᾳ (HG 3.1.16, Cyr. 2.3.24), once more in Xenophon ἐν τῇδε τῇ μιᾷ ἡμέρᾳ (Cyr. 3.1.17). If one combines these parallels with two other facts – first, that there are many other examples of ἐν marking limitative expressions with modifiers other than εἷς; second, that there are no other parallels in these authors in which the dative of time marks limitative constructions – there is good reason to emend passage (48) by inserting an ἐν before μιᾷ. The passage already shows one sign of textual disturbance – ἡ τετράγωνος ἐργασία is a good candidate for interpolation[51] – and it is not hard to imagine, especially in the absence of the punctuation mark of a parenthesis, an ἐν dropping out after the immediately preceding ἐν ἰδίοις προθύροις καὶ ἐν ἱεροῖς.

---

[51] The Patmos scholia, as they gloss Ἑρμαῖ λίθινοι with τετράγωνος ἐργασία (Hude 1927: 341), have been interpreted (including by Stuart Jones) as evidence that τετράγωνος ἐργασία did not stand in the MS the scholiast had in front of him. Dover, however, argues that they might be genuine Thucydides after all (1955).

Far more frequent is the genitive of time νυκτός: it occurs thirty-five times in Thucydides, nearly always in punctual constructions. The clearest examples are the following two:

(49) οἱ δὲ τριακόσιοι τῶν Σκιωναίων **τῆς ἐπιούσης νυκτὸς** ἀπεχώρησαν ἐπ' οἴκου

And the three hundred Scionaeans left the following night for home (Th. 4.130.1)

(50) καὶ **τῆς αὐτῆς ταύτης νυκτὸς** ὡς εἶχον τάχους ὑπομείξαντες τῇ Χερσονήσῳ παρέπλεον ἐπ' Ἐλαιοῦντος

And that same night, just as they were, keeping close to the Chersonese, they quickly sailed past to Elaeus (Th. 8.102.1)

These two passages stand out because the time noun has the sort of modifier one would expect in a punctual construction: (49) looks like (47), (50) like (46). By contrast, most examples of punctual νυκτός are modified either by the definite article (15×) or by nothing at all (15×):

(51) ἐπὶ τοὺς τριακοσίους, οἳ τὴν φυλακὴν διεξῆλθον **τῆς νυκτός**

To the three hundred, who slipped through the guard at night (Th. 7.85.2)

(52) οἱ ... ἐπίκουροι βιασάμενοι παρὰ θάλασσαν τὴν φυλακὴν **νυκτὸς** ἀφικνοῦνται

The troops forced their way through the guard to the sea and arrived at night (Th. 4.131.3)

Because they lack the telltale modifiers like ordinal numbers that make the punctual expressions with ἡμέρα and ἔτος so clear, one might well question whether these should be included under this heading. In particular, they appear to bear some affinity to the genitives of time of ἡμέρα that belong in the modal, rather than punctual, category, viz. (34) through (36). Yet there remains a subtle difference: in the case of most of the examples of (τῆς) νυκτός, the contrast with a daytime action is not as explicit as is the contrast with a night-time action when (τῆς) ἡμέρας is used. Accordingly, examples like (51) and (52) will be labeled as punctual.

In fact, apart from the one habitual example of τῆς νυκτός (4.23.2 = (33)), there are only two other constructions with νυκτός that clearly fall outside the range of uses typified by (51) and (52). One is the following:

(53) εἰ οὖν προσπέσοιμεν ἄφνω τε καὶ **νυκτός**

So, if we were to attack quickly and by night (Th. 3.30.3)

Because νυκτός occurs here in a conditional clause in which potential future courses of action are being considered, it has rather more of the modal quality of (34) and (35) than passages like (51) and (52) do. Indeed, passage (34) itself offers the second example of modal τῆς νυκτός – a rather clear one as it is in parallel with τῆς ἡμέρας. Another handful of examples also has some cause to be taken out of the strictly punctual category, primarily because the temporal phrase is further modified by ἔτι, giving them an appearance like that of (36):[52]

(54) καὶ ἀφικόμενος **νυκτὸς ἔτι** καὶ περὶ ὄρθρον τῷ στρατῷ ἐκαθέζετο πρὸς τὸ Διοσκόρειον

And, arriving when it was still night, at about daybreak, he halted with his army by the temple of the Dioscuri (Th. 4.110.1)

Particularly noteworthy in this example is the coordination of νυκτὸς ἔτι with περὶ ὄρθρον. In (53), νυκτός is in parallel with the adverb of manner ἄφνω, making a modal reading more plausible; here, it is conjoined with περὶ ὄρθρον, favoring a more purely temporal interpretation. In short, the use of νυκτός may be summarized thus: (i) twice it is used in prototypical punctual constructions; (ii) once it is used in a habitual construction; (iii) twice it is used in modal constructions; (iv) thirty times it is used in constructions that are best labeled punctual, as their chief purpose is to indicate when an event happened. Still, it must be added that examples from this last category share some characteristics with the temporal expressions of ἡμέρα that, though potentially punctual, take the genitive of time. In particular, they are modified by only the article or by nothing at all, and they specify not which night the verbal event took place, but that it took place during the hours of darkness.

Before attempting to pin this last category down any further, we must also look at the eight temporal constructions where νύξ is governed by ἐν. As a whole, they are very close in use to the

---

[52] See also 2.5.1, 4.26.6, 8.101.3.

genitives of time, but with a heavier weighting towards the modal type. Four of the eight are best seen as modal, for example:

(55) ὅπως μὴ κατὰ φῶς θαρσαλεωτέροις οὖσι προσφέροιντο ... ἀλλ' ἐν **νυκτὶ** φοβερώτεροι ὄντες ἥσσους ὦσι

> So that they would not attack during daylight against a fairly confident enemy ... but so that the enemy, being more fearful by night, would be defeated (Th. 2.3.4)

Here there is an explicit contrast with a daytime attack, and a modal reading is preferable. Both here and in the other three examples that I assign to the modal category, the temporal expression is virtually equivalent to a causal phrase and, as such, more critical to the understanding of the sentence than in the typical punctual construction:[53]

(56) ἄλλως τε καὶ ἐν **νυκτὶ** τε καὶ διὰ πολεμίας καὶ ἀπὸ πολεμίων οὐ πολὺ ἀπεχόντων ἰοῦσιν, ἐμπίπτει ταραχή

> Especially as they were traveling by night, over hostile ground, and away from enemies who were not far distant, confusion fell over them (Th. 7.80.3)

Granted, in this instance, ἐν **νυκτί** is causal with respect to the main verb of the sentence rather than the participle that it is directly modifying, but the phrase is still more essential to the overall meaning of the sentence than is the case with most punctual constructions, as in the following:

(57) καύσαντες οὖν πυρὰ πολλὰ ἐχώρουν ἐν τῇ **νυκτί**

> So they lit many fires and moved forwards during the night (Th. 7.80.3)

Occurring just before (56), this is the only good candidate for a punctual construction with ἐν (τῇ) **νυκτί**: the emphasis of the temporal phrase lies more on simply indicating when the event took place than in the previous two examples. Of the remaining three examples of ἐν (τῇ) **νυκτί** that might be considered punctual, one is better viewed as limitative because of the future time-reference:

---

[53] See the discussion of modal example (34). The other two examples I classify as modal are 2.3.1 and 7.44.4.

(58) δεδιὼς μὴ οἱ Ἀθηναῖοι καθ᾽ ἡσυχίαν προφθάσωσιν **ἐν τῇ νυκτὶ** διελθόντες τὰ χαλεπώτατα τῶν χωρίων

Afraid that the Athenians would get a head start and quietly pass through the most difficult parts of the terrain during the night (Th. 7.73.3)

A modal reading is probably the best interpretation of the other two:

(59) οἱ δὲ πλείους ἐς φυγὴν κατέστησαν, φοβηθέντες **ἐν νυκτὶ** τε πολεμίων προσπεπτωκότων καὶ τῶν προδιδόντων Μεγαρέων ἀντιμαχομένων

And most turned in flight, afraid because the enemy had attacked by night and the Megarians who betrayed them were now fighting against them (Th. 4.68.2)

(60) καὶ ἀδοκήτου τοῦ τολμήματος σφίσιν **ἐν νυκτὶ** γενομένου προσέβαλόν τε τοῖς Ἀθηναίοις ἐκπεπληγμένοι καὶ βιασθέντες ὑπ᾽ αὐτῶν τὸ πρῶτον ὑπεχώρησαν

And as they had not expected this daring during the night, they attacked the Athenians in a state of panic and were forced to draw back at first (Th. 7.43.6)

In both of these examples, one might argue that the fact that the attack took place at night is less critical to the clause than in (55) and (56), but they are still a far cry from the sort of punctual constructions typical of (τῆς) νυκτός (cf. (51) and (52)). As a side note, the article also seems to play more of a role in affecting the meaning of the constructions with ἐν than it did with the genitive of time. Both νυκτός and τῆς νυκτός occur regularly in the punctual examples (again, cf. (51) and (52)), but it is perhaps significant that the two *least* modal constructions with ἐν, (57) and (58), both have the definite article, whereas the more modal constructions generally do not.[54]

When all these temporal constructions with νύξ are taken together, the picture is very different from that presented by the expressions with ἡμέρα. Two broad lines of interpretation are then open. On the one hand, one could argue that the genitive is simply the preferred marker of the punctual event-type with this noun, with ἐν used instead to mark the limitative and modal types. The occasional use of the dative would result from the influence of the constructions found with ἡμέρα and ἔτος. On the other, it might be

---

[54] The only exception is that the modal construction at 2.3.1 does have the article.

more significant that the vast number of punctual genitives of time of νύξ are very different from those with ἡμέρα, in that they simply specify that an event took place at night, rather than which night it took place. Perhaps the line between punctual and modal should be redrawn. If we extend the modal category to include examples like (51) and (52), then we could eliminate much of the discrepancy between ἡμέρα and νύξ by simply noting that νύξ, because it is not used in timekeeping the way ἡμέρα is, is not prone to occur in the sort of punctual construction that would elicit the dative of time. With this model, the occurrence of the genitive in (49) and (50), where the punctual dative is expected, could be attributed to contamination from the frequent use of the genitive of νύξ in modal expressions. It will be necessary to look at temporal expressions with θέρος and χειμών before deciding which of these two models explains the data better.

Expressions of time with the seasons pattern, at least superficially, like those with νύξ: with θέρος, the genitive of time occurs forty-eight times,[55] ἐν nineteen times, but the dative only twice; with χειμών, the genitive occurs thirty-five times, ἐν seventeen times, and the dative not once. Again, the vast majority of the examples with the genitive are straightforward punctual examples:

(61) **τοῦ δ' ἐπιγιγνομένου θέρους** οἱ Πελοποννήσιοι . . . αὐτοὶ ἐς τὴν Ἀττικὴν καὶ οἱ ξύμμαχοι ἐσέβαλον

And the following summer, the Peloponnesians . . . and their allies invaded Attica (Th. 3.26.1)

(62) **τοῦ δ' αὐτοῦ χειμῶνος** καὶ Δῆλον ἐκάθηραν Ἀθηναῖοι κατὰ χρησμὸν δή τινα

And the same winter, the Athenians also conducted a purification of Delos in accordance with an oracle (Th. 3.104.1)

Like the punctual datives of time with ἡμέρα and ἔτος, these expressions all specify the particular instance of the given time noun during which the verbal event took place. They are different, however, in the modifiers of the time noun (see Table 8). Instead of

---

[55] As noted in Ch. 1, the numbers for the genitive of time of θέρος include constructions where the genitive may be dependent on phrases like ὑπὸ τοὺς αὐτοὺς χρόνους and thus adnominal rather than adverbial. If these are excluded, there are only forty-two genitives of time of θέρος. This is a small enough difference that the general picture remains the same whether or not they are included.

EXPRESSIONS OF TIME IN THUCYDIDES

Table 8. *Modifiers of* θέρος *and* χειμών *in genitive of time constructions in Thucydides*

Modifier	θέρος	χειμών
τοῦ αὐτοῦ	23	16
τοῦ ἐπιγιγνομένου	15	15
τοῦ ... τούτου	7	–
τοῦ	1	2
none	2	2

ordinal numbers and demonstratives, one finds overwhelmingly τοῦ αὐτοῦ and τοῦ ἐπιγιγνομένου.

The preponderance of τοῦ αὐτοῦ and τοῦ ἐπιγιγνομένου is in fact even greater than the table suggests, as the seven examples of τοῦ θέρους τούτου include five of the six genitives of time that are more likely to be adnominal genitives than adverbial, for example:[56]

(63) κατὰ δὲ τὸν αὐτὸν χρόνον **τοῦ θέρους τούτου** Ἀθηναῖοι καὶ περὶ Πελοπόννησον ναῦς ἀπέστειλαν τριάκοντα

And at about the same time of or during this summer, the Athenians also sent thirty ships around the Peloponnesus (Th. 3.7.1)

The sixth passage with τοῦ θέρους τούτου possibly falls in this category as well (2.31.1 = ex. (51) in Chapter 1), and it is only the last one which is clearly adverbial:

(64) Ὀλύμπια δ᾽ ἐγένετο **τοῦ θέρους τούτου**

And the Olympic Games took place this summer (Th. 5.49.1)

Still, even though this difference in the typical modifier must be acknowledged, it remains the case that representative examples like (61) and (62) are closer to the punctual constructions with ἡμέρα and ἔτος than those with νύξ are.

Only four of these eighty-three genitives of time fall into the heterogeneous network of usages that would also elicit the genitive of ἡμέρα:

(65) **θέρους** γὰρ δι᾽ ἀνυδρίαν ἀδύνατα ἦν ἐπιστρατεύειν

For it was impossible to attack it during the summer for lack of water (Th. 3.88.1)

---

[56] See also 3.52.1 (= ex. (59) in Ch. 1), 5.32.1, 6.105.1, 8.99.1.

96

(66) καὶ θέρους καὶ χειμῶνος ἐταλαιπωροῦντο

And they suffered hardship both during summer and winter (Th. 7.28.2)

(67) ἀλλὰ τὸ θέρος τοῦτο ἀντικαθεζόμενοι **χειμῶνος ἤδη** ἀνεχώρησαν ἐπ᾽ οἴκου ἑκάτεροι

But after staying opposite each other for the summer, when it was now winter both sides withdrew home (Th. 1.30.4)

In (65), θέρους is modal (cf. the very similar (35) with ἡμέρας); both genitives in (66) are habitual (cf. (33)); and the phrase χειμῶνος ἤδη in (67), like ἡμέρας ἤδη in (36), looks like a defective genitive absolute.

The only two datives of time are the following:

(68) μέχρι οὗ Κορίνθιοι **περιιόντι τῷ θέρει** πέμψαντες ναῦς καὶ στρατιάν . . . ἐστρατοπεδεύοντο ἐπὶ Ἀκτίῳ

Until the Corinthians, as summer came around, sent ships and an army . . . to be stationed at Actium (Th. 1.30.3)

(69) ἀνέστησαν δὲ καὶ Αἰγινήτας **τῷ αὐτῷ θέρει τούτῳ** ἐξ Αἰγίνης Ἀθηναῖοι

And the Athenians also drove the Aeginetans out of Aegina during this same summer (Th. 2.27.1)

Both of these passages resemble the two datives of time with νύξ, (46) and (47), in being rare examples of the expected punctual construction. The second example is particularly similar in that the time noun is modified by a demonstrative, making it more proto-typically like the examples of the dative of time than is the case with most of the punctual genitives of time with θέρος.

More numerous are the constructions with ἐν. As was the case with ἐν (τῇ) νυκτί, they are more limitative and modal than the genitive of time, but there remain many examples that are just as punctual as the genitives. Consider first the nineteen examples with θέρος. One is modal, and, significantly, it is one of only two not to have the definite article:

(70) καὶ οὐδ᾽ **ἐν θέρει** οἷοί τε ὄντες ἱκανὰ περιπέμπειν

[The Athenians were afraid of what would happen during the winter when conditions were more difficult . . .] Nor were they able even in summer to send around enough provisions (Th. 4.27.1)

The other construction without the definite article is the following:

(71) ὥστε αἱ πᾶσαι ἅμα ἐγίγνοντο **ἐν ἑνὶ θέρει** διακόσιαι καὶ πεντήκοντα

> So the total number of ships in one summer came to two hundred fifty
> (Th. 3.17.3)

This is a good limitative construction: the time noun is modified by εἷς, and it brackets into a time frame a number of discrete events just mentioned (in this case, the enumeration of which ships were where). Closely related are three passages with anaphoric pronouns, for example:[57]

(72) τοσαῦτα μὲν **ἐν τῷ θέρει** ἐγένετο

> All this happened during the summer (Th. 2.68.9)

But there need not be a pronoun like τοσαῦτα or ταῦτα to indicate that multiple events are being wrapped up in the temporal expression. Derivatives of πολύς can also act as signs of the limitative:

(73) πολλάκις δὲ καὶ πολλῶν λόγων γενομένων **ἐν τῷ θέρει τούτῳ**

> And since lengthy discussions had taken place at many times during the summer (Th. 5.35.7)

Twice, adverbial πρότερον and τὸ δεύτερον might justify categorizing the construction as a limitative:

(74) πρότερον δὲ **ἐν τῷ αὐτῷ θέρει τῷδε** ἑκκαίδεκα ἐς αὐτὸν νῆες ἐσέπλευσαν

> And earlier in this same summer sixteen ships had already sailed there
> (Th. 8.99.1)

(75) ἢν ὑμεῖς **ἐν τῷ θέρει τῷδε** ναυσί τε καὶ πεζῷ ἅμα ἐπεσβάλητε τὸ δεύτερον

> If you attack a second time during this summer simultaneously with your navy and army (Th. 3.13.4)

In both these passages, the additional adverbial element highlights the fact that multiple events are taking place in the given period of time. True, this is already suggested in (74) by the modifier ὁ αὐτός, but the distribution of this modifier with the genitive and ἐν itself suggests that the latter is more inclined to mark the limitative type: ὁ αὐτός modifies θέρος in eleven of the nineteen ἐν-phrases (58% of

---

[57] See also 2.32.1, 4.88.2, in both of which the verb is ἐγένετο, and its subject ταῦτα.

the time), but in only twenty-three out of the forty-eight genitives of time (48%). This is admittedly not an impressive distinction at first glance. What is more significant is the nature of the rest of the examples: the bulk of the remaining genitives of time have ἐπιγιγνόμενος as the modifier, but this is never found in ἐν-phrases, which instead most often have demonstratives in constructions like (73) and (75) in which contextual clues hint at a limitative reading.

It remains the case that many constructions with ἐν are virtually indistinguishable from those with the genitive:

(76) ἐν δὲ τῷ αὐτῷ θέρει μετὰ τὴν Λέσβου ἅλωσιν Ἀθηναῖοι . . . ἐστράτευσαν ἐπὶ Μινῷαν τὴν νῆσον

And in the same summer after the capture of Lesbos, the Athenians attacked the island Minoa (Th. 3.51.1)

(77) τοῦ δ' αὐτοῦ θέρους Ἅγνων ὁ Νικίου καὶ Κλεόπομπος ὁ Κλεινίου . . . λαβόντες τὴν στρατιὰν ἥπερ ἐκεῖνος ἐχρήσατο ἐστράτευσαν εὐθὺς ἐπὶ Χαλκιδέας τοὺς ἐπὶ Θρᾴκης

And in the same summer, Hagnon son of Nicias and Cleopompus son of Clinias took the army which [Pericles] had used and immediately attacked the Chalcidians in Thrace (Th. 2.58.1)

In the light of such similarities, one can only conclude that there was considerable overlap between the genitive of time and ἐν. But two differences are still significant: (i) summing-up constructions like (72) always have ἐν, never the genitive; (ii) those, like (61), with ἐπιγιγνόμενος as the modifier always have the genitive, never ἐν. Both of these differences suggest that, when a distinction can be made, the expressions with ἐν are more limitative than those with the genitive. This is consistent with the behavior of νύξ, in which ἐν-phrases were more modal and limitative, genitives of time more punctual.

As for χειμών, it also patterns like θέρος, as seen in example (62) and the table of modifiers (Table 8) that follows. Indeed, it presents an even stronger case for the view that the preferred marker of the punctual event-type is the genitive, as it never occurs in the dative of time. The distribution of ἐν-phrases and the genitive of time is also similar: the only summing-up construction has ἐν (2.70.4; possibly also 2.47.1), and ἐπιγιγνόμενος only occurs with the genitive (although ἐν τῷ ἐπιόντι χειμῶνι does occur once at 4.134.1). But again there is a great deal of overlap: of the seventeen constructions

99

with ἐν, two are best considered limitative (2.70.4, 6.72.4), two modal (2.102.2, 4.108.6), and the remaining thirteen are all punctual enough that one could equally well expect the genitive of time. Finally, while neither μετόπωρον or φθινόπωρον occurs in the genitive or dative of time, or with ἐν, there are four examples of ἔαρ as a genitive of time. Two of these may be adnominal, and so do not tell us much (4.2.1, 7.21.1). But the other two passages are punctual and resemble those with θέρος or χειμών (6.95.1, 7.50.1).

Summary

With the words for night and the seasons (see Table 9):

1. The dative of time is used only in punctual constructions, but it is a very rare construction.
2. The most common punctual construction is the genitive of time, which only rarely is modal or habitual, and apparently never limitative.
3. The limitative and modal event-types are instead most often expressed with ἐν.

Table 9. *Punctual and limitative expressions in Thucydides: Night and the seasons*

Construction	νύξ	θέρος	χειμών
genitive	32× punctual	46× punctual	33× punctual
	1× habitual	1× habitual	1× habitual
	2× modal	1× modal	1× modal[a]
ἐν[+D]	6× modal	1× modal	2× modal
	1× limitative	5× limitative	2× limitative
	1× punctual	13× punctual[b]	13× punctual
dative	2× punctual[c]	2× punctual	–

Note:

[a] This is example (67), which perhaps should be considered punctual. In that case, the genitive of time of χειμών would be even more homogeneous.
[b] The figure for punctual constructions includes examples (74) and (75), which perhaps should be considered limitative instead.
[c] I omit (48) from this table.

4. But with θέρος and χειμών, even ἐν is still more often used in punctual than in limitative or modal constructions.

Clearly, these nouns act differently than the first group, of day, month, and year, which, for simplicity's sake, we may call calendrical time nouns. But is this because the nature of these time nouns is such that they will simply be used in different circumstances, and this is all that is reflected in the different distribution of the various temporal expressions? Or is this second group of time nouns so different that even under the same circumstances, they would not behave in the same way as the nouns of the first group?

In favor of the first explanation is the fact that the overwhelming use of the genitive of time in punctual constructions – the chief hallmark of the second group – might well be due to the different nature of these punctual constructions compared to those of the first group. The dative of time is used with calendrical time nouns because it is used to specify the particular unit of time during which an event occurred; it prototypically distinguishes that unit of time from other potential temporal locations by virtue of ordinal numbers or demonstratives. The punctual constructions with νύξ, by contrast, indicate that the action in question happened during the night, as opposed to during the day. Which night the event took place is understood from context. As such, these constructions could perhaps all be reclassified as modal, assuming an increase in the range of what is considered modal at the expense of the punctual event-type. The latter category would then include only those expressions of Time When that single out one unit of the time noun in question as distinct from other units.

There are, however, several problems with this position. One is that there are a couple of genitives of time of νύξ, examples (49) and (50), that would still be considered punctual even under this more restricted definition. Another is that it still does not get us any further in explaining the occurrence of the genitive of time in the numerous τοῦ αὐτοῦ/ἐπιγιγνομένου θέρους/χειμῶνος constructions, for these would all still count as punctual as well. Third, there is the distribution of genitive absolutes with time nouns, discussed in

Chapter 1: they are much more likely to be formed with nouns of the second than of the first group. That suggests not only that there is something real about the division of these nouns into two groups, but that that division is such as to promote the use of the genitive with the second group. A fourth problem is caused by the expressions with ἐν: here too, night and the seasons pattern differently than the calendrical time nouns, with ἐν regularly available, at least with θέρος and χειμών, for marking the punctual event-type. In the end, there is no getting around the fact that not all time nouns act alike. But even if we simply acknowledge that there is a lexically-based division in the behavior of time nouns, there remains the question of how this heterogeneity arose in the first place. The best answer to this question is likely to involve the first of the alternative explanations just assessed. At an early stage, the distribution of the genitive and dative would indeed have depended less on the time noun, and more on the event-type. Punctual expressions of the shape *on the* ORDINAL TIME NOUN would have taken the dative, whether it were *on the third day* or *on the tenth night*. There are not nearly enough examples in Homer to establish his practice with anything like the thoroughness with which Thucydides' can be determined, but the following examples are still suggestive:[58]

(78) εἰ δέ κεν εὐπλοίην δώη κλυτὸς ἐννοσίγαιος
ἤματί κε τριτάτῳ Φθίην ἐρίβωλον ἱκοίμην

And if the glorious Earthshaker should grant good sailing, I'd reach fertile Phthia on the third day (*Il.* 9.362–3)[59]

(79) ἐννῆμαρ φερόμην· δεκάτῃ δέ με νυκτὶ μελαίνῃ
νῆσον ἐς Ὠγυγίην πέλασαν θεοί

I was carried for nine days, and on the tenth, black night, the gods brought me to the island Ogygia (*Od.* 7.253–4)[60]

The genitive of time, by contrast, would have been used with events not associated with a particular day or night, presumably because this limitative-modal use would be more naturally

---

[58] Chantraine observes that the temporal dative in Homer is found "notamment" with ordinals (1953: 81).
[59] There are also examples with past-tense verbs as well, e.g. *Il.* 11.707, *Od.* 6.170, as well as many with demonstrative τῷδε and κείνῳ.
[60] See also *Od.* 12.447, 14.314.

expressed with a partitive genitive than with a locatival dative. While no examples of a genitive of time ἥματος occur in Homer, νυκτός is found once:[61]

(80) κεῖθεν δὲ πλαγχθέντες ἱκάνομεν ἐνθάδε **νυκτός**

And drifting away from there, we arrived here at night (*Od.* 13.278)

Constructions like (80) will have predominated, if it is sound to assume that, in the post-Homeric period when the two time nouns diverged in their behavior, it was less common to reckon time by nights than by days.[62] Gradually, the association of the limitative-modal genitive with νύξ will have become fossilized and extended to constructions like (49) and (50), in which the dative would have originally been the more natural choice. But even though this narrative is eminently plausible, it must remain speculative, as there simply is not enough evidence of these constructions in the archaic period for any clear diachronic change to be tracked.

Limitative expressions in Thucydides: χρόνος

There remains one time noun whose behavior has not yet been worked into this account of the distribution of the genitive, dative, and ἐν in temporal expressions: χρόνος. I have left it out until now because its semantics are not as easily pinned down as those of the time nouns already covered. In particular, it does not specify a discrete unit of time in the way that day, night, month, year, and the seasons all do. But, given that it occurs three times as a genitive of time, sixteen times in the dative, and twenty-two times after ἐν, it would be rash to ignore it.

---

[61] The other examples of the genitive of time cited by Chantraine are also compatible with this explanation (1953: 59); they will be discussed in Ch. 5.

[62] At any earlier period, one would not want to make this assumption. Modern English *fortnight* still attests to a once widespread practice of counting by nights, as does Caesar's observation on the Gauls: *spatia omnis temporis non numero dierum sed noctium finiunt* (*BG* 6.18). For more examples, including from non-IE peoples, see Nilsson (1920: 13–15). Nevertheless, in the texts that actually show this divergence between νύξ and ἡμέρα, the transition has already taken place to pinpointing events according to days, rather than nights.

In fact, the raw figures promise too much. The datives, in particular, can be dismissed right from the start, as already noted in Chapter 1.[63] They are not punctual datives indicating time when, but datives of degree of difference: despite the obvious English gloss, χρόνῳ 'in time' means not 'at some time', but 'after some time', anomalous behavior similar to that exhibited by χρόνος after διά[+G].[64] The genitives of time, however, are more interesting:

(81) Ἕλληνος δὲ καὶ τῶν παίδων αὐτοῦ ἐν τῇ Φθιώτιδι ἰσχυσάντων, καὶ ἐπαγομένων αὐτοὺς ἐπ᾽ ὠφελίᾳ ἐς τὰς ἄλλας πόλεις, καθ᾽ ἑκάστους μὲν ἤδη τῇ ὁμιλίᾳ μᾶλλον καλεῖσθαι Ἕλληνας, οὐ μέντοι **πολλοῦ γε χρόνου** [ἐδύνατο] καὶ ἅπασιν ἐκνικῆσαι

And since Hellen and his sons grew powerful in Phthiotis, and they were brought in for help to the other cities, one by one because of their association [the Greeks] were increasingly called Hellenes – still, within a great length of time, it would not prevail for all of them (Th. 1.3.2)

(82) καὶ ἡ μὲν μάχη τοιαύτη καὶ ὅτι ἐγγύτατα τούτων ἐγένετο, **πλείστου δὴ χρόνου** μεγίστη δὴ τῶν Ἑλληνικῶν καὶ ὑπὸ ἀξιολογωτάτων πόλεων ξυνελθοῦσα

And the battle was of this sort or as close to this as possible, the greatest battle of the Greeks in a very long time and contested by the most noteworthy cities (Th. 5.74.1)

(83) καὶ μηνὸς μὲν τροφήν, ὥσπερ ὑπέστη ἐν τῇ Λακεδαίμονι, ἐς δραχμὴν Ἀττικὴν ἑκάστῳ πάσαις ταῖς ναυσὶ διέδωκε, **τοῦ δὲ λοιποῦ χρόνου** ἐβούλετο τριώβολον διδόναι, ἕως ἂν βασιλέα ἐπέρηται

And, as he promised in Sparta, he paid out to all the ships for a month's provisions an Attic drachma for each man, but in the future he wanted to give three obols, until he could ask the king about it (Th. 8.29.1)

The first two of these genitives are best construed as limitative. In (81) and (82), this interpretation is aided by the presence of πολύς and πλεῖστος as modifiers: that yields the combination of a temporal phrase designating a stretch of time and a telic event that we expect of the limitative type. The chief wrinkle is that it is not clear in (82) what verb the phrase is modifying. Probably we should understand γενομένη with μεγίστη, as it is awkward to take ξυνελθοῦσα with πλείστου δὴ ... τῶν Ἑλληνικῶν. In (83), however,

---

[63] See the discussion in that Ch. 1 of examples (67) through (75).
[64] See (19) in this chapter.

it is striking that Thucydides uses the genitive rather than a durative accusative. After all, the future payment of three obols is atelic: it should last indefinitely, coextensive with the λοιπὸς χρόνος of the temporal phrase. Probably the best solution is to assume that ὁ λοιπὸς χρόνος was considered as a rule to be so unbounded an extent of time that nothing could last for the entire extent of it. Even a relatively atelic event such as a regular disbursement of money can only ever last for a part of the future (note the ἕως-clause), so a limitative genitive is preferred to the durative accusative.[65]

Much more common are phrases with ἐν. As one might expect, these are typically limitative (18×), but there are four where one might instead expect a durative accusative. Most of the limitative examples have the expected modifiers: ὀλίγῳ, πολλῷ, παντί. They are distinguished from the accusatives of time by having clearly telic verbs:[66]

(84) τούτῳ τῷ τρόπῳ οἱ Ἀθηναῖοι τὴν πόλιν ἐτείχισαν ἐν ὀλίγῳ χρόνῳ

In this way the Athenians walled their city in a short time (Th. 1.93.1)

As for the four durative examples, three have either τῷ πρὸ τοῦ or τῷ πρίν as modifiers:[67]

(85) ὥστε καὶ τοὺς προτέρους στρατιώτας νοσῆσαι τῶν Ἀθηναίων ἀπὸ τῆς ξὺν Ἅγνωνι στρατιᾶς, ἐν τῷ πρὸ τοῦ χρόνῳ ὑγιαίνοντας

Such that even the soldiers of the Athenians who were already there caught the plague from Hagnon's army, even though they had been healthy in the period before this (Th. 2.58.2)

Neither of these modifiers ever occurs with the accusative of time, and the use of the limitative construction can be justified on the same grounds as the limitative genitive in (83), but in the reverse temporal direction: all of past time is too unbounded a period for anything to be coextensive with it. Even otherwise durative events are thus treated as limitative. The final example is rather different:

(86) οἱ γὰρ Ἀθηναῖοι ἐσεκομίζοντο ἐν τῷ χρόνῳ τούτῳ, καὶ ἐδόκουν οἱ Πελοποννήσιοι ἐπελθόντες ἂν διὰ τάχους πάντα ἔτι ἔξω καταλαβεῖν

---

[65] Further evidence for this line of argument comes from Plato: see ex. (81) in Ch. 3.
[66] For a typical accusative of time, see example (16).
[67] See also 4.21.1 (with ἐπιθυμεῖν), 4.41.3 (with ἀμαθεῖς ὄντες ... λῃστείας).

For the Athenians were bringing in their property at this time, and the Peloponnesians thought that if they had come upon them quickly they would have captured everything still outside (Th. 2.18.4)

On the one hand, the modifier οὗτος does not itself exclude a durative reading in the way ὁ πρίν seems to. On the other, ἐσκομίζομαι does not align as neatly with the usual verbs in durative constructions: rather than a strictly continuous activity, like μένειν, the securing of the property can be viewed as discrete, countable instances of bringing in various objects. This would bring (86) in line with the constructions of ἐν τῷ χρόνῳ that more clearly fall under the limitative rubric of a multiplicity of events occurring in a time frame:

(87) ἃ ἐν τῷ παντὶ χρόνῳ ὀλίγοις δὴ ἅμα πάντα ξυνέβη

Which things have happened all at once to few people in the whole of time

(Th. 1.33.2)

In the end, χρόνος is remarkably straightforward: it simply does not occur in punctual constructions, which makes sense given its open-ended semantics, and ἐν is the default limitative construction. The limitative genitive is restricted to three examples, in which twice – (81) and (83) – it is probably preferred because the temporal expression looks forward to a time not yet reached by the main narrative.[68] As for the last genitive, example (82), it is perhaps influenced by potentially being a partitive genitive with μεγίστη. As a final observation, it should be noted that καιρός behaves similarly to χρόνος. Whereas glosses like 'critical time' might suggest that it would occur in punctual constructions, in fact the καιρός was more of a window than a point. When an event occurs at the καιρός, it occurs ἐν (τῷ) καιρῷ (10×), not τῷ καιρῷ.[69]

---

[68] Compare examples (29) and (30) with (37) through (39), and see the discussion on pp. 87–8.

[69] See 1.121.1, 3.56.4, 4.59.3, 5.61.2, 5.66.2, 6.9.3, 6.31.1, 6.69.1, 7.64.2, 8.67.1; παρὰ τῷ ἐντυχόντι αἰεὶ καὶ λόγου καὶ ἔργου καιρῷ occurs at 2.43.2. While Wilamowitz-Moellendorf sees the καιρός as "die scharfe Trennungslinie, welche das richtige vom verkehrten ... scheidet" (1880: 507–10), the fact that a καιρός is not just a point can also be seen in partitive constructions, namely κατὰ τοῦτο τοῦ καιροῦ (7.2.4) and ἐν τῷ τοιούτῳ ἤδη τοῦ καιροῦ ὄντες (7.69.2). For the spatial sense of καιρός, see also Trédé (1992: 38–41). For the (similar) behavior of καιρός in Xenophon, see n. 59 in Ch. 3.

Distributive and approximative expressions
in Thucydides

The final cluster of temporal constructions that deserve attention contains those prepositions that, at least some of the time, express that an event took place at approximately a certain time: κατά$^{+A}$ (found 60× in temporal expressions), ὑπό$^{+A}$ (32×), περί$^{+A}$ (17×). We may call such constructions approximative. Particularly difficult to assess is the difference between constructions such as the following:

(88) **κατὰ δὲ τὸν αὐτὸν χρόνον** Σιμωνίδης Ἀθηναίων στρατηγὸς Ἠιόνα τὴν ἐπὶ Θράκης Μενδαίων ἀποικίαν . . . προδιδομένην κατέλαβεν

And at about the same time, the Athenian general Simonides captured Eion, the colony of the Mendaeans in Thrace, through treachery (Th. 4.7.1)

(89) εἷλον δὲ καὶ Πάνακτον Ἀθηναίων ἐν μεθορίοις τεῖχος Βοιωτοὶ **ὑπὸ τὸν αὐτὸν χρόνον** προδοσίᾳ

And the Boeotians also captured Panactum, a fort in the Athenian border territory, at about the same time, through treachery (Th. 5.3.5)

(90) οἱ δ᾽ ἐν τῇ Πελοποννήσῳ ἀπέστελλον **περὶ τὸν αὐτὸν χρόνον** ταῖς ὁλκάσι τοὺς ὁπλίτας ἐς τὴν Σικελίαν

And those in the Peloponnesus were sending the hoplites off to Sicily at about the same time in merchant ships (Th. 7.19.3)

In the attempt to detect some difference between these three prepositional phrases, the most promising lead is to look first at those constructions in which the prepositions do have clearly distinct functions.

(i)

κατά$^{+A}$ is very common, second only to ἐν in prepositional temporal expressions. Apart from with χρόνος, its most characteristic use is in distributive constructions:

(91) θαρσεῖν τε ἐκέλευε προσιόντων μὲν ἑξακοσίων ταλάντων ὡς ἐπὶ τὸ πολὺ φόρου **κατ᾽ ἐνιαυτὸν** ἀπὸ τῶν ξυμμάχων τῇ πόλει

And he told them to have confidence, because for the most part they had six hundred talents of tribute coming to the city every year from the allies (Th. 2.13.3)

How does it differ from the distributive genitive? Generally, it is used in less strictly distributive constructions than that of example (91). It is often used adjectivally (when the genitive would be more ambiguous; compare μηνός in (83)):

(92) τῆς τε **καθ' ἡμέραν** ἀναγκαίου τροφῆς πανταχοῦ ἂν ἡγούμενοι ἐπικρατεῖν

And believing that they could get hold of the necessary daily provisions anywhere they wanted (Th. 1.2.2)

Such adjectival expressions are necessarily further removed from the distributive prototype insofar as there is no longer a verbal event that takes place in a one-to-one correspondence with the time noun. Furthermore, there are also examples where, even though the preposition's object is a time noun, the phrase as a whole does not specify when an event took place:[70]

(93) γέγραφε δὲ καὶ ταῦτα ὁ αὐτὸς Θουκυδίδης Ἀθηναῖος ἑξῆς, ὡς ἕκαστα ἐγένετο, **κατὰ θέρη καὶ χειμῶνας**

And the same Thucydides of Athens has also written this in order, as the individual events took place, by summers and winters (5.26.1)

In (93), one might conceivably repunctuate so as to take the prepositional phrase with ἐγένετο, in which case it could still be temporal, but the general context, as seen in the next example, suggests that it is more likely to modify γέγραφε as a reference to Thucydides' organization of his history:

(94) **κατὰ θέρη δὲ καὶ χειμῶνας** ἀριθμῶν, ὥσπερ γέγραπται, εὑρήσει ...

And counting by summers and winters, as it has been written, one will find ...

(Th. 5.20.3)

Here the relationship marked by κατά⁺ᴬ is clearly no longer temporal, but rather that of a manner adverbial.

Even before we turn to χρόνος, we find that κατά is not restricted to distributive expressions equivalent to English *by* (including the type *day by day*). One example with ἐνιαυτός stands out:

---

[70] See also 2.1.1.

108

Table 10. *Function of* κατά$^{+A}$ *with time nouns in Thucydides*

Time noun	Function of κατά$^{+A}$
ἡμέρα	11× distributive
ἐνιαυτός	4× distributive, 1× durative (ex. 95)
ἔτος	5× distributive
θέρος	3× distributive
χειμών	3× distributive, 1× limitative (ex. 96)
χρόνος	29× approximative, 3× distributive (1.117.3, 5.20.2, 5.26.3)

(95) ὑπῆρκτο δ᾽ αὐτοῦ πρότερον ἐπὶ τῆς ἐκείνου ἀρχῆς ἧς κατ᾽ ἐνιαυτὸν Ἀθηναίοις ἦρξε

And that had been started earlier during his archonship, which he held among the Athenians for a year (Th. 1.93.3)

Presumably κατά$^{+A}$ is used here in what might otherwise call for a durative accusative of time because the office is held on a yearly basis. More mysterious is the following:

(96) ταῦτα μὲν κατὰ τὸν χειμῶνα τοῦτον ἐγένετο

These events happened during this winter (Th. 3.116.3)

One would by all rights expect ἐν to be used here, as it is a perfect limitative context, paralleled by (72). At any rate, there does not seem to be a trace of distributive sense,[71] and it is thus the closest parallel to the many examples of κατά with χρόνος.

In conclusion, the overall distribution of κατά$^{+A}$ is as shown in Table 10.

(ii)

ὑπό$^{+A}$ is more restricted in scope than κατά$^{+A}$. Apart from the twenty examples with χρόνος, it occurs only with ἡμέρα (1×) and νύξ (11×). The eleven constructions with νύξ all have the set phrase ὑπὸ νύκτα:

---

[71] Given that Dewald treats this year of the *History* as paradigmatic for how Thucydides structures the narrative of the Archidamian war and remarks of this sentence merely that it contains "a formulation that Thucydides often uses to conclude the account of a year" (2005: 27–33, esp. 30), it is difficult to attribute the use of κατά here to an anomaly in the wider context.

(97) μετὰ δὲ ταῦτα φοβούμενοι τὴν ἀπὸ τῶν Ἀθηναίων βοήθειαν **ὑπὸ νύκτα** ἐσέπλευσαν ἐς τὸν κόλπον τὸν Κρισαῖον καὶ Κόρινθον

And after this, fearing the reinforcements coming from the Athenians, they sailed at night to the Crisaean gulf and to Corinth (Th. 2.92.6)

All of these constructions look very much like the genitives of time with (τῆς) νυκτός. Now, according to LSJ, ὑπὸ νύκτα should mean specifically 'at nightfall', but in fact there is no internal indication that this is the case.[72] Indeed, some of the events described by ὑπὸ νύκτα seem unlikely to be restricted to just the beginning of the night:

(98) αὐτοὶ δὲ (*sc.* βουλόμενοι) ταῖς ναυσὶν ἐν τοσούτῳ **ὑπὸ νύκτα** παραπλεύσαντες στρατόπεδον καταλαμβάνειν ἐν ἐπιτηδείῳ καθ᾽ ἡσυχίαν

And they themselves wanted in the meantime to sail past with their ships at night and to take suitable ground for a camp at their leisure (Th. 6.64.1)

(99) τῇ δ᾽ ὑστεραίᾳ αὖθις προσέβαλλον, καὶ ὡς ἄμεινον φαρξαμένων αὐτῶν **ὑπὸ νύκτα** . . . οὐκέθ᾽ ὁμοίως ἔβλαπτον

And on the next day they attacked again, and as they had built better fortifications during the night . . . they no longer caused as much damage (Th. 8.35.4)

(100) οἱ δ᾽ Ἀθηναῖοι ὡς ᾔσθοντο αὐτοὺς προσιόντας, ἀναλαβόντες τό τε στράτευμα ἅπαν τὸ ἑαυτῶν καὶ ὅσοι Σικελῶν αὐτοῖς ἢ ἄλλος τις προσεληλύθει καὶ ἐπιβιβάσαντες ἐπὶ τὰς ναῦς καὶ τὰ πλοῖα, **ὑπὸ νύκτα** ἔπλεον ἐπὶ τὰς Συρακούσας. καὶ οἵ τε Ἀθηναῖοι ἅμα ἕῳ ἐξέβαινον ἐς τὸ κατὰ τὸ Ὀλυμπιεῖον ὡς τὸ στρατόπεδον καταληψόμενοι

And the Athenians, when they found out that they were approaching, gathered together their whole army and as many of the Sicels – or anyone else – as had joined them, boarded them on their ships and boats, and sailed during the night to Syracuse. And the Athenians, at dawn, were disembarking opposite the Olympieium in order to occupy the ground for a camp (Th. 6.65.2–3)

---

[72] LSJ here apparently follows Kühner–Gerth: 525, which, after stating initially that ὑπὸ νύκτα means "gegen die Nacht hin, bei Einbruch der Nacht" – without actually citing a passage where it does so – moves on to a much larger section of passages in which ὑπό[+A] means simply 'während', including two with νύκτα (*Il.* 22.102, Hdt. 9.58.2). Presumably the misconception that ὑπὸ νύκτα means "at nightfall" stems from confusion with *sub noctem*, which Schwyzer–Debrunner points out has a different force; for their part, they take ὑπὸ νύκτα to be an accusative of extent in origin ("unter der N. hin"), p. 532, esp. n. 2. Chantraine (1953: 144), Horrocks (1981: 263–4), and Luraghi (2003: 235–6) all see the Homeric example as denoting a stretch of time. Note also the scholion on Th. 2.92.6: ὑπὸ νύκτα· ἀντὶ τοῦ κατὰ τὴν νύκτα (Hude 1927: 157).

In (98), the action of sailing along the coast to find a place to set up a camp and, in (99), the improvements to the fortifications would both probably have taken more time than just nightfall. To be sure, one cannot exclude an ingressive reading for the aorist παραπλεύσαντες, in which case the shorter time-period would again be a possibility, but a nuance like 'under cover of night' for the prepositional phrase is at least equally conceivable. Similarly, in (100), one might be able to argue that ὑπὸ νύκτα ἔπλεον indicates simply that they started off at nightfall, but the use of the imperfect, combined with the fact that the next event to be temporally marked, the Athenians' disembarking, takes place at dawn, again inclines one towards the view that the act of the sailing is not being pinned down to a precise point at the beginning of the night.

In fact, the characteristic that most distinguishes the constructions with ὑπὸ νύκτα is that they are more likely to modify verbs of sailing – six times out of the eleven (55%),[73] as opposed to only nine out of thirty-three (27%) for the punctual constructions with (τῆς) νυκτός. It is therefore perhaps not too fanciful to propose that a local sense of ὑπό is still in play: when sailing by night, one would have paid close attention to the stars, and one's movement could be envisaged as proceeding beneath the canopy of the sky. In support of this position, one might compare the relatively frequent (10×) Homeric use of διὰ νύκτα in contexts that blend the spatial with the temporal:

(101) πῇ δὴ οὕτως ἐπὶ νῆας ἀπὸ στρατοῦ ἔρχεαι οἶος
      νύκτα δι' ὀρφναίην, ὅτε θ' εὕδουσι βροτοὶ ἄλλοι;
      Why do you come alone to the ships like this, away from the camp, through
      the dark night, when other men are sleeping? (*Il.* 10.385–6)

On the one hand, a spatial reading is suggested both by the visual epithet ὀρφναῖος and by the use of διά[+A], which, as a temporal preposition, should mean 'throughout the night' – which is not the sense here – but, as a spatial preposition, can easily mean 'through

---

[73] In addition to (97), (98), and (100), see 1.115.4, 3.91.3, and 4.67.1.

the darkness of night' – which does fit the context.[74] On the other, the prepositional phrase appears to be reinforced by the clearly temporal ὅτε-clause.[75] As this ambiguous use of διά[+A] is restricted to νύξ,[76] there is good cause to see a similar factor as explaining the anomalous use of ὑπὸ νύκτα.

The one example of ὑπό[+A] with ἡμέρα is the following:

(102) ἀπέθανε δὲ καὶ Σιτάλκης Ὀδρυσῶν βασιλεὺς **ὑπὸ τὰς αὐτὰς ἡμέρας** τοῖς ἐπὶ Δηλίῳ

And Sitalces king of the Odrysians died during the same days as the events at Delium (Th. 4.101.5)

At first glance, this appears to be a limitative construction: the death occurs at some point during the time frame expressed by the prepositional phrase. But it is also very close to the twenty examples of ὑπό with χρόνος, sixteen of which have τὸν αὐτόν or τοὺς αὐτούς as a modifier, and these are all constructions generally seen as approximative. This highlights the potentially close relationship between the two: because an approximative expression cannot pin down an event to a particular point, it will often designate the sort of extensive time frame that characterizes the limitative type. The difference between the two lies in the degree of accuracy with which the event in question can be assigned to that time frame. Assessment of whether a construction is limitative or approximative must therefore depend to some extent on broader contextual clues and historical judgments. With how much certainty will Thucydides have been able to synchronize Sitalces' death with the battle at Delium? Even if he is certain of both dates, is he saying

---

[74] For the potential significance of the visual quality of the epithet, cf. Hoekstra (followed by Edwards 1997: 281), who observes that the epithet in νύκτα διὰ δνοφερήν in *Od.* 15.50 is not merely ornamental: "without good visibility a journey through the Peloponnese must have been a risky affair" (1989: 234). See also the references in n. 76.

[75] Ruijgh, classifying this as "l'emploi digressif-permanent régulier" of ὅτε τε, notes that ὅτε τε clauses are more amenable to analysis as coordinate clauses than ὅς τε clauses are (1971: 488–9). This would further enhance the temporal nuance of the preceding prepositional phrase.

[76] Chantraine on διά[+A]: "Au sens temporel, seulement avec νύκτα, pour exprimer la durée" (1953: 96), followed by de la Villa (1994b: 334–5); but Palmer observes that, even here, "the predominant notion is spatial" (1962: 141–2), as noted by Horrocks (1981: 255) and strongly seconded by Luraghi (2003: 173). That the anomalous prepositional usages with νύξ are due to a more spatial conception of night is explored at greater length by Dyer (1974).

that they were simultaneous or just nearly simultaneous? It does not seem possible to answer these questions on linguistic grounds.[77]

(iii)

περί[+A] occurs less often than ὑπό[+A] in temporal expressions, but it is found with a wider range of time nouns. Of the seventeen examples, six are with χρόνος, six with ἡμέρα, three with φθινόπωρον, and one each with ἔαρ and ὥρα. Leaving aside the constructions with χρόνος for the time being, we find that those with ἡμέρα fall into two broad categories. First, there are three with telic verbs that look much like the approximative constructions already seen:[78]

(103) καὶ περὶ τὰς αὐτὰς ἡμέρας καὶ οἱ Καμαριναῖοι ἀφικνοῦνται

> And during about the same days, the Camarinaeans also arrived
> (Th. 7.33.1)

The other three, however, while still presumably approximative, modify atelic verbs. Thus, rather than being a less precise version of a temporal phrase with ἐν, they are related to the accusative of time:

(104) τούτων (*sc.* ἡμερῶν) περὶ εἴκοσιν ἡμέρας, ἐν αἷς οἱ πρέσβεις περὶ τῶν σπονδῶν ἀπῆσαν, ἐσιτοδοτοῦντο, τὰς δὲ ἄλλας τοῖς ἐσπλέουσι λάθρα διετρέφοντο

> Of these days, they received food for about twenty days, during which the envoys were off to see about the treaty, and the other days they lived off what was brought in secretly (Th. 4.39.2)

In (104), the parallelism with τὰς ἄλλας shows the close relationship of the περί-phrase to the accusative of time. In the other two examples, the word order suggests even more strongly that the construction is, underlyingly, an accusative of time with the preposition governing the numeral alone:[79]

---

[77] Hornblower observes that it is unusual for the death of a non-Greek ruler to be mentioned in passing in this way, rather than woven more organically into the narrative (1996: 318–19).
[78] See also 2.83.1, 4.120.1.
[79] See also 6.74.2. For the syntax whereby the preposition in effect governs only the modifier in a noun phrase, with the result that the noun then raises out of the prepositional phrase, see Basset 1994: 160.

(105) καὶ τῆς θαλάσσης τῆς καθ᾽ ἑαυτοὺς ἐκράτησαν **ἡμέρας περὶ τέσσαρας καὶ δέκα**

And they controlled their part of the sea for about fourteen days (Th. 1.117.1)

More straightforwardly, the constructions with φθινόπωρον (2.31.1, 3.18.3, 3.100.2), ἔαρ (3.116.1), and ὥρα (7.81.1) all align with the first group of examples with ἡμέρα: the verbs modified by the temporal expression are punctual, but the construction as a whole is marked as approximative because of the use of περί:

(106) ἐν τούτῳ δ᾽ οἱ Συρακόσιοι καὶ οἱ ξύμμαχοι, ὡς ἥ τε ἡμέρα ἐγένετο καὶ ἔγνωσαν τοὺς Ἀθηναίους ἀπεληλυθότας, ... κατὰ τάχος διώκοντες ... καταλαμβάνουσι **περὶ ἀρίστου ὥραν**

And meanwhile, the Syracusans and their allies, when day broke and they realized that the Athenians had left, ... pursued them quickly ... and caught up with them at around lunchtime (Th. 7.81.1)

This example shows another feature that marks several of the phrases with περί: the object of the preposition offers a relatively precise indication of when the event took place. In (106), the broader temporal framework is already established earlier in the sentence with ἐν τούτῳ and ὡς ἡ ἡμέρα ἐγένετο, and περὶ ἀρίστου ὥραν focuses in on a narrower segment of the day; compare also the following:

(107) **περὶ δὲ τὸ φθινόπωρον** τοῦ θέρους τούτου Ἀθηναῖοι ... ἐσέβαλον ἐς τὴν Μεγαρίδα

And in the autumn of this summer *or* during this summer,[80] the Athenians ... invaded the Megarid (Th. 2.31.1)

Again, the object of περί is a noun that provides more temporal precision than the broader τοῦ θέρους τούτου. Nor is it surprising that a fairly specific noun like φθινόπωρον should be at home in an approximative construction (indeed, these three examples of περὶ τὸ φθινόπωρον are the *only* temporal phrases with this noun in Thucydides): the more precise the time noun, the less likely it is that the historian will be able to pin down the event described as

---

[80] For the ambiguity of the construction, see the discussion following example (51) in Ch. 1.

occurring at exactly the same time as that noun. That approximative constructions somewhat paradoxically point to a more specific time than do other temporal expressions in the vicinity can be seen in two of the six examples with χρόνος as well:[81]

(108) περὶ δὲ τοὺς αὐτοὺς χρόνους τοῦ θέρους τούτου Σκιωναίους μὲν Ἀθηναῖοι ἐκπολιορκήσαντες ἀπέκτειναν τοὺς ἡβῶντας

And at about the same time this summer, the Athenians, after capturing the Scionaeans in a siege, killed the young men (Th. 5.32.1)

The other four examples with χρόνος are also clear-cut approximative constructions (3.89.2, 5.116.2, 7.19.3, 7.34.1).

At this point, we may step back and summarize the use of κατά[+A], ὑπό[+A], and περί[+A] in those constructions where a contrast is obvious: κατά is used above all in distributive expressions, ὑπό chiefly with νύξ as its object, and περί marks approximative constructions even with time nouns other than χρόνος. So much is clear, but what is the distinction between these prepositions when they govern χρόνος? First, we must clear the field by eliminating potential explanations that do not work: all three prepositions can govern both singular χρόνον and plural χρόνους (but κατά, at least, has a strong preference for the singular);[82] the modifier ὁ αὐτός can occur after all three, as can demonstrative pronouns; phrases with all three prepositions can modify standard punctual aorists like ἐστράτευσαν or ἀπέκτειναν; they can all be used at the beginning of the clause as a single constituent. That there should be so many points of agreement suggests that, whatever differences between the prepositions may be detected, considerable overlap will remain.[83] Still, there need not be complete despair. As in the phrases with νύξ as the object, so too with χρόνος, ὑπό is disproportionately common in constructions that refer explicitly to

---

[81] See also 3.94.1. This is not, incidentally, a pattern restricted to περί[+A]: examples with ὑπό[+A] occur at e.g. 2.95.1 and 3.52.1, and with κατά[+A] at 3.7.1 and 4.78.1. In nearly all of these constructions (3.94.1 is the exception), it is possible that the genitive phrase does not modify the verb directly but is rather adnominally dependent on χρόνος. Cf. n. 80.

[82] κατά occurs 24× with χρόνον, 5× with χρόνους (counting only the 29 approximative expressions); ὑπό occurs 11× with χρόνον, 9× with χρόνους; περί occurs 3× with χρόνον, 3× with χρόνους.

[83] That κατά and ὑπό should be used nearly interchangeably in their temporal sense is in line with Bortone's observation that they come to be virtually synonymous in their local use as well (2010: 163–4).

sailing: seven of the twenty examples (35%), as opposed to only three of the twenty-nine with κατά (10%) and one of the six with περί (17%).[84] There is also evidence of a shift in Thucydides' preferences over the course of writing his work: κατά is preferred to ὑπό in the first six books, ὑπό in the last two.[85] The final difference that may be significant is the preference of κατά, already mentioned, for singular χρόνον over plural χρόνους. But even this is difficult to interpret properly. Are we to assume that, as a singular object, ὁ αὐτὸς χρόνος, like φθινόπωρον, denotes a shorter period of time, is therefore likely to require a fuzzier construction if Thucydides is not to be unduly specific, and so κατά is more approximative than ὑπό?[86] Or is the historian throwing his hands up in the air when he chooses the vaguer, plural object οἱ αὐτοὶ χρόνοι, meaning that ὑπό is the more approximative of the two? I would suggest – tentatively – that the second option is the better choice: when not used in these particular expressions, κατά occurs in distributive constructions that reflect a relatively precise relationship between the temporal phrase and the verbal event. Accordingly, it seems unlikely to be the less precise of the two prepositions when governing χρόνος. But, regrettably, in the absence of any clear non-linguistic indications that Thucydides' sources are more accurate in one set of examples than in the other (both (88) and (89), for instance, synchronize events in which the Athenians were directly involved with other events in which they were directly involved), we cannot avoid a certain amount of *aporia*.

Conclusion

By now, it should be clear that we cannot just shrug off temporal expressions by saying that the genitive of time denotes time within which, and the dative of time, time when. Even if we are only

---

[84] As temporal expressions referring to sailing I count 2.26.1, 4.129.2, 5.4.1, 8.13.1, 8.20.1, 8.99.1, 8.108.1 (all with ὑπό), 3.7.1, 3.99.1, 8.91.2 (with κατά), and 7.34.1 (with περί). They include constructions that modify not only πλεῖν and its compounds, but also ναῦς ἐκπέμπειν, ὁρμέω, and similar verb phrases.

[85] Taking pairs of books together, and discounting distributive κατά, we find that 1–2 have κατά 7×, ὑπό 3×; 3–4 have κατά 12×, ὑπό 4×; 5–6 have κατά 7×, ὑπό 3×; while 7–8 have κατά 3×, ὑπό 10×.

[86] See the discussion on (107) above.

explaining Thucydides' usage, we must set up much finer semantic categories to elucidate the nuances conveyed by the different constructions. Furthermore, we cannot assume that all nouns will behave the same way. The reader is referred to the summaries presented earlier in the chapter for the details, but the following broad trends may be noted here. (i) The genitive of time is of much wider application than it is generally given credit for. Far from only denoting time within which, it is found regularly in distributive, modal, and habitual constructions as well. (ii) Furthermore, with νύξ, θέρος, and χειμών, the genitive of time becomes the default means of expressing time when. As a result, with these nouns (and with χρόνος) time within which is marked by ἐν instead. (iii) As a corollary to the first two points, the dative of time is extremely restricted in use: it is only with ἡμέρα, μήν, and ἔτος that it is the usual means of marking when an event took place. Moreover, even with these nouns, the dative is only employed to specify in an almost calendrical fashion the day, month, or year during which the event occurred. To reiterate the first point: if Thucydides is contrasting a daytime happening with a night-time one (the modal type), or remarking that it took place repeatedly during the daytime (the distributive and habitual types), he opts for the genitive. The next task is to determine the extent to which these patterns hold true in other prose authors as well.

EXPRESSIONS OF TIME: STYLE, GENRE, AND DIACHRONY

The expressions of time in Thucydides show a remarkable amount of subtle variation that belies the broad-stroke characterizations of the standard grammars. Given such richness of construction in a single author, we have all the more reason to expect different authors to exhibit an even wider range of usage. Accordingly, the following chapter will consider several more authors in order to determine how much of the behavior of these phrases is consistent from author to author, from genre to genre, from period to period, and how much the patterning of these expressions varies, depending on who was writing what when. In the first few sections, we will look at Xenophon, Plato, and Demosthenes in turn, in order to set up a base-line of some stylistically significant Attic authors. After a Herodotean intermezzo that assesses the extent to which Ionic differed from Attic, we then turn to later texts – Polybius, Diodorus, Plutarch, Epictetus, and documentary papyri – to gain some sense of the diachronic development of temporal expressions.

Xenophon

Mention has already been made of the relative strangeness of Xenophon's syntax, compared to other Attic authors.[1] Prepositional usage is clearly important to this study, and this is one of the respects in which Xenophon differs from his Attic peers: he uses σύν[+D] more often, in place of μετά[+G], and he is also unusually fond of ἀμφί.[2] It would therefore be no surprise if he were also to prove slightly aberrant in his temporal expressions as well. But, as it happens, despite the variety of different genres to which his work

---

[1] See Gautier (1911), Bers (1984: 13).
[2] See Mommsen (1895: 351–3, 361–8), Gautier (1911: 48–50).

belongs (from history to philosophical dialogue, from encomiastic biography to technical treatises), the Thucydidean case and prepositional usage detailed in Chapter 2 by and large holds good in Xenophon as well. The chief difference will be the use of a couple of additional constructions beyond those found in Thucydides, owing in part to the somewhat more extensive set of temporal circumstances which must be described in works of a relatively wider generic range. To aid comparison, we will proceed through the types of construction in the same order as followed in Chapter 2.

Durative expressions in Xenophon

As in Thucydides, the chief means of marking the durative event type is the accusative of time. There are 248 examples with the time nouns considered in this study (give or take a few that might be direct objects), and nearly all of these (about 221) are clear durative constructions. Twenty-one of the remaining examples are still close to the durative type, but refer to repeated activities, and so might also be counted as habitual:

(1) ἔρρει αὐτῷ **νύκτα τε καὶ ἡμέραν** τὸ αἷμα

[Agesilaus'] blood flowed night and day (X. *HG* 5.4.58)

In this particular passage, we also have the contrast of night and day, thus raising the further possibility of a modal reading. Moreover, the genitive, which, based on Thucydides, we might expect in such modal-habitual contexts, is found in similar passages:

(2) πόσα ...οἴει ταύτῃ καὶ τῇ φωνῇ καὶ τοῖς ἔργοις ἐκ παιδίου δυσκολαίνων **καὶ ἡμέρας καὶ νυκτὸς** πράγματα παρασχεῖν ...;

How much trouble do you think you caused [your mother], peevish since infancy with your crying and behavior, both day and night? (X. *Mem.* 2.2.8)

Are there any characteristics shared by borderline constructions like (1) that would favor the use of accusative of time over the genitive of time seen in (2)? The most obvious difference between the two constructions is that the genitive of time is much more common in such contexts than the accusative of time: (τὴν) ἡμέραν occurs five times, (τὴν) νύκτα three times, while (τῆς) ἡμέρας occurs sixteen times, (τῆς) νυκτός twenty-six times. The combination of this distribution (which suggests that the accusative of time is the marked construction) and the general use of the accusative in the durative type prompts us to look for ways in which passages like (1) opt for the less common usage because the duration of the verbal event is somehow emphasized.

This seems a plausible enough explanation for passage (1) itself: what is important about the flow of Agesilaus' blood by day and night is not so much the contrast of two different settings for the bleeding as the continuity of the event – as if one could paraphrase: 'through the entirety of both the day and the night'. Contrast passage (2), where the type of trouble that can be caused during the day is potentially different in kind from that caused during the night.[3] The other four habitual uses of (τὴν) ἡμέραν can be justified along similar lines (as can the three of (τὴν) νύκτα, which is always parallel with (τὴν) ἡμέραν, as in (1)). (a) At *Hier.* 7.10, we find οὕτως ... καὶ νύκτα καὶ ἡμέραν διάγει. The time nouns here may well be better construed as objects of a transitive διάγω, but even if they are not, the semantics of the verb suggest an action that takes place during the entirety of the day, thus eliciting the accusative rather than the genitive. (b) At *An.* 5.8.24, Xenophon writes: τοῦτον δὲ ... τὴν νύκτα μὲν δήσετε, τὴν δὲ ἡμέραν ἀφήσετε. The use of the accusative rather than the genitive reinforces the idea that Boiscus should be kept under lock and key during the entirety of the night so that he will not continue his thieving. (c) At *Cyr.* 1.2.9, the idea of guarding is again in play: the ephebes have to sleep in a particular location so that they might watch over the city and, in turn, be seen to practice self-control (φυλακῆς ἕνεκα τῆς πόλεως καὶ σωφροσύνης), so, in the following clause, it is not surprising that their offering of their services during the day is expressed with an accusative of time (παρέχουσι ... καὶ τὴν ἡμέραν ἑαυτοὺς τοῖς ἄρχουσι). (d) Finally, at *Cyr.* 1.6.40, hounds have to be trained to hunt hares by smell because their prey only come out at night, hiding away during the (*sc.* entire) day (τὴν δ᾽ ἡμέραν ἀποδιδράσκει).

---

[3] The presence of the interrogative πόσα also helps to articulate the troubles Lamprocles caused his mother into a sequence of discrete events (as if it were: 'on how many occasions did you cause trouble?'), rather than portraying it as one continuous, unbroken stretch of bad behavior.

Another difference between the genitive and the accusative is that only the former is used in negated expressions: οὔτε νυκτὸς οὔτε ἡμέρας or some variation thereof occurs five times, whereas the accusative is not found in the same turn of phrase.[4] This distribution is consistent with the view that the genitive is a neutral marker of the habitual-modal event-type, readily negated, while the accusative retains a durative sense that was apparently at odds with the negative. This clash is a result of how Greek dealt with the potential alternatives in expressing negated temporal phrases: instead of saying that the non-occurrence of an event lasted for a particular length of time (eliciting a durative accusative), it preferred to say that the event did not occur at any point in the time (calling for a limitative genitive).[5] In οὔτε νυκτὸς οὔτε ἡμέρας, the genitive is thus doubly motivated by coalescence of the limitative and habitual-modal event types.

Still, other passages suggest that there is something close to free variation between the accusative and genitive in habitual-modal expressions. First, while acts of guarding naturally associate with the accusative, it being important that they take place without intermission, there is one passage where φυλάττω construes with the genitive of time, at *Cyr.* 7.5.68 (δορυφόρους, οἳ κύκλῳ μὲν νυκτὸς καὶ ἡμέρας ἐφύλαττον περὶ τὰ βασίλεια, ὁπότε ἐπὶ χώρας εἴη· ὁπότε δὲ ἐξίοι ποι, ἔνθεν καὶ ἔνθεν τεταγμένοι ἐπορεύοντο). Perhaps here we are simply to take νυκτὸς καὶ ἡμέρας as a less emphatic way of saying 'both night and day' than καὶ νύκτα καὶ ἡμέραν would provide.[6] Also instructive is one passage where the accusative occurs in parallel with the genitive:

(3) ἀγέσθωσαν δὲ **θέρους** μὲν μέχρι μεσημβρίας, **χειμῶνος** δὲ δι' ἡμέρας, **μετοπώρου** δ' ἔξω μεσημβρίας, ἐντὸς δὲ ἑσπέρας τὸ ἔαρ

---

[4] These occur at *HG* 7.5.19, *Mem.* 3.11.16, *Smp.* 4.48, *Ap.* 31, and *Cyr.* 8.1.45. The variations include μήτε for οὔτε and the reversal of the order of the two constituents.

[5] For other examples of the association of the genitive with negativity, see Chanet (1994); note also the contrast between ἐτόξευσε θηρίων and ἐτόξευσε θηρία discussed by Ruijgh (1994: 138). That said, there is the occasional counter-example, e.g. *An.* 3.1.3 (= ex. (26) in Ch. 1).

[6] That the temporal phrase is relatively unemphatic is also suggested by where the contrastive focus lies in the μέν- and δέ-clauses: the bodyguards form a *circle* when Cyrus is home, but are stationed *on this side and that* when he is traveling.

And let them be brought out during the summer until noon, during winter throughout the day, during fall apart from at noon, and until evening in the spring (X. *Cyn.* 4.11)

Why is τὸ ἔαρ in the accusative of time, but the other seasons in the genitive? As both cases seem to be used to express parallel semantic roles, our best clue lies in the change of word order in the last of the four clauses. The three genitives of time all come just before the succession of particles μὲν ... δὲ ... δέ, and they are thus separated from the subsidiary temporal expressions marking when in the day it was suitable for the dogs to be let out. But in the last clause, Xenophon felt it important to put the subsidiary expression first (for the stylistic effect of a chiasmus?[7]); a genitive of time ἔαρος (which does occur elsewhere in Xenophon: *Oec.* 16.12) would then come directly after the genitive ἑσπέρας, a sequence of two genitives that was perhaps felt to be awkward. But despite such borderline cases, on the whole the evidence suggests that, even in habitual constructions, the accusative of time still emphasizes the duration of the event described.

The other important question regarding durative constructions is the relationship between the accusative of time and prepositional phrases with διά$^{+G}$ and ἐπί$^{+A}$. Here we see the potential for stylistic differences between authors to affect temporal expressions: as noted in Chapter 2, Thucydides prefers ἐπί$^{+A}$ by a 10 : 3 ratio, while Xenophon prefers διά$^{+G}$ by 21 : 4. But in fact, both authors use these prepositions in more or less the same environments, and the different distribution results from Xenophon's greater use of the sorts of phrases that would contain διά$^{+G}$ even in Thucydides. Consider first the four examples of temporal ἐπί$^{+A}$ in Xenophon. Two of these have the preposed modifiers that Thucydides also uses with ἐπί$^{+A}$: θυομένῳ αὐτῷ ἐπὶ τρεῖς ἡμέρας (*An.* 6.6.36) and ὄζει τῶν ἰχνῶν ἐπὶ πλείω χρόνον (*Cyn.* 5.7). A third has a forward-looking reference also found in Thucydides (cf. ex. (24) in Chapter 2):

(4) τὸ δ' **ἐφ' ἡμέραν** ἀρκέσον ὀλίγοι τινὲς οἳ οὐχ ἱκανοὶ ποιῆσαι

There are few who cannot make what will suffice for a day (X. *Cyr.* 6.2.34)

---

[7] The wider context does not offer any strong reason for singling out spring in contrast to the other three seasons, and it is difficult to see any pragmatic motivation for the reversal in the final clause. For pragmatic motivation for chiasmus in Greek, see Slings (1997: 184–92), Bakker (2009: 58–60); for Latin: Devine–Stephens (2006: 242–9, 330).

This example also borders on the distributive type – not just 'sufficient for a day' but 'sufficient for their everyday needs' – and thus provides a link to the final example:[8]

(5) οὐ μόνον δὲ κρατεῖ τοῖς ἐπ' ἐνιαυτὸν θάλλουσί τε καὶ γηράσκουσιν, ἀλλὰ καὶ ἀΐδια ἀγαθὰ ἔχει ἡ χώρα

And the land is not only unsurpassed in those items that flourish and fade year by year, but also has goods that are permanent (X. *Vect.* 1.4)

Here we see the combination of the distributive force of the preposition with the usual durative sense of ἐπί$^{+A}$ (i.e. both 'flourishing year by year' and 'over the course of a year'), rather than with the use of ἐπί$^{+A}$ to mark a goal seen in (4). In short, Xenophon employs ἐπί$^{+A}$ in much the same way that Thucydides does, but simply does not find as much need for it. That he uses it infrequently, compared to Thucydides, with cardinal numerals in relatively precise durative expressions may be due, one suspects, to his lesser interest in ἀκρίβεια.

The situation is similar with διά$^{+G}$. One of the three examples in Thucydides was διὰ χρόνου in the sense 'after some time'. This phrase also accounts for eight of the twenty-one examples in Xenophon, in five of which passages it has this same meaning.[9] Three times, however, a distributive interpretation is forced by an iterative context. This is clearest in *Oec.* 9.10, where the fact that the noun modified by διὰ χρόνου is plural implies a repeated action that recurs periodically (that is, after some time):[10]

(6) ὅσοις δ' εἰς ἑορτὰς ἢ ξενοδοκίας χρώμεθα ἢ εἰς τὰς **διὰ χρόνου** πράξεις

And whatever we use for festivals or entertaining or for occasional activities (X. *Oec.* 9.10)

Nor is this distributive use of διά$^{+G}$ limited to διὰ χρόνου. Twice it is elicited by an ordinal modifier, for example, ἄγειν διὰ τρίτης ἡμέρας 'every other day' (*Cyn.* 6.3) or τοῦτο γίγνεται ... δι' ἔτους πέμπτου 'every fourth year' (*Ath.* 3.5). The second of these two examples is particularly typical in coming from the pseudo-Xenophontic

---

[8] Ex. (4) also helps explain the use of ἐπί$^{+A}$ in Th. 4.69.3 (ἐφ' ἡμέραν γὰρ ἐκ τῆς ἄνω πόλεως ἐχρῶντο), where ἐπί can be used in a distributive construction because it also carries the nuance of a goal expression: the provision they needed *for* the day.

[9] See *Mem.* 2.8.1, 4.4.5, *Cyr.* 1.4.28 (*bis*), 5.5.41.

[10] The other two examples are *Cyn.* 5.3 and *Ath.* 3.5.

Constitution of the Athenians, which provides three further examples, all with δι᾽ ἐνιαυτοῦ (1.16, 3.6 (*bis*)). Given the content of this work (and indeed that of the *Cynegeticus* and *Oeconomicus* as well), it is not surprising to find greater need for distributive expressions than in the more temporally linear historical narrative of Thucydides. But that διά⁺ᴳ occurs in these distributive expressions in (pseudo-)Xenophon is the only real difference (and a slight one at that) between his and Thucydides' use of this preposition. For the remaining eight examples of temporal διά⁺ᴳ in Xenophon are all emphatic durative expressions, which thus match the other two examples of temporal διά⁺ᴳ in Thucydides.¹¹ In three examples, the presence of a modifier indicates that the durativity of the expression is being emphasized: δι᾽ ὅλης τῆς ἡμέρας (*Oec.* 20.17), δι᾽ ὅλης τῆς νυκτός (*An.* 4.2.4), διὰ παντὸς ἀεὶ τοῦ χρόνου (*Cyr.* 8.2.1). In the other five, context suggests that Xenophon needed a stronger expression than the accusative of time. (a) In example (3) above, Xenophon contrasts the hours of the day during which one's dogs can be let out in different seasons of the year; that this can take place during the whole day in the winter is emphasized through the use of διά⁺ᴳ. (b) Similarly at *HG* 5.4.58 (ἠρρώστει τό τε λοιπὸν θέρος καὶ διὰ χειμῶνος), the preposition highlights the fact that, while the illness only lasted for the remainder of the summer, it then continued throughout the entirety of the winter. (c) At *Lac.* 2.4 (καὶ ἀντί γε τοῦ ἱματίοις διαθρύπτεσθαι ἐνόμιζεν ἑνὶ ἱματίῳ δι᾽ ἔτους προσεθίζεσθαι), the prepositional phrase again expresses a duration that is unexpectedly long: instead of changing their garments to match the seasons, Lycurgus' Spartans were instructed to use a single cloak (note ἑνί) throughout the year. (d) At *HG* 3.2.9, the prepositional construction appears to have been necessary to clarify the construction after καθάπερ: ἐπήρετο πότερα βούλοιτο σπονδὰς ἔχειν καθάπερ διὰ τοῦ χειμῶνος ἢ πόλεμον. (e) Finally, at *An.* 4.6.22, διά⁺ᴳ is used as in example (21) in Chapter 2, in conjunction with a noun modified by πολλ-, with the prepositional phrase further emphasizing that much was taking place throughout an extended period: ἐγρηγόρεσαν καὶ ἔκαιον πυρὰ πολλὰ διὰ νυκτός.

---

¹¹ See exx. (20) and (21) in Ch. 2.

Punctual and limitative expressions in Xenophon: day, month, year

As with Thucydides, it will again be important to consider the calendrical time nouns separately, as they alone occur frequently in the dative of time, as well as with the genitive of time and ἐν⁺ᴰ. To begin with ἡμέρα, the dative is again the most common of these three constructions (37×), but in contrast to Thucydides followed more closely by the genitive (35×) and ἐν⁺ᴰ (22×). With only one exception, the dative of time is again used exclusively in stereotypical punctual expressions, with the expected modifiers: 16× demonstrative or relative pronouns, 14× ordinal numbers, 3× τῇ αὐτῇ, and once each with τῇ ἄλλῃ, τῇ ἐπιούσῃ, and τῇ πρόσθεν. The sole anomaly is the following:

(7) ταῦτα δὲ γνοίη ἄν τις μάλιστα ἐνθυμούμενος ὡς οἵ τε ἐνέδραις ἐμπίπτοντες ἐκπλήττονται, καὶ ἐὰν πολὺ πλείους ὦσι, καὶ ὅταν πολέμιοι ἀλλήλοις ἀντικάθωνται, ὡς πολὺ **ταῖς πρώταις ἡμέραις** φοβερώτατα ἔχουσιν

And anyone would recognize this if he considered in particular that those who fall into an ambush are terrified, even if they are much more numerous, and, when enemy armies are facing each other, that they are especially fearful in the first days (X. *Eq.Mag.* 8.20)

As ἡμέραι is here plural, the last sort of construction we should expect is the punctual dative of time, which is almost invariably used of singular time nouns. Rather, this context should call for either (i) the accusative of time, if Xenophon wished to emphasize the duration of the fear, or (ii) the genitive or ἐν⁺ᴰ, if he instead understood it as akin to the nexus of habitual-modal expressions that set one span of time against another (more often 'at night' contrasted with 'by day', but perhaps here 'during the first days' implicitly contrasted with 'later on'). Given the complete absence of parallels in Xenophon (and Thucydides) for the dative of time with a plural noun, it might at first be tempting to assume textual corruption,[12] as the whole clause would fit the general pattern of Xenophon's usage much better if we were to restore the preposition ἐν to head the temporal phrase. But the existence of a close parallel

---

[12] We may compare ex. (48) in Ch. 2, where there are also good grounds for believing that ἐν has been lost over the course of textual transmission.

in Plato suggests that it is better to accept the text as it stands, the best explanation for the simple dative being the influence of the ordinal πρώταις.[13]

As for the genitive of time, that it is comparatively more common in Xenophon than in Thucydides is due to Xenophon's preference for the sorts of environments that called for a genitive of time even in Thucydides, not to an extension of its use in non-Thucydidean ways. In particular, Xenophon has a greater predilection for distributive and modal constructions than is seen in Thucydides, where the limitative is more common. The distributive occurs 11× (8× τῆς ἡμέρας, 3× ἑκάστης ἡμέρας) and the modal 18× (16× ἡμέρας, 1× τῆς ἡμέρας, all paired explicitly with (τῆς) νυκτός; in the remaining example, Cyn. 9.17, χρὴ δὲ καὶ τῆς ἄλλης ἡμέρας answers μάλιστα μὲν ἕωθεν). This leaves six examples, all good limitative constructions: twice motivated by a future-tense verb (ὀλίγων ἡμερῶν at HG 7.5.18, πέντε ἡμερῶν at An. 4.7.20), once by a conditional that, like a future, leaves the exact time of the event open, thus eliciting a limitative construction (τῶν προειρημένων ἡμερῶν at Cyr. 6.2.38), twice by a negative (δέκα ἡμερῶν at An. 1.7.18, τῆς ἡμέρας ὅλης at An. 3.3.11),[14] and once in a ταῦτα ἐγένετο construction (An. 7.4.14).[15]

Constructions with ἐν[+D] in Xenophon also match those in Thucydides fairly closely. The greatest degree of overlap is again with the genitive of time, as both constructions are found in both limitative and modal expressions. But a more pronounced division of labor is evidenced in Xenophon, where the genitive of time is usually distributive-modal (83% of the time), and only occasionally limitative (17%), while ἐν is used overwhelmingly in limitative expressions (20 out of 22 examples, or 91%), with only two modal examples.[16] What is less clear, however, is the explanation for the

[13] See ex. (78) below; ex. (130), in Herodotus, is similar (τῇσι προτέρῃσι ἡμέρῃσι). Cf. also (86) in Demosthenes (ταύταις ταῖς ἡμέραις).

[14] In the second of these two examples, the negative is of restricted scope (διῆλθον οὐ πλέον πέντε καὶ εἴκοσι σταδίων), but the contrast between the restricted ground covered (οὐ πλέον) and the extended period during which the journey took place (ὅλης) is still sufficient to justify calling this a limitative expression.

[15] Cf. the discussion of example (72) and n. 57 in Ch. 2. In the passage from Xenophon, there is also the hint of a modal expression, as the clause in question is followed by εἰς δὲ τὴν ἐπιοῦσαν νύκτα.

[16] Traces of the same distribution can be seen in Thucydides, but the overall figures are not high enough to show it as clearly.

passages that go against the grain. The two modal uses of ἐν were perhaps motivated by one-off considerations:

(8) εἴ τις αὐτὴν ἐν μέσῳ τῷ θέρει καὶ **ἐν μέσῃ τῇ ἡμέρᾳ** κινοίη τῷ ζεύγει

If someone should plow it (sc. the earth) up in the middle of the summer and in the middle of the day (X. Oec. 16.14)

(9) καὶ τὸ ταραχθῆναι δὲ **ἐν τῇ**[17] **νυκτὶ** πολὺ μεῖζόν ἐστι πρᾶγμα ἢ **ἐν τῇ ἡμέρᾳ** καὶ δυσκαταστατώτερον

And confusion at night is a much bigger deal and harder to put right than it is during the day (X. Cyr. 5.3.43)

In (8), the time nouns in both temporal expressions are additionally specified by μέσος, a feature unparalleled with the genitive of time. Perhaps Xenophon chose ἐν as somehow more compatible with a modifier pinning down a particular time of the day and season. Example (9) is different from the modal examples of τῆς ἡμέρας in that ἐν τῇ ἡμέρᾳ is not linked as syntactically closely with ἐν τῇ νυκτί as in the passages with the genitive (where one generally finds καὶ ἡμέρας καὶ νυκτός, οὔτε ἡμέρας οὔτε νυκτός, and the like). Given the presence of a comparative, the prepositional construction might have been used to clarify the role of the noun, as τῆς νυκτός just before μεῖζον could have been misunderstood as a genitive of comparison.

With the limitative expressions, however, the (less common) constructions with the genitive do not appear to share any common traits that set them off against those with ἐν. In Thucydides, the genitive was more common with future time reference, ἐν with past time reference, but this pattern is not seen in Xenophon, where there are several examples of the prepositional construction modifying future (or future perfect) verbs (HG 1.4.12, An. 1.5.16, 1.7.18, Cyr. 3.3.29). What distinguishes these four examples, however, from the two examples of the genitive of time with the future are the modifiers of the time noun: in all four examples with ἐν, the time noun is modified by a demonstrative (1× each τῇδε, ταύταις, 2× ταύτῃ), while those with the genitive of time are modified by more prototypical limitative modifiers (ὀλίγων, πέντε). Indeed, the

---

[17] This article is omitted in some MSS.

genitive of time of ἡμέρα is never modified by a demonstrative, while the limitative constructions of this noun with ἐν have a demonstrative eight out of twenty times. Of these, the four mentioned above, because they occur with future time reference (and in three of the four, with a negative), are well-signposted as limitative. But the other four occur with past-tense verbs and come somewhat closer to the punctual type:[18]

(10) καὶ ἀπέθανον αὐτῶν **ἐν ἐκείνῃ τῇ ἡμέρᾳ** περὶ τριακοσίους

And about three hundred of them died on that day (*HG* 4.6.11)

(11) καὶ πάντες δὲ οἱ στρατιῶται **ἐν ταύτῃ τῇ ἡμέρᾳ** πολλὰ τὰ ἐπιτήδεια ἐκ τῶν χωρίων ἐλάμβανον

And all the solders on that day took many supplies from the countryside (*HG* 4.5.5)

On the one hand, there are good grounds for considering both (10) and (11) limitative constructions. In both, multiple events take place within a time period, as signaled by the numeral τριακοσίους in (10) and the modifier πολλὰ and the imperfect ἐλάμβανον in (11). On the other, it is not such a great step from passages like these to those with the punctual dative of time: in translation, at any rate, the punctual English preposition *on* appears to work best. Nevertheless, there are not in fact any particularly close parallels to these passages with the dative,[19] and it remains best to view these constructions as limitative – but occupying an intermediate position between the punctual dative of time and the more prototypical limitative constructions of the genitive of time.

---

[18] See also *HG* 7.1.42 and *Cyr.* 3.1.17, which are more clearly limitative than (10) and (11), the former because the temporal expression involves a plural noun (ἐν ταύταις ταῖς ἡμέραις), the latter because it also has μία as a modifier (ἐν τῇδε τῇ μιᾷ ἡμέρᾳ).

[19] Verbs modified by the dative of time tend to have either a singular subject or, if the subject is plural, the action occurs more or less in unison, e.g. καὶ ἀφικνοῦνται ἐπὶ τὸ ὄρος τῇ πέμπτῃ ἡμέρᾳ (X. *An.* 4.7.21). The imperfect is also relatively uncommon with datives of time, found in only 7 of the 37 examples with ἡμέρᾳ in Xenophon. Of these, three are verbs that lack an aorist (2× ἧκον, 1× ἦν), and none of the others appear to involve multiple actions the way that ἐλάμβανον does: ἡγοῦντο (*HG* 7.4.30), ἦγε (*HG* 4.5.3), ἠθύμουν (*HG* 3.5.21), οὐκ ἐκαλλιέρει οὐδὲ διεμέτρησεν (*An.* 7.1.40). With the last of these, as we might expect a limitative construction because of the negatives, the dative is best explained as due to the presence of an ordinal number in the expression: τῇ πρώτῃ ἡμέρᾳ.

Turning to μήν, we see a much clearer picture. The dative of time is the least common construction (4×), and is again limited to unambiguous punctual expressions. In all four examples, μηνί is modified by an ordinal number.[20] The five constructions with ἐν are similarly uniform: they are all past-time limitative expressions; in four, the noun is plural and modified by a cardinal number; in the final example, the comparative expression in which the phrase is situated makes clear that the temporal expression marks a boundary:[21]

(12) καὶ ἦν ἐνιαυσίαν ὁδὸν ὁ βάρβαρος ἐποιήσατο, ταύτην μεῖον ἢ **ἐν μηνὶ** καθήνυσεν ὁ Ἀγησίλαος

And the road that the Persian had traveled in a year, Agesilaus covered it in less than a month (*Ages.* 2.1)

Numbering eight examples, the genitive of time is the most common of the three constructions with μήν. While less homogeneous than the other two, it is still mostly found in fairly restricted contexts: six times as τοῦ μηνός in distributive expressions;[22] once in a modal-habitual expression (ὅσα ἄλλα ἢ νυκτὸς ἢ μηνὸς ἢ ἐνιαυτοῦ πράττεται, *Mem.* 4.7.4). The final example is somewhat harder to characterize exactly:

(13) ἀνάγκη μὲν γὰρ ἐγένετο αὐτῷ μετὰ τὴν κρίσιν τριάκοντα ἡμέρας βιῶναι διὰ τὸ Δήλια μὲν **ἐκείνου τοῦ μηνὸς** εἶναι

For it was necessary for him to live for thirty days after the trial because the Delian festival took place that month (*Mem.* 4.8.2)

On the one hand, the context seems to call for a punctual expression: that the yearly festival in Delos actually took place that month is the reason for the delay of Socrates' execution.[23] That we find the genitive of time, on the other, suggests that Xenophon had a different, habitual nuance in mind – this was the month in which the festival regularly occurred – and the phrase as a

---

[20] See *HG* 1.4.21, 2.2.17, 3.3.2, 5.1.5.
[21] For the other 4, see *HG* 1.1.37, 2.4.21, 3.2.11, 5.3.25.
[22] See *HG* 1.5.5, *An.* 1.3.21, 5.6.23, 7.6.1, 7.6.7, *Cyr.* 1.2.9.
[23] The reference is to the yearly festival at Delos in honor of Theseus' successful journey to Crete, not the one that took place every four years (Dindorf 1862: 194, Breitenbach 1878: 240). Cf. Pl. *Phd.* 58a–c.

whole, with εἶναι, comes close to being a possessive genitive ('the Delian festival was a fixture of that month'). This relatively straightforward distribution of the constructions with μήν extends to ἔτος and ἐνιαυτός, which pattern very much the same way: the dative occurs in punctual constructions,[24] ἐν in limitative ones,[25] and the genitive, with one exception, in distributive or habitual-modal ones.[26]

Summary

Xenophon employs a fairly clear division of labor in choosing his temporal constructions:

1. With only one exception, punctual expressions take a dative of time.

2. Of these three constructions, distributive expressions can only take a genitive of time;[27] so too, with only two exceptions, habitual-modal expressions.

3. The only real complication lies with the limitative expressions, which, with μήν, ἐνιαυτός, and ἔτος invariably take ἐν. With ἡμέρα, they usually do as well, but the genitive is available as an alternative, but not if the time noun is modified by a demonstrative, in which case ἐν is obligatory (see Table 11).

Punctual and limitative expressions in Xenophon: night and the seasons

Once again, the numbers on their own suggest that these time nouns behave differently from those just discussed: νύξ occurs

---

[24] There are two examples with ἐνιαυτός (HG 2.1.8 and 3.2.25) and eleven with ἔτος. The modifiers of the time noun are ἐπιόντι (4×), demonstratives (3×), ὑστέρῳ (2×), πρόσθεν, ἄλλῳ, περιόντι (predicative position), and an ordinal (1× each).

[25] There is one example with ἐνιαυτός (HG 5.3.25) and there are two with ἔτος, at HG 5.4.63 (limitative because of the negative) and Vect. 4.23.

[26] There are four distributive examples, three with ἐνιαυτός (Vect. 4.23, Eq. Mag. 1.19, Ath. 3.4), one with ἔτος (An. 5.3.13); and there is one habitual construction with ἐνιαυτός (Mem. 4.7.4). The only anomaly is the inexplicable genitive of HG 1.3.1 (τοῦ δ' ἐπιόντος ἔτους ὁ ἐν Φωκαίᾳ νεὼς τῆς Ἀθηνᾶς ἐνεπρήσθη). One expects the dative of time, on the basis of HG 1.6.1, 2.1.10, and 2.3.1, all of which begin τῷ δ' ἐπιόντι ἔτει.

[27] The distributive event type is also often expressed by κατά[+A].

Table 11. *Temporal constructions with calendrical time nouns in Xenophon*

	ἡμέρα	μήν	ἐνιαυτός	ἔτος
genitive	11× distrib. 18× habitual-modal 6× limitative	6× distrib. 2× habitual[a]	3× distrib. 1× habitual	1× distrib. 1× punctual
ἐν[+D]	20× limitative 2× modal	5× limitative	1× limitative	2× limitative
dative	36× punctual[b]	4× punctual	2× punctual	11× punctual

Note: [a] This counts example (13) as habitual.
[b] Example (7) is omitted from this table.

94× as a genitive of time, but only 3× as a dative; θέρος occurs 16× and χειμών 17× as a temporal genitive, but neither is ever used as a dative of time. But once again, the raw data are to some extent misleading, as the contexts in which these nouns are used are also different from those favored by the calendrical nouns. We begin with θέρος and χειμών, both far more restricted than νύξ in their range of expressions. The genitive of θέρος occurs 16× in temporal expressions, in phrases with ἐν, 5×. All but one of these are modal-habitual expressions (only twice, at *Mem.* 2.1.30 and one of the two examples at *Oec.* 16.14, is θέρος not paired explicitly with another contrasting time noun, nearly always χειμών). The one exception is *HG* 3.2.30, where Xenophon uses the genitive of time in a punctual expression:

(14) τοῦ δ' ἐπιόντος θέρους πέμψας Θρασυδαῖος εἰς Λακεδαίμονα συνεχώρησε . . .

And the next summer, Thrasydaeus sent word to Sparta and agreed . . .
(*HG* 3.2.30)

So too with χειμών (17× as a genitive of time, 8× with ἐν), nearly all the constructions are modal-habitual. Of the three exceptions, one is a punctual genitive of time, similar to (14):

(15) ἐξῆλθον δέ τινας καὶ ἄλλας ἐξόδους τοῦ χειμῶνος εἰς τὴν ἤπειρον καὶ ἐπόρθουν τὴν βασιλέως χώραν

And they went out on some other raids during the winter into the mainland and laid waste to the king's land (*HG* 1.2.17)

131

The other two, both with ἐν, are also probably best labeled as punctual, although they deviate from the prototypical construction. In (16), the situation of the phrase in an ἐπειδάν-clause might incline one to viewing it as habitual; still, as it indicates the particular moment at which the sun changes direction, a punctual reading seems preferable:

(16) τὸ δὲ τὸν ἥλιον, ἐπειδὰν **ἐν χειμῶνι** τράπηται, προσιέναι

> And the fact that the sun, when it turns at the winter solstice,[28] draws nearer
>
> (*Mem.* 4.3.8)

In (17), the presence of ἰσχυρῷ suggests that the noun refers to winter less as a period of time than as a general condition of extreme cold.[29] Even so, the action in question is pinned down to a specific time, so the punctual label again seems best:

(17) **ἐν γὰρ τῷ ἰσχυρῷ χειμῶνι** καὶ αὐτός ποτε ἀναμένων τινὰς συσκευαζομένους καθεζόμενος συχνὸν χρόνον κατέμαθον ἀναστὰς μόλις καὶ τὰ σκέλη ἐκτείνας

> For in the extreme cold, when I myself was once waiting for some men who were packing up, when I'd been sitting for a long time, I realized that I got up and stretched out my legs with difficulty (*An.* 5.8.14)

Now, examples (14) and (15) give us some slight evidence to corroborate the view that, with these nouns, the genitive, and not the dative, is the default construction in punctual constructions. Furthermore, (16) and (17) hint that even ἐν could also be used in such expressions. But there remains the question: what difference is there between the genitive and ἐν? Some possibilities may be discarded from the start. Both constructions are used with and without the definite article; both are nearly always found with the present tense, as is expected of the modal-habitual type. A more promising starting point for detecting a difference may be found in the modifiers (excluding the article) that occur in the respective constructions: the genitive only occurs once with a modifier, the τοῦ ἐπιόντος θέρους of example (14); ἐν occurs three times: ἐν μέσῳ τῷ θέρει καὶ ἐν μέσῃ τῇ ἡμέρᾳ (*Oec.* 16.14), ἐν τῷ ἰσχυρῷ χειμῶνι

---

[28] For the translation, see Smith (1903: 217).
[29] Masqueray translates: "Dans le froid intense de l'hiver" (1954: 86).

(ex. (17)), and ἐν τῷ ἰσχυροτάτῳ χειμῶνι (*Cyr.* 1.6.39). Insofar as ἐπιών acts like a demonstrative in simply specifying which summer is referred to, while μέσος and ἰσχυρός give additional information about the season or part of the season in which the event took place, it is tempting to see the prepositional construction as favored when the temporal expression is given relatively heavy semantic weight.

This position is borne out by the other four passages with ἐν (τῷ) θέρει (three of which also contain ἐν (τῷ) χειμῶνι), where the emphasis of the clause is again on the temporal construction:

(18) ἀλλὰ μὴν **καὶ ἐν τῷ χειμῶνι** οὐ μόνον κεφαλὴν καὶ σῶμα καὶ πόδας ἀρκεῖ αὐτοῖς ἐσκεπάσθαι, ἀλλὰ καὶ περὶ ἄκραις ταῖς χερσὶ χειρῖδας δασείας καὶ δακτυλήθρας ἔχουσιν. **ἐν γε μὴν τῷ θέρει** οὐκ ἀρκοῦσιν αὐτοῖς οὔθ᾽ αἱ τῶν δένδρων οὔθ᾽ αἱ τῶν πετρῶν σκιαί, ἀλλ᾽ ἐν ταύταις ἑτέρας σκιὰς ἄνθρωποι μηχανώμενοι αὐτοῖς παρεστᾶσι

Indeed, also in the winter it was not enough for only their heads, bodies, and feet to be sheltered, but also up to the ends of their hands they wear thick gloves and finger-coverings. By contrast, in the summer, the shade of trees and of rocks is not enough for them, and, while in this shade, men stand by and contrive other sources of shade for them (*Cyr.* 8.8.17)

(19) ἢν μὲν **ἐν θέρει** ὦσι, τὸν ἄρχοντα δεῖ τοῦ ἡλίου πλεονεκτοῦντα φανερὸν εἶναι· ἢν δὲ **ἐν χειμῶνι**, τοῦ ψύχους

If they take place during the summer, the officer must clearly have a greater share of the sun; if during the winter, of the cold (*Cyr.* 1.6.25)

(20) τάδε μέντοι πλεονεκτῶν οὐκ ᾐσχύνετο, **ἐν μὲν τῷ θέρει** τοῦ ἡλίου, **ἐν δὲ τῷ χειμῶνι** τοῦ ψύχους

But he was not ashamed to have the greater share of these things: in the summer of the sun, and in the winter of the cold (*Ages.* 5.3)

(21) ταῦτ᾽ οὖν, ἔφη, σὺ ἄλλως πως νομίζεις μᾶλλον ἂν γίγνεσθαι ἢ εἰ **ἐν τῷ θέρει** ὅτι πλειστάκις μεταβάλοι τις τὴν γῆν;

He said, "So do you think that this happens other than if, during the summer, one turns the soil as often as possible?" (*Oec.* 16.14)

In (18), the temporal phrases are emphatic in that they are used as contrastive settings at a comparatively large-scale level of text organization (as indicated both by the amount of information conveyed in the two halves of the passage and by the particularly bulky particle combinations: ἀλλὰ μὴν καὶ ... γε μήν). In the next example, their importance is shown by the fact that Xenophon creates conditional clauses (ἢν μὲν ... ὦσι) whose sole purpose is to house them – not unlike cleft sentences in English. With (20), we reach an example where the genitive would probably also be possible (see below), but the semantic content is so close to that of (19) that it is reasonable to account for it along the same lines. Finally, in (21), ἐν τῷ θέρει is again a prominent setting constituent, this time in a conditional clause thrown into relief by the immediately preceding μᾶλλον ἤ.

What we do not see among these prepositional phrases are passages like the following, with the temporal genitive:

(22) ἱμάτιον ἠμφίεσαι οὐ μόνον φαῦλον, ἀλλὰ τὸ αὐτὸ **θέρους τε καὶ χειμῶνος**

You wear a cloak that is not only plain, but the same one both summer and winter (*Mem.* 1.6.2)

(23) ἀλλὰ ψύχη τε **χειμῶνος** καὶ θάλπη **θέρους** ἐθίζει καρτερεῖν

But it gets people used to enduring cold in the winter and heat in the summer (*Oec.* 5.4)

Here, the phrases with summer and winter are linked by τε ... καί, and they do not come first in their clause; thus, they do not have the strong pragmatic marking of the prepositional examples.[30] That said, there are still examples of the genitive used with contrastive phrases of the sort that also take ἐν; twice, for example, in the following passage:

(24) καὶ διαιτητήρια δὲ τοῖς ἀνθρώποις ἐπεδείκνυον αὐτῇ κεκαλλωπισμένα **τοῦ μὲν θέρους** ἔχειν ψυχεινά, **τοῦ δὲ χειμῶνος** ἀλεεινά. καὶ σύμπασαν δὲ τὴν οἰκίαν ἐπέδειξα αὐτῇ ὅτι πρὸς μεσημβρίαν ἀναπέπταται, ὥστε εὔδηλον εἶναι ὅτι **χειμῶνος μὲν** εὐήλιός ἐστι, **τοῦ δὲ θέρους** εὔσκιος

And I showed her the rooms for the men, decorated, that were cool during the summer, and warm during the winter. As for the house as a whole, I

---

[30] In Dik's model (2007: 31–7) (cf. also the refinements of Dik (1995) in Matić (2003)), this contrastive marking would presumably fall into more than one category: setting in (18), (20), and (probably) (21), but focus in (19). As for (23), one could potentially analyze ψύχη and θάλπη as contrastive topics, χειμῶνος and θέρους as contrastive foci, but this goes against the overall sense of the passage, where the new, salient information is the cold and the heat, not the seasons when they happen to occur. I am thus inclined to view χειμῶνος and θέρους as unmarked, at least compared to the phrases with ἐν; one cannot exclude the possibility that they are actually adnominal genitives.

showed her that it opened to the south, so it was clear that in the winter it was sunny, in the summer, shady (*Oec.* 9.4)

As there is little to distinguish these two pairs from that of example (20), where the preposition is used instead, it seems impossible draw a firm line between the usage of the genitive and ἐν. Nevertheless, that all five of the modal-habitual examples of ἐν (τῷ) θέρει are emphatic, whereas only half of the fifteen with (τοῦ) θέρους are,[31] remains good evidence that, despite a certain amount of free variation, the prepositional construction was perceived as weightier.

With νύξ, the data are far richer: the genitive occurs 94×, ἐν 12×, the dative 3×, and there is also the isolated word νύκτωρ (14×) that must be taken into account. The expressions with the genitive show an exceptionally wide range of uses: 51× in punctual constructions and 43× in constructions that cover the spectrum of the habitual, modal, and limitative event-types in such a smooth continuum that it would not be sensible to attempt to work out discrete figures. What is more, νύκτωρ occupies much the same functional territory, with six punctual examples and eight modal ones; the twelve examples of ἐν are little different, though only two of these are punctual. The three datives of time are the most homogeneous: all are punctual, and have a demonstrative or ἐπιοῦσα as a modifier. But even this does not serve to distinguish them from the genitive of time, as it too is found in punctual constructions with these same modifiers.

To sort through this jumble of temporal expressions, these punctual expressions with demonstratives are a good starting point, as they form a group that can be detached relatively easily from the rest. First, the examples with the dative of time:

(25) Λύσανδρος δὲ **τῇ ἐπιούσῃ νυκτί**, ἐπεὶ ὄρθρος ἦν, ἐσήμηνεν εἰς τὰς ναῦς ἀριστοποιησαμένους εἰσβαίνειν

And Lysander, on the next night, when it was dawn, signaled that, after breakfast, they would embark on the ships (HG 2.1.22)

---

[31] I count as emphatic *Mem.* 3.8.9, *Oec.* 9.4 (2×), 16.11, *Cyn.* 4.11, 5.1, 10.6; non-emphatic: *Mem.* 1.6.2, 3.8.9, *Oec.* 5.4, *Cyr.* 5.1.11, 8.5.2, *Cyn.* 5.5, 5.6. There remains *Mem.* 2.1.30, which is probably also emphatic, but to a much lesser extent than the other examples.

(26) φανερὸς δὲ ἐγένετο καὶ ὁ νεὼς τοῦ Ποσειδῶνος **ταύτῃ τῇ νυκτὶ** καόμενος

And the temple of Poseidon was conspicuous as it burned that night (*HG* 4.5.4)

(27) κωμάζει γὰρ ἡ πόλις πᾶσα **τῇδε τῇ νυκτί**[32]

For the whole city is celebrating on this night (*Cyr.* 7.5.25)

Next, those with the genitive of time:

(28) ὥστ' **ἐκείνης τῆς νυκτὸς** οὐδεὶς ἐκοιμήθη

And so no one slept on that night (*HG* 2.2.3)

(29) καὶ **ταύτης τῆς νυκτὸς** σφενδονῆται μὲν εἰς διακοσίους ἐγένοντο, ἵπποι δὲ καὶ ἱππεῖς ἐδοκιμάσθησαν **τῇ ὑστεραίᾳ** εἰς πεντήκοντα

And on this night, the slingers came to two hundred, and about fifty horses and cavalry were approved on the next day as fit to serve (*An.* 3.3.20)

All of the remaining examples of the genitive of time of νυκτός have either no modifier at all or only the definite article, apart from three examples with τῆς ἐπιούσης, of which the following is representative:[33]

(30) ἀθρόαι δὲ γενόμεναι αἱ νῆες ἅπασαι ἐν Παρίῳ ἓξ καὶ ὀγδοήκοντα **τῆς ἐπιούσης νυκτὸς** ἀνηγάγοντο, καὶ **τῇ ἄλλῃ ἡμέρᾳ** περὶ ἀρίστου ὥραν ἧκον εἰς Προκόννησον

And all eighty-six ships, assembling at Parium, put to sea on the next night, and on the next day, around breakfast time, they reached Proconnesus (*HG* 1.1.13)

One might like to distinguish between the genitive and dative by finding the former to be used in more limitative situations, the latter in more prototypical punctual contexts. And indeed examples (25) through (27) fit this view of the dative, and (28), with the genitive, could be seen as more limitative, thanks to the presence of the negative οὐδείς. The genitives in passages (29) and (30), however, resist this interpretation, as neither really contains the hallmarks of the limitative type. Both have plural subjects, to be sure, and thus

---

[32] The text here depends on Stephanus' conjecture of κωμάζει for the garbled readings of the MSS. But they are all at least consistent in having the dative of time (though some omit the article τῇ).

[33] See also *HG* 1.2.4 (καὶ τῆς ἐπιούσης νυκτὸς ἐνέβαλον εἰς τὴν Λυδίαν) and *Cyr.* 7.2.3 (τῆς ἐπιούσης νυκτὸς ἀναβιβάζει Χαλδαίους τε καὶ Πέρσας).

might potentially be seen as describing the multiplicity of events that can trigger the limitative. But a plural verb is clearly not enough on its own to warrant such a reading;[34] nor do either of the two further passages with τῆς ἐπιούσης νυκτός (see n. 33) call for a limitative reading. On the whole, the similarity of the passages with the genitive and dative provides credible evidence that there is something close to free variation in the case usage here: the genitive is the preferred case for the punctual expressions of νύξ (recall that there are 46× with (τῆς) νυκτός without a further modifier), presumably because this is a noun that occurs so readily in modal-habitual constructions; but, when a demonstrative is also present, this tendency can be overridden by assimilation to the datives of time with ἡμέρα.

The factors that condition the use of ἐν instead of the genitive are, if anything, even more difficult to determine, largely because these are constructions that often overlap even when they are at their most distinct. In the case of (τῆς) νυκτός and ἐν (τῇ) νυκτί, perhaps the clearest differentiating feature is the almost complete absence of the prepositional construction in punctual expressions. While such expressions account for over half of the genitives of time, only two of the twelve constructions with ἐν belong under this heading, and one of these only tenuously at that:

(31) οὐκοῦν καὶ ἐπειδὴ ὁ μὲν ἥλιος φωτεινὸς ὢν τάς τε ὥρας τῆς ἡμέρας ἡμῖν καὶ τἄλλα πάντα σαφηνίζει, ἡ δὲ νὺξ διὰ τὸ σκοτεινὴ εἶναι ἀσαφεστέρα ἐστίν, ἄστρα **ἐν τῇ νυκτὶ** ἀνέφηναν, ἃ ἡμῖν τῆς νυκτὸς τὰς ὥρας ἐμφανίζει . . . ;

Since the sun, being bright, distinguishes for us the hours of the day as well as everything else, but the night, because it is dark, is less clear, did they not cause the stars to shine at night, which show us the hours of the night?
(*Mem.* 4.3.4)

This is an unusual passage in several respects, primarily because of the extent to which the concept of time is itself the subject of

---

[34] In fact, the genitives of both (29) and (30) are followed by further plural verbs (in (30) with the same subject) that construe with temporal datives, τῇ ὑστεραίᾳ and τῇ ἄλλῃ ἡμέρᾳ. Even if one objects to using these two particular examples as parallels on the grounds that the events modified by these datives (approval of the cavalry, an arrival pinned down specifically to 'around breakfast time') are more instantaneous in nature than those with the genitive, other examples (e.g. ταύτῃ μὲν τῇ ἡμέρᾳ . . . ἀπῆλθον οἱ βάρβαροι, *An.* 3.4.18) show that the dative, not the genitive, is still regular with ἡμέρα in such contexts.

discussion. As a result, the constructions do not fall into the proto-typical event-types as easily as elsewhere; note, for instance, the ambiguity as to whether τῆς ἡμέρας and τῆς νυκτός are adnominal genitives, dependent on τὰς ὥρας, or adverbial genitives, dependent on σαφηνίζει and ἐμφανίζει respectively.[35] What sort of expression, then, is ἐν τῇ νυκτί?

Potentially punctual, as it modifies the aorist ἀνέφηναν that refers to the gods' initial placement of the stars in the night sky – though in that case, the expression is almost more spatial than temporal. Indeed, a better case can be made for assigning it to the modal category, as the passage emphasizes more the contrast between the repeated shining of the stars in the night and that of the sun during the day than it does the first night on which the gods set the stars in the sky. If we discard (31), then we are left with only one punctual example of ἐν τῇ νυκτί:

(32) ὡς δὲ τοῦτο ἐγένετο, τὸ ὕδωρ κατὰ τὰς τάφρους ἐχώρει **ἐν τῇ νυκτί**

And when this happened, the water went down the ditches during the night
(*Cyr.* 7.5.16)

Here the temporal phrase does seem just as punctual as in passages with the genitive, such as:

(33) ἐμβιβασάμενος αὐτοὺς εἰς τὰς ναῦς ἔπλει **τῆς[36]νυκτὸς** εἰς τὸν λιμένα τῶν Ἀθηναίων

After putting them on board the ships, he sailed during the night to the harbor of the Athenians (*HG* 5.1.19)

Still, this instance of apparent free variation notwithstanding, we can at least observe that, with this noun in this author, ἐν is less available as a punctual marker than the genitive is.

With the modal and habitual types, there is even less difference between the two markers, other than that the prepositional construction is rarer than the genitive on its own. This is largely

---

[35] Word order leads me to translate the former as adnominal, as it is much closer to τὰς ὥρας than to σαφηνίζει; it is harder, though, to exclude an adverbial reading for the latter expression. That said, there is textual uncertainty here: τῆς ἡμέρας is omitted by MS B, placed before ἡμῖν in other MSS, and after it in still others; τῆς νυκτός is placed before τὰς ὥρας in B, after it in others. Dindorf (1862: 168) and Breitenbach (1878: 213) print the second order for τῆς νυκτός and take it as an adnominal genitive. In any event, the exact syntax of these genitives is not critical to the argument.

[36] The article is present in MS B, but absent in the others.

the result of the one significant divergence between the two: (τῆς) νυκτός, especially without the article, is regularly preferred to ἐν (τῇ) νυκτί when night and day are conjoined as a single unit:[37]

(34) **καὶ ἡμέρας καὶ νυκτὸς** πράγματα παρασχεῖν

To cause trouble both day and night (*Mem.* 2.2.8)

The construction with ἐν that comes closest to this is the following:

(35) καὶ τὸ ταραχθῆναι δὲ **ἐν τῇ**[38] **νυκτὶ** πολὺ μεῖζόν ἐστι πρᾶγμα ἢ **ἐν τῇ ἡμέρᾳ** καὶ δυσκαταστατώτερον

And confusion during the night is a much more serious affair than it is during the day and harder to put right (*Cyr.* 5.3.43)

But even these two examples are not quite comparable, in that the temporal phrases in (35) show a contrastive emphasis not found in (34) and nearly all of the numerous constructions that resemble it.[39] It is thus likely that Xenophon uses the lengthier construction when the temporal phrase bears a heavier pragmatic load. Still, as suggestive as this point of difference is, it remains the case that many pairs show free variation, where, if anything, one-off considerations will have determined the choice of construction. In looking at these pairs, since the prepositional constructions are so much rarer than those with the genitive, it is fair to treat the latter as the default, and therefore to look for special factors that would favor a switch to ἐν. Examples (36) and (37), for instance, show that either expression may occur in a ὅταν-clause, in both cases in a preverbal focal position:[40]

---

[37] Other examples of the two nouns connected by (καὶ …) καί occur at *Mem.* 2.2.5, *An.* 2.6.7, 6.1.18, *Cyr.* 2.3.23, 7.5.68, 8.1.3; at *Lac.* 2.7, one finds καὶ νυκτός … καὶ μεθ' ἡμέραν. The nouns are joined by εἴτε … εἴτε (καί) at *An.* 3.1.40, *Cyr.* 2.2.30; by ἤ at *Cyr.* 1.6.43, 8.5.14. Negative examples, with οὔτε … οὔτε, are found at *Mem.* 3.11.16, *Smp.* 4.48, *Ap.* 31, *Cyr.* 8.1.45; with μήτε … μήτε, at *HG* 7.5.19. Somewhat more loosely connected are the examples with μὲν … δὲ at *Mem.* 2.1.30 and οὐ μόνον τῆς νυκτός … ἀλλὰ καὶ μεθ' ἡμέραν at *Cyn.* 9.17. In total, this amounts to 19 examples.

[38] The article is omitted by MSS C and E, and D and F.

[39] The main exceptions are the last two passages cited in n. 37; *Cyn.* 9.17 is particularly interesting, as it apparently shows an intermediate level of emphasis, where the genitive τῆς νυκτός is retained, but Xenophon upgrades τῆς ἡμέρας to μεθ' ἡμέραν.

[40] These examples also show how slight the difference between a modal and a punctual construction can be; I count these as modal because their occurrence in a ὅταν-clause means that they do not so much specify the time at which a particular event happened as give a general condition for the event.

(36) ὅταν μέλλητε **νυκτός** ἀναστήσεσθαι

When you are going to get up at night (*Cyr.* 5.3.44)

(37) ὥσπερ ὅταν φέγγος τι **ἐν νυκτὶ** φανῇ

Just as when a light shines in the night (*Smp.* 1.9)

Given the tendency for the temporal expressions with νύξ to show spatial features,[41] one may reasonably speculate that the preposition is used in (37) because the night sky is presented as a sort of background against which the star is seen. A similar consideration is probably at work in (38), where the choice of the prepositional construction allows Xenophon to treat night as parallel to fear:

(38) μάλα δὲ χαλεπῶς πορευόμενοι, οἷα δὴ **ἐν νυκτί τε καὶ ἐν φόβῳ** ἀπιόντες καὶ χαλεπὴν ὁδόν

And, marching with difficulty, as they were leaving at night and in fear and along a difficult road (*HG* 6.4.26)

At other times, however, the constructions really do seem alike; there is no apparent reason why νυκτός could not have been used in (40) as it is in (39):

(39) πονηρὸν γὰρ **νυκτός** ἐστι στράτευμα Περσικόν

For a Persian army is terrible at night (*An.* 3.4.35)

(40) ἴσασι γὰρ ὅτι ἱππικὸν στράτευμα **ἐν νυκτὶ** ταραχῶδές ἐστι καὶ δύσχρηστον ἄλλως τε καὶ βάρβαρον

For they know that the cavalry of the army are prone to confusion at night and difficult to control, especially if they are not Greek (*Cyr.* 3.3.26)

Before moving on, one final observation is perhaps significant: modal-habitual (τῆς) νυκτός occurs eight times in the *Anabasis*, but ἐν (τῇ) νυκτί not once; for the *Cyropaedia*, the figures are 12× and 4× respectively. While these numbers are too low to prove anything, it seems just possible that Xenophon's reluctance to use the prepositional construction in the *Anabasis*, but not in the

---

[41] Cf. ex. (31) and, in Ch. 2, (97) through (101), with ὑπό (and διά) νύκτα.

Cyropaedia, represents a changing stylistic preference over the course of his career.[42] The final expression that must be considered is the isolated form νύκτωρ, not found in either Herodotus or Thucydides, which Xenophon uses fourteen times, eight times in modal constructions, six times in punctual ones.[43] As a modal example, consider (41), which comes at the end of the section opened by example (39):

(41) ταῦτα δὲ πάντα χαλεπὰ **νύκτωρ** καὶ θορύβου ὄντος

And all these things are difficult at night and when there's commotion

(*An.* 3.4.35)

It is hardly obvious why νύκτωρ should have been chosen here, rather than the genitive of (39) or the ἐν of (40).[44] In the features where one can perceive some slight difference between the genitive and ἐν, it aligns sometimes with ἐν, sometimes with the genitive. Like ἐν, it is generally not used in straightforward pairs with ἡμέρα, the closest it comes being (42), in which the two temporal phrases serve as contrastive settings:

(42) καὶ **νύκτωρ** ἀμαχεὶ μᾶλλον ἂν τὰ πρὸ ποδῶν ὁρῴη τις ἢ **μεθ᾽ ἡμέραν** μαχόμενος

And at night, when not fighting, one may see better what lies at one's feet than during the day, when fighting (*An.* 4.6.12)

But νύκτωρ is more like the genitive in its compatibility with the punctual event-type. Compare examples (43) and (44), which have no close counterparts with ἐν (τῇ) νυκτί:

---

[42] The dating of Xenophon's works is far from straightforward. In favor of a relatively wide gap between the *Anabasis* and the *Cyropaedia*, Breitenbach offers the 380s for the former (1967: 1644) and puts the latter after 362/1 ("jedenfalls für das Schlußkapitel, eher aber für das ganze Werk") (1967: 1742; cf. also col. 1902). Others, however, would put them closer together: in Dittenberger's assessment of the usage of μήν, both the *Anabasis* and the *Cyropaedia* fall into the same group (1881: 331), and Dillery assigns the *Anabasis* to the period after the battle of Leuctra in 371 (1995: 59).

[43] I count as modal *HG* 6.2.29, *An.* 3.4.35, 4.6.12, 7.3.37, 7.3.41, *Cyr.* 3.3.25, 4.5.6, *Lac.* 12.3; as punctual *HG* 3.1.7, 5.3.24, 6.4.33, 7.1.41, *An.* 4.4.9, 7.8.20.

[44] Marchant's *deteriores* MSS do in fact have νυκτός here.

(43) ὅμως μέντοι ὅ γε Δελφίων καὶ στιγματίας τις μετ' αὐτοῦ ... ἀπέδρασαν **νύκτωρ**

Nevertheless, Delphion and a branded outlaw with him escaped at night
(*HG* 5.3.24)

(44) οἱ δ' ἐν Σηστῷ Ἀθηναῖοι ... **νυκτὸς** ἀπέδρασαν εἰς Καρδίαν

And the Athenians at Sestus escaped at night to Cardia (*HG* 1.1.11)[45]

The fact that νύκτωρ comes after the verb, νυκτός before it, is unlikely to be significant: two of the punctual examples of νύκτωρ are pre-verbal (*HG* 3.1.7, 6.4.33), and many of the punctual examples of νυκτός are post-verbal (e.g. *HG* 2.2.3, 7.4.27, *An.* 4.4.15). Furthermore, as these examples also suggest, there is no tendency for verbs of a particular semantic field to prefer one construction to the other.[46] Nor, to consider only the punctual expressions, is νύκτωρ a stylistic tic that shows a different distribution in Xenophon's work from (τῆς) νυκτός: νύκτωρ occurs 4× in the *Hellenica*, 2× in the *Anabasis*; (τῆς) νυκτός is found 27× in the *Hellenica*, 15× in the *Anabasis*, and 4× in the *Cyropaedia*. It is hard to reach a verdict other than free variation. While disappointing, such a conclusion has a parallel in the ease with which one can interchange *at night*, *by night*, and *during the night* in the translations of the examples above.

Summary

The non-calendrical time nouns are found in the following distribution of constructions (see Table 12):

1. With θέρος and χειμών, there is limited evidence (examples (14) and (15)) that these nouns preferred the genitive to the dative in punctual constructions; the absence of temporal datives is hardly a smoking gun, however, as these nouns are simply extremely rare in such constructions. Examples (16) and (17) are not prototypically punctual enough to suggest that ἐν was freely available as an alternative.

---

[45] There is a very similar example at *HG* 1.1.10.
[46] In Plutarch, by contrast, verbs of motion overwhelmingly favor the genitive over νύκτωρ (see Table 21 on p. 255).

2. With θέρος and χειμών, both the genitive and ἐν are used in modal-habitual constructions, but while the genitive is used freely in both focalized and unemphatic contexts (especially phrases of the type θέρους τε καὶ χειμῶνος, where the two nouns are coordinated), ἐν is only used when the temporal phrase bears particular semantic weight.

3. With νύξ, punctual constructions are again found not only with both the genitive and ἐν, but also with the dative and with νύκτωρ. The genitive is by far the most common, but all but five of these examples simply state that the event occurred at night (with (τῆς) νυκτός) without giving any further specification. Of the other five, three have τῆς ἐπιούσης νυκτός (ex. (30)), and one each ἐκείνης τῆς νυκτός (ex. (28)) and ταύτης τῆς νυκτός (ex. (29)). By contrast, all three with the dative have a demonstrative or ἐπιοῦσα as a modifier (exx. (25) through (27)). There thus appears to be free variation between the genitive and dative in punctual expressions with these modifiers. As with θέρος and χειμών, ἐν is only marginally available to mark punctual constructions, and most often competes with the genitive in modal-habitual contexts; here too, the genitive is preferred in paired expressions (καὶ ἡμέρας καὶ νυκτός), and the prepositional construction tends to be more emphatic. The isolated form νύκτωρ shares functions with both the genitive and ἐν: like the genitive, it can be used in punctual expressions; like ἐν, it is not used in paired expressions.

Table 12. *Temporal constructions with non-calendrical time nouns and νύξ in Xenophon*

	θέρος	χειμών	νύξ
genitive	15× modal-hab.	16× modal-hab.	43× mod.-hab.-limitv.
	1× punc. (ex. (14))	1× punc. (ex. (15))	51× punctual
ἐν^{+D}	5× modal-hab.	6× modal-hab.	10× mod.-hab.-limitv.
		2× punc. (exx. (16), (17))	1× punctual
			1× adjl. (*Cyr.* 5.3.56)
dative	0×	0×	3× punctual
νύκτωρ	NA	NA	8× modal
			6× punctual

EXPRESSIONS OF TIME: STYLE, GENRE, AND DIACHRONY

Punctual and limitative expressions in Xenophon: χρόνος

The final time noun to consider, χρόνος, does not fall into either of the two groups already discussed as it does not refer to a discrete unit of time; as such, it is only seldom found in prototypical punctual expressions. In temporal constructions, it is most commonly found as the accusative of time, in durative expressions (94×), and with ἐν, in limitative ones (about 19×), but it can also occur as a genitive (4×) and dative (5×) of time. It is also found an additional 20× with ἐν in expressions that extend from the limitative category into the punctual (and at times even come close to being durative) – normally distinct categories that are brought closer to each other because of the comparatively vague semantics of χρόνος. Most of the questions raised by this distribution revolve around the constructions with ἐν. When limitative, how do they differ from those with the genitive of time? When punctual, what distinguishes them from those with the dative (and those with κατά⁺ᴬ and περί⁺ᴬ)? When durative, is there a reason why Xenophon has not used the accusative instead?

The limitative event type is most often expressed by ἐν, but there are also four limitative genitives of time.⁴⁷ These all bear the obvious hallmarks of the limitative: three occur in negative constructions (*Mem.* 1.2.35, *An.* 1.9.25, *Ages.* 2.23), and the fourth modifies a future-tense verb (*Cyr.* 1.4.28). The modifiers, too, are the usual suspects: twice πολλοῦ, once each ὀλίγου and ὅσουπερ. Similar constructions with ἐν can also be found: of the nineteen examples that may provisionally be called limitative, ὀλίγῳ occurs four times as a modifier, πολλῷ twice, and ὅσῳ once; while there are no examples with morphological futures, the conditional at *Cyr.* 2.1.23 certainly has future semantics: εἴ τι ἐν τῷ ἐπιόντι χρόνῳ ἀγαθὸν μεῖζον φανοῖτο; and negative constructions are found at *HG* 7.4.32 and *Vect.* 4.3. But this overlap is not in fact a sign of complete free variation, for such prototypical examples account for all four of the genitives of time, but only half of those with ἐν. That ἐν is freer in usage than the genitive can be seen in constructions where the

---

⁴⁷ I do not take into consideration the three limitative expressions with ἐντός (all ἐντός ὀλίγου χρόνου), as they all come from the spurious *Ath. Pol.* (3.11, 3×).

limitative idea is confined to the fact that multiple events have taken place within a definite period, without the additional signals of a typically limitative modifier or future-tense verbs:[48]

(45) ἐκεῖνα μέντοι ἃ ἐν τῷ χρόνῳ ἐκείνῳ ἔπραξε

However, those actions that he carried out during that time (*HG* 6.5.51)

Indeed, the phrases with ἐν can go much further in this direction, leading to the use of this preposition to mark punctual and perhaps even durative expressions as well:

(46) καὶ ἐν τούτῳ τῷ χρόνῳ ἦλθεν Ἀρχαγόρας ὁ Ἀργεῖος πεφευγώς

And at this time came Archagoras of Argos, in flight (*An.* 4.2.17)

(47) ὥστε ἔν γε ἐκείνῳ τῷ χρόνῳ πολὺ ᾤοντο κράτιστοι εἶναι

And so at that time at least they thought they were far the most powerful (*HG* 7.1.25)

Example (46) shows none of the signs of the limitative type and is best labeled as punctual.[49] The atelic nature of the event in (47) renders this construction nearly durative, although the presence of the modifier ἐκεῖνος probably means that it too is best understood as punctual, singling out this χρόνος against other χρόνοι, rather than stretching out the state to refer to all of the current χρόνος. (While other time nouns, like ἡμέρα, also partake of this ambiguity, the distinction is harder to draw with χρόνος because its referent is that much more indefinite.)

But while ἐν is clearly in play as a punctual marker, it is not the only possibility. One finds the simple dative used as well, four or, possibly, five times. Unlike the temporal genitive of χρόνος, these datives do not form a cohesive group. One of the five (*HG* 4.1.34) is best disregarded for the same reason as the sixteen temporal datives of χρόνος in Thucydides: it means not 'at some time', but

---

[48] See also *HG* 5.2.10, *Oec.* 11.19, *Vect.* 5.12.
[49] It is true that the sentence then continues with Archagoras as subject of a second verb (καὶ λέγει), but this does not constitute the sort of multiplicity of events that would shift this example into the limitative category. The punctual dative is regularly used in such contexts, e.g. καὶ ταύτῃ τῇ ἡμέρᾳ ἀφικνεῖται Βίων καὶ Ναυσικλείδης ... καὶ ξενοῦνται τῷ Ξενοφῶντι καὶ ἵππον ... λυσάμενοι ἀπέδοσαν καὶ τὴν τιμὴν οὐκ ἤθελον ἀπολαβεῖν (*An.* 7.8.6).

'after some time'.[50] The second probably also belongs in this category, as the temporal phrase can be understood as equivalent to 'after the passage of half as much time':[51]

(48) εἴ τι παραγγεῖλαι χρήζοιεν, ἡμίσει ἂν χρόνῳ αἰσθάνεσθαι τὸ στράτευμα

If they should need to give an order, the army would hear in half the time
(*An.* 1.8.22)

In the third, we might expect an accusative of time, partly because the verbal event is atelic, partly because it occurs in a static μέν-clause that sets up a following punctual clause with ἐπεὶ δέ:

(49) τῷ μὲν οὖν πρώτῳ χρόνῳ ὁ Κριτίας τῷ Θηραμένει ὁμογνώμων τε καὶ φίλος ἦν· ἐπεὶ δὲ αὐτὸς μὲν . . .

During the first period, Critias was on good political and personal terms with Theramenes; but when Critias for his part . . . (*HG* 2.3.15)

Xenophon presumably uses the dative because the modifier, an ordinal number, is of a sort often associated with the temporal dative. The next two examples show datives that are comparatively predictable, as a straightforward punctual dative is not out of place (even if an expression with ἐν would also be possible):[52]

(50) τῷ δ' αὐτῷ χρόνῳ καὶ Λακεδαιμόνιοι τοὺς εἰς τὸ Κορυφάσιον τῶν Εἱλώτων ἀφεστῶτας ἐκ Μαλέας ὑποσπόνδους ἀφῆκαν

---

[50] See the discussion of examples (67) and (68) in Ch. 1. Moreover, in Xenophon, as in Thucydides (see ex. (19) in Ch. 2), one may note the similar use of διὰ χρόνου, which suggests that this behavior is associated with an instrumental force (cf. Luraghi (2003: 69–72), with another example of the similarity of the dative and διά[+G]). A good example of an intermediate construction occurs at *An.* 3.4.12: ταύτην δὲ τὴν πόλιν πολιορκῶν ὁ Περσῶν βασιλεὺς οὐκ ἐδύνατο οὔτε χρόνῳ ἑλεῖν οὔτε βίᾳ. The parallelism with βίᾳ brings the instrumental element to the fore, but it is also clearly a short step from 'to capture the city by means of the passage of time' to 'to capture the city after the passage of some time'.

[51] Given the translation, one might also be tempted to see this as a limitative construction, with the expected ἐν dropped by haplology after the -εν of the preceding verb. Indeed, MS D and the *deteriores* have ἐν instead of ἄν, and Bisschop added ἐν before ἡμίσει. But the broader context of the clause speaks against this. Persian commanders are described as stationing themselves in the center of the line for various reasons, including quicker communication with the ends of the line. As there is thus an implicit contrast with a position at the end of the line, the idea is not that the army hears *within* (i.e. at some point sooner than) half the time, but rather that the army can be informed in more or less *exactly* half the time it might otherwise take.

[52] For a parallel with ἐν to (50), see *HG* 2.3.5; ἐν τῷ αὐτῷ χρόνῳ also occurs at *Oec.* 11.19, but there is a better case to made there that the expression is limitative rather than punctual. There are no exact parallels to (51) with ὕστερος as the modifier, but one does find e.g. ἐν τῷ πρόσθεν χρόνῳ at *An.* 2.3.22.

And at the same time, the Spartans also released under a truce those of the Helots who had fled in revolt from Malea to Coryphasium (*HG* 1.2.18)

(51) ὑστέρῳ δὲ χρόνῳ ἀκούσαντες ξένους μισθοῦσθαι τοὺς Ἐλευσῖνι, στρατευσάμενοι πανδημεὶ ἐπ' αὐτοὺς τοὺς μὲν στρατηγοὺς αὐτῶν εἰς λόγους ἐλθόντας ἀπέκτειναν

And when they heard at a later time that the Eleusinians had hired mercenaries, they marched against them in their full numbers and, when their commanders came to speak with them, they killed them (*HG* 2.4.43)

The general picture is that Xenophon occasionally still uses the dative of time for punctual constructions with χρόνος, but that this has been largely superseded by phrases with ἐν. Nor, for that matter, is ἐν the only competitor to the dative. There are also four examples of κατά⁺ᴬ in roughly the same function:[53]

(52) ἦν δέ τις Ἀπολλοφάνης Κυζικηνός, ὃς καὶ Φαρναβάζῳ ἐτύγχανεν ἐκ παλαιοῦ ξένος ὢν καὶ Ἀγησιλάῳ **κατ' ἐκεῖνον τὸν χρόνον** ἐξενώθη

And there was a certain Apollophanes of Cyzicus, who, as it happened, had been a guest-friend of Pharnabazus for a long time and became a guest-friend of Agesilaus at that time (*HG* 4.1.29)

While expressions with κατά⁺ᴬ are often glossed as approximative ('at about', rather than simply 'at'),[54] it takes more work to justify such a translation for this preposition than for περί, which, three of the four times in Xenophon that it governs χρόνος, is preceded by σχεδόν ('more or less').[55] Still, the constructions of κατ' ἐκεῖνον τὸν

53 The other examples are *HG* 3.2.13, 3.2.21, 6.4.10. The 5th and final example of κατά⁺ᴬ with χρόνος in Xenophon, while also somewhat punctual, is better classified as distributive because of the presence of ἕκαστος: ὦν κατὰ χρόνον ἕκαστος ὑπὸ θεῶν ἐτιμήθη (*Cyn.* 1.3).
54 Kühner–Gerth, p. 478: 'zur Zeit, um'; Schwyzer–Debrunner, p. 478: "als *ungefähre* Zeitbestimmung"; and LSJ *s.v.* B.VII.2.: 'about'. (In none of these sources, to be sure, is this claimed as the *sole* temporal meaning of κατά⁺ᴬ.)
55 These are found at *HG* 6.1.2, 7.3.1, 7.4.12 (all σχεδόν περὶ τοῦτον τὸν χρόνον), and the verb in all three is a historical present (ἀφικνεῖται, συγκαλεῖ, πέμπει). That an approximative expression should favor the HP makes sense if we view the HP as marking an event that is presented as taking place particularly quickly (see George 2011), as an event of comparatively short duration would be harder to align precisely with the preceding temporal landmark (τοῦτον τὸν χρόνον). The fourth example stands out because χρόνος is plural, again an indication that the time in question is not narrowly circumscribed: περὶ τούτους τοὺς χρόνους (*HG* 1.1.33).

χρόνον (2×), κατὰ τοῦτον τὸν χρόνον (1×), and κατὰ τὸν αὐτὸν χρόνον (1×) are likely to refer to a more open-ended period of time than those with ἐν. This can be seen by contrasting the temporal constructions of κατά, which are closer to the prototypical punctual event type, with those of ἐν, which are more limitative.[56] Consider first the constructions with ἐκεῖνος as modifier. The two examples with κατά are (52) and the following:

(53) τοῖς δὲ Λακεδαιμονίοις **κατ᾽ ἐκεῖνον τὸν χρόνον** πονηρότατον ἦν τὸ ἱππικόν

And the most inferior part of the Spartans' army at that time was the cavalry
(*HG* 6.4.10)

Those with ἐν include (47) and these three:[57]

(54) εἰ μὴ οἱ πρὸ αὐτοῦ μαχόμενοι ἐπεκράτουν **ἐν ἐκείνῳ τῷ χρόνῳ**

If those fighting in front of him had not held the upper hand at that time
(*HG* 6.4.13)

(55) εἰ δὲ καὶ σὺ πολεμικῶν ἔμπειρος εἶ, ὦ Σιμωνίδη, καὶ ἤδη ποτὲ πολεμίᾳ φάλαγγι πλησίον ἀντετάξω, ἀναμνήσθητι ποῖον μέν τινα σῖτον ᾑροῦ **ἐν ἐκείνῳ τῷ χρόνῳ**, ποῖον δέ τινα ὕπνον ἐκοιμῶ

And if you too have any experience of war, Simonides, and were ever previously stationed near an enemy line, remember what sort of food you had at that time, and what sort of sleep you enjoyed (*Hier.* 6.7)

(56) ἐκεῖνα μέντοι ἃ **ἐν τῷ χρόνῳ ἐκείνῳ** ἔπραξε

However, all those things that he did at that time (*HG* 6.5.51)

Clearly, there is some overlap between the two: (47) and (53), both with superlatives, are particularly similar, at least superficially. But the examples of ἐν all fix the verbal event within a more bounded period of time than do those with κατά. In (54), the situation of the phrase within a negative conditional is akin to one common context for limitative expressions ('If this does not happen within ten days'); in (55), reference is made to what Simonides' experiences

---

[56] Despite the label, punctual constructions are actually more open-ended than limitative ones when they occur with a time noun like χρόνος: to say that an event took place 'at this time' simply synchronizes it, with no particular precision, with the events just mentioned; to say that it happened 'within this time' evokes the idea of the limits of the time period, which, accordingly, must be established somehow by other information in the text.

[57] The fifth example with ἐν falls into the same category as (56): καὶ ταῦτα μὲν αὖ περὶ τῶν Φλειασίων φυγάδων ἐν ἐκείνῳ τῷ χρόνῳ ἐπέπρακτο (*HG* 5.2.10).

had been under the circumstances of war just specified; in (56), we again have a familiar environment for the limitative, a clause with a semantically neutral verb wrapping up into a single bundle the events that took place within a given time frame. Furthermore, a close look at (47) shows that, even here, there is good reason to consider the expression with ἐν more bounded than that with κατά in (53): the presence of γε draws a line between the period when the Argives felt they were most powerful and other periods, when they did not.[58] By contrast, the time periods specified by κατά are more open-ended: in (52), the start of the *xenia* between Apollophanes and Agesilaus is not fixed within any specific time period; and in (53), the weakness of the Spartans' cavalry happens to be true at that point of time in question, but there is no contrast made with greater strength at other times.

So too with the temporal phrases κατά τὸν αὐτὸν χρόνον (1×) and ἐν τῷ αὐτῷ χρόνῳ (2×), the former is less bounded than the latter. In (57), we see κατά used to place an action in the fairly open-ended time frame set up by the preceding genitive absolute τούτων πραττομένων:

(57) τούτων δὲ πραττομένων ἐν τῇ Ἀσίᾳ ὑπὸ Δερκυλίδα, Λακεδαιμόνιοι **κατὰ τὸν αὐτὸν χρόνον**, πάλαι ὀργιζόμενοι τοῖς Ἠλείοις καὶ ὅτι ... ἐκ τούτων οὖν πάντων ὀργιζομένοις ἔδοξε τοῖς ἐφόροις καὶ τῇ ἐκκλησίᾳ σωφρονίσαι αὐτούς

And while these actions were carried out in Asia by Dercylidas, the Spartans, at the same time, long angry at the Eleans both because [omitted: two sections' worth of reasons for Spartan anger] ... ; so, angry for all these reasons, the ephors and assembly decided to punish them (*HG* 3.2.21, 23)

In the first of the two examples with ἐν, however, approximative κατά would not work, as the whole point of the sentence is that Socrates admires Ischomachus' ability to pursue multiple goals all at the same time; thus, the clear boundedness of a limitative construction is required:

(58) τὸ γὰρ **ἐν τῷ αὐτῷ χρόνῳ** συνεσκευασμένοις χρῆσθαι τοῖς τε πρὸς τὴν ὑγίειαν καὶ τοῖς πρὸς τὴν ῥώμην παρασκευάσμασι καὶ τοῖς εἰς τὸν πόλεμον ἀσκήμασι καὶ ταῖς τοῦ πλούτου ἐπιμελείαις, ταῦτα πάντα ἀγαστά μοι δοκεῖ εἶναι

---

[58] Admittedly, MSS D and F lack the γε, but the contrast is still present even if not made explicit with the particle.

That you engage at the same time in your exercises for health and for strength and your training for war and your diligent attention to money – all this seems marvelous to me (*Oec.* 11.19)

In the second example, the sentence that begins with ἐν τῷ αὐτῷ χρόνῳ is immediately preceded by one that opens with κατὰ τοῦτον τὸν καιρόν:

(59) **κατὰ δὲ τοῦτον τὸν καιρὸν** περὶ ἡλίου ἔκλειψιν Λυκόφρων ὁ Φεραῖος ... τοὺς ἐναντιουμένους αὐτῷ τῶν Θετταλῶν ... μάχῃ ἐνίκησε καὶ πολλοὺς ἀπέκτεινεν.

ἐν δὲ τῷ αὐτῷ χρόνῳ καὶ Διονύσιος ὁ Συρακόσιος τύραννος μάχῃ ἡττηθεὶς ὑπὸ Καρχηδονίων Γέλαν καὶ Καμάριναν ἀπώλεσε

And at this moment, about the time of the eclipse of the sun, Lycophron of Pherae defeated in battle those of the Thessalians who opposed him, and he killed many of them. And at the same time Dionysius, tyrant of Syracuse, was also defeated in battle by the Carthaginians and lost Gela and Camarina

(*HG* 2.3.4–5)

The first sentence is preceded by the coming to power of the Thirty, and the use of κατά makes sense if Xenophon does not want to synchronize the two events exactly.[59] In the second sentence, because these two different events are already in play, a broader time of reference has been established, so it is then easier to pinpoint the next event as taking place within this general period. Moreover, the switch from κατά to ἐν is also stylistically welcome in eliminating the need for starting two successive sentences with the same preposition.

As for the phrases with οὗτος, here the numbers are skewed far more in favor of ἐν, with only one example of κατά but nine with ἐν.[60] The phrases with ἐν fall into two broad categories. First, there

---

[59] We might expect καιρός to construe more with κατά than ἐν insofar as it is generally thought of as a decisive moment, but in fact, as seen in Ch. 2 (see n. 69), it is treated more as a bounded window of opportunity. Phrases with ἐν (...) καιρῷ occur 20× in Xenophon (11× without any modifier, 6× with οὗτος, 2× with τοιοῦτος, 1× with just the article), while κατά ... καιρόν only occurs 3× (2× with οὗτος, 1× with ὁ αὐτός). That the καιρός is not an instantaneous point but rather a (limited) period of time is nicely shown by *An.* 3.1.44: ἐν τοιούτῳ γὰρ καιρῷ ἐσμεν.

[60] The overall numbers are too low to be statistically significant, but it is perhaps no coincidence that, with the demonstratives, ἐν is more common, but with ὁ αὐτός, κατά is: if the temporal landmark is as exact as 'the same time' (as opposed to the vaguer 'at this *or* that time'), then there will be fewer circumstances in which a 2nd event can be precisely fit within it. In other words, even if we know that an event happened on the same day as another, we do not necessarily know that it happened at the same hour; but if we know it happened at the same hour (viewing hours in absolute terms, rather than as

are seven where the event described by the phrase is relatively discrete and punctual, often an arrival:[61]

(60) καὶ Ξενοφῶν μὲν σὺν τοῖς νεωτάτοις ἀνέβαινεν ἐπὶ τὸ ἄκρον, τοὺς δὲ ἄλλους ἐκέλευσεν ὑπάγειν ... καὶ προελθόντας κατὰ τὴν ὁδὸν ἐν τῷ ὁμαλῷ θέσθαι τὰ ὅπλα εἶπε. καὶ **ἐν τούτῳ τῷ χρόνῳ** ἦλθεν Ἀρχαγόρας ὁ Ἀργεῖος πεφευγώς

And Xenophon, together with his youngest soldiers, climbed up to the peak, and he ordered the others to move on ... and when they had advanced along the road he told them to take up a position under arms on the level ground. And at this time came Archagoras of Argos, in flight (*An.* 4.2.16–17)

Also typical of these examples is the lack of a break in the narrative between what precedes and follows: ἐν τούτῳ τῷ χρόνῳ simply marks the next stage of the action.[62] In the second category are two

---

indicating time on a repeating 24-hour cycle), we can be sure it happened on the same day. Thus one can have a construction of the sort: 'on the same day at about the same hour', but not 'on about the same day at the same hour'. As a result, we expect to find the equivalent of *at about*, κατά, more with the narrower time noun (ὁ αὐτός χρόνος), and the equivalent of *on*, ἐν, with the broader one (οὗτος or ἐκεῖνος ὁ χρόνος).

61 The most similar examples are found at *HG* 1.1.27 (ἠγγέλθη), *An.* 5.6.15 (καλὸν αὐτῷ ἐδόκει εἶναι χώραν καὶ δύναμιν ... προσκτήσασθαι πόλιν κατοικίσαντας: despite the imperfect ἐδόκει, the sentence still marks a fairly punctual decision taken by Xenophon), 7.6.1 (ἀφικνεῖται; the historical present is an additional sign of punctuality), *Cyr.* 3.1.7 (προσῄει), 6.2.1 (ἦλθον). Slightly different is *HG* 3.4.20: ἐν δὲ τούτῳ τῷ χρόνῳ καὶ ὁ ἐνιαυτὸς ἤδη ἀφ' οὗ ἐξέπλευσεν ὁ Ἀγησίλαος διελήλυθει. Here the verbal phrase does not refer to the action of an individual, but simply to the ending of the year, and is thus all the more instantaneous.

62 The narrative continuity is particularly clear in this example, where the connective particle is καί, rather than δέ (see Bakker 1993, 1997b (esp. ch. 4)). The other examples, to be sure, do have δέ (apart from *An.* 7.6.1, which has no connective particle), but there is still no strong break with the preceding content. In *HG* 1.1.27, a message is received by Syracusan generals, and those same Syracusans had already been active in the previous sentence. Prior to *HG* 3.4.20, Xenophon has told us of Agesilaus' activities, and this sentence provides the temporal landmark of the end of the year in reference to Agesilaus' expedition. With *An.* 5.6.15, there is at first glance more of a break, as 5.6.14 tells of the sending out of messengers – but, in fact, it merely resumes Xenophon's thoughts of 5.6.13, with the intervening sentence acting as a parenthesis. The best candidate for an expression with ἐν that provides a real narrative discontinuity is that found in *An.* 7.6.1 (it is no coincidence that it occurs in the first section of a chapter): ἐν τούτῳ τῷ χρόνῳ σχεδὸν ἤδη δύο μηνῶν ὄντων ἀφικνεῖται Χαρμῖνός τε ... καὶ Πολύνικος. Here, the arrival of the messengers brings new participants onto the scene. Still, this sentence is relatively closely anchored to what precedes through the inclusion of σχεδὸν ἤδη δύο μηνῶν ὄντων, which acts as a further temporal connection to the earlier events. In the final two examples, *Cyr.* 3.1.7 and 6.2.1, we again see the natural continuation of what has just preceded (in the former, Xenophon presents the next stage in the captivity of Tigranes; in the latter, he signals the narrative cohesion through the use of καί: ἦλθον δ' ἐν τούτῳ τῷ χρόνῳ καὶ παρὰ τοῦ Ἰνδοῦ χρήματα ἄγοντες). For more examples of how Xenophon's linguistic expressions are affected by the articulation of the text, see Buijs 2005, esp. ch. 4.

examples where the event is drawn out enough (in both cases, the verb modified is an imperfect) that the temporal phrase is almost best interpreted as durative:

(61) ἐν δὲ τούτῳ τῷ χρόνῳ οἱ Κερκυραῖοι οὕτω σφόδρα ἐπείνων ὥστε . . .

And at this time the Corcyraeans were so hungry that . . . (HG 6.2.15)

(62) οὕτω δὴ γιγνώσκων πρῶτον μὲν τὰ περὶ τοὺς θεοὺς μᾶλλον ἐκπονοῦντα ἐπεδείκνυεν ἑαυτὸν ἐν τούτῳ τῷ χρόνῳ, ἐπεὶ εὐδαιμονέστερος ἦν

With this in mind, in the first place he showed himself more assiduous in his attending to the gods at this time, since he was more fortunate (Cyr. 8.1.23)

There is an even stronger connection between the preceding sections and that with the ἐν-phrase in these two examples, as the long-lasting events described in these two passages have what precedes as a precondition: in (61), military actions against Corcyra are what lead to famine there; in (62), it is Cyrus' views on the proper behavior of a ruler that lead to his increased observance of religious ritual.

The expression with κατὰ τοῦτον τὸν χρόνον is somewhat different:

(63) ἐτύγχανε δὲ κατὰ τοῦτον τὸν χρόνον καὶ Φαρνάβαζος πρὸς Τισσαφέρνην ἀφιγμένος

And Pharnabazus too, as it happened, was visiting Tissaphernes at this time (HG 3.2.13)

What distinguishes it from the examples with ἐν is that there is less of a connection between the host clause and the preceding section. True, there is the continued presence of Tissaphernes as an actor in the narrative (signaled in this sentence with καί), but it is presented as mere chance (ἐτύγχανε) that Pharnabazus is visiting him, and this looser connection is consistent with the use of κατά instead of ἐν. While this example is certainly not enough on its own to establish a difference between the two prepositions, the combined weight of the contrasts seen in examples (52) through (63) suggests that κατά[+A] does indeed introduce a temporally less precise phrase than does ἐν.

It remains to consider briefly those constructions with ἐν that border on the durative type.[63] We have seen several examples already, such as (61) and (62), where the verbal event seems to last for the entire duration of the temporal phrase.[64] Should such phrases be classified as durative in the final analysis? Probably not: first, the construction with ἐν^{+D} is strongly associated with the limitative or punctual types elsewhere, and it would be uneconomical to attribute a durative value to it here. Still, as has already been seen, languages need not have a one-to-one relationship between event-type and the surface expression, so the better reason not to view these as durative constructions lies in the difference between them and the true durative expressions with the accusative of time: the latter do not have the telic boundedness associated with the limitative type. This can most easily be seen by comparing constructions with like modifiers. First, if we consider only constructions where χρόνος is modified by ὀλίγος or πολύς, then there is far less scope for confusion between the two, as all the expressions with ἐν ὀλίγῳ or πολλῷ χρόνῳ are clearly limitative. The contrast between the two is nicely illustrated in the following clause:

(64) ὁπόταν χρημάτων μὲν ἕνεκα παρῶσιν οἱ φυλάττοντες, ἐξῇ δ' αὐτοῖς **ἐν ὀλίγῳ χρόνῳ** πολὺ πλείω λαβεῖν ἀποκτείνασι τὸν τύραννον ἢ ὅσα **πολὺν χρόνον** φυλάττοντες παρὰ τοῦ τυράννου λαμβάνουσιν

Whenever the guards are present because of the money and it is possible for them in a short time to take far more money by killing the tyrant than they get from the tyrant if they protect him for a long time (*Hier.* 6.11)

Here, the aspectual contrast between perfective λαβεῖν and imperfective φυλάττοντες ... λαμβάνουσιν highlights the distinction between the limitative construction with ἐν, which must be telic, and the durative one with the accusative of time πολὺν χρόνον, which must modify an atelic verb. With other modifiers, the contextual clues may not point as clearly to a limitative reading with ἐν ... χρόνῳ, but the limitative reading is always possible, and,

---

[63] The constructions with ἐπί$^{+A}$ and διά$^{+G}$ are discussed on pp. 122–3 and 124 respectively.

[64] Other potential durative examples with ἐν are *HG* 1.4.15, 6.4.13 (= ex. (54)), 7.1.25 (= ex. (47)), *An.* 2.3.22 (= ex. (65)), *Cyr.* 8.8.20, *Hier.* 6.7, *Vect.* 4.25.

given its function elsewhere, the presence of ἐν makes it the preferred reading:

(65) ἐπεὶ μέντοι ἤδη αὐτὸν ἑωρῶμεν ἐν δεινῷ ὄντα, ἠσχύνθημεν καὶ θεοὺς καὶ ἀνθρώπους προδοῦναι αὐτόν, **ἐν τῷ πρόσθεν χρόνῳ** παρέχοντες ἡμᾶς αὐτοὺς εὖ ποιεῖν

However, when we saw that he was in danger, we were ashamed, before gods and men, to betray him, since we kept recommending ourselves in earlier time for him to benefit us (*An.* 2.3.22)

At first glance, we might expect a durative construction here, given the atelicity one would generally associate with the present participle παρέχοντες. But the use of ἐν τῷ πρόσθεν χρόνῳ shows that a telic interpretation is required – a bounded number of discrete instances of self-recommendation – and that the imperfective participle is here triggered by iterativity.

Summary

Apart from the durative expressions with the accusative of time, the construction found most often with χρόνος is ἐν[+D] (39×). These phrases are most often limitative, but also extend into the punctual category. Both the genitive (4×) and dative of time (5×)[65] are also found, but only rarely; the former is confined to prototypical limitative phrases, the latter to punctual ones. The other constructions that compete with ἐν ... χρόνῳ are those with περί[+A] and κατά[+A] (4× each). The former is clearly approximative, the latter somewhat more ambiguously so.

Xenophon and Thucydides: a comparison

At this point, we can step back and compare Xenophon's and Thucydides' usage to get a rough indication of the amount of variation we can expect to find from author to author. The overwhelming impression is one of similarity.

1. **Durative** constructions are essentially the same in both authors: the accusative of time is the default construction; ἐπί[+A] is often used when the time noun is modified by a cardinal number, and

---

[65] Two of these are best seen as datives of degree of difference.

$\delta\iota\acute{\alpha}^{+G}$ when the author wishes to underline that the verbal event lasted for the entire extent of the time.

2. The difference between the **punctual and limitative** constructions of calendrical time nouns (day, month, year) and those of non-calendrical time nouns (night, summer, winter) is present in both authors, although it is less obvious in Xenophon than it is in Thucydides. With the **calendrical time nouns**, both authors:

a. use the dative exclusively for punctual constructions.

b. use the genitive for the whole continuum of distributive, habitual, and modal constructions, as well as for limitative constructions, though these amount to less than half the examples.

c. use $\dot{\epsilon}\nu^{+D}$ primarily for limitative constructions; in Thucydides, $\dot{\epsilon}\nu^{+D}$ and the genitive are roughly equally common; in Xenophon, $\dot{\epsilon}\nu^{+D}$ has largely superseded the genitive of time in this function.

With the **non-calendrical time nouns**, both authors largely avoid the dative of time in favor of the genitive of time or $\dot{\epsilon}\nu$ in punctual constructions; that said, Xenophon has so few punctual constructions with $\theta\acute{\epsilon}\rho\sigma\varsigma$ (1× genitive) and $\chi\epsilon\iota\mu\acute{\omega}\nu$ (2× $\dot{\epsilon}\nu^{+D}$, 1× genitive), that dividing the time nouns into these two categories is largely based on extrapolating from Xenophon's treatment of $\nu\acute{\upsilon}\xi$ and Thucydides' treatment of the seasons.

3. In both authors, $\chi\rho\acute{\sigma}\nu\sigma\varsigma$ occurs most often as an accusative of time in durative expressions, and its second most common construction is with $\dot{\epsilon}\nu^{+D}$. The latter phrases are most often limitative (especially in Thucydides). Both authors use $\chi\rho\acute{\sigma}\nu\sigma\varsigma$ in approximative constructions with $\kappa\alpha\tau\acute{\alpha}^{+A}$ and $\pi\epsilon\rho\acute{\iota}^{+A}$.

Still, within this general picture of similarity, there remain differences:

1. While the durative constructions are extremely similar in both authors, the different ideas expressed by the two authors mean that different constructions come to the fore: Thucydides, who has more opportunity for giving precise lengths of time, uses $\dot{\epsilon}\pi\acute{\iota}^{+A}$ more than Xenophon; Xenophon's content, in turn, elicits a greater use of $\delta\iota\acute{\alpha}^{+G}$, both in distributive expressions and in circumstances where it must be emphasized that an event lasted for the entire length of time denoted by the phrase.

2. With the punctual and limitative constructions of the non-calendrical time nouns, there is a clearer division of labor between the genitive and ἐν in Thucydides (the former preferred in punctual constructions, the latter in limitative and modal ones) than in Xenophon (both are used freely in modal-habitual constructions, but when the temporal construction bears particular semantic weight, ἐν is favored). Furthermore, Xenophon has an additional option with νύξ not found at all in Thucydides: the isolated adverb νύκτωρ.

3. Conversely, Xenophon only uses ὑπό⁺ᴬ once in a temporal construction (with νύκτα, *Ages.* 2.19), whereas Thucydides uses it frequently not only with νύκτα, but also as an approximative marker with χρόνος.

As the similarities are so much more pronounced than the differences, in turning to the next authors in the study, we can now focus more on the latter, allowing a faster run through the data.

Plato

We will concentrate on four questions that are raised by the evidence from Thucydides and Xenophon, largely because they involve expressions where there are discrepancies between the two authors. (i) Do ἐπί⁺ᴬ and διά⁺ᴳ show the same difference from the accusative of time as already seen? (ii) Do different time nouns behave differently in preferring the genitive or dative in punctual expressions? (iii) Where do expressions with ἐν fall? Are they more like the genitive or more like the dative? And does νύκτωρ show a more distinct usage than it does in Xenophon? (iv) Does Plato shed any light on the use of the different approximative constructions?

Durative expressions in Plato

The data are given Table 13.

These numbers offer few surprises. Once again, the accusative of time is the default durative marker, with διά⁺ᴳ and ἐπί⁺ᴬ as occasional alternatives. Here too διά⁺ᴳ is found in contexts where it is emphasized that the event lasts for the entire length of time expressed by the phrase. For instance, in three of the five examples

Table 13. *Durative expressions in Plato*

Time noun	Accusative of time	διά$^{+G}$	ἐπί$^{+A}$
ἡμέρα	23	5	1
νύξ	11	3	–
μήν	–	1	1
θέρος	–	–	–
χειμών	–	1	–
ἔτος	51^a	[4]^b	–
ἐνιαυτός	20	[1]^b	2
χρόνος	92	[9]^b	5

Note:
^{a} This includes three slightly anomalous constructions, *R*. 414e7, *Lg*.
656e5 (= ex. (110)), 677d2, discussed below, where the accusative of time
is used in expressions with the sense '*x* years ago'.

^{b} In contrast with διά$^{+G}$-phrases with other time nouns, none of those with
ἔτους, ἐτῶν, or ἐνιαυτοῦ is actually durative. Only one of the nine with
χρόνος is, and it is an anomaly.

with ἡμέρα, the noun is modified by ὅλη or πᾶσα (*Ly*. 208e5, *Lg*.
790c8, 947c2), and in a fourth, the phrase occurs in a sequence
explicitly describing the need for officials to replace one another in
a continuous succesion:

(66) δεῖ δὴ **δι' ἡμέρας** τε εἰς νύκτα καὶ ἐκ νυκτὸς συνάπτειν πρὸς ἡμέραν ἄρχοντας
ἄρχουσιν, φρουροῦντάς τε φρουροῦσιν διαδεχομένους ἀεὶ καὶ παραδιδόντας
μηδέποτε λήγειν

It is necessary that one official follow another throughout the day into night
and from night-time on towards day, that guards follow guards in continuous
succession and never cease handing the watch over to the next (*Lg*. 758a8)

Furthermore, all three of the phrases with διὰ νυκτός are paired with
expressions for daytime as well, indicating particular emphasis on the
uninterrupted progression of the event in question.[66] The expressions
with ἐπί$^{+A}$ also share features with those seen in the other authors: in
the one example with ἡμέρα, the time noun is modified by πολλάς; of
the five with χρόνος, the time noun is twice modified by πολύν and
once by πάντα. That the choice of expression may to some extent be

---

[66] The three occur at *R*. 343b7, *Criti*. 117e8, and *Lg*. 790c7. In the last example, νύξ is
further modified by πᾶσα.

correlated with the modifier is also suggested by the other two phrases with χρόνος, which have only τινα as a modifier, one that does not occur once in the ninety-two accusatives of time.[67] The phrases with μήν and ἐνιαυτός also resemble another class of examples previously seen, those in which ἐπί[+A] has a forward-looking reference that comes close to expressing goal, especially in a distributive context (cf. (4) and (5) from earlier in the chapter):[68]

(67) τὸ δὲ δωδέκατον μέρος αὐτῶν **ἐπὶ δώδεκα μῆνας** νείμαντας

Allotting the twelfth part of [the *boulētai*] for each of the twelve months
(*Lg.* 758b7)

There remain the non-durative expressions with διά[+G] in square brackets in the table above. These too are largely variations on the distributive type and thus mirror usage already seen. Of the nine phrases with χρόνος, all but one are of the form διὰ χρόνου and indicate that the action takes place after the passage of time. Normally, these can be translated 'after some time',[69] but occasionally a vestige remains of this preposition's use to indicate path:

(68) οὐ μὴν ἐβουλήθην παραχρῆμα εἰπεῖν· **διὰ χρόνου** γὰρ οὐχ ἱκανῶς ἐμεμνήμην

Yet I didn't want to say it on the spot, for, through the passage of time, I didn't remember it very well (*Ti.* 26a1)

The odd one out is the following:

(69) τὸ δὲ ἀληθές ἐστι τῶν περὶ γῆν κατ᾿ οὐρανὸν ἰόντων παράλλαξις καὶ **διὰ μακρῶν χρόνων** γιγνομένη τῶν ἐπὶ γῆς πυρὶ πολλῷ φθορά

But the truth is that there is an alteration in the bodies that revolve through the sky around the earth, and, at great intervals, a destruction of what is on earth takes place in a great conflagration (*Ti.* 22d2)

Because διά[+G] so often marks durative constructions, some translators have treated it thus in this passage too (e.g. Zeyl: "across vast stretches

---

[67] That said, πολύς and πᾶς do both occur modifying χρόνος as an accusative of time. Clearly they do not trigger the use of ἐπί[+A], but they are particularly compatible with it, just as πολύς is in Thucydides. Also, as in both Thucydides and Xenophon, these modifiers are preposed.

[68] The two examples with ἐνιαυτός are at *Lg.* 945b4 and 955e3. In the former it is again a question of officials being appointed for a period of time; in the latter, the distributive force is reinforced by ἑκάστοτε.

[69] For example, *Phdr.* 247d3, *Chrm.* 153a2, *Euthd.* 273c1.

of time" (1997: 1230)). But as διά$^{+G}$ with χρόνος regularly marks an *interval* of time, this is the better way to interpret the phrase in (69) – a reading, moreover, that fits in well with the cyclical nature of the content of the *Timaeus*, a dialogue in which the root κυκλ- occurs no fewer than thirty-eight times.[70] The phrases with δι' ἔτους or ἐτῶν,[70] especially example (70), provide good parallels. Three of the four examples are modified by an ordinal number and are of the type 'every *x*th year';[71] so too the one phrase with δι' ἐνιαυτοῦ (*Criti.* 119d2). The fourth comes closer to the standard διὰ χρόνου phrases in meaning 'after an interval of time':

(70) πάλιν **δι' εἰωθότων ἐτῶν** ὥσπερ νόσημα ἥκει φερόμενον αὐτοῖς ῥεῦμα
οὐράνιον

Again, after the usual number of years, there comes, like a disease, a heavenly flood rushing upon them (*Ti.* 23a7)

All in all, the data from Plato conform to the patterns found in Thucydides and Xenophon as well: accusative of time as the default construction; ἐπί$^{+A}$ used with a limited number of modifiers, especially πολύς; and διά$^{+G}$ emphasizing that the event lasts for the entire extent of time – except with χρόνος or when modified with ordinal numbers, when it instead marks that an event occurs after an (often regularly repeating) interval of time.

Punctual and limitative expressions in Plato

The figures are set out in Table 14.

As in Xenophon, these data support the view that the calendrical nouns behave differently from the non-calendrical nouns, but they are hardly conclusive in their own right, because there are so few punctual constructions with the non-calendrical nouns. What is more, only two of the three phrases with νύξ that I have labeled punctual are prototypically so:

(71) τεκμαίρομαι δὲ ἔκ τινος ἐνυπνίου ὃ ἑώρακα ὀλίγον πρότερον **ταύτης τῆς**
νυκτός

---

[70] Both Taylor (1929: 19) and Cornford (1937: 14) translate it 'at long intervals'.
[71] These are *Min.* 319e3 and *Lg.* 624b2 (δι' ἐνάτου ἔτους) and *Lg.* 834e7 (διὰ πέμπτων ἐτῶν).

Table 14. *Punctual and limitative expressions in Plato*

	genitive	dative	ἐν^{+D}	νύκτωρ
ἡμέρα	14× distrib. 6× limitative 3× modal	16× punc. 1× limitv.^{a} 1× durative	5× limitative	–
μήν	5× distributive 1× limitv.	3× punc.	1× limitative.^{b}	–
ἔτος	7× limitative 1× distributive	3× punc.^{c}	8× limitative	–
ἐνιαυτός	2× distributive	2× punc.	1× limitative	–
νύξ	5× modal 2× limitative 2× punctual	–	1× habitual	18× hab.-mod. 1× punc.
θέρος	8× hab.-mod.	–	–	–
χειμών	8× hab.-mod.	–	2× hab.-mod.	–

Note:

^{a} While potentially limitative, this construction (ex. (77)) is probably better labeled as punctual as well; see the discussion below.

^{b} I count ἐν τῷ τοῦ Πλούτωνος μηνὶ τῷ δωδεκάτῳ κατὰ τὸν νόμον ἀποδίδοντας (*Lg.* 828d1), as more a spatial than a temporal construction ('placing the former celebration by law in the twelfth month'), but it could be added here as an additional, habitual construction.

^{c} I omit a fourth example at *Men.* 81b9 because it is a quotation from Pindar.

And I conclude this from a dream which I saw[72] a little earlier during this night (*Cri.* 44a7)

(72) τῆς γὰρ παρελθούσης νυκτὸς ταυτησί, ἔτι βαθέος ὄρθρου, Ἱπποκράτης ... τὴν θύραν τῇ βακτηρίᾳ πάνυ σφόδρα ἔκρουε

During this past night, when it was still early dawn, Hippocrates came banging on the door rather loudly with his staff (*Prt.* 310a8)

---

[72] In passing, note the remarkable combination of the perfect of ὁράω with a past-time punctual phrase (commented on by neither Stallbaum (1846) nor Burnet (1924)). This construction is often used as a diagnostic to show that a perfect tense has started to be used as a simple past: ^{x}*I have seen it yesterday* is not grammatical, but *ich habe es gestern gesehen* is (Comrie 1976: 54–5). Cf. (98) in Demosthenes.

These two examples stand apart from the other temporal expressions with νύξ, θέρος, and χειμών in that the demonstratives modifying the time noun show that the phrase in question indicates the specific night on which the event takes place. They are thus closer to the sort of ταύτῃ τῇ ἡμέρᾳ construction where the dative might particularly be expected than the one punctual construction with νύκτωρ:

(73) ἐμβαλὼν εἰς ἅμαξαν, **νύκτωρ** ἐξαγαγὼν ἀπέσφαξέν τε καὶ ἠφάνισεν ἀμφοτέρους

After putting them on the wagon and leading them out at night, [Archelaus] slaughtered them and did away with the bodies (*Grg.* 471b5)

While νύκτωρ does not explicitly say which night the event took place, the event in question is a one-off historical event, and the phrase does little more than note the time at which Archelaus' victims were led out, so the punctual label is appropriate. In short, punctual constructions with the non-calendrical time nouns are extremely rare in Plato – but, given that the two best examples have the genitive of time, and that none of these nouns ever occurs in the dative of time – the data still suggest that day, month, and year are treated differently from other time nouns.

Perhaps the most interesting question raised by these calendrical nouns lies in the behavior of the limitative type. For, were it not for the split of the limitative constructions between the genitive of time and ἐν^{+D}, one could very nearly summarize the upper half of the chart with the rule: use the dative of time for the punctual type, the genitive for everything else. As it happens, the difference between the two constructions in Plato is closer to that seen in Thucydides than to the usage of Xenophon: the genitive is preferred in constructions that somehow point to the future, ἐν^{+D} in those that look back to the past. To begin with ἡμέρα, both limitative constructions with morphological futures have the genitive of time.[73] A further three of the six genitives of time

---

[73] These are οὐ τοίνυν τῆς ἐπιούσης ἡμέρας οἶμαι αὐτὸ ἥξειν ἀλλὰ τῆς ἑτέρας (*Cri.* 44a5) and τοῦτο δ' ἔσεσθαι μάλα ὀλίγων ἡμερῶν (*1 Alc.* 105b1).

are in directive expressions that also look forward.[74] The final limitative genitive of ἡμέρα occurs in the present-tense statement of a general truth; that is, it is not bound to a specific occurrence and so is contextually similar to the legal apodoses in which the directives occur.[75] What we do *not* find with the genitive of time are the expressions with past-tense verbs referring to one-off events that account for three of the five limitative expressions with ἐν⁺ᴰ.[76] The remaining two examples, while they do occur in the *Laws*, do not set a legal time limit for the accomplishment of an action in the way that the directives of note 74 do, and are instead closer to the general truth cited in note 75.[77] The two limitative expressions with μήν also split along these lines: the genitive, at *Lg.* 915d4, occurs in the same imperative construction as one of the examples with ἡμέρα, and the phrase with ἐν almost counts as a punctual expression in its reference to a past time.[78] With ἔτος, however, the picture is more complicated, as it makes a difference whether or not the verb is negated. The two examples of affirmative past-tense limitative expressions again

---

[74] Two of these are imperatives: τριάκοντα ἡμερῶν ἀπὸ ταύτης τῆς ἡμέρας λαβὼν ἀπίτω τὰ ἑαυτοῦ (*Lg.* 915b7) and ἀναγέτω ... ἡμερῶν τριάκοντα (*Lg.* 915d4). The third is also found in a legal context, forbidding merchants from changing their prices: ταύτης τῆς ἡμέρας μὴ τιμήσῃ πλέονος μηδὲ ἐλάττονος "he must not assess it as worth more or less within the course of the day" (*Lg.* 917c2).

[75] Of Love: ἀλλὰ τοτὲ μὲν τῆς αὐτῆς ἡμέρας θάλλει τε καὶ ζῇ, ὅταν εὐπορήσῃ, τοτὲ δὲ ἀποθνῄσκει (*Smp.* 203e2).

[76] These are (a) Socrates' rhetorical rejection of the possibility that the events of his trial invalidated his previous lines of reasoning: ἢ πᾶσαι ἡμῖν ἐκεῖναι αἱ πρόσθεν ὁμολογίαι ἐν ταῖσδε ταῖς ὀλίγαις ἡμέραις ἐκκεχυμέναι εἰσίν ... ; (*Cri.* 49a9); (b) a description of what happened when the universe started rotating in its present direction: τὸ τοῦ νεκροῦ σῶμα τὰ αὐτὰ ταῦτα πάσχον παθήματα διὰ τάχους ἄδηλον ἐν ὀλίγαις ἡμέραις διεφθείρετο (*Plt.* 271a1); and (c) Datis' defeat of the Eretrians, in the funeral oration of the *Menexenus*: τούτους ἐχειρώσατο μὲν ἐν τρισὶν ἡμέραις (*Mx.* 240b4).

[77] These are θειότατα δὲ δῶρα ὄρνιθές τε καὶ ἀγάλματα ὅσαπερ ἂν ἐν μιᾷ ζωγράφος ἡμέρᾳ εἰς ἀποτελῇ (*Lg.* 956b2) and χῶμα δὲ μὴ χοῦν ὑψηλότερον πέντε ἀνδρῶν ἔργον, ἐν πένθ' ἡμέραις ἀποτελούμενον (*Lg.* 958e7), both sumptuary laws aimed more at limiting the size of an object than at giving a deadline.

[78] The latter is ἀγαπῴη ἂν ἐν ὀγδόῳ μηνὶ ὅσα ἔσπειρεν τέλος λαβόντα "he would be happy if what he had sowed reached its end in the eighth month" (*Phdr.* 276b7). It is true that this example also occurs in the broader context of a general truth, but here the use of the ordinal number in a phrase modifying the aorist participle λαβόντα emphasizes the success of the planting as a point on a particular time-line.

PLATO

have ἐν^{+D}.[79] The prepositional construction is also found in the affirmative examples of the two general statements and even in one future-tense passage.[80] By contrast, all seven examples with the genitive of time are negated, and these range from negated perfects[81] and an aorist[82] to two negated general statements,[83] a future,[84] and a purpose clause.[85] What prevents us, however, from setting up a simple rule that negative expressions take the genitive, affirmative ones ἐν^{+D} is that there are also three negated verbs with the prepositional construction. One of these can be explained away fairly easily:

(74) ἐξ ὧν **οὐκ ἐν πολλοῖς ἔτεσιν** αὐτοί καὶ παῖδες καὶ σύμπασα ἡ πόλις ἀντ' ἐλευθέρων πολλάκις ἔλαθον αὐτοὺς γενόμενοι δοῦλοι

As a result, in a few years, they themselves and their children and the whole city, instead of being free, have often become slaves without their knowing it   (*Plt.* 307e10)

Here, the negative only has scope over πολλοῖς, and the verb itself remains affirmative. In the second, the modifier may have played some role in the selection of the prepositional construction:

(75) πρὸς τάχος δὲ ἢ κάλλος ἀπηκριβῶσθαί τισιν, οἷς μὴ φύσις ἐπέσπευσεν **ἐν τοῖς τεταγμένοις ἔτεσιν**, χαίρειν ἐᾶν

But any whose nature has not hastened them in the assigned years so as to be polished in speed or in penmanship, one must let slide (*Lg.* 810b4)

The genitives of time of ἔτος have a fairly restricted set of modifiers: 3× δέκα, 2× πολλῶν, 1× τοσούτων (all preposed) and

---

79 These are οὐδὲ ἐν ὀλίγῳ χρόνῳ ἀναγκασθεὶς βουλεύσασθαι, ἀλλ' ἐν ἔτεσιν ἑβδομήκοντα, ἐν οἷς ἐξῆν σοι ἀπιέναι (*Cri.* 52e3) and πολλῶν οὖν γεγονότων καὶ μεγάλων κατακλυσμῶν ἐν τοῖς ἐνακισχιλίοις ἔτεσι (*Criti.* 111a8).
80 These are ὥστε καὶ ἔριν πολλοῖς παρέσχηκεν μὴ γίγνεσθαι τά γ' ἀνθρώπινα μήκη διπλάσια ἀπὸ πέντε ἐτῶν ἐν τοῖς λοιποῖς εἴκοσιν ἔτεσιν αὐξανόμενα (*Lg.* 788d7), ἐὰν δ' ἐν τοῖς ἔτεσι τούτοις αὐτῷ συμβῇ λόγου ἀξίῳ πρὸς εὐεργεσίαν τῆς πόλεως γεγονέναι τινὰ ἱκανήν (*Lg.* 850b6), and τοῖς μέλλουσιν ἐν τρισὶν ἔτεσιν τὸ τῆς μουσικῆς χρήσιμον ἐκλήψεσθαι διὰ τάχους (*Lg.* 812e4).
81 These are οὐκ οἶσθ' ὅτι πολλῶν ἐτῶν Ἀγάθων ἐνθάδε οὐκ ἐπιδεδήμηκεν ... ; (*Smp.* 172c4) and καὶ λέγω ὅτι οὐδεὶς μέ πω ἠρώτηκε καινὸν οὐδὲν πολλῶν ἐτῶν (*Grg.* 448a3).
82 ἐγὼ δὲ τοσούτων ἐτῶν οὐδὲ προσεῖπον (*I Alc.* 106d3).
83 εἰς μὲν γὰρ τὸ αὐτὸ ὅθεν ἥκει ἡ ψυχὴ ἑκάστη οὐκ ἀφικνεῖται ἐτῶν μυρίων (*Phdr.* 248e6), ἄν τις δέκα ἐτῶν μὴ ἐπιθυμήσῃ θετὸν ὑὸν ποιήσασθαι (*Lg.* 929c7).
84 εἶπεν ὅτι δέκα μὲν ἐτῶν οὐχ ἥξουσιν (*Lg.* 642e2).
85 ἵνα αὐτοῦ δέκα ἐτῶν μὴ ἀκούσειαν τῆς φωνῆς (*Grg.* 516d7).

163

ι × μυρίων (postposed). By contrast, the expressions with ἐν show more variety: preposed, we find τρισίν, πέντε, πολλοῖς, which parallel the genitives of time, but also τοῖς ἐνακισχιλίοις, τοῖς λοιποῖς εἴκοσιν, and (here in (75)) τοῖς τεταγμένοις, and, postposed, ἑβδομήκοντα and τοῖς ... τούτοις. All in all, the genitives of time give the impression of being somewhat more fossilized in set phrases than the expressions with ἐν; this may have led to the choice of the latter construction in (75). The third and final example of ἐν in a negated clause is difficult to interpret definitively:

(76) ἐὰν δὲ κατ᾽ ἄστυ μὲν μὴ μηδὲ κατ᾽ ἀγορὰν χρῆται, κατ᾽ ἀγροὺς δὲ φανερῶς, μὴ
προστυχὴς δὲ **ἐν πέντε ἔτεσιν** γένηταί τις, τῶν πέντε ἐξελθόντων ἐτῶν, μηκέτι
τοῦ λοιποῦ χρόνου ἐξέστω τούτῳ τοῦ τοιούτου ἐπιλαβέσθαι

And if he uses it neither in the city nor in the market, but openly in the
countryside, and no one approaches him about it within five years, when the
five years have passed, no longer in future time should it be allowed for him
to take possession of such a thing (*Lg.* 954d5)

A couple of anomalies in this passage may have led to the use of ἐν even with a negative expression. First, the negatives themselves are unusual: the first μή in the sentence is postponed after the phrase that it negates and so would normally precede, κατ᾽ ἄστυ, presumably to highlight the contrast with the κατ᾽ ἀγρούς of the δέ clause. More importantly, the placement of the Wackernagel particle δέ after προστυχής suggests that μὴ προστυχής is to be taken prosodically as a single unit.[86] In that case, the scope of μή may again, as in (74), be limited enough for this not to count as a negated example where we otherwise expect the genitive of time. It is also possible that, given the presence of two other genitive phrases, τῶν πέντε ἐξελθόντων ἐτῶν and τοῦ λοιποῦ χρόνου, a third might have been stylistically undesirable.[87] All in all, Plato offers a remarkably

---

[86] For the (to some extent limited) utility of postpositives in determining the boundaries of intonation units, see Dik (1995: 31–7, 2007: 17–22).

[87] These two phrases are interesting in their own right. The first is apparently a genitive absolute even though the participle is, superficially at least, in attributive position; but as only a genitive absolute is semantically plausible in this context, it is best to take ἐτῶν as a clarifying afterthought, τῶν πέντε ἐξελθόντων on its own being a well-formed absolute. The second phrase is a limitative construction of the sort that might potentially take ἐν[+D], but, compared with the preceding ἐν πέντε ἔτεσιν, this is the one that is more likely to have the genitive of time as the modifier λοιπός inherently looks forward to the future.

complicated picture in the distribution of the limitative constructions between the genitive of time and ἐν^{+D}. No absolute rules can
be established, but certain conditions favor one or the other: the
genitive of time refers more to the future, ἐν more to the past; the
genitive is preferred in negative phrases, ἐν in affirmative ones.

The other puzzle posed by the calendrical nouns is that the dative
of ἡμέρα is once used in an apparent limitative construction, once in
a durative one:

(77) μιᾷ μὲν ἡμέρᾳ πάσας τὰς τῶν πολεμίων ἐλόντες ναῦς, πολλὰς δὲ καὶ ἄλλας
νικήσαντες

Having captured all the enemies' ships on one day, and winning the battle on
many others (*Mx.* 243a8)

(78) ἆρ᾽ οὖν, εἶπον, οὐ ταῖς μὲν πρώταις ἡμέραις τε καὶ χρόνῳ προσγελᾷ τε καὶ
ἀσπάζεται πάντας ... ;

So, I said, isn't it the case that, during the first days and period of time, he
smiles at and welcomes everyone ... ? (*R.* 566d8)

Taken on its own, μιᾷ ἡμέρᾳ in example (77) looks like a prototypical limitative phrase: a multiplicity of events takes place
(πᾶσας ... ἐλόντες ναῦς), and these are limited to a bounded
time frame (μιᾷ ... ἡμέρᾳ). The wider context, however, shows
that this is better seen as punctual: the emphasis is not on the fact
that *all* the ships were captured on (only) *one* day, but rather in
the gentle contrast between the one day when they captured all
the ships, and all the other days when they won without doing so.
Because μιᾷ ἡμέρᾳ thus singles out which day an event took
place, rather than confining an event to that day, the punctual
dative of time is the natural expression to use. The dative in (78)
is more unusual, as the noun is plural, which is extremely rare
with the dative of time: there are no parallels at all in
Thucydides. Still, the one example of a plural dative of time in
Xenophon (example (7) above) is sufficiently similar (in both,
the phrase is ταῖς πρώταις ἡμέραις) that it is probably best to
accept that Attic Greek of this period could on rare occasions use
this sort of construction in a habitual-modal expression – perhaps
motivated by the ordinal number, which is usually associated
with the punctual type.

It remains to take one last look at νύκτωρ: we have already seen that its punctual construction differs from those with the genitive νυκτός by being closer to the modal type. But νυκτός itself can occur in modal expressions: is there any difference between the two? In fact, there is very little. Both νυκτός and νύκτωρ are paired with μεθ' ἡμέραν; both occur freely in both positive and negative expressions; both occur nearly always with present-tense verbs.[88] The main distinction seems to be one of distribution: of the sixteen modal-habitual examples of νύκτωρ, eleven occur in the *Laws*; of the five with νυκτός, only one does. That νύκτωρ is particularly common in the *Laws* is probably no coincidence, given the nature of the texts in which it is found most frequently. A crude estimate of an author's propensity for νύκτωρ can be made by dividing the instances of νύκτωρ in the corpus by the total number of examples of νυκτ-. Major fifth- and fourth-century authors line up as shown in Table 15.

While νύκτωρ is extremely rare in tragedy and completely absent from Herodotus and Thucydides, it is particularly common in oratory and in comedy – a distribution that makes it look sensitive to genre and dialect, avoided as it is by those writing Ionic or Ionicizing Attic. Accordingly, it makes sense that it is in the comparatively parochial and legalistic *Laws* that Plato uses it the most.

Expressions with χρόνος in Plato

Plato, as a philosopher, apparently had less reason to speak of the occurrence of an event at an inexact time than did the historians: he never uses περί[+A] with time nouns in approximative expressions.[89] As for χρόνος in particular, the accusative is again the most common construction (93×), with ἐν[+D] coming in a close second (88×). While the accusative is limited to durative, atelic situations, ἐν[+D]

---

[88] νυκτός τε καὶ μεθ' ἡμέραν (*Ti*. 71a6), οὔτε νυκτὸς ... οὔτε μεθ' ἡμέραν (*Phdr*. 251e1); νύκτωρ τε καὶ μεθ' ἡμέραν (*Lg*. 633c3), νύκτωρ τε καὶ μεθ' ἡμέραν (*Lg*. 779a2), οὔτε νύκτωρ οὔτε μεθ' ἡμέραν (*1 Alc*. 106e9); νύκτωρ and μεθ' ἡμέραν occur at greater distance from each other, but still in parallel, at *R*. 516a9 and *Lg*. 674b5 and 854a7. When the two words are paired right next to each other with correlatives like οὔτε ... οὔτε, νύκτωρ or νυκτός always comes first.
[89] When Plato does use this preposition with a time noun (e.g. *Smp*. 188a8), it has the sense 'concerning'.

166

Table 15. Νύκτωρ *in fifth- and fourth-century authors*

Author	# uses of νύκτωρ	# uses of νυκτ-	νύκτωρ frequency
Antiphon	6	11	55%
Aristophanes	16	46	35%
Lysias	4	13	31%
Aeschines	5	16	31%
Plato	19	82	23%
Demosthenes	5	29	17%
Sophocles	2	17	12%
Xenophon	14	203	7%
Euripides	3	57	5%
Aeschylus	0	31	0%
Herodotus	0	89	0%
Thucydides	0	97	0%

extends rather far beyond telic events, both limitative and punctual, to atelic contexts where one might expect the accusative. Some of these should be discounted as more spatial than temporal in sense, especially in the *Parmenides* where it is discussed whether certain things exist in time or not.[90] Many of the others can be understood as limitative, even if this reading is not initially obvious:

(79) **ἐν ἐκείνῳ τῷ χρόνῳ**, ἐν ᾧ ἡ πᾶσα γῆ ἀνεδίδου καὶ ἔφυε ζῷα παντοδαπά, θηρία τε καὶ βοτά, ἐν τούτῳ ἡ ἡμετέρα θηρίων μὲν ἀγρίων ἄγονος καὶ καθαρὰ ἐφάνη

In that time, in which the whole earth produced and gave life to all sorts of creatures, wild animals and domesticated ones – in that time our land did not give rise to wild beasts and was clearly free from them (*Mx.* 237d3)

Here one might expect an accusative on the grounds that the speaker's praise of Athens would be strongest if it were emphasized that there were no unpleasant creatures there throughout the

---

[90] See the examples of ἐν χρόνῳ at *Prm.* 141a5, 141a6, 141c8, 156d1, 156e1, all with different forms of εἶναι. The phrase occurs with modifiers as well, e.g. ἐνί at 156c2, οὐδενί at 156e6.

whole of the time in question. But, as indicated in my translation, even though the verb is not explicitly negated with οὐ or μή, the negative semantics of ἄγονος are sufficient for this example to count as a limitative construction: at no point during the time frame of this period did the telic event of the appearance of a wild beast trouble Attica. Furthermore, the use of ἐν may also have been favored by the presence of a demonstrative as a modifier. The accusative of time of χρόνος occurs only four times with ἐκεῖνος or οὗτος,[91] whereas temporal ἐν is found with them fifteen times.[92] This distribution makes sense in that demonstratives, by singling out one period of time in contrast to others, are less compatible with durative expressions[93] than they are with these past-time limitative expressions that are comparatively close to the punctual type – and, as noted in the discussion of Xenophon, ἐν . . . χρόνῳ had certainly come to be used in punctual constructions as well.

But even if these crypto-limitative phrases are excluded, there remain perhaps a dozen examples where it is particularly surprising not to find the accusative:

(80) πάντα ταῦτά ἐστι μεστὰ ἀπορίας ἀεὶ **ἐν τῷ πρόσθεν χρόνῳ** καὶ νῦν

All these things are full of uncertainty, always in past time and now

(*Sph.* 236e3)

In this example, the temporal phrase with ἐν . . . χρόνῳ is coordinated with καὶ νῦν, in a sort of merism that is typically used to express 'for all time', a sense further elicited here by the presence of ἀεί.[94] It is hard to square this sense with the idea that ἐν⁺ᴰ

---

[91] With ἐκεῖνος at *Prm.* 146e1, with οὗτος at *Thg.* 128e7, and, in longer expressions, at *Phd.* 91b4 (in full: τοῦτόν γε τὸν χρόνον αὐτὸν τὸν πρὸ τοῦ θάνατον), *Grg.* 512e5 (τοῦτον ὃν μέλλοι χρόνον βιῶναι). Neither the accusative nor ἐν occurs with ὅδε modifying χρόνος.

[92] With ἐκεῖνος at *Cra.* 439e2, *Hipparch.* 229c6, *Ly.* 213a2, *Mx.* 237d3, 239d5, *R.* 461d7, 538a6; with οὗτος at *Euthphr.* 4d1, *Phd.* 58b5, 87b2, 116c5, *1 Alc.* 103b3, and in a longer expression, at *Men.* 91e8 (ἐν ἅπαντι τῷ χρόνῳ τούτῳ); in the plural, with οὗτος, at *Phlb.* 50a9 (possibly also at 36b6, but this is textually suspect) and *Criti.* 111b1.

[93] Because durative expressions serve chiefly to express a length of time, it is generally already clear which particular period of time is referred to.

[94] Cf. the durative expressions with δι᾿ ἡμέρας and νυκτός at *R.* 343b7, *Lg.* 758a8 (= (66)), and 790c8. That said, it is perfectly possible for an expression to be limitative, even though it specifically includes ἀεί or πᾶς and thus refers to all time: ἡ γὰρ εἰωθυῖά μοι

168

should mark a limitative phrase, an event-type characterized by a telic verbal event, the completion of which only occupies a part of the time frame established by the temporal expression: neither of these conditions holds here. Nor is (80) an isolated example. In (81), Plato again uses ἐν in a situation otherwise conducive to the accusative of time, with a μέν-clause describing a static initial period, contrasted with a change of the state of affairs in the subsequent δέ-clause:

(81) ἐγὼ γὰρ **ἐν μὲν τῷ ἔμπροσθεν χρόνῳ** ἡγούμην οὐκ εἶναι ἀνθρωπίνην ἐπιμέλειαν ᾗ ἀγαθοὶ οἱ ἀγαθοὶ γίγνονται· νῦν δὲ πέπεισμαι

For previously I thought that there was no human practice through which good people become good, but now I am persuaded of it (*Prt.* 328e2)

The choice of ἐν in these examples must in part have been motivated by the modifier. Certainly, most of these strangely durative ἐν-phrases have πρόσθεν or ἔμπροσθεν as modifiers;[95] conversely, this is true of none of the ninety-three accusatives of time with χρόνον. The preference for ἐν with these modifiers is probably due to the same motivation that caused Thucydides to use the genitive τοῦ λοιποῦ χρόνου in example (83) of Chapter 2: the past is treated as so unbounded a period of time that nothing could be coterminous with its entire extent, so a limitative expression is inevitable.

Demosthenes

The final Attic author to consider is Demosthenes.[96] Again, the focus of the following section will be limited to the issues that have come to the fore in the other authors: the difference between the

μαντικὴ ἡ τοῦ δαιμονίου ἐν μὲν τῷ πρόσθεν χρόνῳ **παντὶ** πάνυ πυκνὴ **ἀεὶ** ἦν καὶ πάνυ ἐπὶ σμικροῖς ἐναντιουμένη, εἴ τι μέλλοιμι μὴ ὀρθῶς πράξειν (*Ap.* 40a5). Here, as the past general conditional clause makes clear, Socrates' *daimonion* was operative during the whole of his past life – but only from time to time, whenever he was about to act incorrectly. A limitative marker is well in order here. By contrast, the general state of uncertainty referred to in (80) cannot be reduced to a finite number of discrete points within the larger time frame of past time.

95 Of the 88 temporal expressions with ἐν . . . χρόνῳ, fully 12 have (ἔμ)πρόσθεν as a modifier, of which only about half are best assigned to the limitative type, the rest being atelic enough to be better labeled as durative.

96 Data were gathered from all speeches in the Demosthenic Corpus, including those not attributed to Demosthenes himself, such as the speeches of Apollodorus, son of Pasion

accusative and prepositional constructions in durative expressions, the varying behavior of calendrical and non-calendrical time nouns in punctual expressions, and the relationship of $\dot{\epsilon}v^{+D}$ to the genitive and dative of time.

Durative expressions in Demosthenes

The data are shown in Table 16.

Demosthenes has less variation in his durative expressions than other authors, but, at least in the five examples of $\dot{\epsilon}\pi\acute{\iota}^{+A}$ with ἡμέρα, the same patterns surface. One of the five is an adnominal phrase that is really more of a goal expression than a standard durative one,[97] and the other four are familiar types: all have either πολλάς or a cardinal numeral preceding ἡμέρας.[98] To be sure, the simple

Table 16. *Durative expressions in Demosthenes*

Time noun	Accusative of time	$\delta\iota\acute{\alpha}^{+G}$	$\dot{\epsilon}\pi\acute{\iota}^{+A}$
ἡμέρα	21[a]	–	5
νύξ	7[b]	–	–
μήν	14	–	–
θέρος	–	–	–
χειμών	–	–	–
ἔτος	39[c]	–	–
ἐνιαυτός	3	1	–

Note:
[a] This does not count one distributive example (59.46) and three punctual accusatives of time (21.31, 21.56, 25.11).
[b] This includes three modal examples (18.259, 19.175, 45.80). There is also one durative genitive of time (58.65).
[c] This does not count the two expressions with ordinal numbers in the sense 'x years ago' (exx. (104) and (105)).

(generally agreed to be 46, 49, 50, 52, 53, 59; see Trevett (1992) and e.g. Usher (1999: 338–9)). They are not sufficiently different in their temporal expressions to merit exclusion from consideration, esp. as they represent Greek of the same genre and time period anyway. On the rare instances where genuine Demosthenes appears to be stylistically different, this will be noted.

97 That is, while the phrase can be translated 'for a day', the sense is more 'food to meet the needs of a day' than 'food that lasts for the duration of a day': ἐπεὶ ὅ γε στρατηγὸς οὐδὲ τὸ ἐφ' ἡμέραν αὐτοῖς τροφὴν διαρκῆ ἐδίδου (50.23).
98 With πολλάς, 21.41 and 56.18; with δύο and τρεῖς, 47.42 and 47.69.

accusative can also be used in such contexts (although πολλάς only occurs once, negated by a narrow-scope μή (42.11)), but the phrases with ἐπί⁺ᴬ still place comparatively more emphasis on the temporal expression. This is most obvious in the following:

(82) ἃ δ' ἂν ἐκ πολλοῦ συνεχῶς **ἐπὶ πολλὰς ἡμέρας** παρὰ τοὺς νόμους πράττων τις φωρᾶται

And as to whatever one is detected doing for a long time, continually, for many days, against the law (21.41)

The piling up of temporal phrases one after another in a pre-verbal position shows that Demosthenes is here interested in highlighting them; furthermore, better balance is achieved by matching ἐκ πολλοῦ with the ἐπί-phrase than with the bare accusative. Use of ἐπί⁺ᴬ could also be driven by the need for clarification in a slightly unusual construction:

(83) ἐκέλευεν εἰσαγγέλλειν με, καὶ τοὺς πρυτάνεις προγράφειν αὐτῷ τὴν κρίσιν **ἐπὶ δύο ἡμέρας**

It ordered me to bring an impeachment, and the *prytaneis* were to give him notice of the trial two days in advance (47.42)

It is tempting to suggest that ἐπί⁺ᴬ was favored here because of the indirect discourse: with τοὺς πρύτανεις and τὴν κρίσιν already in the clause, a third accusative might have seemed unclear. But while a stylistic consideration of this sort may have played some role in the decision to use ἐπί⁺ᴬ, there is in fact no categorical restriction against such accusatives of time, as the nature of the nouns in question and the presence of a cardinal number are sufficient to prevent ambiguity.[99] What probably played a greater role in triggering the prepositional construction is the unusual semantic relationship of the temporal phrase to the verb it modifies. Whereas

---

[99] Accusatives of time of ἡμέρα in accusative+infinitive constructions are found at 1.27, 18.180, 24.105 and 114, 42.11, 59.47. That said, most of these are not very good parallels to (83), for they only have one accusative in addition to the accusative of time and are thus that much less ambiguous. The exception is 18.180: καίτοι τίνα βούλει σέ, Ἀισχίνη, καὶ τίν' ἐμαυτὸν ἐκείνην τὴν ἡμέραν εἶναι θῶ; "And now, Aeschines, who would you like me to say that you were, and who that I was, over the course of that day?" A rhetorically prominent question in the *De corona*, even this might be seen as marked syntax (though the gapping is certainly easier in Greek than in English), so one cannot entirely exclude the possibility that Demosthenes was reluctant under normal circumstances to put in a row three accusatives, each with a different syntactic function.

such durative expressions normally indicate the length of time that the verbal event lasts, in this case it gives the interval between the notice of the trial (the προγράφειν proper) and the trial itself. A verb like μένω, which construes so naturally with a durative expression, has little need of a preposition like ἐπί⁺ᴬ to signal that grammatical relationship, but προγράφω calls for a bit more clarification – especially when there are two other accusatives already in play. That ἐπί⁺ᴬ is elicited by verbs that less obviously collocate with durative expressions is also suggested by the other verbs that take durative phrases with ἐπί⁺ᴬ – πράττειν, πρόκλησιν ἐκτιθῆναι (particularly close to (83)), and φυλάττω. While φυλάττω to be sure construes rather easily with a durative expression, this set of verbs still lacks some of the verbal roots that are the most common in such constructions: μένω, βιόω, εἰμί, ἐπέχω, ὁρμέω.¹⁰⁰ All in all, one may reasonably regard the use of ἐπί⁺ᴬ instead of the accusative as a means of highlighting a durative expression where the audience might not otherwise expect it.

Rather more difficult to determine is the reason that Demosthenes once chooses διά⁺ᴳ rather than the accusative:

(84) πρὸς γὰρ τῇ ἄλλῃ οὐσίᾳ τῇ Φαινίππου . . . καὶ αὕτη πρόσοδος μεγάλη ἐστὶν αὐτῷ· ἓξ ὄνοι **δι᾽ ἐνιαυτοῦ** ὑλαγωγοῦσιν

For in addition to Phaenippus' other property, he also has this large source of revenue: six donkeys carry wood for him throughout the year (42.7)

At first glance, this looks like another candidate for a prepositional usage that is triggered by the need for emphasis and clarity: substitute τὸν ἐνιαυτόν, and it is no longer as clear that Demosthenes is saying that it is the donkeys' year-round transport of wood that enriches Phaenippus. But this runs up against the problem that the accusative of time can in fact be used in this way, as long as ὅλον is added as a modifier:

---

¹⁰⁰ For these verbs with the accusative of time of ἡμέρα in Demosthenes, see 35.13, 50.19 ((περι)μένω), 41.18 and 19 (ἐπιβιόω), 18.112 and 180 (εἰμί), 21.12 (ἐπέχω), 35.29 (ὁρμέω).

(85) ἃ σὺ πάντ' ἐποίεις **ἐνιαυτὸν ὅλον** μετ' Ἀνδροτίωνος

This is what you did with Androtion for a whole year (24.197)

As the other two accusatives of time of ἐνιαυτόν are not modified by ὅλον and are not emphatic,[101] the best solution is to assume that either the addition of ὅλον or the use of διά[+G] was potentially available as a means of emphasizing the duration of time.

Although there is not enough evidence to prove it, it seems likely that the constructions in (84) and (85) differ because of what in particular is being emphasized: in (84), the speaker stresses that Phaenippus could bring in this revenue at all times in any given year, whereas the focus in (85) lies on the actions of the addressee during the length of one particular year.

Punctual and limitative expressions in Demosthenes

The figures are presented in Table 17.

Again, Demosthenes' usage does not diverge very much from that of other Attic authors. The dative of time is almost entirely restricted to punctual constructions. In the one exception, a limitative construction, the surrounding syntax is generally choppy:

(86) ἅμα γὰρ τῷ Δημοσθένει καὶ ὁ χορηγὸς ὑβρίζετο, τοῦτο δ' ἐστὶ τῆς πόλεως, καὶ τὸ **ταύταις ταῖς ἡμέραις**, αἷς οὐκ ἐῶσιν οἱ νόμοι

> For, at the same time as Demosthenes, the chorus master was also assaulted, and that is a concern for the city, and it happened on those days that the laws prohibit it (21.34)

As Demosthenes is referring to a multiplicity of discrete events (the assault upon him and that upon the *chorēgos*) that took place over a period of time (ταύταις ταῖς ἡμέραις, in the plural), it seems best to characterize this as a limitative phrase. But it would be misleading simply to take it as an unmarked limitative construction modifying ὑβρίζετο, given the presence of τοῦτο δ' ἐστί and καὶ τό, both of which, with their articulating connective particles, break up the flow of the syntax enough that there could well be independent

---

[101] ἐνιαυτὸν ἀτόκῳ χρῆσθαι τῷ ἀργυρίῳ (53.12), ἐνιαυτὸν συνοικήσας αὐτῇ (59.51).

173

Table 17. *Punctual and limitative expressions in Demosthenes*

	genitive	dative	$\dot{\epsilon}v^{+D}$	νύκτωρ
ἡμέρα	14× limitative[a] 3× distributive	10× punc. 1× limitative	9× limitative[b] 3× punctual[c] 1× modal	–
μήν	14× punctual[d] 7× distributive 3× limitative	5× punctual	3× punctual 1× limitv.	–
ἔτος	3× limitative	7× punctual	11× limitv.	–
ἐνιαυτός	13× distrib. 2× punctual	–	3× limitv. 1× punctual	–
νύξ	9× punctual[e] 3× modal 1× limitative	–	–	3× punc.[e] 1× modal
θέρος	–	–	–	–
χειμών	–	–	1× modal	–

Note:
[a] This excludes two spurious examples in a *nomos* and a *syngraphē*.
[b] This excludes one example in a spurious *nomos*.
[c] These are examples (96) through (98), which, as will be seen below, lie at the boundary between the limitative and punctual type.
[d] This does not include an additional eight examples in the spurious *psēphismata* and the like, but it does include eight examples where the genitive μηνός could be either adverbial or adnominal. In the latter case, it would be dependent on the particular day of the month, which itself is a dative of time, e.g. ἅπαξ γὰρ τοῦ ἐνιαυτοῦ ἀνοίγεται, τῇ δωδεκάτῃ τοῦ ἀνθεστηριῶνος μηνός 'on the twelfth of the month Anthesterion' or 'in the month A.' (59.77).
[e] This excludes one spurious example in a *martyria*.

reasons for choosing the dative by this point in the sentence. Here there is perhaps attraction to the relative αἷς, which in turn could be in the dative as a sort of indirect object after οὐκ ἐῶσιν. Whatever the reason for this dative of time, it is an outlier.

As for the division of time nouns into calendrical and non-calendrical, Demosthenes offers the first evidence of a different distribution than in the other authors. In particular, the genitive is used for punctual constructions even with the calendrical nouns:

DEMOSTHENES

twice with ἐνιαυτός and fourteen times with μήν. Both punctual genitives of ἐνιαυτός are modified by τοῦ ὑστέρου:

(87) ἐὰν δ' ἐπὶ τῆς ἐνάτης <ἢ δεκάτης> πρυτανείας ὄφλῃ, **τοῦ ὑστέρου ἐνιαυτοῦ** ἐπὶ τῆς ἐνάτης ἢ δεκάτης πρυτανείας ἐκτίνειν

And if he incurs it in the ninth or tenth presidency, he should pay it off in the next year in the ninth or tenth presidency (24.40)

(88) **τοῦ δὲ ὑστέρου ἐνιαυτοῦ**, ἐπὶ Ἀλκισθένους ἄρχοντος, ἀφικνεῖται ὁ Φιλώνδας ἄγων τὰ ξύλα ἐκ τῆς Μακεδονίας

And in the following year, when Alcisthenes was archon, Philondas arrived with the wood from Macedonia (49.60)

For several reasons, example (87) is not valid evidence on its own. First, it occurs in the quotation of a *nomos*, and such passages are considered generally to be spurious;[102] second, as the apodosis of a law, it refers to a potentially recurring situation, so the similarity to the habitual event-type may have encouraged the genitive over the dative; finally, it is subject to interpretation as an adnominal genitive dependent on ἐπὶ τῆς ἐνάτης ἢ δεκάτης πρυτανείας.[103] Passage (88), however, is less susceptible to such objections: it occurs in the narration of a one-time event, and it cannot be adnominal. Yet, even here, given the tendency of the closely related ἔτος still to take a dative of time, it is probably better not to see the genitive as an unmarked punctual construction for two reasons: adjectives like ὕστερος that refer to future time can trigger the use of the genitive;[104] insofar as ἐνιαυτός, as opposed to ἔτος, designates the year as a recurring period of time (Demosthenes uses only ἐνιαυτός, never ἔτος, in distributive constructions), the frequent use of the distributive genitive may have bled over to the punctual type.

This may in part account for the punctual genitives of μήν as well, as it is second only to ἐνιαυτός in the number of times it occurs

---

[102] For the untrustworthiness of the documents, see e.g. MacDowell (1990: 43–7), Yunis (2001: 29–31).
[103] Indeed, this is how it is translated in Murray's Loeb.
[104] See the discussion of τοῦ ἐχομένου ἔτους in ex. (43) in Ch. 2.

175

in distributive constructions (7×). But with this time noun the punctual genitives are numerous enough to be considered unmarked. As indicated in note *d* of Table 17, eight of the fourteen examples can be interpreted as adnominal, but the remaining six include several good punctual constructions:

(89) τούτου τοῦ μηνὸς μόγις μετὰ τὰ μυστήρια δέκα ναῦς ἀπεστείλατ' ἔχοντα κενὰς Χαρίδημον καὶ πέντε τάλαντ' ἀργυρίου

During this month, after the mysteries, with some difficulty you sent Charidemus with ten unmanned ships and five talents of silver (3.5)

(90) ἐγήματο μὲν γὰρ ἐπὶ Πολυζήλου ἄρχοντος **σκιροφοριῶνος μηνός**, ἡ δ' ἀπόλειψις ἐγράφη **ποσιδεῶνος μηνὸς** ἐπὶ Τιμοκράτους

For she married during the archonship of Polyzelus in the month Scirophorion, and the divorce was drawn up in the month Posideon during Timocrates' archonship (30.15)

In (89), the time noun is modified by a demonstrative; in the two examples in (90), as well as three of the other four,[105] the month is specified by name. In this instance, the modifier does seem to have affected the choice of construction, as the five datives of time all occur with either τίνι or δευτέρῳ:[106]

(91) ἅπαντες γὰρ ἴσμεν **τίνι μηνὶ καὶ τίνι ἡμέρᾳ** ἡ εἰρήνη ἐγένετο

For we all know in what month and on what day the peace was made (7.36)

(92) **δευτέρῳ μηνὶ** τὴν ἀπόφασιν ἔδωκέ μοι τῆς οὐσίας

In the second month he gave me the declaration of his property (42.26)

In short, the dative of time is still used where expected (especially with the ordinal δεύτερος), while the unexpected genitive is correlated to the presence of the month name. This genitive is characteristic of legal language: it is found eight times in the spurious

---

[105] These occur at 37.6, 49.6, 56.5. The fourth is modified by τοῦ ἐξελθόντος (37.39).

[106] The other examples (perhaps not to be counted as fully independent, since they occur with the same modifiers in the same speeches as the passages cited): τίνι μηνί at 7.37 and δευτέρῳ μηνί at 42.2 and 42.28.

documents that worked their way into the textual tradition of Demosthenes and becomes common in the Ptolemaic papyri.[107] The next problem is the use of the preposition ἐν. On the whole, it shows more affinity to the genitive than to the dative: it is more often a limitative marker (24×) than a punctual one (7×). Indeed, it is only with μήν that it is more likely to be punctual – not surprising considering that this is, of the four time nouns in question, the one that shows the most fully developed punctual genitive as well. With ἡμέρα, there is a relatively clear division of labor between the genitive and ἐν in limitative constructions. Of the fourteen genitives, all are modified by a cardinal numeral, and they often also refer to the future, setting a limit by which time an event has to take place:

(93) καὶ ἀκούσεσθε **δυοῖν ἢ τριῶν ἡμερῶν**, οἷς μὲν ἐχθρὸς ἥκει, φίλον αὐτὸν γεγενημένον, οἷς δὲ φίλος, τοὐναντίον ἐχθρόν

And you will hear within two or three days that he has become a friend to those for whom he arrived as an enemy, and, vice versa, to those for whom he came as a friend, he has become an enemy (18.35)

By contrast, not one of the limitative constructions with ἐν has a cardinal number; furthermore, they generally look back to the past and derive their limitative sense from the fact that the verbal event is a composite one:[108]

(94) καὶ ἐκλήθην ὕστατος ἁπάντων τῶν **ἐν ἐκείνῃ τῇ ἡμέρᾳ** κληθέντων

And I was called last of all those who were called on that day (57.10)

The presence of a negative can also motivate a limitative construction with ἐν:

(95) οὐ νομίμου ὄντος **ἐν ταύτῃ τῇ ἡμέρᾳ** ἱερεῖα θύειν

Although it is not lawful to sacrifice animals on that day (59.116)

Because these constructions frequently occur with demonstratives,[109] they form a bridge between the stricter limitatives of the

---

[107] Mayser lists seven examples of months in the genitive of time, but none in the dative (1934: 224, 296); that said, the dative enjoys a resurgence in the Roman period: cf. p. 237.
[108] Cf. 57.15.
[109] In addition to (94) and (95), see 21.10, 21.11, 21.12, and 57.15. Xenophon, too, often uses ἐν with demonstratives at the boundary between the punctual and limitative type: see exx. (10) and (11).

genitive of time and the true punctual constructions of the dative of time. Indeed, there are three passages where a phrase with ἐν ἐκείνῃ τῇ ἡμέρᾳ has moved more or less entirely into punctual territory. One of these could perhaps still be considered limitative:

(96) καίτοι τρί' **ἐν ἐκείνῃ τῇ ἡμέρᾳ** πᾶσιν ἀνθρώποις ἔδειξαν ἐγκώμια Θηβαῖοι καθ' ὑμῶν τὰ κάλλιστα, ἓν μὲν ἀνδρείας, ἕτερον δὲ δικαιοσύνης, τρίτον δὲ σωφροσύνης

And the Thebans on that day, before all men, offered you praise on three counts, the finest ones: one for your courage, another for your justice, a third for your moderation (18.215)

Demosthenes here relates how the Thebans' welcome of their Athenian allies was tantamount to great praise of them. As the behavior of the Thebans on the day of the Athenians' arrival is seen as rendering this praise in three different respects, the temporal phrase could be considered limitative on the grounds that multiple actions are distinguished as having transpired on that day. Still, this interpretation would extend the limitative event-type somewhat further than in other cases (if not so very much beyond (94)), and it seems better to classify (96) alongside the next two examples, both harder to explain away as potentially limitative:

(97) ἐφάνην τοίνυν οὗτος **ἐν ἐκείνῃ τῇ ἡμέρᾳ** ἐγὼ καὶ παρελθὼν εἶπον εἰς ὑμᾶς

So I appeared as that man on that day, I did, and when I came forward, I spoke to you (18.173)

(98) ὑπὲρ τῶν ἐν τῇ χώρᾳ καὶ τοῦ πρὸς τὴν Ἀττικὴν πολέμου, ὃς λυπήσει μὲν ἕκαστον, ἐπειδὰν παρῇ, γέγονεν δ' ἐν[110]**ἐκείνῃ τῇ ἡμέρᾳ**

On behalf of what you have in your country and the war in Attica, which will pain each of you, when it comes, but it came into being[111] on that day (6.35)

In the first example, also from *On the crown* and one of the most famous sentences in Demosthenes,[112] the temporal phrase describes the orator's coming to the rescue after news of Philip's capture of Elatea reaches the Athenians. One expects a dative of time in what should be a punctual construction, but Demosthenes

---

[110] The preposition is omitted in S[a], but present in the other MSS.
[111] For the perfect combined with a past-time temporal phrase, cf. ἑώρακα in (71) and Tarbell (1880: 79).
[112] See Kennedy (1963: 235).

knows what he is doing: by using what is normally a limitative marker, he expands the day in question, treating it as a *period* of time during the turmoil of which he came forward, rather than as a simple *point* in time at which he happened to do something. This reading is well in line with the preceding four sections, in which Demosthenes has painstakingly detailed the events that took place that day and the sort of man they called for. Example (98) is similar: Demosthenes is again speaking of a particularly significant day, that on which, in his view, Athens' war with Philip really began. There is, to be sure, less emphasis on describing the day than in the lead-up to (97), but, through the use of ἐν, the speaker can zoom in on the true outbreak of the war as a decisive point within that day. The simple dative of time, by contrast, would not have been strong enough here, as it would only register that the event had occurred then.

With ἔτος, the situation is less complicated, as the dative is the only punctual construction, and the main concern is the split expression of the limitative type, usually with ἐν, but sometimes with the genitive. But the same differences seen elsewhere between these two variant limitative markers do not obtain here. In contrast to the phrases with ἡμέρα, both constructions occur readily with cardinal numbers: this is true of all three of the genitives of time with ἔτος, and of nine of the eleven constructions with ἐν. That said, it is probably significant that all of the genitives have only the number as modifier, whereas all the phrases in which further modifiers are present take ἐν.[113] As elsewhere, one is left with the impression that the genitive is an older, more restricted construction, and that with ἐν, more productive. Unfortunately, the sorts of verbs modified by the respective phrases are not distinct enough to confirm this impression. One would like to see the genitive of time found either with verbs that look forward to the future or with negatives, the phrases with ἐν with past-tense verbs with which a limitative construction would be less expected and therefore require more prominent marking. Again, the predicates that occur

---

[113] ἐν τοῖς τριάκοντ' ἐκείνοις ἔτεσιν, ἐν τρισὶ καὶ δέκ' οὐχ ὅλοις ἔτεσιν (both in 9.25), ἐν πλεῖν ἢ διακοσίοις ἔτεσιν (24.141), ἐν τοῖς δέκ' ἔτεσιν (27.36), as well as the constructions without a numeral, ἐν πολλοῖς πάνυ ἔτεσι (24.140) and ἐν τούτοις τοῖς ἔτεσιν ἅπασιν (55.4).

with the genitive do fall into a fairly narrow range: at 25.42 the verb is negated; at 38.18 the phrase is in a forward-looking conditional protasis; at 36.37, the genitive in some sense modifies the εἰσπέπρακται of the preceding clause, but in reality is better seen as an adnominal phrase dependent on the preceding τῶν μισθώσεων. But ἐν is also found freely with negatives (at 27.24, 30.33, 40.3, and 55.4), and, while there are not any examples in conditionals or other forward-looking clauses, we cannot adduce the fact that the one forward-looking limitative construction with ἔτος takes the genitive as independent evidence that the genitive is favored in this context.

The constructions with μήν are similarly inconclusive: it is welcome that the three limitative genitives (50.1, 50.12, 52.7; all speeches attributed to Apollodorus) are all modified just by a cardinal number, and that two of these are negated, but the one limitative construction with ἐν is unusual enough that there is hardly a clear contrast between the two markers:

(99) τοὺς μισθοὺς οὓς ταῖς ὑπηρεσίαις καὶ τοῖς ἐπιβάταις κατὰ μῆνα ἐδίδουν, παρὰ τῶν στρατηγῶν σιτηρέσιον μόνον λαμβάνων, πλὴν δυοῖν μηνοῖν μόνον μισθὸν **ἐν πέντε μησὶν καὶ ἐνιαυτῷ**

The wages that I gave to the rowers and the marines each month, taking from the generals only food supplies, except for two months' pay only in a period of five months and a year (50.10)

Had the speaker used the genitive rather than the preposition ἐν, the construction would presumably have been too opaque, as there is already the genitive δυοῖν μηνοῖν; the slightly weightier construction with ἐν helps place an emphasis on the small fraction of time for which he received pay beyond the *sitērésion* – an emphasis that calls for an expansion to 'in a period of' in the translation.

The final question raised by Table 17 is the relationship between the three punctual phrases with νύκτωρ and the nine with νυκτός. As with Xenophon, there seems to be free variation, with both constructions used in phrases that range from the more strictly punctual to the more modal. Compare, for example:[114]

---

[114] A similar example of νύκτωρ occurs at 57.65.

(100) ἐπεβούλευσεν ... διαφθεῖραί μοι **νύκτωρ** ἐλθὼν ἐπὶ τὴν οἰκίαν τὴν τοῦ χρυσοχόου

He plotted to destroy them, to harm me, by going at night to the house of the goldsmith (21.16)

(101) ἐλθὼν εἰς τὸ χωρίον **τῆς νυκτός**, ὅσα ἐνῆν φυτὰ ἀκροδρύων γενναῖα ἐμβεβλημένα καὶ τὰς ἀναδενδράδας ἐξέκοψε

Having come to my land at night, he cut down all the excellent fruit-tree plants that were grafted there as well as their vines (53.15)

In both passages, the temporal phrase notes that an event described by the aorist participle ἐλθών has taken place at night. True, the phrase in (101) has the definite article, whereas νύκτωρ in (100) does not, but there is no greater singling out of a particular night in (101) than in (100). Nor is it the case that νύκτωρ is restricted to punctual constructions, while νυκτός extends to modal contexts:

(102) εἰ μέν τις μεθ' ἡμέραν ὑπὲρ πεντήκοντα δραχμὰς κλέπτοι ... εἰ δέ τις **νύκτωρ** ὁτιοῦν κλέπτοι

If someone were to steal over fifty drachmas by day ... But if someone were to steal anything by night (24.113)

(103) διαβῆναι οὐ ῥᾴδιον ἦν, ἄλλως τε καὶ **νυκτός**

It wasn't easy to cross, especially by night (59.99)

While νυκτός does not occur in contrastive focus in quite the same way as νύκτωρ in (102), it can be focalized by ἄλλως τε καί, and there is no obvious syntactic reason why these two examples should take νύκτωρ and νυκτός respectively, rather than the other way around. To some extent, the difference between the two may result simply from stylistic preferences, as we have here one instance where the speeches of Apollodorus behave differently from genuine Demosthenes. Apollodorus uses νυκτός eight times (once each in 49 and 53, twice in 50, and four times in 59), but never uses νύκτωρ, while in genuine Demosthenes, the balance is even: νύκτωρ occurs twice in 21, and once each in 24 and 57; νυκτός occurs once each in 18, 21, 32, and 54.[115] But the distribution of the latter eight examples remains unexplained.

---

[115] A final example of νυκτός occurs in speech 58, of unknown authorship (Usher 1999: 265).

One final set of expressions, which have very few close parallels in the authors already studied, requires comment. Three times with ἡμέρα, and twice with ἔτος, Demosthenes uses accusatives of time in what look very much like punctual constructions. Those with ἔτος form one group:

(104) ἔχοντος δέ μου οὕτως ὡς λέγω, κατέπλευσαν δεῦρο **τρίτον ἔτος** οὗτός τε καὶ πολίτης αὐτοῦ Παρμένων

I was in such a position as I've said, when they sailed here, two years ago, both this man and his fellow citizen Parmenon (33.5)

(105) ἐξῆλθον **ἔτος τουτὶ τρίτον** εἰς Πάνακτον φρουρᾶς ἡμῖν προγραφείσης

This is the third year since I went out to Panactum, as guard duty had been assigned to us (54.3)

Here, the sense of τρίτον ἔτος is not 'in the third year (from an earlier starting point)', in which case we would expect the dative, but rather 'two years ago', 'this is now the third year since'. Accordingly, these passages are reminiscent of how French and Portuguese express when a past event occurred relative to the present:[116]

(106) *Il est venu il y a trois ans*
Ele veio há três anos
He came three years ago

In both languages, the temporal expression is formally an independent clause that is simply juxtaposed with the main clause, without any explicit subordinating conjunction, roughly as if one were to say 'He came, it's been three years' in English. It is thus tempting to view the Greek expressions as nominatives, with ellipsis of ἐστί and a subordinator, somewhat akin to the following construction, where, to be sure, there is also an explicit subordinator:

(107) καὶ οἱ πρεσβύτεροι αὐτοῖς τῶν εὐδαιμόνων διὰ τὸ ἁβροδίαιτον οὐ **πολὺς χρόνος** ἐπειδὴ χιτῶνάς τε λινοῦς ἐπαύσαντο φοροῦντες

---

[116] A trace of such a construction is perhaps also found in Latin *si nox furtum faxit*, if Watkins (1965) is right to see in *nox* the nominative of a reduced clause rather than a syncopated genitive; even if one does not believe this particular example, he cites several other parallels.

And the older men of their wealthy classes because of their sumptuous lifestyle – it has not been a long time since they stopped wearing linen tunics (Th. 1.6.3)

But other evidence points to taking these as accusatives of time:

(108) οἱ μὲν τὸ δεξιὸν ἔχοντες οὓς ὑμεῖς **ἡμέραν πέμπτην** τρεψάμενοι ἐδιώξατε

Those on the right wing, whom you routed and pursued four days ago (X. *HG* 2.4.13)

(109) καὶ ἐχθὲς δὲ καὶ **τρίτην ἡμέραν** τὸ αὐτὸ τοῦτο ἔπραττον

And both yesterday and the day before they were doing this same thing (X. *Cyr.* 6.3.11)

Although such constructions are very rare, these examples are sufficient to make clear that one way of expressing 'x days ago' is to use the ordinal number with the singular accusative of time, leading to the same interpretation of (104) and (105), as well as a couple of examples from Plato:[117]

(110) σκοπῶν δὲ εὑρήσεις αὐτόθι **τὰ μυριοστὸν ἔτος** γεγραμμένα ἢ τετυπωμένα

And if you look, you'll find there what was painted or carved ten thousand years ago (Pl. *Lg.* 656e5)

Rather different, however, are the three anomalous accusatives of time with ἡμέρα:

(111) ὅπως μὴ τὸν ἐστεφανωμένον καὶ λῃτουργοῦντα τῷ θεῷ **ταύτην τὴν ἡμέραν** καλῇ μηδ' ἐπηρεάζῃ μηδ' ὑβρίζῃ μηδεὶς ἐξεπίτηδες

So that no one would deliberately summon or insult or outrage on that day one who had been crowned and was performing a service for the god (21.56)

(112) οὐ γὰρ εἰς Δημοσθένην ὄντα μ' ἠσέλγαινε μόνον **ταύτην τὴν ἡμέραν**, ἀλλὰ καὶ εἰς χορηγὸν ὑμέτερον

For it wasn't just me personally, as Demosthenes, that he outraged on this day, but also your chorus sponsor (21.31)

(113) πάντα τὰ ἐν τῇ πόλει καλὰ καὶ δίκαια καὶ συμφέροντα [φυλάττων καὶ] **ταύτην τὴν ἡμέραν** παρακαταθήκην ἔνορκον εἰληφὼς παρὰ τῶν νόμων καὶ τῆς πολιτείας καὶ τῆς πατρίδος

---

[117] See also *R*. 414e7.

183

Having received under oath, for safekeeping on that day, from the laws and the state and the fatherland everything in the city that is fine and just and beneficial (25.11)

In these passages, the use of the accusative requires explanation, as one rather expects the dative, as in the following:

(114) τὸν δ᾽ Εὔεργον οὐδ᾽ ἤδειν εἰσεληλυθότα μου εἰς τὴν οἰκίαν **ταύτῃ τῇ ἡμέρᾳ**

And neither did I know that Evergus had gone to my house on that day

(47.65)

Two potential solutions present themselves: either these constructions are in fact durative, despite the similarity to punctual constructions like (114), or they are punctual constructions, and the accusative has started to expand its range to cover this type. (That the latter option is plausible is due to the presence of a punctual accusative of time in certain post-Classical texts.) Example (111) is perhaps the most susceptible of the three to the former explanation. If one takes the temporal phrase as modifying the preceding participle λῃτουργοῦντα, the day could be viewed as an extended period of time during which the atelic service of the god takes place.[118] If, on the other hand, it modifies the following subjunctives, then it is hard to take as durative a phrase that modifies such telic verbs. Passage (112), from earlier in the same speech, is similar: the phrase in question again refers to the day during which it was particularly forbidden to attack the sponsor of the chorus. If ταύτην τὴν ἡμέραν can be understood as modifying atelic ὄντα – "I, who was not just Demosthenes for the extent of that day, but *chorēgos* as well" – then it is an ordinary durative accusative. But if, as the word order suggests, the phrase instead modifies ἠσέλγαινε, then this reading is far more difficult, as this act of outrage does not in fact last for the entirety of the day, but refers

---

[118] It might be objected that the demonstrative in ταύτην τὴν ἡμέραν suggests that the temporal phrase should modify the sequence of subjunctives, on the grounds that it is only with the mentioning of the state of being crowned and service to the god that it becomes clear which day is referred to. In fact, however, the day in question has been present in the discourse since the previous section (τὰς μὲν ἡμέρας ἐκείνας ἃς συνερχόμεθ᾽ ἐπὶ τὸν ἀγῶνα), so the demonstrative need not signal a break in sense before the temporal phrase. Even so, as my translation indicates, I am inclined to take the phrase with the following subjunctives, as they require the specification of the day more than the participles do.

more specifically to a particular attack.[119] Finally, in (113), given the telicity of the phrase πάντα ... παρακαταθήκην ἔνορκον εἰληφώς, it is very difficult to avoid a punctual interpretation of ταύτην τὴν ἡμέραν. True, it is tempting to explain the accusative by assuming that εἰληφώς, as a perfect participle, is somehow stative enough to trigger the more open-ended durative construction, but (114) shows that the dative of time is still entirely compatible with a perfect. Taking (111) through (113) together, it is hard to avoid the conclusion that we have here the first tentative steps towards a punctual accusative of time.

Herodotus

Or, to be more accurate, the first punctual accusatives of time in *Attic*. For, having established a clear picture of the behavior of Classical Attic prose, we can now cast our net more widely, and, turning first to Herodotus, one curiosity that comes to light is that this seemingly aberrant Demosthenic accusative of time is already anticipated in Herodotus:

(115) νηυσὶ μέν νυν Ἴωνες ἄκροι γενόμενοι **ταύτην τὴν ἡμέρην** ὑπερεβάλοντο τοὺς Φοίνικας, καὶ τούτων Σάμιοι ἠρίστευσαν

With their ships, then, the Ionians that day were outstanding and defeated the Phoenicians; of the Ionians, the Samians fought the best (5.112.1)

What makes Herodotus' usage look especially like Demosthenes' is that here, and in the other four examples, the accusative of time is ταύτην τὴν ἡμέρην. The other examples, in connection with (115), also suggest a possible motivation for this accusative, both here and in Demosthenes:[120]

---

[119] To be sure, Demosthenes does specify at the start of the speech that Midias was violent for an extended period of time (21.1 παρὰ πᾶσαν τὴν χορηγίαν), but the fact that he here specifies ταύτην τὴν ἡμέραν shows that he is in this instance referring to the main attack on him at the Dionysia.

[120] See also 7.181.1 (ἀνδρὸς ἀρίστου γενομένου ταύτην τὴν ἡμέρην), 8.86.1 (καίτοι ἦσάν γε καὶ ἐγένοντο ταύτην τὴν ἡμέρην μακρῷ ἀμείνονες αὐτοὶ ἑωυτῶν ἢ πρὸς Εὐβοίῃ), 8.107.1 (ταύτην μὲν τὴν ἡμέρην ἐς τοσοῦτο ἐγίνετο, τῆς δὲ νυκτὸς ... τὰς νέας ... ἀνῆγον ὀπίσω ἐς τὸν Ἑλλήσποντον). In the last of these examples, the accusative is certainly further motivated by its occurring in a μέν-clause that sets up a δέ-clause with punctual τῆς νυκτός. Still, the presence of ἐς τοσοῦτο with the verb makes the context telic enough to

(116) εἰ μέν νυν οἱ παρεόντες Λακεδαιμονίων ὅμοιοι ἐγένοντο <πάντες> **ταύτην τὴν ἡμέρην** Ἀρχίῃ τε καὶ Λυκώπῃ, αἱρέθη ἂν Σάμος

If, then, those of the Spartans who were present had <all> been like Archias and Lycopes on that day, Samos would have been taken (3.55.1)

In all of the Herodotean examples, the verb modified by the temporal phrase is (or is likely to be)[121] a form of γίγνομαι (4× the aorist, once the imperfect). These constructions thus sit halfway between the punctual and the durative type. On the one hand, the aorist of γίγνομαι is often unquestionably telic, as it refers complexively to the event in question taken as a whole. This usage is particularly evident in the various ταῦτα ἐγένετο constructions that sum up the events that have just taken place; it is also hinted at by the fact that the temporal phrases that modify these aorists are more readily translated with punctual than with durative constructions in English.[122] On the other hand, γίγνομαι can also have the open-ended semantics of εἰμί or μένω, so an accusative of time is often more natural, as seen in atelic contexts such as:

(117) Κύπριοι μὲν δὴ **ἐνιαυτὸν** ἐλεύθεροι γενόμενοι αὖτις ἐκ νέης κατεδεδούλωντο

So the Cypriots, after being free for a year, were again enslaved anew (5.116.1)

(Here, the fact that ἐνιαυτόν is indefinite – in contrast to the demonstrative ταύτην in the other examples, which, while certainly compatible with the durative type, is more characteristic of the punctual – further accentuates the appropriateness of the atelic interpretation.) Triangulating between these two points, we can see the accusative of time in (115) and (116) as an extension of the usage with atelic γενέσθαι in (117) to passages where broader

have potentially warranted a punctual dative instead. Note also the similar examples of ταύτην τὴν ἡμέρην at 7.54.1, 7.55.2, and 8.25.3, in each of which a clause with τῇ δὲ ὑστεραίῃ follows. In these passages, the action described by the accusative of time is open-ended enough that it is easier to label these simply as ordinary durative expressions.

[121] In ex. (115) one cannot exclude the possibility that phrase goes more closely with ὑπερεβάλοντο.

[122] The latter are not entirely excluded, but if, say, ex. (115) were translated 'The Ionians were outstanding for that day', it would imply a contrast with a subsequent day on which they did less well, whereas the immediate context of the Greek requires instead a contrast with the poor performance of the Greeks' land army. (It is true that the Ionian navy is defeated later on, in 5.116, but this occurs in a different episode, after the Ionians have sailed back to Ionia from Cyprus, where they had been victorious.)

contextual clues, the presence of the demonstrative, and the translation as an English punctual construction would rather lead us to expect the dative.[123] As for the examples in Demosthenes, while they do not form nearly as coherent a group on their own, it is still possible that they were motivated by the same general principle, especially (111) and (112), where relatively atelic verbs are at least lurking in the near vicinity, if not directly modified by the accusatives in question.

In other respects too, Herodotus' temporal expressions are not so different as to require a completely separate treatment in their own right, but can rather be seen as following the same general rules as in Attic. Accordingly, in the remainder of this section we can attend briefly to the main themes that have already been raised: the difference between durative expressions with the accusative of time and those with prepositions; the respective domains of the punctual genitive and dative of time; the contrast between the genitive and ἐν as markers of the limitative type.

Durative expressions in Herodotus

The data are as shown in Table 18.[124]

Table 18. *Durative expressions in Herodotus*

Time noun	Accusative of time	διά$^{+G}$	ἐπί$^{+A}$
ἡμέρη	41	4	7
νύξ	4	1	1
μήν	12	–	3
θέρος	–	–	–
χειμών	1	–	–
ἔτος	45	1	24
ἐνιαυτός	5	–	–

[123] Just to be clear: the English translations do not prove on their own that these constructions should be considered punctual. But, taken together with the other evidence, they do provide additional support for this view.
[124] For the distribution of the accusative of time and temporal ἐπί$^{+A}$ in Herodotus, Basset (2009) is valuable. He observes that there is no correlation between these two constructions and aspect; both can be used with imperfective constructions ('for how many years had he been reigning at that time?') and perfective ones ('for how many years did he reign in total?') (2009: 207–10).

The raw figures are generally in line with what one expects on the basis of Attic, although Herodotus employs the prepositional constructions more often. This difference should not be exaggerated, though, as he does so in the same sorts of contexts as the Attic authors. The preposition διά$^{+G}$, for instance, is used in somewhat emphatic expressions, in which the accusative on its own would probably not suffice to indicate that the event lasted for the whole of the time period; it is thus closer to English 'throughout' than 'for':[125]

(118) ἰκτῖνοι δὲ καὶ χελιδόνες **δι' ἔτεος** ἐόντες οὐκ ἀπολείπουσι

And kites and swallows never fail to stay there throughout the year (2.22.4)

Nor, it seems, could Herodotus have expressed this sense through simply adding a form of πᾶς to the accusative of time, as πᾶσαν ἡμέρην conveys the special meaning 'any day now', the two times it occurs in Herodotus:[126]

(119) τῷ δ' ἄρα καὶ αὐτῷ ἡ γυνή, ἐπίτεξ ἐοῦσα **πᾶσαν ἡμέρην**, τότε κως κατὰ δαίμονα τίκτει

And his wife, as she was expecting to give birth any day now, gave birth to his child as well at that time, in accordance with some god's plan (1.111.1)

(120) λέγοντες δι' ἀγγέλων ὡς αὐτοὶ μὲν ἥκοιεν πρόδρομοι τῶν ἄλλων, οἱ δὲ λοιποὶ τῶν συμμάχων προσδόκιμοι **πᾶσαν** εἶεν **ἡμέρην**

---

[125] The example with νύξ (further strengthened by πάσης τῆς) occurs at 8.12.1; the four examples with ἡμέρη, all δι' ἡμέρης, are at 1.97.1, 2.173.2, 6.12.1, and 7.210.2. Of these, the phrase at 1.97.1 is the only possible odd one out: οὐ γάρ οἱ λυσιτελέειν τῶν ἑωυτοῦ ἐξημελεηκότα τοῖσι πέλας δι' ἡμέρης δικάζειν ('for it was not advantageous to him to neglect his own affairs because he was judging his neighbors throughout the day *or* day after day'). While one cannot entirely exclude the latter translation (it is perfectly in line with the sense διά$^{+G}$ can take on in other authors; see e.g. the discussion of ex. (6)), Herodotus' practice elsewhere inclines one towards the first translation (so Stein: "den (ganzen) Tag hindurch" (1901: 121) and Antelami's translation in Asheri: "tutto il giorno" (1988: 115)).

[126] In a third instance, 9.52.1, ἡμέρην is modified by κείνην τὴν in addition to πᾶσαν, which blocks the indefinite reading. There are no examples of πᾶν ἔτος. By contrast, one does find (once each) πᾶσαν τὴν νύκτα (7.217.1; τὴν νύκτα πᾶσαν occurs at 2.68.1, but there the durative sense would be inevitable given that the verb is διατρίβει) and τὸν χειμῶνα ἄπαντα (2.19.2). One wonders whether the 'any day now' sense of πᾶς + time noun is chiefly possible with calendrical time nouns, as only they are likely to be used to denote the random point at which a hypothetical future event will occur. Certainly, 'any winter now' or 'any night now' are more strained in English than 'any day now' or 'any year now'.

Saying through messengers that they would come before the others, and that the rest of the allies were expected any day now (7.203.1)

Likewise, Herodotus employs ἐπί⁺ᴬ in esssentially the same way that Attic authors do. Of the thirty-five examples, in only one is the time noun not modified by a cardinal number.[127] That said, this is a less significant fact than it would appear at first glance: so too in most of the simple accusatives of time, the time noun is modified by a cardinal number (only 18 out of the 41 accusatives with ἡμέρη and none of the five with ἐνιαυτός, to be sure, but still 10 out of the 12 examples of μήν, and 43 out of the 45 with ἔτος). With ἔτος, then, what triggers the addition of ἐπί? Two factors distinguish the prepositional constructions. First, as presented in Table 19, they show different word order, with the accusative favored when the numeral comes first, ἐπί when ἔτεα comes first.

Second, the two constructions favor different verbs. Consider, for instance, the common construction in which a ruler is said to βασιλεύειν for a given number of years. These account for 15 of the 45 accusatives of time, but at most two of the 24 with ἐπί;[128] most of the time, no information is given in the clause beyond the mere length of the rule:

Table 19. *Word order in selected durative constructions in Herodotus*

Word order	accusative of time	ἐπί⁺ᴬ
numeral – ἔτεα	34	6
ἔτεα – numeral	9	17
other[a]	2	1

Note:

[a] These are the two accusatives of time with a non-numeral modifier (one preposed ἴσα (7.155.1), the other postposed ὀλίγα (3.22.4)) and the sole example of ἔτεα ἐπί + numeral order (2.140.2).

---

[127] The exception is ἐπὶ μῆνας συχνούς at 7.119.2.

[128] The exceptions are exx. (123) and (124) below. In fact, the preposition is not textually reliable in (124); if it is a later addition, then (123) is the only exception.

(121) ἀλλ' οὐδὲν γὰρ μέγα ἀπ' αὐτοῦ ἄλλο ἔργον ἐγένετο βασιλεύσαντος **δυῶν δέοντα τεσσεράκοντα ἔτεα**, τοῦτον μὲν παρήσομεν τοσαῦτα ἐπιμνησθέντες

But, as no other great deed was done by him, who ruled for thirty-eight years, we will move on from him, having mentioned only this much

(1.14.4)

Furthermore, τυραννεύω is also found with the accusative three times, but with ἐπί⁺ᴬ only once. That said, these figures overstate the case for explaining the difference with reference to verbal semantics, as the two constructions are much more evenly distributed – seven of each – with ἄρχω, which ought to line up with the other verbs of ruling.

Now these two factors, word order and collocations with particular verbs, do not appear to have anything in common, but it is just possible that they both fall out from the same communicative goal. As a starting-point, Dik's work on adjective-noun word order (1997) leads us to expect that the numeral will generally be more salient in the accusative of time constructions (where it is usually preposed) than it is in the prepositional phrases (where it is usually postposed).[129] On the whole, the sort of context in which the numeral would be more salient is easy to understand: it is the straightforward type seen in (121), where Herodotus' sole aim in the clause is to say how many years the ruler was in power for; as the specific number of years is important, that is placed first, and, in this construction, he prefers the simple accusative of time. Less intuitive is the pragmatic scenario in which ἔτος would be more salient than the numeral: 'He ruled for some years, twenty-five of them as it happens'.[130] Still, a few examples do suggest how this situation can arise:

---

[129] This position is seconded by Bakker (2009: 38–66); note esp. her example (52) on p. 59.

[130] Incidentally, we can also rule out the possibility that the numeral is postposed when it is a compound and therefore phonologically bulky (cf. Bakker 2009: 62–6, esp. n. 37): ex. (121) shows that Herodotus is perfectly happy to end a clause with a light ἔτεα after a heavier compound numeral. Other examples occur at 1.14.4, 1.102.1, 4.1.3. That said, once further modifiers have been added, then it becomes plausible that this additional complexity causes the numeral to be placed after ἔτεα; see the discussion of the second temporal phrase in ex. (124).

(122) μετὰ δὲ ἐξεχώρησαν ἐς Σίγειον τὸ ἐπὶ τῷ Σκαμάνδρῳ, ἄρξαντες μὲν Ἀθηναίων **ἐπ᾽ ἔτεα ἕξ τε καὶ τριήκοντα**, ἐόντες δὲ καὶ οὗτοι ἀνέκαθεν Πύλιοί τε καὶ Νηλεῖδαι

And afterwards they went to Sigeum-on-Scamander, after ruling the Athenians for thirty-six years, and being themselves Pylians in origin and descendants of Neleus (5.65.3)

Here, the Pisistratids have been expelled from Athens, and the communicative weight of the sentence apparently lies less on the exact number of years they ruled than was the case in (121), insofar as the temporal expression is nestled in the first half of a μέν . . . δέ opposition, rather than forming the blunt conclusion to the discussion of one ruler, before proceeding to the next. Even more so in the following example, the ἐπί-phrase, far from concluding a section, is further modified by a relative clause:

(123) τὸν μὲν δὴ τυφλὸν τοῦτον οἴχεσθαι φεύγοντα ἐς τὰ ἕλεα, τὸν δὲ Αἰθίοπα βασιλεύειν Αἰγύπτου **ἐπ᾽ ἔτεα πεντήκοντα**, ἐν τοῖσι αὐτὸν τάδε ἀποδέξασθαι

And this blind king fled off to the marshes, and the Ethiopian ruled Egypt for fifty years, in which he accomplished the following (2.137.2)

The only other potential example of ἐπ᾽ ἔτεα with βασιλεύειν is, as in example (122), in a μέν-clause; that said, the preposition is textually dubious, only occurring as a correction in manuscript D:

(124) Ἀστυάγης μέν νυν βασιλεύσας **ἐπ᾽ ἔτεα πέντε καὶ τριήκοντα** οὕτω τῆς βασιληίης κατεπαύσθη, Μῆδοι δὲ ὑπέκυψαν Πέρσῃσι διὰ τὴν τούτου πικρότητα, ἄρξαντες τῆς ἄνω Ἅλυος ποταμοῦ Ἀσίης **ἐπ᾽ ἔτεα τριήκοντα καὶ ἑκατὸν δυῶν δέοντα**, παρὲξ ἢ ὅσον οἱ Σκύθαι ἦρχον

Astyages, after ruling for thirty-five years, lost his kingdom in this way, and the Medes fell under Persian control because of his harshness, after ruling the part of Asia beyond the Halys river for 128 years, apart from as long as the Scythians ruled (1.130.1)

As for the second ἐπί-phrase in (124), with ἄρξαντες, here it is plausible to propose that the heaviness of the numeral constituent has caused it to gravitate to a later position: not just τριήκοντα καὶ ἑκατὸν δυῶν δέοντα, already fairly long on its own, but also the παρὲξ ἢ ὅσον clause, which further specifies the time range. A couple more examples show the relative complexity of the information being conveyed in clauses with ἐπί-phrases:

191

(125) ὃς μετὰ Ψαμμήτιχον τὸν ἑωυτοῦ προπάτορα ἐγένετο εὐδαιμονέστατος τῶν
πρότερον βασιλέων, **ἐπ' ἔτεα πέντε καὶ εἴκοσι** ἄρξας, ἐν τοῖσι ἐπί τε Σιδῶνα
στρατὸν ἤλασε καὶ ἐναυμάχησε τῷ Τυρίῳ

Who, after Psammetichus, his ancestor, was most fortunate of the kings up
to his day, having ruled for twenty-five years, during which he led an army
against Sidon and fought a sea-battle against Tyre (2.161.2)

(126) ἐπείτε δὲ ἐς τὴν Κύρνον ἀπίκοντο, οἴκεον κοινῇ μετὰ τῶν πρότερον
ἀπικομένων **ἐπ' ἔτεα πέντε** καὶ ἱρὰ ἐνιδρύσαντο

And when they arrived at Cyrnus, they lived there together with those who
had arrived earlier for five years and they established temples (1.166.1)

In (125), a relative clause is dependent on the temporal phrase; in
(126), the phrase is separated from the verb it modifies by a
prepositional phrase with an additional verbal element. With
these, contrast two more typical examples of the plain accusative
of time; in the first, the clause in which the phrase occurs serves no
purpose other than to indicate the length of the rule:

(127) ἀπικόμενοι δὲ ἐς τὸν Ταρτησσὸν προσφιλέες ἐγένοντο τῷ βασιλέι τῶν
Ταρτησσίων, τῷ οὔνομα μὲν ἦν Ἀργανθώνιος, ἐτυράννευσε δὲ Ταρτησσοῦ
ὀγδώκοντα ἔτεα, ἐβίωσε δὲ <τὰ> πάντα εἴκοσι καὶ ἑκατόν

And when they arrived at Tartessus, they became friends with the king of
the Tartessians, whose name was Arganthonius, and he ruled Tartessus for
80 years, and he lived in total for 120 (1.163.2)

The numeral-first word order is particularly understandable here
given the contrast between the length of Arganthonius' rule and
that of his life. In the second, the phrase occurs in a genitive
absolute, in a dry, detail-free sentence that does nothing beyond
state the bare facts of how the rule passed from one king to the next:

(128) Δηιόκεω δὲ παῖς γίνεται Φραόρτης, ὃς τελευτήσαντος Δηιόκεω,
βασιλεύσαντος **τρία καὶ πεντήκοντα ἔτεα**, παρεδέξατο τὴν ἀρχήν

And Deioces' son was Phraortes, who, when Deioces died, after ruling for
53 years, took over the kingdom (1.102.1)

In a final example, both the prepositional phrase and the simple
accusative occur in quick succession:

(129) ἐπὶ μέν νυν Βάττου τε τοῦ οἰκιστέω τῆς ζόης, ἄρξαντος **ἐπὶ τεσσεράκοντα
ἔτεα**, καὶ τοῦ παιδὸς αὐτοῦ Ἀρκεσίλεω, ἄρξαντος **ἑκκαίδεκα ἔτεα**, οἴκεον οἱ
Κυρηναῖοι ἐόντες τοσοῦτοι ὅσοι ἀρχὴν ἐς τὴν ἀποικίην ἐστάλησαν

During the life of Battus, the founder, who ruled for 40 years, and his son
Arcesilaus, who ruled 16 years, the Cyrenaeans who lived there numbered
as many as had been sent to the colony in the first place (4.159.1)

Here, both numerals occur before the modified noun, probably
because they show contrastive focus, but ἐπί is only used in the
first phrase. Its absence in the second expression can be attributed
to the general information structure of the sentence: in the first
phrase, the temporal phrase comes after a preceding prepositional
phrase with ἐπί$^{+G}$, the main verb is not yet in sight, and additional
specification of the role of τεσσεράκοντα ἔτεα is more helpful here
than in the second phrase, which is parallel to the first, and therefore less in need of being marked with ἐπί$^{+A}$. In conclusion, while
space does not permit an exhaustive look at the remainder of these
phrases, the passages discussed are representative of the basic
difference between the constructions with the accusative and
those with ἐπί:[131] the former typically occur when little more
information is being conveyed than the length of a rule, the latter
when the communicative goals are more complex.

Punctual expressions in Herodotus

Herodotus, like Attic authors, shows variation between both the
genitive and the dative – but the conditions are not quite the same.
Here, there is less of a categorical distinction between nouns that
favor the genitive and those that favor the dative, and, in its place, a
more fluid alternation based on subtle distinctions of event type, as
indicated by modifiers of the time nouns (see Table 20).

---

[131] As evidence that I have not skewed the examples in my favor, it should be noted that exx.
(124), (125), (129), are, together with 5.92ζ.1 (which, like the others, does *not* occur in a
bare-bones description of the succession passing from one king to another), the only four
passages out of the ten with a verb of ruling + ἐπί$^{+A}$ + ἔτεα in which the clause with the
temporal phrase consists only of the verb and the temporal phrase. Everywhere else,
additional information, such as what land is ruled, is conveyed. By contrast, constructions with the same pattern, but with the simple accusative, are found not only in (121),
(128) and the second temporal phrase in (129), but also at 1.16.1 (2×), 1.25.1, 1.86.1,
1.102.2, 2.127.1, 2.127.3, and 3.10.2. It is also reasonable to include four additional
constructions in this category, as the only constituent in the clause with the temporal
accusative besides the verb of ruling is an adverbial τὰ πάντα; all of these occur in
skeletal summaries of kings' successions: 1.214.3, 2.159.3, 3.66.2, 7.4.1.

Table 20. *Punctual and limitative expressions in Herodotus*

	genitive	dative	ἐν^{+D}

ἡμέρη	9× distributive
	8× limitative
	8× modal
		24× punctual
		21× w. ordinals, 1× each w. the relative pronoun, μιῇ, and τῇ ὑστεραίῃ
		1× limitative
		  w. μιῇ
		1× durative
		  w. τῇσι προτέρῃσι
			11× limitative
			1× punctual
			1× 'after'

μήν	3× distributive 1× limitative^{a}	4× punctual all w. ordinal numbers	2× limitative
ἔτος	9× distributive 3× limitative 1× punctual	27× punctual 23× w. ordinals, 3× w. τῷ προτέρῳ, 1× w. τῷ ὑστέρῳ	3× limitative
ἐνιαυτός	4× distributive	1× distributive w. τῷ . . . ἑκάστῳ	2× limitative 1× distributive 1× non-temporal
νύξ	1× distributive 1× habitual 1× limitative 6× modal 17× punctual	3× punctual 2× w. ordinal, 1× w.o. modifier	3× punctual 1× limitative 1× habitual
θέρος	11× modal	–	2× modal
χειμών	8× modal	1× punctual w. the article	3× modal

Note: ^{a} This phrase (9.101.2) is deleted in the OCT.

The dative is, once again, the more limited of the two in scope. Nearly all of the datives of time are neatly categorized as punctual, and most of the exceptions are easily explained. The most striking outlier is the durative expression with ἡμέραις:

(130) ἰδόντες δὲ τὸν χῶρον κεινὸν ἐν τῷ ἐτετάχατο οἱ Ἕλληνες **τῇσι προτέρῃσι ἡμέρῃσι,** ἤλαυνον τοὺς ἵππους αἰεὶ τὸ πρόσω

And, upon seeing that the land where the Greeks had been stationed on the previous days was empty, they kept riding their horses forward (9.57.3)

There are only a couple of parallels for the temporal dative of a plural noun,[132] but this phrase matches them closely enough to suggest that, though extremely rare, this construction was not impossible. Also noteworthy are the two constructions with μιῇ ἡμέρῃ, one of which I have labeled punctual, the other limitative:

(131) **μιῇ δὲ ἡμέρῃ** τοῦ ἐνιαυτοῦ, ἐν ὀρτῇ τοῦ Διός, κριὸν ἕνα κατακόψαντες καὶ ἀποδείραντες κατὰ τὠυτὸ ἐνδύουσι τὤγαλμα τοῦ Διὸς καὶ ἔπειτα ἄλλο ἄγαλμα Ἡρακλέος προσάγουσι πρὸς αὐτό

And on one day of the year, during the festival of Zeus, after chopping up and flaying one ram, in the same way they dress up the statue of Zeus and then bring up to it another statue, of Heracles (2.42.6)

(132) **μιῇ δὲ ἡμέρῃ** ἀπέδυσε πάσας τὰς Κορινθίων γυναῖκας διὰ τὴν ἑωυτοῦ γυναῖκα Μέλισσαν

And on one day [Periander] stripped all the Corinthian women of their clothing because of his own wife, Melissa (5.92η.1)

In (131), the temporal clause simply indicates that this act occurs on one day of the year and is thus best called punctual, even though the presence of the modifier 'one' is often associated with the limitative type.[133] Indeed, example (132) illustrates why this is so: very often, when one says that something happened 'on one day', the force of the numeral is similar to that of English 'a single', and the event in question is so described because it is contrary to the audience's expectation that so much could take place within the

---

[132] See esp. (7) and (78) (ταῖς πρώταις ἡμέραις in Xenophon and Plato, respectively). Ex. (86), in Demosthenes, is not as close a parallel.

[133] It comes close to the habitual type, but because it specifies that the event takes place on one day of the year, rather than repeatedly occurring during any generic day, the punctual category is more appropriate.

confines of a single day. That Periander burns the clothing of all the women of Corinth in order to satisfy the ghost of his wife certainly falls under this heading. The final anomalous dative of time is, unfortunately, textually uncertain, as manuscripts D R S V add ἐν. If we can trust that the preposition is a later addition (reasonable enough, insofar as the reading with the preposition would be *facilior*), the dative is here used, as in (131), of a repeating event:

(133) αὐτοὶ δὲ τὰ γινόμενα **τῷ ἐνιαυτῷ ἑκάστῳ** χρήματα διενέμοντο

And they distributed among themselves the money that came in each year

(3.57.2)

Here, however, the construction is better classified as distributive as the emphasis really is on the regular recurrence of the distribution, as shown by ἑκάστῳ. While it is easy to understand why the dative would have been an option in such a context – in the end, the phrase does say when the event occurred – it remains an unusual construction by Attic standards, and, together with some of the other examples seen below (constructions (143) and (144) with νύξ and (146) with χειμών),[134] hints that the dative of time might have still had a slightly wider range in Herodotus than in the Attic authors.

That said, the overwhelming impression given by the comparison of the genitive and dative columns in the table above is the same as in Attic: while the dative is mostly restricted to punctual expressions, often with ordinal numbers, the genitive has a much wider range of uses, primarily distributive, limitative, and modal, but also (though this is almost exclusively limited to νύξ) punctual. But before contrasting νυκτός and νυκτί, it is first important to mention a few of the limitative and modal examples of ἡμέρη, as these classifications require some justification. First, there are the eight limitative constructions with ἡμέρη. Two of these (2.115.6, 6.58.3) have ἡμερέων in the plural, modified by a cardinal number, and are thus unproblematic. A further four fall into this class because the time noun is modified by τῆς αὐτῆς (of these, one also has the demonstrative ταύτης), and thus assign multiple events to the same period of time, a scenario that favors the limitative

---

[134] The third construction with νύξ, (145), is an outlier better seen as an indirect object.

HERODOTUS

(5.77.2, 7.166.1, 9.90.1, 9.101.2). The seventh is limitative because it modifies a future tense: αὐτοὶ οὐκ ἐν νόῳ ἔχοντες ταύτης τῆς ἡμέρης τοῖσι Ἕλλησι ἐπιθήσεσθαι (8.7.2); the eighth, though not morphologically future, still refers to a coming event and actually comes close to being a predicative genitive:

(134) ὥρη μηχανᾶσθαι καὶ μὴ ἀναβάλλεσθαι, ὡς **τῆς ἐπιούσης ἡμέρης** ὁ ἀγὼν ἡμῖν ἔστι

It is time to plan and not to delay, as our contest is tomorrow (3.85.2)

As for the modal genitives, four have an explicit contrast with νυκτός or, once, τὴν νύκτα (2.133.4, 5.23.2, 8.71.2, and 2.95.2). Two more, both in the same episode, have an implied contrast with νυκτός, as they juxtapose what happened during the day with dreams seen at night (7.12.2, ὥσπερ τῆς ἡμέρης ἐβουλεύσαο ποιέειν, with ἐν τῇ νυκτί in the previous sentence, and 7.16β.2). In the seventh, the genitive is triggered by a combination of factors: it is partly a partitive genitive after πρωί, partly a defective genitive absolute (with ἔτι, but lacking ἐούσης), and partly modal because of the contrast with another time of day:

(135) τὸ μὲν γὰρ ἐν Πλαταιῇσι <τρῶμα> **πρωὶ ἔτι τῆς ἡμέρης** ἐγίνετο, τὸ δὲ ἐν Μυκάλῃ περὶ δείλην

For the battle at Plataea took place early, while it was still day, and that at Mycale in the late afternoon (9.101.2)

The final example perhaps comes the closest of the eight to being a simple punctual construction:

(136) ᾔδεσαν δὲ οὔκω ὅτι σφέας περιεκυκλοῦντο τῇσι νηυσὶ οἱ βάρβαροι, ἀλλ' ὥσπερ **τῆς ἡμέρης** ὥρων αὐτοὺς τεταγμένους ἐδόκεον κατὰ χώρην εἶναι

But they did not yet know that the Persians had surrounded them with their ships, but rather thought that they were still stationed in place just as they saw them during the day (8.78.1)

Now, there is some reason to consider this a punctual construction, insofar as the phrase refers to a one-time event: the commanders had seen the enemies' ships in a particular position that day. Nevertheless, a modal label is better, for a contrast between the daytime sighting and the night-time deliberations of the Greeks is still the more prominent function of the phrase. Even if the sentence

197

lacks the clear hallmark of a καὶ ἡμέρης καὶ νυκτός phrase, the nocturnal setting had been clearly established two paragraphs earlier: οἱ μὲν δὴ ταῦτα τῆς νυκτὸς οὐδὲν ἀποκοιμηθέντες παραρτέοντο (8.76.3). The constructions with νυκτός have, on the whole, a different profile from those with ἡμέρη, as the punctual type predominates (17×). Still, as in Attic, these are not prototypical punctual phrases, but share characteristics of the modal type, largely because they do not occur with ordinal numbers or demonstratives that specify which night the event took place; instead, usually (14×) νυκτός simply occurs on its own, without even an article. Typical are the following:

(137) ἐπελθόντας δὲ ἐπὶ τὰ βασιλήια **νυκτὸς** καὶ τὸν λίθον ἐπὶ τῷ οἰκοδομήματι
ἀνευρόντας ῥηιδίως μεταχειρίσασθαι καὶ τῶν χρημάτων πολλὰ ἐξενείκασθαι

And they came to the palace at night and, finding the stone in the building,
handled it easily and took out many of the valuables (2.121α.3)

Here, one could argue for a modal reading, as it is characteristic of thieves to operate at night, for darkness suits their activities better; moreover, the king will open the room up, presumably during the day, and discover that items have been stolen. But the situation is still different from the modal genitives of ἡμέρη, as this is – at this point in the narrative, at least – a single event, and there has not been any explicit contrast with daytime happenings. Furthermore, rather than being placed in a focal position before the verb (contrast (134) through (136)),[135] νυκτός is tucked away relatively late in the clause, suggesting that it is simply adding the incidental detail that the thieves came at night, rather than setting up an opposition with another time of the day. That said, there are other examples of punctual νυκτός where it does come before the verb:

(138) οἷα δὲ **νυκτός** τε ἀπικόμενοι καὶ λελυμένης τῆς γεφύρης ἐντυχόντες ἐς πᾶσαν
ἀρρωδίην ἀπίκοντο μή σφεας οἱ Ἴωνες ἔωσι ἀπολελοιπότες

But as [the Persians] arrived at night and found the bridge broken up, they
were caught up in a total panic that the Ionians had left them (4.140.4)

---

[135] See Dik (2007: 38).

In this passage, there is a stronger case for taking νυκτός as modal, as the fact that the Persians' arrival takes place at night is seen as contributing to their fear. Still, there is no real contrast with a daytime event, and it thus remains slightly closer to the punctual type than do examples of ἡμέρης like (136). Finally, a more neutral example:

(139) ἐλόχησαν τὴν ἐν Πηδάσοισι ὁδόν, ἐς τὴν ἐμπεσόντες οἱ Πέρσαι **νυκτός** διεφθάρησαν καὶ αὐτοὶ καὶ οἱ στρατηγοὶ αὐτῶν

> They waited in ambush on the road at Pedasa, and the Persians, stumbling upon it at night, were annihilated, both the men and their generals (5.121.1)

It is not entirely clear whether νυκτός goes more closely with ἐμπεσόντες or διεφθάρησαν. One might at first prefer the latter option, given that it is placed directly in front of the finite verb. But this throws a focal emphasis[136] on the temporal expression that does not seem justified by the context – unlike the instance in (138), νυκτός is not in a causal participial phrase – and the English reads more smoothly if we translate it with ἐμπεσόντες instead. In either case, that it is so difficult to assess which verb νυκτός modifies suggests that it provides a comparatively incidental piece of information and is therefore better classified as a punctual expression.

The three examples of punctual νυκτός where the time noun is modified are the following; first, one with the definite article:

(140) ταύτην μὲν τὴν ἡμέρην ἐς τοσοῦτο ἐγίνετο, **τῆς δὲ νυκτὸς** κελεύσαντος βασιλέος τὰς νέας οἱ στρατηγοὶ ἐκ τοῦ Φαλήρου ἀνῆγον ὀπίσω ἐς τὸν Ἑλλήσποντον

> Over the course of this day, events only amounted to that much, but at night, on the king's orders, the generals went about sailing the ships from Phalerum back to the Hellespont (8.107.1)

This construction follows the regular pattern of a durative accusative in a μέν-clause followed by a punctual phrase in a δέ-clause.[137]

---

[136] Naturally, constituents that occur before verbs need not be focal; they can also be settings or topics. But neither of these possibilities is plausible here: οἱ Πέρσαι is here an excellent candidate for topic assignment, and a setting constituent in this position is unexpected; contrast the temporal expressions of (140), which are much farther forward in their clauses.

[137] Looking back at ex. (136), one might object that τῆς νυκτός should be considered modal in light of the contrast between ταύτην τὴν ἡμέρην and τῆς νυκτός. But there is an important difference: here, τῆς νυκτός simply introduces a new stage in the sequence of

Even more typical of punctual constructions are the other two, both with τῆς παροιχομένης:

(141) ἅμ' ἡμέρῃ δὲ διαφωσκούσῃ οἱ ἓξ κατὰ συνεθήκαντο παρῆσαν ἐπὶ τῶν ἵππων· διεξελαυνόντων δὲ [κατὰ] τὸ προάστειον, ὡς κατὰ τοῦτο τὸ χωρίον ἐγίνοντο ἵνα **τῆς παροιχομένης νυκτὸς** κατεδέδετο ἡ θήλεα ἵππος, ἐνθαῦτα ὁ Δαρείου ἵππος προσδραμὼν ἐχρεμέτισε

And, at the first light of day, the six, as they had agreed, were there on their horses; and, as they were riding through the outer parts of the city, when they were at the place where the mare had been tied up the previous night, then Darius' horse ran up and neighed (3.86.1)

(142) τοῖσι δὲ βαρβάροισι κατηγέετο Ἱππίης ὁ Πεισιστράτου ἐς τὸν Μαραθῶνα, **τῆς παροιχομένης νυκτὸς** ὄψιν ἰδὼν ἐν τῷ ὕπνῳ τοιήνδε

And Hippias, son of Pisistratus, led the barbarians to Marathon, after seeing the following vision in his sleep the previous night (6.107.1)

Both of these passages are signposted as punctual by the presence of a modifier that specifies which night the event took place. However, the potential ambiguity between the punctual and the modal can be seen by comparing (141) with (136). In both passages, the temporal expression occurs in a subordinate clause that takes a chronological step back to give information about an earlier state of affairs. This, of course, raises the worrying possibility that the assignment of (136) to the modal type, and (141) to the punctual type is due to circular reasoning about the expected role of the genitive with ἡμέρης as opposed to νυκτός. But there is in fact no cause for alarm: in (141), the modifier τῆς παροιχομένης creates an important difference between the two passages, for it is the prototypical role of the punctual, not the modal expression, to single out one particular instance of the time noun in question as the setting for the event; and in (136), the use of ὥσπερ as a subordinating conjunction establishes a greater degree of parallelism – and hence, more of a modal contrast – between the events of day and those of night than ἵνα does in (141). These subtle differences, combined with the center of gravity of the rest of the data (many examples of

events (much as the indisputably punctual τῇ ὑστεραίᾳ often does) and is therefore not contrastive in the specific sort of way that would elicit a modal construction. In (136), by contrast, there is a juxtaposition of the two times: the earlier daytime disposition of the ships is considered at a time when the narrative has already reached the night. See also the discussion of (141) below.

νυκτός that are closer to the punctual type than are any of the expressions with the genitive ἡμέρης), are sufficient to establish the divergent behavior of the two time nouns.

Even so, Herodotus also offers a glimpse of a system in which temporal expressions are slightly less lexically determined than in Classical Attic prose. For there are also the three punctual expressions with the dative νυκτί. The first two, with ordinal numbers, show that νύξ can behave exactly like ἡμέρη in selecting for the dative.[138] Of these, example (143) is a fairly straightforward punctual construction, but (144) is more striking, as it refers to a customary practice rather than a one-time event, so one might expect a habitual expression. That one has the dative instead of the genitive shows the extent to which singling out the fact that the event occurs on the first night trumps the regularity of the custom:

(143) ὥς με ἠγάγετο Ἀρίστων ἐς ἑωυτοῦ, **νυκτὶ τρίτῃ** ἀπὸ τῆς πρώτης ἦλθέ μοι
φάσμα εἰδόμενον Ἀρίστωνι

When Ariston had brought me to his place, on the third night after the first, there came to me a phantom that looked like Ariston (6.69.1)

(144) πρῶτον δὲ γαμέοντος Νασαμῶνος ἀνδρὸς νόμος ἐστὶ τὴν νύμφην **νυκτὶ τῇ πρώτῃ** διὰ πάντων διεξελθεῖν τῶν δαιτυμόνων μισγομένην

And when a Nasamonian man first marries, it is the custom for the bride to have sex with all the guests in turn on the first night (4.172.2)

The third example, with no modifiers, is a marginal construction at best:

(145) μετὰ δὲ εὐφρόνη τε ἐγίνετο καὶ Ξέρξην ἔκνιζε ἡ Ἀρταβάνου γνώμη· **νυκτὶ δὲ** βουλὴν διδοὺς πάγχυ εὕρισκέ οἱ οὐ πρῆγμα εἶναι στρατεύεσθαι ἐπὶ τὴν Ἑλλάδα

And afterwards it was night, and Artabanus' opinion bothered Xerxes; and taking counsel at or with night, he fully realized that it was not in his interest to go to war against Greece (7.12.1)

From a communicative standpoint, νυκτί is superfluous as a temporal expression: that the event takes place at night has already been established by the preceding clause with εὐφρόνη. It is probably better, then, to see it as an indirect object of διδούς, comparable

---

[138] Cf. the Homeric exx. (5) and (6) in Ch. 5.

to the expression ἑωυτῷ λόγον ἔδωκε 'he thought the matter over to himself' (1.34.3), where the dative that occurs after the combination of δίδωμι with an abstract direct object really must be an indirect object.[139] The one potential dative of time with χειμών is superficially similar:

(146) ὃς ἦγε μὲν δυώδεκα νέας ἐκ Πάφου, ἀποβαλὼν δέ σφεων τὰς ἕνδεκα **τῷ χειμῶνι τῷ γενομένῳ κατὰ Σηπιάδα**, μιῇ τῇ περιγενομένῃ καταπλέων ἐπ' Ἀρτεμίσιον ἥλω

> [Penthylus,] who brought twelve ships from Paphos, but, after losing eleven of them in or to the storm that took place off Sepias, was sailing to Artemisium with the one that survived when he was captured (7.195.1)

Here, however, the naturalness of the English gloss with 'to' is misleading: unlike δίδωμι in (145), ἀποβάλλω does not regularly occur with datives, so the better label is the temporal dative.

Before leaving the comparison of the temporal genitive and dative behind, one final construction merits attention, the single punctual genitive with ἔτος:

(147) **τοῦ προτέρου ἔτεος** ἐπεὰν ἀπολίπῃ ὁ Νεῖλος, οἱ ἰχθύες ἐντεκόντες ᾠὰ ἐς τὴν ἰλὺν ἅμα τῷ ἐσχάτῳ ὕδατι ἀπαλλάσσονται

> In the year before, when the Nile recedes, the fish lay eggs in the mud, then depart with the last of the water (2.93.6)

While a dative might be expected here, given the singling out of a particular year, τοῦ προτέρου, the recurring nature of the event apparently shifts Herodotus towards using the genitive – even though the similar context in (144) elicits the dative. Given that there are so few comparanda, a definitive explanation of the difference between the two will remain elusive, but it seems probable that the dative is favored in (144) because of the ordinal number, a more constant companion of the dative of time than is the modifier ὁ πρότερος.

Overall, the picture is thus rather different from Thucydides: looking just at Herodotus, there is far less call for making a division between calendrical and non-calendrical time nouns. Rather, the

---

[139] Stein on 7.12.1 translates "der Nacht die Beratung überlassend"; of the parallels he adduces, Plut. *Them.* 26.2 (νυκτὶ φωνήν, νυκτὶ βουλήν, νυκτὶ τὴν νίκην δίδου, admittedly metrical) is the closest (1908: 26).

situation is closer to that described in the standard grammars, with the genitive used in punctual constructions primarily when they diverge from the prototypical examples of this class: while the majority of passages with punctual νυκτός are less modal than those with ἡμέρης, they still fall short of the punctual ideal, as there are no demonstratives or ordinals specifying the night in question. While there remain counter-examples, especially (141) and (142), and possibly also (140), where the genitive of νύξ is used in what is reasonably labeled a punctual construction, the strength of these is weakened by the existence of (147), where use of the genitive can extend to a relatively punctual non-calendrical time noun as well. It is easy to see how Thucydides' practice could have developed out of a lexicalized fossilization of Herodotean usage, and that the two thus show slightly different stages of development.

The final problem is the relationship of the expressions with ἐν to those with the genitive and dative. On the whole, they are closer to the genitive than they are to the dative. Especially with the calendrical time nouns, ἐν is used almost exclusively in limitative constructions. As in other texts, the main question then becomes: why do some limitative constructions take the genitive, others ἐν? With ἡμέρη, the modifiers of the time noun in the respective constructions are different. Four of the eight with the genitive are τῆς αὐτῆς (ταύτης) ἡμέρης; none of the eleven with ἐν have this modifier. Of the genitives, a further two also have the singular noun, and only two (25%) have the plural, both times modified by a cardinal number, both in prototypical (i.e. negative or future) limitative contexts.[140] With ἐν, however, seven of the eleven (64%) have the plural (again, all modified by cardinals), and, while some of these occur in the same sort of context as those with the genitive of time, they also extend to simple past-time events as well.[141] As the

---

[140] In 6.58.3, there is a negative (ἀγορὴ δέκα ἡμερέων οὐκ ἵσταταί σφι), in 2.115.6 a clear future sense (αὐτὸν δέ σε ... τριῶν ἡμερέων προαγορεύω ἐκ τῆς ἐμῆς γῆς ... μετορμίζεσθαι).

[141] Prototypical limitative passages with ἐν: 2.22.3 (ἐπὶ δὲ χιόνι πεσούσῃ πᾶσα ἀνάγκη ἐστὶ ὗσαι ἐν πέντε ἡμέρῃσι), 5.65.2 (ὥστε ἐν πέντε ἡμέρῃσι ἐκχωρῆσαι ἐκ τῆς Ἀττικῆς); passages with ἐν which extend beyond this usage: 1.185.2 (τρίς τε ἐς τὴν αὐτὴν ταύτην κώμην παραγίνονται καὶ ἐν τρισὶ ἡμέρῃσι, i.e. those sailing down the Euphrates go past the same village three times on three days), 2.29.6 (διεξελθὼν δὲ ἐν τῇσι τεσσεράκοντα

other time nouns are less frequent, the data are less conclusive, but some of the same trends are still apparent: in the only other construction with ὁ αὐτός, the genitive is used (with μηνός, at 9.101.2).[142] Of the six limitatives with ἔτος, the only one with the singular has the genitive, and of the five with the plural, the two that are genitives are both prototypical limitatives, and the only nonnegative, non-future-time construction has ἐν.[143] All in all, the usage seen in the Attic authors extends to Herodotus in this respect as well.

Polybius, Diodorus, Plutarch, Epictetus

On turning to later authors, we find that the patterning of temporal expressions is relatively stable diachronically as well, as the following brief sketches illustrate.

Polybius

There are thirty-one datives of time in books 1–5. Twenty-five of these are unproblematic punctual constructions, of which the most common subtypes are expressions with τῇ κατὰ πόδας ἡμέρᾳ (10×) and ἔτει + ordinal (9×). More interesting are the other six, all of which have some claim to be limitatives. Twice, the dative is less unusual, as the construction is a type of limitative that borders on the punctual, namely a clause with γίνεσθαι that sums up the events just described.[144] In the other four, however, the combination of a

---

ἡμέρῃσι τοῦτο τὸ χωρίον), 7.56.1 (διέβη δὲ ... ἐν ἑπτὰ ἡμέρῃσι καὶ [ἐν] ἑπτὰ εὐφρόνῃσι), 8.66.1 (καὶ ἐν ἑτέρῃσι τρισὶ ἡμέρῃσι ἐγένοντο ἐν Φαλήρῳ), 8.115.1 (καὶ ἀπικνέεται ἐς τὸν πόρον ... ἐν πέντε καὶ τεσσεράκοντα ἡμέρῃσι).

[142] This is not, to be sure, an independent example: it occurs in parallel with τῆς αὐτῆς ἡμέρης.

[143] The one construction with the genitive singular is 6.42.1; the prototypical limitatives with the genitive plural are 4.151.1 (negative: ἑπτὰ δὲ ἐτέων μετὰ ταῦτα οὐκ ὗε τὴν Θήρην) and 9.26.4 (in the provisions of a treaty, thus future-time: ἑκατόν τε ἐτέων μὴ ζητῆσαι κάτοδον ἐς Πελοπόννησον); the non-negative, non-future-time construction with a plural is 2.123.2 (τὴν περιήλυσιν δὲ αὐτῇ γίνεσθαι ἐν τρισχιλίοισι ἔτεσι). The other two constructions with ἐν are 2.142.3 (negative, past-time) and 7.149.1 (in a purpose clause).

[144] ταῦτα δὲ συνέβαινεν γίνεσθαι τῷ τρίτῳ πρότερον ἔτει τῆς Πύρρου διαβάσεως εἰς τὴν Ἰταλίαν (2.20.6), ταῦτά τ' ἐγίνετο τῷ πρότερον ἔτει τῆς Καρχηδονίων ἥττης (2.43.6). In both, the modifiers of the time noun bring the construction closer to other, more prototypical examples of the punctual type (e.g. 1.6.5, 2.43.3).

telic aorist with a plural time noun is much less typical of the dative; one instead expects ἐν or, possibly, the genitive:[145]

(148) γνῶναι πῶς καὶ τίνι γένει πολιτείας ἐπικρατηθέντα σχεδὸν ἅπαντα τὰ κατὰ τὴν οἰκουμένην **οὐχ ὅλοις πεντήκοντα καὶ τρισὶν ἔτεσιν** ὑπὸ μίαν ἀρχὴν ἔπεσε τὴν Ῥωμαίων

To know how and conquered by what sort of constitution nearly all the inhabited world fell under Roman rule alone in not quite fifty-three years
(1.1.5)

While earlier authors occasionally use the simple dative with plural time nouns (Hdt. 9.57.3 = ex. (130) and the examples in n. 132) or in limitative constructions (Hdt. 5.92η.1 = ex. (132); possibly also Pl. *Mx.* 243a8 = ex. (77)), these appear to be the first examples where both of these conditions are fully satisfied.[146] As noted by others, Polybius' extension of the temporal dative, considering that the dative was generally in retreat in the Hellenistic era, might well be the result of interference from the Latin ablative of time.[147]

The temporal genitive, however, is still the more widely used of the two, with forty-eight examples in the first five books. But even it seems relatively unflexible when compared to the wide range of uses seen in Herodotus and other authors. Fully forty-one of them are punctual constructions, thirty-one of these with νυκτός, another seven with τῆς νυκτός, two more with τῆς νυκτὸς τῆς αὐτῆς and τῆς

---

[145] Indeed, Pédech in the Budé prints Heyse's emendation, adding the expected ἐν; he opts for the simple dative, though, in the remaining 3 examples in these books: 3.56.3 (ἡμέραις δεκαπέντε), 5.26.16 (ταῖς ἑξῆς ἡμέραις), and 5.92.2 (ταῖς αὐταῖς ἡμέραις). In the first of these, it is just possible that the omission of ἐν is rendered easier by ἐν πέντε μησί in the preceding μέν-clause, but the phrase with the simple dative occurs after the articulation of a new clause with δέ, so the force of the preposition cannot really carry over.

[146] D. 21.34 = ex. (86) does not really count, as there are too many complicating factors.

[147] Dubuisson is happy to ascribe this usage to Latin influence (1985: 238–9). Adams is more cautious (2003: 507–8), but Ward, with additional data from Josephus, has probably tipped the balance in favor of interference from Latin (2007: 640–1). Cf. also Langslow (2002: 43–4, 2012: 96–8). In favor, however, of a more organic development of this construction from a native Greek origin is the fact that Polybius still uses ἐν[+D] to mark the vast majority of his limitative phrases, and it is striking how many of the anomalous datives occur with verbs of accomplishing and conquering, with which the dative can be read as a relatively easy extension of the instrumental (as is regularly the force of the dative χρόνῳ 'in time'), e.g. exx. (159), (169)–(173), and (182) below; but cf. also n. 205. The two explanations need not be mutually exclusive, with Latin influencing Greek first in those contexts where the construction is somehow compatible with existing Greek syntax.

EXPRESSIONS OF TIME: STYLE, GENRE, AND DIACHRONY

ἐπιούσης νυκτός, and one with μέσου χειμῶνος. The constructions
with νύξ are all familiar from other authors, but the one with χειμών
offers further evidence that seasons could trigger a punctual
genitive:

(149) τὴν δ᾿ ἀποσκευὴν ἀναλαβὼν ἐκ τῆς Ἡραίας ἦλθε **μέσου χειμῶνος** εἰς Μεγάλην
πόλιν

And when he had taken up the baggage from Heraea, he came in the middle
of the winter to Megalopolis (4.80.16)

That said, this one example is balanced by a lone punctual dative
with θέρος (τῷ δ᾿ ἐπιγινομένῳ θέρει πάλιν ὁρμήσας ἐπὶ τοὺς
Οὐακκαίους, 3.14.1), so there is insufficient evidence to determine
Polybius' preferred practice with these time nouns. Of seven non-
punctual genitives of time, five are modal (καὶ θέρους καὶ χειμῶνος
at 3.55.9, μήθ᾿ ἡμέρας μήτε νυκτός at 5.100.4, and ποτὲ μὲν ἡμέρας,
ποτὲ δὲ νύκτωρ at 1.73.7), one is distributive (ἑκάστου μηνός,
5.1.12), and only one is limitative:

(150) συνήθεις δ᾿ ἐκ τῶν κατὰ Σικελίαν ἀγώνων πολλάκις **τῆς αὐτῆς ἡμέρας** ποτὲ
μὲν ὑποχωρεῖν, ποτὲ δὲ πάλιν ἐκ μεταβολῆς ἐγχειρεῖν τοῖς πολεμίοις

And accustomed after the battles in Sicily to withdraw many times on the
same day, then turning around, to attack the enemy again (1.74.9)

That the genitive is used only here in a limitative expression is
probably due to the fossilization of the phrase τῆς αὐτῆς ἡμέρας: as
just seen, this particular phrase is disproportionately common in
Herodotus with the genitive, with ἐν otherwise the more common
limitative marker.

Generally, the preference for ἐν has become much more marked
in Polybius 1–5, where, compared to the sole limitative genitive,
there are thirty limitatives with ἐν (twenty-three with ἡμέρα, three
with νύξ, and two each with μήν and ἔτος), including such usual
suspects as constructions with future-time reference and negatives
(e.g. 3.40.4 and 4.86.2 respectively) and past-time telic events said
to occur within a time frame rather than at a particular time (e.g. six
examples of ἐν ὀλίγαις ἡμέραις). Of the four remaining temporal
expressions with ἐν, three are punctual constructions with νυκτί,
where the preposition is apparently preferred to the genitive on
syntactic grounds: in all three with ἐν, and in none with the genitive,

the phrase occurs with an attributive participle (always from (προ)γίνομαι) itself introduced by a preposition: ἐκ τῆς προγεγενημένης ἐν τῇ νυκτὶ πορείας (2.25.10), διὰ τὸν ἐν τῇ νυκτὶ γενόμενον ἐν τοῖς ὑπὲρ τὰ στρατόπεδα τόποις ὄμβρον (3.72.4), διὰ τὴν ἐν τῇ νυκτὶ προγεγενημένην ἀλογίαν (5.53.7). There are, to be sure, three examples of (τῆς) νυκτός modifying definite attributive participles, but in all of these the participle is an animate sentence subject, which gives them a rather different feel: οὗτος δ᾽ ἦν ὁ τὰς δυνάμεις ἐκκλέψας νυκτὸς ἐκ τῆς τῶν Ἀκραγαντίνων πόλεως (1.23.4), ὁ δὲ κατὰ τύχην εἰσπλεύσας νυκτός (1.47.7),[148] οἱ τῆς νυκτὸς ἀποβάντες (3.19.2). Probably, a sort of syntactic hierarchy is in play: in the latter three passages with the genitive, the nominative outranks the genitive, and so the genitive, clearly preferred on purely numerical grounds, can stand; in the passages with ἐν, on the other hand, the temporal phrase is itself dependent on a prepositional object that does not outrank the genitive, and, as a result, Polybius opts for the clearer marker, ἐν.[149] The final punctual expression with ἐν sits at the intersection of several event types:

(151) Ἀντίοχος δὲ μεγάλῃ παρασκευῇ χρησάμενος **ἐν τῷ χειμῶνι**, μετὰ ταῦτα τῆς θερείας ἐπιγενομένης ὑπερέβαλε τὸν Ταῦρον

And Antiochus, after getting a lot of preparation done during the winter, afterwards, when summer came on, crossed the Taurus mountains (5.107.4)

One could argue for a modal reading here (there is a contrast between wintertime and summertime activity) or for a limitative one (a great deal of preparation is accomplished in the bounded time frame of the winter), but on the whole a punctual reading seems best. Winter and summer are not presented as balanced alternatives, as is typical of the modal type, but as different stages in a sequence (note μετὰ ταῦτα); and μεγάλῃ, unlike πάσῃ or τοσαύτῃ, does not carry the implication that the preparation

---

[148] This example only barely falls into this category, as ὁ is really the anaphoric pronoun.

[149] For other examples of such case hierarchies, consider the fact that relative pronouns that would otherwise be in the accusative are attracted to the more marked genitive or dative, but not vice versa (Smyth 1920: §2522). That constructions in Polybius are sensitive to the case of a head participle can also be seen in his agent expressions: with εἰρημένος and πεπραγμένος, if the participle was in the genitive, he preferred the dative of agent to ὑπό[+G] by a 16 : 3 ratio; if it was in the dative, he preferred ὑπό[+G] to the dative by an 8 : 1 ratio (George 2005: 99–100).

consisted of multiple activities that all had to be fit into a limited period. The morphological singleton νύκτωρ again occupies ambiguous ground. On the one hand, it is clearly the preferred marker for explicit modal constructions, occurring in five (4× paired with μεθ᾽ ἡμέραν, 1× with ἡμέρας, 1.73.7), while ἐν τῇ νυκτί is not used in this way, and νυκτός only occurs once (5.100.4). On the other hand, the remaining three examples of νύκτωρ are punctual constructions that can hardly be distinguished from the numerous examples with νυκτός. That said, they do conform to a coherent pattern, in that all occur directly after an aorist verb of motion: ἐξέπλευσε νύκτωρ ἔτι ... εἰς τὰ Δρέπανα (1.46.1), τῇ τρίτῃ τῶν ἡμερῶν κατῆρε νύκτωρ εἰς Καφύας (4.70.1), ὁρμήσας νύκτωρ μετ᾽ ὀλίγων ἐποιήσαντο τὴν εἰς πόλιν πάροδον (5.23.5). But, since the genitive, found with many other types of verbs as well, can also be found under the same conditions (ὥστε ... φυγεῖν νυκτὸς εἰς τὰς Συρακούσας (1.15.3), ἐξεπήδησαν νυκτὸς ἐκ τῆς πόλεως ἐπὶ τὸ στρατόπεδον (1.43.1)), it remains unclear what triggers νύκτωρ instead.[150] A further complication is the existence of three accusatives of time which are unusually punctual, a usage of the accusative found in Polybius only with νύκτα:[151]

(152) ὑπολαμβάνοντες τοὺς περὶ τὸν Αἰμίλιον περιπεπορεῦσθαι **τὴν νύκτα** τοῖς ἱππεῦσι καὶ προκαταλαμβάνεσθαι τοὺς τόπους

Supposing that Aemilius' cavalry had marched past during the night and occupied those places in advance (2.27.6)

---

[150] The favored conditions for punctual νύκτωρ in Xenophon are similar, but not as homogeneous: four out of the six examples occur directly after a verb (HG 5.3.24, 7.1.41, An. 4.4.9, 7.8.20); but in only two of those is the verb one of motion. In Plato, νύκτωρ is found in only three punctual constructions; in none of these does it occur immediately after the verb, but in all three, the verb is one of motion: περιιόντες (Cra. 433a7), ἐξαγαγών (Grg. 471b5), ἰόντος (R. 574d4). Just to confuse the picture, though, in Plutarch, the one author where νύκτωρ and νυκτός do show a difference, it is νυκτός that is preferred with verbs of motion; see below.
[151] The closest that Polybius comes to marking the punctual event type with the accusative of another time noun is the following: οἱ πρότερον ἔτος ὕπατοι γεγονότες (3.116.11). Usually the punctual dative is found with a modifier like πρότερον – e.g. οἱ τῷ πρότερον ἔτει στρατηγοῦντες (3.114.6) – as it is generally a sign that the temporal phrase specifies which year an event took place, not how long it lasted. Still, insofar as the event in 3.116.11 is the durative state of being consul for the whole year, the choice of the accusative is understandable.

(153) τοὺς δ' ἐπιτηδειοτάτους εὐζώνους ποιήσας διῆλθε τὰ στενὰ **τὴν νύκτα** καὶ κατέσχε τοὺς ὑπὸ τῶν πολεμίων προκαταληφθέντας τόπους

And after setting up the most appropriate of his men as light soldiers, he crossed the narrows at night and occupied the places that had been held earlier by the enemy (3.50.9)

(154) ἀναλαβὼν τοὺς προκατασχόντας **τὴν νύκτα** τὰς ὑπερβολὰς ὥρμησε παραβοηθήσων τοῖς τῇ πορείᾳ προλαβοῦσιν

Taking those who had occupied the passes in advance during the night, he set out to help those who had gotten started on the march (3.51.6)

In all three of these passages, the subject of the verb modified by τὴν νύκτα has made some forward movement during the night, as indicated by the verbal prefixes in each case (περι-, δι-, προ-). The situation again resembles that with punctual νύκτωρ: while they form a coherent group, it is unclear what triggers this accusative, when Polybius is content to use the genitive in such examples as ὃς ἐπιπλεύσας νυκτὸς ἐν τῷ λιμένι συνέκλεισε τοὺς περὶ τὸν Γνάιον (1.21.7), προσπλέουσιν τῆς νυκτὸς ἑκατὸν λέμβοι πρὸς τὴν Μεδιωνίαν (2.3.1), or παρῆλθε νυκτὸς ὡς ὀγδοήκοντα σταδίους ὑποκάτω τῆς τοῦ Μόλωνος στρατοπεδείας (5.46.11). In any case, examples (152) through (154) are important as further evidence[152] for an incipient punctual accusative of time.

Another factor that apparently plays a role in Polybius' temporal expressions is phonotactics. In distributive expressions with ἑκάστην ἡμέραν, one finds καθ' ἑκάστην ἡμέραν seven times, ἀν' ἑκάστην ἡμέραν five times. Neither preposition shows a particular affinity with one tense or another (all seven with κατά occur with the present; so too all but one with ἀνά, the exception modifying an imperfect). Nor do they associate with verbs of a particular semantic field: ἀνά occurs with πονέω, ποιέω (once with (ἀντ)ενέδρας as object, once with ἀναπείρας καὶ μελέτας), ἐνδίδωμι, and γίνομαι (with συμπλοκαί as subject), κατά with ἀκροβολίζομαι, ἐπιπορεύομαι, ἐπινοέομαι, προσδοκάω, ἀναφέρω, ἀθροίζομαι, and διαμάχομαι. Phrases with both prepositions occur regularly with both participles and infinitives. The chief difference seems to be that four of the five examples of ἀνά are

---

[152] In Attic, the first steps towards this usage are found in Demosthenes (examples (111) through (113) above); cf. also exx. (115) and (116) from Herodotus.

preceded by the syllable -ων (once ὤν, once ποιῶν, and twice participles in -ντων), whereas this is never true of the counterpart expressions with κατά. Given the gradual decline of ἀνά in the Greek prepositional system,[153] it is reasonable to assume that κατά would have been the preferred preposition in such constructions and that ἀνά is motivated by some additional consideration. That this consideration was the desire to avoid the sequence -ων καθ- is possible;[154] however, it must remain tentative, insofar as Polybius had no absolute stricture against this combination.[155]

Polybius' temporal expressions also show, for the first time, a noticeable extension of κατά[+A] beyond the distributive and habitual types with time nouns other than χρόνος. There are sporadic examples of this in earlier authors, especially the following summing-up limitative constructions:[156]

(155) καὶ **κατὰ τὸ ἔτος τοῦτο** ἐκ τῶν Περσέων οὐδὲν ἐπὶ πλέον ἐγένετο τούτων

And in this year, nothing more was done by the Persians along these lines
(Hdt. 6.42.1)

(156) καὶ **κατὰ τὸ ἔτος τοῦτο** οὐδὲν ἐπὶ πλέον τούτων ἐγένετο

And in this year, nothing more happened along these lines (Hdt. 9.121.1)

But in Polybius 1–5 there are eight good examples, which probably build on the Herodotean constructions above. Closest are the two examples with ἐνιαυτός, both of which sum up what did (or did not) happen in a particular year:

(157) **κατὰ μὲν τὸν ἑξῆς ἐνιαυτὸν** οὐδὲν ἄξιον ἔπραξαν λόγου

In the following year, they did nothing worthy of note (1.24.8)

---

[153] For the decline of ἀνά, see Bortone (2010: 162, 185).

[154] Certainly, variation between the spatial uses of κατά[+A] and ἀνά[+A] in Homer seems due more to metrical factors than to a semantic difference; see George (2006).

[155] A *TLG* search reveals only 32 instances of -ων καθ- in Polybius 1–5, compared to 232 of -ων αν-, a ratio of 1 : 7.25. To test whether this is sufficiently few examples of -ων καθ- to merit description as a dispreferred combination, consider as a control group the number of words in book one that begin with καθ- and αν-: 86 and 402 respectively, a ratio of 1 : 4.67. This ratio is indeed different enough to suggest that Polybius avoided -ων καθ-. If he had been indifferent to what syllable preceded καθ- and αν-, the 232 examples of -ων αν- should have been matched by roughly 50 of -ων καθ-.

[156] Herodotus also offers one punctual example, κατὰ ταύτην τὴν ἡμέρην ἠρίστευσαν Ἀθηναῖοι (8.17.1). In Thucydides, there is one durative and one limitative example (1.93.3 and 3.116.3 (= exx. (95) and (96) in Ch. 2)). There are no examples in Xenophon, Plato, or Demosthenes.

(158) ταῦτα δὲ πάντα συνέβη γενέσθαι **κατὰ τὸν τρίτον ἐνιαυτὸν τῆς ἑκατοστῆς καὶ τετταρακοστῆς ὀλυμπιάδος**

And all this happened to take place in the third year of the 140th Olympiad (5.105.3)

There are also three examples with ἔτος, all of which again assign events to the 140th Olympiad, though in these passages it is specific events that take place: Λεύκιον τὸν Αἰμίλιον ἐξαπέστειλαν ... ἐπὶ τὰς κατὰ τὴν Ἰλλυρίδα πράξεις κατὰ τὸ πρῶτον ἔτος τῆς ἑκατοστῆς καὶ τετταρακοστῆς ὀλυμπιάδος (3.16.7), τούτου δὲ τοῦ δόγματος κυρωθέντος κατὰ τὸ πρῶτον ἔτος τῆς ἑκατοστῆς καὶ τετταρακοστῆς ὀλυμπιάδος (4.26.1), ἐγένετο δ' ἡ συμπλοκὴ τῶν πράξεων περὶ τὴν τοῦ πολέμου συντέλειαν κατὰ τὸ τρίτον ἔτος τῆς ἑκατοστῆς καὶ τετταρακοστῆς ὀλυμπιάδος (4.28.5). A further two examples, with χειμῶνα, recall one of the two Thucydidean examples (ταῦτα μὲν κατὰ τὸν χειμῶνα τοῦτον ἐγένετο, Th. 3.116.3): τὰς παρασκευάς ... ἃς ἐπεποίητο κατὰ χειμῶνα πρὸς τὴν πολιορκίαν (5.99.1), ἀκούων κατὰ χειμῶνα λέμβους ναυπηγεῖσθαι τὸν Φίλιππον πλείους (5.110.8). The final example, with ἡμέρα, again has a partial precedent in Herodotus (8.17.1; see n. 156): κατὰ δὲ τὴν ἐπιοῦσαν ἡμέραν ... προῆγε μετὰ τῆς λοιπῆς δυνάμεως ἐπὶ τὴν προκειμένην χρείαν (5.68.11). Still, even though all these Polybian passages have some precedent in earlier language, their concentration in one text is something new in Greek.

Diodorus

In books 11–15 of Diodorus Siculus' universal history, there are only five datives of time, all with ἡμέρα. Four of these are straight-forward punctual constructions (11.24.1, 14.115.6, 15.79.4, 15.91.3). Though rare, they do not give the impression of being a fossilized relic, as the modifier of ἡμέρα is different in each instance (τῇ αὐτῇ, τῇ τετάρτῃ, τεταγμένῃ, τῇ πρότερον). The fifth example is striking, as it is a limitative construction with the time noun in the plural:

(159) Ἱμίλκων δὲ **δυσὶν ἡμέραις** κατανύσας εἰς τὸν τῶν Καταναίων αἰγιαλόν

But Himilcon, having made it to the Catanian shore in two days (14.61.4)

We see here the continuation of a possibly Latinate dative of time, already present in Polybius (see ex. (148) and n. 147). The genitive of time is much more common (66×), but hardly more flexible: all but one of these involve νυκτός. The one exception is a modal example of ἡμέρας, in parallel with νυκτός, at 15.48.2. Two more passages with νυκτός also count as modal, one where it is contrasted with ἐφ᾽ ἡμέρας (13.108.8), one with καθ᾽ ἡμέραν (15.26.4). In a further two passages (both in 13.18.3), νυκτός, both times with the definite article, occurs in limitative constructions. The remaining sixty examples of temporal νυκτός are all punctual, and, in all but five of these, the time noun has no modifiers whatsoever,[157] resulting in a very homogeneous usage of the genitive of time.

Nor is ἐν used in a wide range of temporal expressions: twelve limitative and four punctual constructions. These do break down more or less in accordance with a division between calendrical time nouns (ten of the limitative constructions are with ἡμέρα, one with ἔτος, and all of those have the noun in the plural; only one is with νύξ (13.2.3), but it is especially clearly limitative because of the presence of μιᾷ as a modifier) and non-calendrical ones (two of the punctual constructions are with χειμών, one with θέρος, and only one with ἐνιαυτός). In effect, ἐν has replaced the genitive of time, apart from with νυκτός: it is the default limitative marker for ἡμέρα, and punctual marker with the seasons.

Diodorus, then, has a comparatively limited use of all three of the major temporal markers of the Classical period, the genitive, dative, and ἐν. In part, this is simply due to a lower number of temporal expressions. But two other constructions are more common than in the authors seen already. First, he is very fond of the genitive absolute: in books 11–15, there are sixty-nine temporal genitive absolutes with νύξ, θέρος, ἡμέρα, ἔτος, and χειμών. Many of these are formulaic, of which the most frequent are τοῦ ἔτους τούτου διεληλυθότος (12×),[158] νυκτὸς οὔσης (10×), and (τῆς)

---

[157] The modifiers in the five exceptions: the definite article twice, and once each τῆς ἐπιούσης, ἀσελήνου, and ἀσελήνου καὶ χειμερίου.

[158] In all of these, the absolute occurs in a δέ-clause that announces a new ruler in Athens – some form of ἄρχω, ἄρχων, or ἀρχή is always present. In all but 2, the absolute is directly followed by Ἀθήνησι μέν.

νυκτὸς ἐπιγενομένης (8×). In such cases, the genitive absolute sometimes appears virtually equivalent to a simple genitive of time (omitting the participle from νυκτὸς οὔσης changes the semantics little), sometimes broadly analogous to the genitive or dative of time, but specifying more precisely the point during the time noun during which the event occurred: τοῦ ἔτους τούτου διεληλυθότος, unlike τῷ ἔτει τούτῳ, draws attention to the fact that the event modified takes place at the close of the year in question, and τῆς νυκτὸς ἐπιγενομένης to its occurrence at the onset of the night. The same is also true of Diodorus' less stereotyped genitive absolutes. For instance, of the six with ἡμέρα, five belong to this type: τῆς ἡμέρας ὑποφωσκούσης (13.18.6, 13.111.2), ἡμέρας γενομένης (11.10.4), ἐπιλαβούσης ἡμέρης (15.48.3), and the following:[159]

(160) οὔσης δὲ τῆς ἡμέρας ταύτης καθ᾿ ἣν ἔμελλε συντελεῖν τὴν θυσίαν Ἀμίλκας, κατὰ ταύτην Γέλων ἀπέστειλεν ἰδίους ἱππεῖς

And, when it was the day on which Hamilcar was to carry out the sacrifice, on this day Gelon sent off his own cavalry (11.21.5)

Here, the presence of οὔσης at the start of the absolute perhaps suggests a causal force that goes beyond what could be conveyed by a simple dative of time, but the resumptive κατὰ ταύτην hints at another explanation for the absolute: Diodorus is communicating enough information in the whole temporal expression – there is, after all, an entire relative clause nested within it – that it is advantageous to have a more syntactically substantial construction to house all of it.

This example also illustrates the other temporal marker that becomes common in Diodorus, κατά$^{+A}$, used twice here in punctual expressions, and, all in all, eighty-three times with ἡμέρα, νύξ, θέρος, ἐνιαυτός, and ἔτος, in books 11–15.[160] As in other respects, here too Diodorus' language is relatively formulaic. Thirty of these are distributive expressions of the sort seen in other authors: 18× καθ᾿ ἡμέραν, 1× καθ᾿ ἑκάστην ἡμέραν, 7× κατ᾿ ἐνιαυτόν, 4× καθ᾿

---

[159] In the sixth example, enough additional information is conveyed by the verb in the absolute construction that it is no longer equivalent to a simple temporal phrase: ταχθείσης δὲ τῆς ἡμέρας, οἱ μὲν Κυμαῖοι ὑπελάμβανον ἑαυτοὺς πλεονεκτεῖν διὰ τὸ τὴν αὐτῶν πόλιν ἐγγυτέρω κεῖσθαι (15.18.3).

[160] For Diodorus' fondness for κατά$^{+A}$, see Palm (1955: 72).

ἕκαστον ἐνιαυτόν. Two more expressions, κατὰ τὸ θέρος (12.58.4) and καθ' ἡμέραν (15.26.4), are closely related, being habitual and modal respectively. But the remaining fifty-one are all of the sort – limitative, punctual, and durative – that are extremely rare in Classical Attic and only start to become common in Polybius. The largest contingent of these phrases consists of those with κατὰ τοῦτον τὸν ἐνιαυτόν (33×). Generally, this phrase is used in limitative summing-up expressions at the end of a year (e.g. 16× directly after ταῦτα μὲν οὖν ἐπράχθη, 3× in τῶν δὲ κατὰ τοῦτον τὸν ἐνιαυτὸν πράξεων) and is thus particularly reminiscent of examples (155) through (158) from Herodotus and Polybius. But in addition to the twenty-five limitative examples of this type, there are eight more where it moves more into punctual territory, as well as another five with different modifiers (or different word order with the demonstrative), for example:

(161) ἤκμασαν δὲ **κατὰ τοῦτον τὸν ἐνιαυτὸν** οἱ ἐπισημότατοι διθυραμβοποιοί

And the most famous poets of dithyrambs were at their height in this year
(14.46.6)

(162) τὴν ἅλωσιν τῆς Ῥώμης ὑπὸ Γαλατῶν, ἥτις ἐγένετο **κατὰ τὸν προηγούμενον ἐνιαυτὸν** τῆς Περσῶν στρατείας εἰς Κύπρον

The sack of Rome by the Gauls, which happened in the year before the Persians' expedition to Cyprus (15.1.6)

Nor are such constructions limited to ἐνιαυτός. There are two very similar examples with ἔτος that also follow directly on ταῦτα μὲν οὖν ἐπράχθη (12.3.4, 12.81.5). (These are primarily different from those with ἐνιαυτός in that ἔτος is modified by an ordinal number rather than the demonstrative and is followed both times by τοῦ (Πελοποννησιακοῦ) πολέμου.) Twice κατά governs τὴν (τεταγμένην) νύκτα; in both instances, the event is simplex enough to merit categorization as punctual rather than limitative (εἶδε ... τοιαύτην ὄψιν 13.97.6, ἦγον τὸ στρατόπεδον ἐπὶ τὴν Κατάνην 13.6.4). Finally, there are another nine relevant constructions with ἡμέραν. Four times in books 11–15, Diodorus writes κατὰ τὴν αὐτὴν ἡμέραν. Here the nature of the modifier makes a limitative interpretation possible.[161] In a fifth passage, the event described is regular and repeating (εὔξασθαι ... ἄγειν κατὰ ταύτην τὴν ἡμέραν τοὺς Ἕλληνας ἐλευθέρια κοινῇ 11.29.1), and so, despite the demonstrative, is perhaps better seen as habitual than punctual, in which case it would represent less of a divergence from Classical Attic practice. The other four examples, however, (one durative, three punctual) show the full flexibility with which Diodorus used this preposition:

(163) καὶ προσεπειπόντος ὅτι **καθ' ὅλην τὴν ἡμέραν**, ἂν ζημιοῦν θέλωσιν, ἐκτίσει τἀργύριον ὑπὲρ αὐτοῦ

And when he added that, if they wanted to keep fining him, he'd pay the money on his behalf for the whole day (13.91.4)

(164) ὁρμηθῆναι δὲ ἐκ τῆς ἰδίας πόλεως ἅμ' ἡλίῳ ἀνιόντι **κατὰ τὴν ἡμέραν**, ἣν ἀμφότεροι συμφώνως ὑποστήσονται

And they would set out from their own city at sunrise on the day that each side would agree in proposing (15.18.2)

(165) Ἀλεξάνδρου δ' ἑλόντος τὴν πόλιν ... **κατὰ τὴν ὁμώνυμον ἡμέραν καὶ τὴν αὐτὴν ὥραν** ἐν ᾗ Καρχηδόνιοι τὸν Ἀπόλλωνα περὶ Γέλαν ἐσύλησαν

And as Alexander conquered the city on the day of the same name and at the same time at which the Carthaginians plundered the Apollo at Gela (13.108.4)

(166) τοὺς δ' ἑτοίμους **κατὰ τὴν συντεταγμένην ἡμέραν** παραγενηθέντας

And those who arrived, prepared, on the day that had been agreed upon (11.81.5)

In the first three of these examples, to be sure, one could quibble about the best assignment of event type: both (163) and (164) have verbal events that take place in the future, and so might be influenced by limitative constructions; in (165), the limitative type is again a possibility given the similarity between ὁμώνυμος and ἡ αὐτή as modifiers. But the presence of ὅλην in (163) makes the durative reading override any limitative force; the exactness with which the two parties are to leave on the proposed day of (164) suggests the punctual more than the limitative; as for (165),

---

[161] See the discussion (preceding ex. (134)) of Herodotus' expressions with τῆς αὐτῆς ἡμέρης.

constructions singled out as limitative on the basis of modification by ὁ αὐτός are already a borderline type, best considered limitative only when other evidence points in that direction (e.g. uniformly occurring with what is otherwise primarily used as a limitative marker). In the end, though, what is important is not the precise classification of the constructions – which, after all, is to some extent an artificial problem, based on the arbitrary division of a continuum of meaning into discrete segments – but rather the sheer existence of so many borderline examples in Diodorus, which shows that, unlike the other constructions, which are more reduced in range, he uses κατά⁺ᴬ with a freedom not found in other authors.

Furthermore, that κατά⁺ᴬ should come to be so common in past-time limitative constructions makes sense considering the spatial semantics of the preposition: it is differentiated from ἐν in typically denoting the scattered location of multiple items within a landmark.¹⁶² Its extension, however, to more punctual constructions requires some explanation. At this point in the history of Greek (the first century BC), it is reasonable to see the gradual decline of the dative at work: not only is the dative in its own right becoming less common, but the prepositions that govern it are also employed with diminishing frequency.¹⁶³

The last preposition of interest to consider is διά⁺ᴳ, which only occurs in three temporal constructions in Diodorus 11–15, all with νυκτός. In one, the preposition is expected, as the phrase is durative and emphasizes that the event lasted for the whole night: τούτοις δ' ἦν παρηγγελμένον πυρὰ καίειν δι' ὅλης τῆς νυκτός (13.111.2). In a second passage, the preposition may also have this force, but a punctual reading is also possible:¹⁶⁴

(167) ἤγγελλόν τινες **διὰ νυκτὸς** εἴδωλα φαίνεσθαι τῶν τετελευτηκότων

Some of them reported that ghosts of those who had died appeared throughout the night (13.86.3)

That a punctual interpretation of διὰ νυκτός in (167) is plausible can be seen from the final example:

---

¹⁶² See Luraghi (2003: 209–10). ¹⁶³ See Bortone (2010: 181–3, esp. n. 26).
¹⁶⁴ Oldfather, in the Loeb edition, translates simply "in the night."

(168) οἱ δὲ Σελινούντιοι τῶν ἱππέων τοὺς κρατίστους ἐπιλέξαντες **διὰ νυκτός** εὐθέως ἀπέστειλαν τοὺς μὲν εἰς Ἀκράγαντα, τοὺς δ' εἰς Γέλαν καὶ Συρακούσας

And the Selinuntians picked the best of their cavalry and sent them immediately in the night, some to Acragas, others to Gela and Syracuse (13.56.1)

Here, it is very hard to view διὰ νυκτός as durative considering that the event it modifies is also described as taking place εὐθέως. That διὰ νυκτός comes to be punctual is not an isolated trait of Diodorus': we will see this as well in the next author in the corpus, Plutarch.

Plutarch

In the first fourteen *Lives* of Plutarch,[165] there are 35 datives of time, all but one with calendrical time nouns (20× ἡμέρα, 9× ἔτος, 5× μήν, 1× νύξ). As in Polybius, most of these are punctual, but as many as ten have some claim to be considered limitative. The constructions with μήν are a typical microcosm: three are stereotypical punctual phrases with ordinals (*Thes.* 27.5, *Rom.* 14.1, *Per.* 28.1), one is an outlier because it is modified both by the month name and by the participle λήγοντι, thus making it look almost like a sort of dative absolute;[166] the fifth, however, in which the plural μησὶν ἐννέα modifies a telic aorist, shows the spread of the dative into the limitative type; it also stands in parallel with the one limitative temporal dative of ἔτος:[167]

(169) θαυμαστὸν δέ τι καὶ μέγα φρονῆσαι καταπολεμήσαντα τοὺς Σαμίους φησὶν αὐτὸν ὁ Ἴων, ὡς τοῦ μὲν Ἀγαμέμνονος **ἔτεσι δέκα** βάρβαρον πόλιν, αὐτοῦ δὲ **μησὶν ἐννέα** τοὺς πρώτους καὶ δυνατωτάτους Ἰώνων ἑλόντος

---

[165] For Plutarch, my corpus includes the *Lives* of Theseus, Romulus, Lycurgus, Numa, Solon, Publicola, Themistocles, Camillus, Pericles, Fabius Maximus, Alcibiades, Coriolanus, Timoleon, and Aemilius Paulus, as well as the associated comparisons. The time nouns included in the database are ἡμέρα, νύξ, μήν, θέρος, χειμών, ἔτος, and ἐνιαυτός.

[166] τὸ μὲν οὖν ἔτος ἱσταμένου θέρους εἶχεν ὥραν καὶ λήγοντι μηνὶ Θαργηλιῶνι πρὸς τὰς τροπὰς ἤδη συνῆπτε τὸν καιρόν (*Tim.* 27.1).

[167] It is unlikely that Plutarch's use of the dative here is due to his source, as Ion of Chios lived in the 5c BC, long before the limitative dative started to flourish (Stadter 1989: lxi).

217

And Ion says that he prided himself on his amazing defeat of the Samians, as Agamemnon took a barbarian city in ten years, but he took the foremost and the most powerful of the Ionians in nine months (*Per.* 28.7)

While the growth of a limitative dative of time is often ascribed simply to the influence of Latin (see n. 147), this example shows an additional impetus for this construction: rather than a locative dative pinpointing the action, it can be read as a perlative, instrumental dative ('over the course of nine months'), much as is regularly the case, even in Attic, with χρόνῳ. Examples with ἡμέρα are more numerous (7×); four are prototypically limitative, with the time noun modified by a cardinal number or ὀλίγαι:[168]

(170) μὴ προπηλακισθεὶς οὕτως ὑπὸ τῶν στρατηγῶν **ὀλίγαις ἂν ἡμέραις** ἠνάγκασε Λακεδαιμονίους διαναυμαχεῖν αὐτοῖς ἄκοντας ἢ τὰς ναῦς ἀπολιπεῖν

Had he not been insulted like this by the generals, in a few days he would have forced the Spartans, against their will, to fight their sea-battle to the end or to abandon their ships (*Alc.* 37.2)

The other three are closer to the punctual type because they are modified by a demonstrative or similar word usually used to pinpoint a particular day. Of these, the first two are still better classified as limitative because the time noun is plural (not characteristic of the punctual dative of time in Classical Attic); the third is borderline but could still be considered limitative because multiple actions are assigned to the day in question:

(171) σημεῖον μὲν λαμβάνων τὸ τοῦ δράκοντος, ὃς ἀφανὴς **ταῖς ἡμέραις ἐκείναις**[169] ἐκ τοῦ σηκοῦ δοκεῖ γενέσθαι

Taking as a sign the matter of the snake, which seems to have gone missing from the sacred enclosure during those days (*Them.* 10.1)

(172) **ταῖς δ' ἑξῆς ἡμέραις** σκηψάμενος ἀρρωστεῖν ἐξωμόσατο τὴν ἀρχήν

And over the next days, pleading illness, he renounced his office (*Cam.* 39.4)

(173) δύο νίκας, ὦ δίκτατορ, **τῇ σήμερον ἡμέρᾳ** νενίκηκας

You have won two victories, dictator, on this day (*Fab.* 13.7)

---

[168] So too δύο ἡμέραις (*Aem.* 24.1), μιᾷ ἡμέρᾳ (*Aem.* 36.4), ἡμέραις ὀλίγαις (*Rom.* 10.3).
[169] Manuscript family Y has the word order ἐκείναις ταῖς ἡμέραις.

While examples like these, based on the traditional understanding of the dative of time when, might seem at first glance unremarkable, they in fact have very few parallels in Attic[170] and, especially considering that they represent a full third of the twenty temporal datives with ἡμέρα in these *Lives* of Plutarch, show an extension of the construction beyond its earlier range.

As for the remaining datives of time, the nine with ἔτος, apart from (169), are all standard punctual constructions (eight modified by ordinal numbers, one by τῷ ἑξῆς), but the one with νύξ – not a noun that frequently took a dative of time in Attic – is limitative (multiple events, all limited to the time frame of a single night):

(174) ἡ μέντοι τῶν Ἑρμῶν περικοπή, **μιᾷ νυκτὶ** τῶν πλείστων ἀκρωτηριασθέντων
τὰ πρόσωπα, πολλοὺς καὶ τῶν περιφρονούντων τὰ τοιαῦτα διετάραξε

The mutilation of the Herms, however, when most of them had their faces disfigured on one night, frightened many even of those who think little of such things (*Alc.* 18.6)

It is worth recalling the Thucydidean parallel (6.27.1 = ex. (48) in Chapter 2), where the dative of time is also found: there, it is very much an anomaly, and one can make a reasonable case for emending it away; in Plutarch, however, the numerous other limitative datives of time make it far more plausible.

By contrast, Plutarch's use of the genitive of time follows Attic models rather closely (18× νύξ, 15× ἡμέρα, 5× μήν, 1× each ἔτος and χειμών in the first fourteen *Lives*). Most (12×) of the examples with νύξ consist solely of νυκτός, and these include both habitual-modal (*Thes.* 25.5, *Lyc.* 12.7) and punctual constructions (e.g. *Sol.* 9.1, *Cam.* 29.5). Several times, an expression with ἡμέρα is in the near vicinity, but the two verbal events are treated sequentially, rather than as alternatives to each other, and they are thus perhaps more punctual than modal:[171]

(175) ὅσοι δὲ **νυκτὸς** ἀπέδρασαν ἐκ τοῦ χάρακος οὐ πολλοί, τούτους **μεθ᾽ ἡμέραν**
σποράδας ἐν τῇ χώρᾳ διαφερομένους ἐπελαύνοντες ἱππεῖς διέφθειρον

---

[170] See the discussion of (148) in Polybius for the Attic parallels.

[171] Other examples where νυκτός and a modal expression with ἡμέρα form a chronological sequence: *C.Per.Fab.* 2.2 (also with μεθ᾽ ἡμέραν), *Alc.* 31.3 (with ἡμέρας); closer to a punctual expression is a passage where νυκτός μέν is paired with ἅμα δὲ τῇ ἡμέρᾳ (*Fab.* 11.3).

As for the few who ran away from the camp by night, the cavalry chased them down by day as they were scattered through the countryside and destroyed them (*Cam.* 23.7)

Still, that the second temporal phrase is μεθ᾽ ἡμέραν, a typical modal expression, means that some modal contrast is still in play. In a further two expressions, the only additional modifier νυκτός has is ἔτι, which makes these look like the defective genitive absolutes seen earlier.[172] The remaining four are all limitative or modal.[173]

With ἡμέρα, most of the examples again fall into categories seen in Attic: three are distributive,[174] three are modal,[175] and seven are limitative. Of these, only one is firmly in the limitative camp (ἡμερῶν ὀλίγων, *Tim.* 21.6); the other six are all only limitative in that the temporal phrase is τῆς αὐτῆς ἡμέρας. Even though a past-time event is described as taking place on a particular day, potentially favoring a punctual construction, the modifier ἡ αὐτή, by assigning a second event to a period of time already established by the preceding narrative, can shunt the speaker towards a limitative construction. That said, it does seem to be a quirk of Plutarch's to be quite so fond of this particular phrase: in the earlier authors studied, it only occurs four times in Herodotus (5.77.2, 7.166.1, 9.90.1, 9.101.2), once in Plato (*Smp.* 203e2) and once in Polybius (1.74.9). The final two examples diverge more from Attic precedent:

(176) οὐκ ἔγνω ποιεῖσθαι τῆς τιμωρίας ἀναβολήν, ἀλλ᾽ εὐθὺς ἦγεν ἐπὶ τὸ Σούτριον **ἐκείνης τῆς ἡμέρας**

He decided not to delay his revenge; rather, he led them immediately to Sutrium on that day (*Cam.* 35.3)

---

[172] *Cam.* 41.3, *Fab.* 7.1. For earlier examples of what look like defective genitive absolutes, see e.g. exx. (36) and (67) in Ch. 2.

[173] Limitative: ὁρῶντα τῆς αὐτῆς ἡμέρας καὶ νυκτὸς τὸν αὐτὸν ἰδιώτην ἐκ βασιλέως γινόμενον (*Num.* 2.7), ἐδόκει δὴ τῆς νυκτὸς ἀποχωρεῖν (*Them.* 12.2), ἐκεῖνον δὲ τῆς ἑτέρας νυκτὸς ἥκειν κελεύσας (*Aem.* 26.3); modal: χρηματίζειν ἐξ μὲν ὥρας τῆς νυκτός, ἐξ δὲ τῆς ἡμέρας (*Num.* 2.6). This last example could also be considered adnominal.

[174] *Sol.* 23.6, *Cam.* 10.3, 27.6.

[175] *Num.* 2.6 (possibly adnominal; see n. 173), *Cam.* 25.2 (ἡμέρας in μέν-clause; contrast with σκοταῖος in the δέ-clause), *Alc.* 31.3 (contrast with νυκτός).

POLYBIUS, DIODORUS, PLUTARCH, EPICTETUS

(177) τῆς δὲ τρίτης ἡμέρας ἕωθεν μὲν εὐθὺς ἐπορεύοντο σαλπιγκταί

And on the third day, at dawn the trumpeters immediately marched out

(Aem. 33.1)

With (176), the text is problematic,[176] and the reading ἄγειν for ἦγεν would be preferable, as, in that case, the verbal event will not yet have taken place, making ἐκείνης τῆς ἡμέρας easier to understand as a limitative genitive. In (177) the genitive is harder to understand – ordinals being particularly prone to elicit a punctual dative – unless we are somehow to take it as limitative because it will serve as a time frame encompassing a sequence of multiple events. This interpretation is well in line with the following ἕωθεν μέν, which sets up precisely this expectation. The only snag is that the passage does not then continue with further temporal subdivisions of the day, each linked with δέ, but rather with more general phrases (e.g. μετὰ δὲ τούτους, εἶτα, τούτοις ἐπέβαλλε). Still, in this paragraph Plutarch does go on to describe the rest of the procession, so one need not completely reject the possibility that τῆς τρίτης ἡμέρας acts as a broad time frame for all of what follows. But even if one can justify a limitative genitive, it remains the case that there are no Classical parallels for this in my corpus: the genitive singular of ἡμέρα is never found modified by an ordinal number, and when it occurs with demonstratives or similar modifiers, it is in clearer limitative constructions, like Th. 7.40.2, Pl. *Cri.* 44a and *Lg.* 917c, where it looks forward to an event or is negated.

As for the remaining genitives of time, the five with μήν include two distributive examples *(Sol. 20.4, Cam. 19.12)* and one habitual construction *(Rom. 4.5)*; in the last two of these, an adnominal reading is also possible. A fourth example is limitative (δέκα μηνῶν οὐκέτι συνῆλθεν αὐτῇ, *Alc.* 23.9), and the fifth is punctual *(Thes. 27.3)* – an event-type well-attested for the genitive of time of μήν in Demosthenes.[177] The temporal genitive of ἔτος is limitative (ἐτῶν εἴκοσι τὸ βῆμα καὶ τὴν ἀγορὰν ἰδεῖν οὐκ ὑπέμεινεν, *C.Tim.Aem.* 2.11), and that with χειμών is perhaps punctual, but more likely to be habitual *(Lyc. 15.1)*; in either case, it conforms with Classical precedent.

[176] Manuscript S reads ἦγεν, while family Y reads ἄγειν.   [177] See e.g. exx. (89) and (90).

221

On turning to ἐν, what is most surprising is that Plutarch does not use it more often than he does: only twenty-two examples in the first fourteen *Lives* (11× ἡμέρα, 4× μήν, 3× ἔτος, 2× χειμών, and 1× each ἐνιαυτός and νύξ). In some sense, this low frequency is simply the corollary of his extension of the dative of time to limitative constructions where one would have otherwise expected ἐν. And when Plutarch does use the construction, it is generally in a limitative context: true of all but one of the examples of ἡμέρα and all of those with ἔτος.[178] These thus conform with Attic usage, as do those with χειμών, where ἐν marks a modal-habitual construction.[179] Also Attic is the use of ἐν with non-calendrical νύξ to mark a punctual construction.[180] Of the four with μήν, two are habitual and thus unremarkable,[181] but the remaining two, as well as the one with ἐνιαυτός, are more noteworthy as punctual constructions with calendrical time nouns; first, the two with μήν:

(178) τὴν μὲν τῇ μητρὶ τοῦ Ῥωμύλου γεγονέναι σύλληψιν **ἔτει πρώτῳ** τῆς δευτέρας ὀλυμπιάδος **ἐν μηνὶ κατ᾽ Αἰγυπτίους Χοιὰκ τρίτῃ καὶ εἰκάδι** τρίτης ὥρας, καθ᾽ ἣν ὁ ἥλιος ἐξέλιπε παντελῶς, τὴν δ᾽ ἐμφανῆ γέννησιν **ἐν μηνὶ Θωὺθ ἡμέρᾳ πρώτῃ μετ᾽ εἰκάδα** περὶ ἡλίου ἀνατολάς

[The astrologer Tarutius said that] the mother of Romulus conceived him in the first year of the second Olympiad in the month the Egyptians call Choeac on the 23rd day at the third hour, at which time the sun was completely eclipsed, and the actual birth took place in the month of Thoth on the twenty-first day at about the rising of the sun (*Rom.* 12.5)

Here, in quick succession, are a couple of useful minimal pairs: ἔτει and ἡμέρα occur as datives of time, but Plutarch feels obliged to use ἐν with μηνί. Now there is some Classical precedent for this: of the fourteen examples of ἐν with μήν in Herodotus, Thucydides, Xenophon, Plato, and the Demosthenic corpus, eight are clearly limitative (all of these but one are plural, e.g. X. *HG* 1.1.37; the one

---

[178] With ἡμέρα: *Pub.* 16.9 (2×), *Cam.* 35.5, *Alc.* 15.2, 18.8, *Cor.* 23.10, 31.7, *Tim.* 16.2, *Aem.* 36.4, 36.7; the expression at *Rom.* 21.4 is habitual (δρᾶται γὰρ ἐν ἡμέραις ἀποφράσι τοῦ Φεβρουαρίου μηνός). With ἔτος: *C.Thes.Rom.* 6.4, *Num.* 8.8, *Tim.* 37.6.

[179] These are ἐν τῷ χειμῶνι at *Lyc.* 16.7 and ἐν χειμῶνι πολλῷ (here 'storm') at *Cor.* 32.1.

[180] ἐν τῇ παρῳχημένῃ νυκτί (*Cam.* 14.3); insofar as this phrase has a modifier that specifies the particular night, it is closer to the prototypical punctual construction than are the corresponding phrases with the genitive.

[181] ὅταν τὰς ἱερὰς πέλτας ἀναλάβωσιν ἐν τῷ Μαρτίῳ μηνί (*Num.* 13.4), ὅθεν καὶ τὴν ἡμέραν ἐκείνην ἐπινίκιον, οὖσαν ἐν τῷ Ἰουλίῳ μηνὶ τὰς εἰδούς, Διοσκόροις ἀνιερώκασι (*Cor.* 3.6).

exception is X. *Ages.* 2.1, but it too is unambiguously limitative), one is habitual (Th. 2.15.4), but the other five have some claim to the punctual label. Of these, two are marginal,[182] but the three that occur in Apollodorus' *Against Timotheus* are a reasonable precedent for Plutarch's usage here.[183] Compared to ἡμέρα and ἔτος, μήν, when combined with the name of the month, apparently avoided the dative of time in favor of the punctual markers more associated with the non-calendrical time nouns, both the genitive and ἐν. Finally, the passage with ἐν . . . ἐνιαυτῷ is the following:

(179) **ἐν δὲ τῷ κατόπιν ἐνιαυτῷ** λοιμώδης νόσος ἐμπεσοῦσα τῇ Ῥώμῃ τὸν μὲν ἄλλον ὄχλον οὐ περιληπτὸν ἀριθμῷ διέφθειρε, τῶν δ' ἀρχόντων τοὺς πλείστους

And in the following year, a plague fell upon Rome and killed an immense number of the people and most of the officials (*Cam.* 43.1)

What stands out here is the attributive use of κατόπιν. This is not a word common in Attic prose (2× in Thucydides, 1× in Xenophon, 2× in Plato; Demosthenes and, for that matter, Herodotus avoided it altogether), but it had become common in Diodorus (9×) and, especially, Polybius (55×). None of these, however, offer an exact parallel to Plutarch's attributive usage, although Plb. 1.46.7 is close (καὶ τὴν κατόπιν [*sc.* ἡμέραν] εὐθέως ἐγίνετο περὶ ἀναγωγήν "and the following day he busied himself with the return trip"). That κατόπιν should be so un-Attic reinforces the comparative novelty of a punctual construction of ἐνιαυτός signaled by ἐν – not

---

[182] Both occur in Plato: σπείρας εἰς τὸ προσῆκον, ἀγαπώῃ ἂν ἐν ὀγδόῳ μηνὶ ὅσα ἔσπειρεν τέλος λαβόντα; "after sowing at the appropriate time, would he be content if everything which he sowed reached its full growth in the eighth month?" (*Phdr.* 276b) and τὸ τῶν τούτοις ἑπομένων οὐ συμμεικτέον ἀλλὰ χωριστέον, ἐν τῷ τοῦ Πλούτωνος μηνὶ τῷ δωδεκάτῳ κατὰ τὸν νόμον ἀποδιδόντας "and what is connected with the two groups of gods are not to be mingled together, but rather to be kept separate, placing it [i.e. worship of the gods of the Underworld] by law in the twelfth month, of Pluto" (*Lg.* 828d). In the first, the temporal phrase is ultimately dependent on a potential optative, making the construction forward-looking enough that it could be considered limitative. In the second, the prepositional phrase is almost more spatial than temporal, with the worship in question in some sense physically separated from other religious celebrations. Furthermore, that this is regularly to be so suggests that ἐν could here be used as a marker of the habitual type.
[183] These are ἐν τῷ μαιμακτηριῶνι μηνί ([D.] 49.22, 49.62) and ἐν τῷ θαργηλιῶνι μηνί (49.60); all three modify telic aorists.

completely unparalleled in Attic, but only found once in Apollodorus in a curiously similar description of a natural event:

(180) ἡ δὲ γῆ οὐχ ὅπως τινὰ καρπὸν ἤνεγκεν, ἀλλὰ καὶ τὸ ὕδωρ ἐν ἐκείνῳ τῷ ἐνιαυτῷ ... ἐκ τῶν φρεάτων ἐπέλιπεν

And the land not only brought forth no crops, but even the water in that year ... disappeared from the wells ([D.] 50.61)

While one could just about assign both (179) and (180) to the limitative category on the grounds that multiple events are said to take place in the time frame (multiple deaths in the first, multiple failures of wells in the second), it is probably better to view Apollodorus as anticipating a relaxing of the conditions under which ἐν could occur, as seen in both (178) and (179).[184] In the final analysis of Plutarch, however, this must be set against the much more pronounced spread of a limitative dative of time.

Given this confusion between the dative and ἐν, it comes as a welcome surprise to find that the particular sphere of νύκτωρ, especially the difference between it and νυκτός, is more sharply defined in Plutarch than elsewhere.[185] In the first fourteen *Lives*, there are fourteen examples of νύκτωρ, as against fourteen of νυκτός (including the two examples with ἔτι) and another two with τῆς νυκτός. Both are used predominantly in punctual constructions modifying aorists, but both are also found in modal expressions. Indeed, either one may be paired with μεθ'

---

[184] Calling these constructions limitative would be unwise because it would open up too many other punctual constructions to being relabeled as limitative: generally, assignment to the limitative type under the 'multiple events' rubric can only be justified if there is a more explicit signal that the temporal phrase is viewed more as a frame than as a point (e.g. a modifier of the sort seen in ἐν ὀλίγαις ἡμέραις), or if the multiplicity of the events is highlighted by a numeral or a quantifier like πάντα or πολλά (e.g. οὐδὲ δύο ἀρχὰς ἄρξαι τὸν αὐτὸν ἐν τῷ αὐτῷ ἐνιαυτῷ D. 24.150). The other example which comes closest to showing a punctual use of ἐν τῷ ... ἐνιαυτῷ in my corpus of Classical authors is a limitative – but borderline punctual – passage at D. 33.25: καίτοι προσῆκεν ... προσελθεῖν αὐτόν μοι ἔχοντα μάρτυρας καὶ ἀπαιτῆσαι τὴν ἐγγύην, εἰ μὴ προπέρυσιν, ἐν τῷ ἐξελθόντι ἐνιαυτῷ. Here the irrealis context (much like a negative) makes it easier to assign this to the limitative heading and, therefore, to understand the use of ἐν.

[185] The dative and ἐν, by contrast, are not in competition with νύκτωρ: the sole dative, ex. (174), is a limitative construction, and the only example with ἐν is a punctual construction specifying the night in question (see n. 180).

Table 21. Νύκτωρ *and* νυκτός *in Plutarch*

Type of verb	νύκτωρ	νυκτός
motion verbs	ἧκε πρὸς αὐτόν (*Fab.* 22.3)	διαπλεύσαντα εἰς τὴν νῆσον (*Sol.* 9.1) ἀπέδρασαν ἐκ τοῦ χάρακος (*Cam.* 23.7) ἀνάψαντας ἐλαύνειν ἐπὶ τὰς ὑπερβολάς (*Fab.* 6.6) εἰς τὰς τάφρους κατέσπειρε τῶν στρατιωτῶν τινας (*Fab.* 11.3) ἐμβαλὼν εἰς τὸ πέλαγος (*Tim.* 8.5) εἰς Πέλλαν εἰσελθών (*Aem.* 23.6)
intermediate verbs	παρεισπεσόντας[a] (*Rom.* 27.5) ἡ φωνὴ τῷ Μάρκῳ προσέπεσε (*Cam.* 30.4) πυρσὸν ἄραι (*Rom.* 29.7)	ἀναστήσας ἅπαντας ἐξέλιπε τὴν πόλιν (*Cam.* 29.5) τῷ Καπιτωλίῳ ἐπέθεντο (*Cam.* 36.2) προέμενος λαθόντα (*C.Per.Fab.* 2.2) ὑποστρέψας (*Alc.* 31.3)
non-motion verbs	ἀνοίξασα πύλην μίαν (*Rom.* 17.3) ἐκβοῆσαι τρίς (*Them.* 28.6) ὑφελέσθαι τὰ ἐγχειρίδια (*Cam.* 33.5) κατατρῆσαι τὴν οἰκίαν (*Alc.* 17.6) ἐμπρῆσαι τὴν οἰκίαν (*Alc.* 39.9) τὰ χρήματα ἀνέλαβεν (*Aem.* 26.3)	(none)

Note: [a] Of enemies breaking into Scipio Africanus' house and smothering him.

ἡμέραν.[186] The chief difference apparently lies in the semantics of the verbs they modify, as the genitive is preferred with verbs of motion, as shown in Table 21.[187] The first row of the table shows the constructions where the verb clearly indicates directional motion, in that a prepositional goal or source expression is present. In such passages, Plutarch favors νυκτός by six to one. Meanwhile, the bottom row lists the passages where there is no such motion: here νύκτωρ is favored by six to zero.[188] With the passages that fall somewhat in between these categories (there is a verb of motion, but no prepositional phrase explicitly indicating goal or source), there is a roughly even division between νυκτός (4×) and νύκτωρ (3×).[189] What is less clear is why νυκτός is favored when there is explicit motion towards or away from a place, and νύκτωρ in other circumstances. Given the numerical balance between the two, it is difficult even to begin by assuming that one or the other was the unmarked expression, and the other triggered by a particular environment. We might be tempted to view νύκτωρ as unmarked, given the wider semantic range of verbs with which it occurs – but that would ignore the fact that νυκτός is flexible enough to occur with the definite article and additional modifiers as well. Still, the best solution perhaps lies with the awareness that in these particular examples, νυκτός does not take advantage of this flexibility and is thus more limited in

---

[186] νυκτός paired with μεθ' ἡμέραν: *Cam.* 23.7, *C.Per.Fab.* 2.2; νύκτωρ paired with μεθ' ἡμέραν: *Thes.* 6.9, *Lyc.* 28.2. The latter examples are closer to the prototypical modal type than those with νυκτός (see the discussion of ex. (175)), but there are enough non-modal examples with νύκτωρ, and enough relatively modal examples with νυκτός that we cannot distinguish between them on the grounds that one is more modal than the other.

[187] The chart only contains punctual constructions.

[188] All of these verbs do, of course, involve some degree of motion, but even in the case of opening a door (probably the most motion of the six), there is not the same sense of a complete translational shift from point A to point B that is conveyed by the verbs in the top row.

[189] In fact, one could reasonably go further in assigning this middle row to the top and bottom row, thereby bringing the distribution of the two constructions into still greater relief: the three motion verbs that occur with νύκτωρ all refer to a comparatively minimal amount of motion along a vertical axis (literal, in the case of lifting a signal light; figurative, when one speaks of 'falling into a house' or having a voice 'fall upon one') and could thus be moved to the bottom row. By contrast, those with νυκτός all refer to the same sort of horizonal translation that, combined with a goal or source expression, belong in the top row.

range. That being so, νύκτωρ, by virtue of being morphologically distinct, might have been favored when it was particularly important to highlight its semantic role (note that the non-motional verbs with which it occurs are often quite dramatic: burning or breaking into a house, hiding daggers, lifting a signal fire), while νυκτός, the genitive having other uses as well, would have been more at home in routine descriptions of the night-time movements of soldiers and the like.

Before leaving νύξ, it should also be noted that Plutarch, like Diodorus (see examples (167) and (168)), extends the use of διά⁺ᴳ beyond the durative with this time noun alone:

(181) ἐκείνη κατὰ τύχην παρεξιόντες ᾗ **διὰ νυκτὸς** ὁ Πόντιος προσέβη τῷ Καπιτωλίῳ

By chance passing by that point where, by night, Pontius had gone up to the Capitoline (*Cam.* 26.2)

One such example on its own could perhaps be somehow explained away as durative, but in combination with the other three examples,[190] one can only conclude that διά⁺ᴳ really had begun to mark punctual constructions with this time noun. This might in turn further support the explanation for the distribution of νύκτωρ and νυκτός given above: somehow the genitive νυκτός was gradually becoming an insufficient marker of the punctual event type and was subject to replacement by διά⁺ᴳ or νύκτωρ. In all four passages, motion is again involved, making these constructions closer to those with νυκτός than those with νύκτωρ. Furthermore, with this particular preposition and this particular time noun, it again[191] seems a real possibility that a spatial metaphor – that of motion through the night as a palpable setting – is in play.

---

[190] Two are punctual: εἰς Βηίους αἱ φυγαὶ διὰ νυκτὸς ἦσαν (*Cam.* 18.9), τοῖς ἡγεμόσι φράσας τὸ ἀληθὲς ἦγε διὰ νυκτὸς τὴν ἐναντίαν ἀπὸ θαλάσσης (*Aem.* 15.8). A final example refers to future time and therefore moves into the limitative category: καὶ λαβὼν μέρος τι τῆς στρατιᾶς ἔμελλεν ὁρμήσειν διὰ νυκτός (*Fab.* 19.8).
[191] See exx. (97) through (101) in Ch. 2, where ὑπό⁺ᴬ (in Thucydides) and διά⁺ᴬ (in Homer) apparently retain some spatial force with νύξ.

Epictetus

While the writings of Epictetus are potentially a useful source of information for the state of Greek in the early second century AD,[192] they are not rich enough in temporal expressions to help this study very much. With ἡμέρα, νύξ, μήν, θέρος, χειμών, ἐνιαυτός, and ἔτος, there are only nine accusatives of time, three datives of time (two of which occur in the same sentence), eight genitives of time, and one temporal use of ἐν. But even with these low numbers, some constructions stand out, especially the datives of time:

(182) οὐδέποτ' οὐδεὶς τύραννος **ἐξ μησίν** τινα ἔσφαξεν, πυρετὸς δὲ **καὶ ἐνιαυτῷ** πολλάκις

No tyrant ever killed someone over the course of six months, but fever has often done so and even taken a year (2.6.19)

(183) εἰ γὰρ ἔδει **πέντε μόναις ἡμέραις** θεραπεῦσαι τὸ τοῦ γείτονος σῶμα, οὐκ ἂν ὑπεμείναμεν

For if one had to tend to the body of a neighbor for just five days, we could not bear it (*Fr.* 23)

In the first passage, the dative of time is limitative, providing further evidence that the similar examples seen in Polybius, Diodorus, and Plutarch are not just a fluke, but part of a real extension of its use into this event type.[193] In the second, the dative has moved even further away from Attic usage, being employed in a durative construction. While these examples give the impression that the system has completely broken down, the genitives and accusatives do follow Classical precedent. Of the nine accusatives of time, five, all with ἡμέρα, are durative. Of these, four are unremarkable,[194] and the fifth shows how much force was still left in the construction:

(184) οὕτως κἂν ἀναπέσῃς **δέκα ἡμέρας**, ἀναστὰς ἐπιχείρησον μακροτέραν ὁδὸν περιπατῆσαι καὶ ὄψει, πῶς σου τὰ σκέλη παραλύεται

So too, if you lie down in bed for ten days, when you get up, try to take a fairly long walk and you'll see how your legs have atrophied (2.18.3)

---

[192] See Horrocks (2010: 146–7).   [193] See n. 147.
[194] Two have ὅλην τὴν ἡμέραν (1.10.9, 2.16.27), I has τριάκοντα ἐφεξῆς ἡμέρας (2.18.2), and one has an ordinal (ἤδη τρίτην ἡμέραν ἔχοντος αὐτοῦ τῆς ἀποχῆς, 2.15.5); while ordinals are a fairly rare modifier of durative accusatives, parallels are found in Classical texts (with ἡμέρα at X. *An.* 4.5.24, *Cyr.* 6.3.11, Pl. *Prt.* 309d, D. 8.2, 50.29).

The verb ἀναπίπτω is relatively common by this period in the sense 'to lie down, recline (for a meal)', and one expects the aorist to refer to the telic act of moving into the reclining position, as it does for instance in the New Testament.[195] Here, however, the accompanying accusative of time is sufficient to force a stative interpretation of the aorist, as required by a durative expression. The remaining four examples also show the Classical force of the accusative: while they are modal-habitual, the idea of durativity is also still present.[196]

The genitives of time, though few in number, again remain close to those of earlier texts: six are modal-habitual,[197] and two are punctual – one with νυκτός (4.1.19), one with χειμῶνος (3.7.3), both time nouns that took a punctual genitive in Attic as well. In none of the eight do any modifiers (including the definite article) occur with the time noun, which perhaps hints at a degree of fossilization. So too the one construction with ἐν follows Classical precedent: a modal construction with χειμών (ἐκεῖνον ἐπικαλοῦ βοηθὸν καὶ παραστάτην ὡς τοὺς Διοσκούρους ἐν χειμῶνι οἱ πλέοντες, 2.18.29). The form νύκτωρ occurs once, paired with μεθ' ἡμέραν in a modal construction (τοῦτο καὶ ὄρθρου καὶ μεθ' ἡμέραν καὶ νύκτωρ ἔστω πρόχειρον, 4.4.39). While this can perhaps be differentiated from the modal construction with the accusative on the grounds that it is not as explicitly durative,[198] it is also extremely

---

[195] For ἀναπίπτω in other literature of the time, see the entry in BDAG. New Testament examples of the aorist include καὶ ὅτε ἐγένετο ἡ ὥρα, ἀνέπεσεν καὶ οἱ ἀπόστολοι σὺν αὐτῷ (Lk. 22:14), which fairly clearly makes the reclining a punctual act synchronized with the hour in question; see also Mk. 6:40, Lk. 11:37, Jn. 6:20, 13:12, where ἀνέπεσαν/-εν marks one stage in a sequence of events, rather than an on-going state.

[196] The modal type is clearest in the pair of examples in 3.26.6 (ῥιγῶντες τὰς νύκτας καὶ τὰς ἡμέρας); that the durative sense persists is clearest in 3.26.2 (τὰς νύκτας ἀγρυπνεῖς), where it is signaled by the prototypically durative verb, and especially 4.4.41 (ὅτι ἀναγιγνώσκει ἢ γράφει, κἂν προσθῇ τις, ὅτι ὅλας τὰς νύκτας "that he reads or writes – even if one adds that he keeps at it all night long"), where the durative force is made clear by the modifier ὅλας – and further emphasized by the accusative of time's being placed in its own separate ὅτι-clause.

[197] Of these, three have νυκτός (3.24.24, 3.24.103, 4.1.18), two have χειμῶνος (3.24.86, 3.24.87), and one has ἡμέρας (3.24.103).

[198] This is problematic because the cumulative sense of the three temporal expressions in 4.4.39 is 'always', which could easily elicit a durative construction. Still, chopping the 24-hour day into three different slices perhaps presents them in this case as three separate modalities that are juxtaposed with one another, rather than as three contiguous stretches of time that form a single whole.

close in nuance to the pair of modal genitives at 3.24.103: ταῦτα νυκτός, ταῦτα ἡμέρας πρόχειρα ἔστω. With so little evidence, one can do little more than speculate about why Epictetus uses the genitive here: given that it is paired with the simple form ἡμέρας, and only that word, whereas νύκτωρ is paired with the heavier constituent μεθ᾽ ἡμέραν in a sequence of three, highlighted by repeated καί, it may well be that νύκτωρ has become a clearer, more emphatic way of saying 'at night' than νυκτός. Such an explanation would be in line with the evidence from Plutarch as well.

In the end, though, there are simply too few temporal constructions in Epictetus of the right diagnostic sort to determine where he stands on many of the more interesting questions of usage. It looks as if the dative of time has lost a lot of ground, but that could be just a mirage caused by the total absence of punctual constructions with ἡμέρα, μήν, ἐνιαυτός, and ἔτος. That, in turn, shows the dependence of a study such as this one on the existence of texts that place particular importance on recording when things happened. And while the philosophy of an Epictetus focuses on general truths and has little interest in historical events, the situation is very different, as the Chapter 4 will show, when we look at the Septuagint and New Testament: for the Judeo-Christian tradition thought the historical manifestations of divinity to be very important indeed.

Papyri

But before turning to these texts, which have to a certain extent been influenced by the Semitic languages, one final source of evidence to consult for the post-Classical period is that provided by the non-literary papyri.[199] These are, of course, extremely useful, in attesting to several centuries of Greek that did not aspire to the belletristic standards of a Thucydides or a Plato; they are also now eminently searchable through the on-line interface of the Duke

---

[199] For recent studies showing the usefulness of the papyri for linguistic research, see the essays collected in Evans & Obbink (2010); Evans (2010) has instructive discussion of the varying degrees of competency found in the Greek of the papyri.

Databank of Documentary Papyri (http://www.papyri.info/browse/ddbdp/). At the same time, they are problematic in that they do not represent as uniform a corpus as that of a single author, and one cannot always secure enough examples of a given construction from a particular register of speech to be sure of the significance of individual phrases – assuming that the papyrus is well-preserved enough that one can be confident of understanding the syntactic and semantic context of the phrase in the first place. Additionally, one must also reckon with the formulaic nature of bureaucratic language: while copious material informs us of the proper phrasing for recording in a legal document what day an event occurred, we cannot be nearly so sure about how the same event-type would be expressed in a less formal register. Because of the uneven nature of the data, the following section will be based more on qualitative assessments of which constructions are most common at which periods in which types of documents than on any strictly quantitative data. In particular, because certain time nouns are more than usually prone to clump together into narrowly defined sets of constructions, it will be organized by time noun rather than by grammatical construction in the first instance. I limit myself to papyri from before AD 150.

Expressions with ἡμέρα

Both the simple dative of time and expressions with ἐν are found, but the former are considerably more common: in the papyri of *BGU*, for instance, they predominate over the latter by eight to two. Several modifiers are particularly associated with the dative of time: ordinals, τῇ αὐτῇ, and τῇ ἐνεστώσῃ.[200] By contrast, with the singular ἡμέρα, the construction with ἐν is found both with modifiers associated elsewhere with the limitative type (including μιᾷ, τῇ αὐτῇ, τῇ αὔριον, and τῇ ἐχομένῃ) and with some that are more commonly punctual (demonstratives, and the relative pronoun).[201]

---

[200] For ordinals, see *BGU* 2.647.10, 23 (AD 130), *BGU* 16.2626.2 (5–4 BC), etc.; for τῇ αὐτῇ, *BGU* 3.959.11 (AD 148), *O. Deiss.* 62.3 (187–163 BC), etc.; for τῇ ἐνεστώσῃ, see *BGU* 11.2050.7 (AD 106), *Chr. Mitt.* 204.17 (= *P. Lond.* 2.299.17) (AD 128), etc.

[201] For μιᾷ, see *P. Cair. Zen.* 4.59741.8 (275–226 BC); τῇ αὐτῇ: *P. Princ.* 2.16.13 (182–158 BC); τῇ αὔριον: *P. Cair. Zen.* 1.59078.8 (257 BC); τῇ ἐχομένῃ: *P. Amh.* 2.50.17 (106 BC);

That said, the simple dative remained an option with at least some of these modifiers.[202] With the plural ἡμέραις, the limitative construction with ἐν is very common, nearly always modified by a cardinal number.[203] Most of these examples occur in documents specifying that a future event is to take place within a certain amount of time, but a past time construction is found at *P. Cair. Zen.* 3.59312 (250 BC): καὶ ἐν ταῖς ἐπαγομέναις ἡμέραις ἀπώλετο α. In one striking passage, the simple dative is used where we might have expected a durative accusative of time: ἀνάγκη ἐστὶν ϲκοπελάριν ἐξ[πε]ῖναι ταύταις ταῖς ἡμέραις (*O. Claud.* 1.175.3–5). Because of the demonstrative, this is not as clearly durative as one modified, for example, by πολλαῖς would be, but it is hard to take this otherwise than that a guard's presence is necessary for the duration of a number of days.[204] Given the Greek–Latin interference seen elsewhere in the Mons Claudianus evidence, this construction is an excellent candidate for a Greek dative of time influenced by the Latin ablative of time.[205]

In Classical Greek, the other leading marker of the limitative is the genitive of time. The papyri also show examples of this construction with ἡμερῶν, but it is much less common than ἐν[+D], and one only finds sporadic examples of its use with cardinal numbers, for example, μόλις γὰρ ἡμερῶν δύο [......]ομεν (*BGU* 1.249.11–12, AD 75–85).[206] The only notable environment in which the genitive was apparently preferred to ἐν was with the modifier ὀλίγοι: ἐν ὀλίγαις ἡμέραις is never found, but ὀλίγων ἡμερῶν occurs four

---

ταύτη (restored): *P. Muench.* 3.1.66.12 (AD 124); ἐκείνη: *P. Thomas* 9.13 (AD 76–100, in a conditional clause that makes the limitative reading easier: εἰ ἐν ἐκείνη τῇ ἡμέρᾳ ἦν); relative: *SB* 12.11016 (AD 13).

202 One has the temporal dative τῇ ἐχομένη ἡμέρᾳ at *P. Tebt.* 3.2.920.26 (200–151 BC) and *P. Diosk.* 1.30 (154 BC), and τῇ ἐπαύριον ἡμέρᾳ at *P. Lille* 1.15.2 (241 BC).

203 See e.g. *BGU* 1.5.14, 1.183.8, 6.1248.4, etc.

204 This seems to hold true even if ἐπεῖναι is not restored correctly.

205 For this particular type of interference, see Adams 2003: 504–8. Note that, unlike most of the examples of the extended dative of time seen in the post-Classical literary texts, which are largely limitative (see exx. (148) for Polybius, (159) for Diodorus, (169)–(173) for Plutarch, and (182) for Epictetus; ex. (183) is the durative exception), this example cannot be easily understood as an outgrowth of the instrumental dative. For more Greek–Latin interference in the Mons Claudianus ostraca, see Adams 2003: 543.

206 This, along with *BGU* 3.699, where the syntactic context is even less clear, are the only two examples of papyri up to AD 150 in *BGU* with ἡμερῶν modified by a numeral. By contrast, there are in this same set of papyri some twelve examples where ἐν ... ἡμέραις is so modified.

times.[207] The genitive also continues to be a regular marker of the distributive event-type.[208] More surprising is a new use of ἐπί[+G] with the singular ἡμέρας in punctual constructions, for example [χ]ειρογράφῳ [ἐ]πὶ τῆς ἐνεστώ[σ]ης ἡμέρας (*BGU* 3.981.2.1, AD 77).[209] While ἐπί[+G] can have a temporal sense in Classical Greek, it never (at least in Herodotus, Thucydides, Xenophon, Plato, or Demosthenes) construes with an actual noun of time.[210] This appears to point forward to constructions that fall beyond the chronological scope of this book, such as εὐθὺς μὲν ἐπ᾽ ἐκείνης τῆς ἡμέρας ἐρωτικῶς τῆς Χλόης διετέθη (Longus 1.15.1) or ἄμφω τεθνᾶσιν ἐπὶ μιᾶς ἡμέρας (Luc. *DMort.* 21.2).[211] That said, one

---

[207] See *P. Cair. Zen.* 4.59538.3–4 (ὀλίγων δ᾽ ἡμερῶν ἀποστελοῦμέν σοι, 257 BC), *P. Col.* 3.19.4 (257 BC), *P. Mich.* 1.55.15 (240 BC), and *UPZ* 2.199.19 (131 BC). A possible fifth instance is the restoration παραγενέσθαι πρὸς σὲ [ὀλίγων ἡμ]ερῶν at *P. Cair. Zen.* 4.59634.6–7 (275–26 BC).

[208] See e.g. *BGU* 7.1508.3–4 (ἔσθουσι χό(ρτου) τῆς ἡμέρας δέσμας ς) (210–187 BC) or *BGU* 3.802.2.18 (AD 42). It is reinforced by ἑκάστης at *BGU* 16.2618.10 (7 BC).

[209] See also *BGU* 4.1053.28, 1055.24, 1151.35 (all 13 BC), all with variants of the clause ἐφ᾽ ἧς ἐὰν ἡμέρας κοιλάνωσιν.

[210] In my database (which includes only prepositional phrases with time nouns as the object), the only examples of temporal ἐπί[+G] come from post-Classical authors, and even there it is vanishingly rare. (i) There are two possible examples in Diodorus; the better of these is modal, with an explicit contrast with νυκτός (13.108.8); at 14.52.5, ἡμέρας is probably accusative plural (thus Oldfather's Loeb: "had lasted some days"), but, given the contrast with αἰεὶ πρὸς τὴν ἑσπέραν in the following main clause, it is just possible that here too it is singular in a modal construction. (ii) Polybius 3.55.1 offers τῆς ἐπ᾽ ἔτους πεπτωκυίας (*sc.* χιόνος), which must mean something like 'the snow that had fallen this year (on top of what remained from last year)'. (iii) Judeo-Christian texts have a few examples with ἔσχατος: ἵνα ἀναγγείλω ὑμῖν, τί ἀπαντήσει ὑμῖν ἐπ᾽ ἐσχάτων τῶν ἡμερῶν "that I might tell you what will befall you in the last of days" (Gen. 49:1; there are nine more examples of ἐπ᾽ ἐσχάτων τῶν ἡμερῶν in the LXX, not counting the Theodotion translation of Daniel) and ἐπ᾽ ἐσχάτου [τοῦ] χρόνου ἔσονται ἐμπαῖκται "there will be mockers in the end time" (Jude 18; cf. 2 Pet. 3:3, with ἐπ᾽ ἐσχάτων τῶν ἡμερῶν). These seem to have been triggered by the modifier, which – note the position of the article, not to mention constructions like ἐπ᾽ ἐσχάτου τῶν ἡμερῶν (Heb. 1:2; cf. 1 Pet. 1:20) – acts as the head of the phrase with the time noun dependent on it. (This is also suggested by the Hebrew antecedent of the Septuagintal example cited: *bə-'aḥărît hay-yāmîm* 'in-(the.)end (of.)the-days', with a construct chain – see Ch. 4, n. 79 – rather than direct dependence of *yāmîm* on *bə.*) That the time noun is not directly dependent on the preposition makes these more like a temporal construction that *was* possible in Classical Greek, namely the construal of ἐπί with the genitive of the person or abstract event that is treated as the circumstances attendant on the verb.

[211] In this particular passage of Longus, the only example with ἡμέρας, Reeve's Teubner prints Courier's emendation ἀπ᾽, perhaps rightly. But there remain a couple of examples with νυκτός the first of which at least is harder to emend away: limitative ἐπὶ μιᾶς νυκτός at 1.7.1, and ἐπράχθη δὲ ἐπ᾽ αὐτῆς (= νυκτός) τάδε at 2.24.4. In the latter passage, MS F has αὐτῇ, but, as Reeve intimates ad 2.9.1, this MS regularly replaces genitives with datives in a pattern that looks like hypercorrection; see esp. 4.16.3, where F has ἑκάστῃ

more often finds ἐπί followed by the accusative plural ἡμέρας in a durative construction, thereby competing with the simple accusative of time, as in Attic prose.²¹²

Expressions with νύξ

Compared to the literary evidence, the dative of time is unusually common, with fifty-three hits for νυκτί – all but a handful datives of time, rather than, for example, prepositional phrases with ἐν – compared to sixty-seven for νυκτός. That said, nearly all of these occur in the dating formula (τῇ) νυκτὶ τῇ φερούσῃ εἰς τὴν NUMERAL ('on the night before the *n*th day'):

(185) τῆι νυκτὶ τῆι | φερούσηι εἰς τὴν ιθ τοῦ ἐνεστῶτος μηνὸς | Παῦνι ἐπιβαλόντες

On the night before the nineteenth of the present month Pauni, when they attacked (*BGU* 8.1832.4–6, 51 BC)

There are also isolated examples of τῇ νυκτὶ ταύτῃ (*O. Claud.* 2.245.4, AD 125–175) and αὐτῇ τῇ νυκτί (*P. Bad.* 2.34.4–5). That the bulk of the examples should resemble (185) supports the position that the dative of time was most closely associated with calendrical expressions. The rarity of ἐν νυκτί expressions is surprising; I found only one (σκεύη . . . μετέφερον ἐν τῆι ἐπιούσηι νυκτί (*P. Cair. Zen.* 4.59620.10–11, 248–239 BC)), where the modifier is one associated elsewhere with the genitive of time, either limitative with ἡμέρα (ex. (134)) or punctual with νύξ (ex. (30)). There is also a solitary example of the plain dative which looks modal, rather than punctual, but the papyrus is too fragmentary to be completely sure (]τειας μὴ νυκτὶ μηδ' ἐν χ[ειμῶνι πλέων (*P. Laur.* 1.6.4, AD 98–103)).

The temporal genitive νυκτός, on the other hand, is common both in explicit modal constructions, where it is parallel with ἡμέρας (sometimes with asyndeton, for example, οὐ καρτε[ρ]ῷ νυκτ[ὸ]ς ἡμέρας ε[ὐ]χ[ο]μένη (*P. Giss. Apoll.* 10.3–5, AD 113–20)), and in

---

ἡμέρα in place of the expected distributive genitive. As for Lucian, other examples are found at *Tox.* 23 and *DMort.* 25.5 (both limitative phrases in which the noun is modified by μιᾶς).

²¹² ἐπί⁺ᴬ is found at e.g. *BGU* 3.892.6 (προσ[έ]δρευσα ἐφ' ἡμέρας δύο) (2C AD); possibly outside our time period, but still clear examples are 7.1648.5 (2–3C AD), 7.1668.7 (1–4C AD), both also with cardinal numbers. For the plain accusative, see e.g. *BGU* 7.1531.4 and 1534.5, 10, and 13 (both 210–187 BC) and *BGU* 4.1141.33 (14–13 BC).

234

punctual constructions where the particular night is not specified
(καὶ νυκτὸς ... ἀπώλετο ἱερεῖον α (*P. Cair. Zen.* 3.59379.18–19,
254–1 BC)). The accusative νύκτα is also found in modal constructions, where there is generally some sort of trigger for the durative
marker, for example, the modifier πᾶσα in νύκταν [*sic*] καὶ ἡμέραν
πᾶσᾳ[ν (*P. Oxy. Hels.* 45.r.2, 1C AD). The plain durative accusative
also occurs, although it is not especially common (*P. Corn.* 1.98
and 1.151, 257 BC; *P. Oslo.* 3.152.3, 1–2C AD in the singular; *Chr.
Wilck.* 237.8 = *P. Lips.* 1.105.8, 1–2C AD, and *P. Hal.* 8.4, 231 BC,
in the plural). Set against these five duratives, there are three papyri
which appear to show a punctual accusative of time, although none
of them are particularly clear. In the first, ὥστε ἐπισκευάσαι τὰ
χαλκία τὴν νύκτα ὅτε ἔπεσσον (*P. Col.* 3.37.21–5, 254–250 BC), the
accusative could perhaps be seen as durative, although the aorist
verb suggests rather a telic punctual construction: 'for preparing the
copper pots at night when they were baking'. The second, καλῶς
ποήσις ἀπελεύσῃ νύκταν [*sic*] μίαν ἀπὸ α ἕως β τοῦ Παοῖνι φρουρω
(*BGU* 6.1467.2–4, 1C BC), occurs in a request that someone depart
on a particular night in the month Pauni, but the modifier μίαν is ill
at ease in a punctual construction. Finally,]τι τὴν νύκτα ἐξαίβαλαν
(= ἐξέβαλον) (*BGU* 7.1673.9, 2C AD) looks like a good example of
the accusative modifying a comparatively instantaneous verb, but
the preceding lacuna makes it unclear what exactly the wider
syntactic context is. As uncertain as these examples may be,
taken together and compared with the relative paucity of clear
durative examples, it is not unreasonable to posit some extension
of the accusative into the realm of the punctual event-type in this
period.

Two of the temporal expressions most associated with νύξ in
particular, ὑπὸ νύκτα and νύκτωρ, are also attested in the papyri.
The former occurs three times, all referring to night-time movement, for example, ἡ (= εἰ) οὖν κομψῶς ἔσχε σοῦ ὄνος [ὑ]πὸ νύκτα
εἴσελθε 'if your donkey has gotten better, come by night' (*O.
Berenike* 2.195.8–10, AD 50–75).[213] There are also three examples

---

[213] The phrase modifies ἀνοίσω at *P. Sorb.* 1.18.8 (256–250 BC) and, with the last three
letters supplied, ἀνα]στάντες ἀνεχώρησαν at *P. Stras.* 2.111.5 (215–214 BC).

of νύκτωρ in the pre–150 AD papyri: in *P. Hal.* 1.194 (259 BC) in a clear modal construction (ὅταν τις ... μεθύων ἢ νύκτωρ ἢ ἐν ἱερῶι ἢ ἐν ἀγορᾶι ἀδικήσηι), in *P. Mich.* 9.525.20 (AD 119–24) in a punctual one (αὐτὸς ἐπεισῆλθε[ν ἐ]ν τῆ [ο]ἰκίᾳ νύκτωρ), and in *P. Aberd.* 177.5 (2C AD) surrounded by lacunae. This distribution, limited though it is, is consistent with its use in literary prose.

Expressions with μήν

Thanks to the use of the word for month in dating formulae, there are many more temporal expressions with μήν in the papyri than in literary texts. Even limiting the search to papyri before AD 150, there are 3401 hits for oblique forms of μήν, compared to 1486 for forms of ἡμέρα. That said, the vast majority of these are trivial adnominal genitives in which the noun is dependent on the designation of a particular day of the month: μηνὸς Γερμανικείου ἑβδόμη καὶ εἰκάδι (*P. Mich.* 3.197.2–3, AD 123). Also unsurprising are examples of the distributive genitive: ἑκάστωι τοῦ μη(νὸς) (τάλαντα) η 'Γ (*Chr. Wilck.* 159.20 = *P. Grenf.* 2.23.20, 108 BC). More interesting uses of the genitive arise when the adnominal genitive is used as a general heading at the start of a list of activities that occurred on different days of the month in question; in such constructions it starts to break away from a particularly close syntactic construction with the individual dates: in *P. Mich.* 2.127 (AD 46), an account of the private expenditures of a certain official Kronion, the heading μηνὸ(ς) Σεβαστοῦ in line 3 is followed in line 4 with the subheading numeral δ, for expenses from day 4, in line 5 with the numeral ι for expenses from day 10, and so forth. Early on, this process had led to the free use of the genitive in dating formulae where otherwise the punctual dative might be used, for example, μηνὸς Ξανδικοῦ in *P. Mich.* 1.66.4 (245 BC), where no individual date is specified.[214] This genitive need not even be in a heading, as seen in *P. Mich.* 3.182.13 (182 BC), where it occurs in the participial phrase τὴν τεθεῖσαν τοῦ κγ (ἔτους) μηνὸς Δαισίου. As with ἡμέρα, so too with

---

[214] That μήν should lend itself to what is prototypically a limitative marker more than its fellow calendrical time nouns ἔτος or ἡμέρα is paralleled in ex. (178) from Plutarch, where ἐν (which, like the genitive, is associated with limitatives) is used with μηνί, while ἔτει and ἡμέρᾳ in the same passage take the simple dative of time.

μήν the punctual event-type can be marked by ἐπί⁺ᴳ: τὴν δὲ δευ[τέρα]ν ἐπὶ τοῦ Φαρμοῦθι μην[ὸς το]ῦ προκ[ει]μένου πρώτου ἔτους (*Chr. Mitt.* 247.6–7 = *P. Flor.* 1.86.6–7, AD 86). Mostly, however, it is the dative μηνί that marks the punctual event-type, for example, ἀνήνεγκαν πρὸς ἑαυτοὺς ... τῷ Φαρμοῦθι μηνὶ τοῦ ἕκτου ἔτους Νέρωνος (*P. Mich.* 3.194.15–17, AD 61).²¹⁵ Still, as is evident from the absence of any examples of this usage in Mayser's syntax (1934), this is apparently a use that only came to the fore in the Roman period, providing further evidence of a resurgence of the dative of time in the first century AD.²¹⁶ There are also many examples with ἐν, but these generally show characteristics of the limitative, habitual, or both, for example, τὰ καθ᾽ ἔτος ἐκφό(ρια) ἀποδώσω σοι ἐν μηνὶ Παῦνι (*P. Mich.* 3.185.19–20, AD 122), which refers to a repeated event in the future, or γεινώσκιν σε θέλω ὅτι τρεῖς σοι ἐπιστολὰς ἔπεμψα ἐν τούτωι τῶι μηνί (*P. Mich.* 3.203.2–3, AD 114–16), which falls under the limitative heading because it refers to the sending of multiple letters within the time frame in question.²¹⁷ That said, the line between the two types is not absolute; *P. Col.* 10.259 (AD 146) has two future-time constructions, each in a different hand; the first has ἐν, the second the plain dative: ἃς καὶ ἀποδώσι ἐν μηνὶ Παῦ[νι τοῦ] ἐνεσ[τ]ῶτος ἔτους (lines 12–13), but ἃς ἀποδώσω μηνὶ Παῦνι τοῦ αὐτοῦ ἐνάτου ἔτους (lines 17–19).²¹⁸ Still, it holds as a general rule that a month in which an event had already taken place will be marked by the plain dative, one in which an event will take place by ἐν⁺ᴰ.

---

²¹⁵ See also *BGU* 1.44.11 (AD 102), *BGU* 1.353.12 (AD 141), *P. Mich.* 5.341.4 (AD 47).

²¹⁶ See n. 107. Of the 226 hits for μηνί in papyri up to AD 1 in the DDBDP, nearly all are governed by ἐν. Only two stand any chance of being temporal datives, *P. Tebt.* 3.1.815.2. r.6 (223–222 BC) (but the reading is not secure) and *BGU* 4.1139.12 (5 BC).

²¹⁷ See also *BGU* 1.339.14 (AD 128), *P. Mich.* 3.182.24 (182 BC), *P. Mich.* 3.184.16 (AD 121); all modify future-tense verbs. Another good example is καὶ γὰρ αἱ ἑορταὶ αἱ μέγισται αἱ ἐν τῶι ἐνιαυτῶι εἰσιν ἐν τῶι μηνὶ τούτωι (*P. Hamb.* 2.182.14, 249 BC): 'the greatest festivals of the year regularly take place in the given month'. Occasionally the plural is also found in future-tense habitual constructions: τὰ δ᾽ ἐκφόρια ἀποδώσομεν κατ᾽ ἔτος ἐν τῷ Παῦνι κ(αὶ) Ἐπεὶφ μησί (*Chr. Wilck.* 370.12–13 = *P. Lond.* 3.1223, AD 121).

²¹⁸ Another example of the future limitative type with the plain dative is found at *P. Mich.* 14.678.8 (AD 98), but here the absence of ἐν may be motivated by the occurrence of another ἐν-phrase between the verb and the temporal expression: ἃς καὶ ἀποδώσω ἐν ἀναφοραῖς ἰσομερέσι μηνὶ Φαμ[εν]ὼθ καὶ μηνὶ Καισαρείῳ.

For the limitative type in which an event like a payment is to take place within a certain number of months, ἐν[+D] is the standard construction.[219] It does not have much competition in this function from the genitive plural μηνῶν, which is primarily used in apposition to prepositional phrases marking the start and end points of a stretch of months: ἀπὸ μηνὸς Φαμενὼθ ἕως Παῦνι μηνῶν δ 'from the month of Phamenoth to Pauni, four months' (*P. Mich.* 1.67.8–9, 243 BC). As for the accusative, the singular is primarily found in distributive expressions: τὸν μῆνα and κατὰ μῆνα both occur, the former especially in formulations of interest rates, and both often reinforced by ἕκαστον.[220] The plural is used in durative expressions, nearly always with the addition of ἐπί[+A] or εἰς[+A], seemingly without distinction.[221] Because nearly all of these phrases occur in documents stipulating that an event is to be carried out for a period of time extending into the future, it is natural that they are headed by prepositions which in their spatial sense mark a goal.

---

[219] See e.g. *BGU* 4.1053.20 (13 BC), *P. Oxy.* 12.1471 (AD 81).
[220] For the former, see e.g. *P. Mich.* 5.328.r.13 τόκου ὡς ἐκ δραχμῆς μιᾶς τῆ μνᾷ τὸν μῆνα ἕκαστον 'at interest of one drachma per mina each month' (AD 29–30). For the latter, see e.g. *P. Mich.* 5.349.7–9 τὰς δὲ λοιπὰς ἀργυρίου δραχμὰς ὀγδοήκοντα τέσσαρες [*sic*] λήμψομαι κατὰ μῆνα τὸ αἱροῦν ἀπὸ μηνὸς Μεχείρ (AD 30).
[221] *P. Mich.* up to AD 150 has one example of each, εἰς μῆνας ιγ at 3.190.17 (172 BC) in the formulaic description of the conditions of a loan (what we might call 'staccato language', given the dry, detached listing of conditions), but ἐφ' ἔτη δύο καὶ μῆνας ἕξ at 5.346.4 (AD 16) in a contract for an apprenticeship that is full of non-standard spellings – not only the φ for π in the preposition, but also the spelling ὁμολογῶ ἐπάνανκαν (for -γκον) ἐκδιδάξιν (for -ειν) in the verbal phrase modified by the temporal expression. That phrases with εἰς may be associated with staccato language in financial documents receives some support from the examples in *BGU*: (i) εἰς is found in 3.741.13 (a staccato loan, AD 143), 6.1232.19 (a receipt for confirmation of a wheat delivery, 111–110 BC; here, the expression is better understood as a goal expression than as indicating a true stretch of time; in other words: 'the amount intended for the months of Pachon and Pauni'), 10.1948.6 (a lease, 213–212 BC), 10.1968.7 (a staccato loan, 184 BC); (ii) ἐπί in 3.855.6 (a contract for training, AD 147), 4.1055.16 (a loan, but described with fuller syntax, 13 BC), 4.1115.44 (similar, 13 BC), 4.1134.11 (similar, but closer to the staccato language of the loans with εἰς, 10 BC). Examples with the plain accusative are found at *P. Cair. Zen.* 3.59368 (ἔδησε πέδαις καὶ εἶχεν ἐν φυλακῆι μῆνας η, 241 BC, with no need for a preposition after ἔχω ἐν φυλακῇ, which easily prompts understanding of the accusative on its own as a durative) and, possibly, *P. Petr.* 3.43.3rp.21 (φάμενοι ἀδικεῖσθαι ἐνταῦ[θα ἤδη] μῆνας ι, 245–240 BC, where the preposition-less supplement would be justified, again given the easy compatibility of the verb with a durative expression).

Expressions with θέρος and χειμών

The chief season words account for very few of the temporal expressions of the papyri up to AD 150: there are only eight examples of θέρος, all singular, several of which occur in contexts too lacunose to provide any useful information. There are two examples dependent on ἐν⁺ᴰ, the first of which is apparently modal, given that it is juxtaposed with κατὰ χειμῶνα and κατὰ τρύγητον (*P. Tebt.* 1.120.135, 94–67 BC), but there is a lacuna after the phrase that makes it difficult to interpret ἐν τῶι θεριρει . . [. The second, at least, is a secure habitual expression: μ]ὴ ἔχειν ἡμᾶς ἐν τῶι θέρει τὸ ἱκανὸν [ὕδωρ ἑαυτοῖ].ς τε κ̣α̣ὶ τοῖς κτήνεσι (*P. Tebt.* 3.1.787.5–6, 138 BC). When the durative component outweighs the modal, as happens at *P. Col.* 4.66.17 (256–255 BC), then the accusative is used instead: ἐγὼ δὲ καὶ θέρος καὶ χειμῶνα ἐν τῶι πόνωι γίνομαι. The only other accusative not surrounded by lacunae is found at *P. Mich.* 5.240.70 (AD 46–7), but this is really a goal expression rather than a temporal one. The final clear example of θέρος in a temporal phrase is ἦν μὲν οὖν διὰ θέρους εὐωνότατον· ἐν δὲ τῷ παρόντι ἡ λυσιτελοῦσα καὶ δικαία τιμὴ πρὸς τέσσαρας μ[νᾶ]ς ἐστιν (*P. Oxy.* 14.1760.4–5, 2C AD), where the general context of the construction is a type familiar from literary Greek: a durative expression in a μέν-clause followed by a punctual one in a δέ-clause.

Examples of χειμών are a little more common, but still rare, often with the meaning 'storm' rather than 'winter'. The genitive of time is not found (although there are two genitive absolutes), and the only possible example with the dative, after ἐν, is lacunose.[222] The plain accusative occurs twice, once conjoined with θέρος (see previous paragraph), once on its own in a typical durative construction: τόν τε χειμῶνα τοῦ λδ (ἔτους) Καίσαρος ἀνα<σ>τ[ρ]αφεὶς καὶ τὴν θερείαν παραμείνας (*P. NYU* 2.3.16–18, AD 5). Apart from the usual examples of goal expressions with εἰς⁺ᴬ and direct object

---

[222] The genitive absolutes occur at *P. Enteux.* 27.3 (with γενομένου, 222 BC) and *P. Oxy.* 45.3250 (with ὄντος, AD 63); the example with ἐν⁺ᴰ:]τειας μὴ νυκτὶ μηδ' ἐν χ[ειμῶνι πλέων (*P. Laur.* 1.6.4, AD 98–103).

accusatives, the only other accusatives are objects of κατά, which range from the punctual to the limitative type.[223]

Expressions with ἐνιαυτός

Given the semantics of ἐνιαυτός, it is not surprising that it is found only once in the plural and that many of the singular examples are distributive.[224] Many of the other constructions are used in patterns similar to the expressions with μήν. The genitive is often used adnominally (although with this noun its head is less often a smaller unit of time and more often a product associated with the year in question);[225] such genitives can then break free and become a sort of genitive of rubric, specifying the year as a topic for the following clause.[226] Some genitives, though, do belong to the standard limitative type,[227] and there is again a continuum of examples connecting these to expressions with ἐν^{+D} and, from there, to those with the simple dative. Of these last two types, ἐν is found both in purer limitative constructions and, once, with ἔσχατος, a modifier that elsewhere occurs with the plain temporal

---

[223] On the punctual end of the cline, we have *P. Cair. Zen.* 4.59643.2–4 (κεραμείωι ἐνέβαλον θεμέλιον κατὰ χειμῶνα, mid 3C BC) and *P. Heid.* 9.422.18–19 (τὰ καὶ προκατανενεμηκότα κατὰ χειμῶνα, 158 BC); at the other end, there are a couple of expressions in conditional clauses which are limitative insofar as they describe future-time contingencies (and also, to a degree, modal, because such conditionals generally imply an alternative against which the given possibility is considered; note μέν in the second example): *P. Koeln* 3.147.5–6 (πλὴν ἐὰν μή τι βίαιον ἐκ θεοῦ γ[έ]νη[τ]αι κατὰ χιμῶνα, 30 BC–AD 15) and *P. Zen. Pestm.* A.14 (ἐὰν μὲν κατὰ χειμῶνα συντελῆται τὰ ἔργα, 258 BC). Other examples are found at *P. Erasm.* 1.1.15 (148–147 BC) and *UPZ* 1.110.108 (164 BC).

[224] The only clear plural example: [διὰ τὸ λί]αν ἐπὶ τρῖς ἐνιαυτοὺς μὴ ἀναβῆναι τὸν πο[ταμόν (*SB* 6.9302.6–7, late 3C BC). The distributive type is marked either by κατά$^{+A}$ (e.g. *BGU* 4.1119.13–14, *P. Bingen* 45.4, *P. Heid.* 9.431.23–4) or by the genitive (e.g. *P. Col.* 3.54.38, *SB* 18.13763.8, 10, *UPZ* 1.35.11). The genitive seems esp. characteristic of staccato language; see n. 221.

[225] See e.g. δότ]ω μοι ἐνιαυτοῦ τόκον (*P. Stras.* 7.652.11–12, AD 136–41), παραδόντ[ας] ἐνιαυτοῦ ἐκφόριον (*P. Tebt.* 1.5.41, 118 BC).

[226] See *P. Oxy.* 8.1102.18 (AD 146), where the word order shows ἐνιαυτοῦ in predicative rather than attributive position: ἐγιαψ[τοῦ] τὰς προσόδους ἀπολήμψεται ἡ πόλις.

[227] Two reasonably good examples are the future-time τούτου δὲ πληρωθέντος εἰς ἅπαξ ἀποδώσει αὐ[τῆι] ὁ Παᾶπις τοῦ ἄλλου ἐνιαυτοῦ [ἀ]ργυρ[ίου δ]ραχμὰς ἑξήκοντα (*C. Pap. Gr.* 1.14.14–15 = *P. Rein.* 2.103, AD 26) and the negated πρὸς τῶι μηδ᾽ εἰληφέναι μηθὲν ἐνιαυτοῦ ἤδ[η] ἀλλ᾽ ἢ τὴν μνᾶν καὶ τρεῖς ἀρτάβας σίτου (*P. Col.* 3.6.9–10, 257 BC). It is sometimes difficult to assess whether a given genitive is dependent on a noun or on the verb (and so properly limitative): [δ]οθήσεται δ[έ] σοι παρ᾽ ἐμοῦ το[ῦ] πρώτου [ἐ]νιαυτοῦ τὸ γινόμενον (*P. Cair. Zen.* 5.59835.6–7, mid 3C BC).

dative associated with the punctual type;[228] in addition to ἔσχατος, temporal datives of ἐνιαυτός can also be modified by ordinal numbers (or, once, a phrase including an ordinal number).[229] In durative expressions, one occasionally finds the plain accusative,[230] but, as with μήν, it is more common to find prepositional phrases with εἰς and ἐπί[+A].[231]

Expressions with ἔτος

Various practical concerns make it particularly difficult to assess the frequency of the different constructions with ἔτος quantitatively. First, there is the sheer amount of data: even with the search limited to papyri up to AD 150, the string ἔτους still pulls up 12,524 hits. Second, those data are themselves greatly skewed by the number of examples in which the word itself does not appear, but is supplied by editors as an expansion of the symbol

[228] Limitative: τὸ δὲ δάνειον [τοῦτο] καὶ τοὺς τόκους ἀποδότω Μενε[σθε]ὺς Πυλάδηι ἐν ἐνιαυτῶι ἀπὸ Δύστρο[υ] τοῦ ις (ἔτους) (CPR 18.14.282–5, 231–206 BC), ἔκαστα ποιήσω ἐν τῷ ἐνιαυτῷ ἐνί (P. Oxy. 2.275.39–40, AD 66). Closer, but not all the way, to the punctual type: ὥστε ἐπὶ μὲν τὰ πρῶτα ἔτη τρία κατ᾽ ἔτος σπεῖραι καὶ ξυλαμῆσαι ταύτας ... ἐν δὲ τῷ ἐσχάτῳ ἐνιαυτῷ σπεῖραι τὸ μὲν ἥμισυ πυρῷ (P. Oxy. 2.280.11–15, AD 88–9). While the modifier ἔσχατος is elsewhere (e.g. P. Oxy. 1.101.13 (AD 142), 38.2874.48–9 (AD 108)) associated with the plain dative and here occurs in a δέ-clause that follows a durative μέν-clause, thus suggesting a punctual construction, a certain limitative nuance is still present given that the wider context is that of a lease of land looking forward to the future. (To be sure, the main verb is past tense ἐμίσθωσεν, but the four years of the lease begin from the present one (lines 5–6).)

[229] The plain dative modified by an ordinal number: P. Oxy. 36.2776.9, 11, 14 (AD 118–9); modified by a phrase with an ordinal number (τῷ μετὰ τὸ εἰσιὸν ἕβδομον ἔτος ἐνιαυτῷ): SB 20.14464.20–1 (2 C AD).

[230] The plain accusative has a less formulaic appearance than the prepositional constructions. In BGU 7.1571.25–6 (AD 74–5), it occurs in a sentence that also has 1st- and 2nd-person pronouns: ἐπιγνοὺς τὸν σ[τρατι]ώτην ἐπ᾽ ὀψώνιον ἀπεληλυθότα, ὃς ὅλο]ν τὸν πέρυσι ἐνιαυτὸν ἐνθάδε ἦν, ἐπὶ σὲ κ[ατ]απέφευγα. Another good example is [ὁ γὰρ ὑ]πάρχων (sc. θησαυρός) οὐχ ἱκαν[ός ἐστι] χωρεῖν τὸν σῖτον τὸν ἐνιαυτὸν [τοῦ]τον (P. Cair. Zen. 3.59509.10–11, mid 3 C BC), again in a comparatively non-formulaic letter, with use of the temporal accusative not blocked by the presence of a direct-object accusative immediately before it.

[231] The two prepositions seem to be used nearly interchangeably; compare [ἡ] μίσθωσις ἥδ᾽ ἥ εἰς ἐνιαυτὸν [ἔ]να ἀπ[ὸ] τῆς ἐνεστώσης ἡμ[έρας] (BGU 3.916.15–16, AD 69–79) against ἀπὸ τοῦ ἐνεστῶτος μηνὸς Φαρμοῦθι ἐφ᾽ ἐνιαυτὸν ἕνα ἐνοικ(ίου) ὅλου τοῦ χρόνου ἀργυ(ρίου) δραχμῶν ἐνενήκοντα ἓξ ἔχι (BGU 3.981.27–9, AD 77). Again as with μήν, these are nearly all forward-looking phrases, so the addition of goal prepositions is understandable. One potential point of difference between the two is that εἰς is apparently preferred to ἐπί when there are no modifiers, which perhaps correlates to the tendency mentioned in n. 221 for εἰς to occur in more staccato language.

for year.[232] Of the seventy-nine hits for ἔτους in *P. Col.* up to AD
150, only ten papyri actually have the word written out. Nor can
one assume that those papyri are a representative sample of those
where the word is only implicit, given that the abbreviation should
be proportionally more common in formulaic texts where the word
can be understood easily from context than in those where its
syntactic role would be less easily parsed by a reader. That said,
even those ten fully-spelled examples in *P. Col.* are extremely
repetitive: all but one are in dating formulae, and the one exception
is an unremarkable adnominal genitive.[233] Perhaps most interesting is one phrase where the genitive does *not* occur: ἀπὸ Παῦνι τοῦ
ἐνάτου καὶ τριακοστοῦ ἔτους ἕως τοῦ Παχὼνς τοῦ ἐν τῶι τρί[τωι ἔτει
(*P. Mich.* 1.66.8–10, 245 BC). Here, the expected genitive is found
in the first half, dependent on Pauni, but when the month name is
itself given the determiner τοῦ, then the genitive is replaced by a
prepositional phrase with ἐν, presumably to avoid repetition of the
τοῦ.[234] In the plural, the genitive is overwhelmingly used in the age
formula: γυναικὶ Θασῶτι ... ὡς ἐτῶν τεσσαράκοντα 'to his wife
Thasos ... forty years of age' (*P. Corn.* 6.7, AD 17).[235]

The accusative plural, as is by now familiar, is nearly always
reinforced by εἰς or ἐπί[+A] to indicate extent of time; so too the
singular is most often headed by εἰς (or πρός[+A]) when durative, or
κατά[+A] when distributive.[236] Turning to the dative, we again find

---

[232] This usually takes the form L. See the examples in Pestman 1990: 35–41.

[233] The use of the genitive in dating formulae arises, as it does with μήν, from constructions of
the form 'on day *x* of month *y* of year *z*'; see e.g. *P. Col.* 3.49.2 (252 BC), 8.210.1 (AD 3),
10.254.14 (AD 129). It is dependent on γενήματι at 4.87.16 (244 BC). The distribution in *P.
Mich.* is similar, with nearly all the examples in dating formulae. Occasionally the
genitive is used even when there is no month name for it to be dependent on (1.66.2,
245 BC).

[234] This assumes, of course, that the supplement is correct, although it seems plausible
enough, given the first two and a half words of the phrase.

[235] Another example, with somewhat more flexible syntax: οὔπω ὄντι μοι τῶν ἐτῶν 'though
I am not yet of the right age' (*P. Mich.* 1.23.3, 257 BC); cf. *P. Mich.* 3.170.6 (AD 49),
3.171.10 (AD 58), both references to minors who are not yet of age.

[236] With ἔτη, it becomes even more difficult to find any factors to distinguish between εἰς and
ἐπί phrases. A couple of examples, the first of which is a near-minimal pair; the second,
while not as close a match, is representative of many other such pairs: (i) both from
Bakchias: βούλομαι μ[ισ]θώσασθαι παρὰ σο[ῦ] εἰς ἔτη τέσσ[α]ρα ... τὰς ὑπαρχούσας
σοι ... ἀρούρας (*P. Mich.* 3.184.3–8, AD 121), but β[ούλο]μαι μ[ι]σ[θ]ῶσαι παρὰ σοῦ ἐφ᾽
ἔ[τη τέσ]σαρα ... τ[ὰς] ὑ[παρχ]ούσας σοι ... ἀρούρας (*P. Mich.* 3.185.5–9, AD 122); the
latter papyrus also has, at lines 17–18, σπείρων ἐπὶ τὰ πρῶτα ἔτη τρία ὡς ἐὰν αἱρῶμαι,
with the same preposition used in a less lacunose context; (ii) both from Karanis:

the simple dative and phrases with ἐν in competition with each other. The preposition is not restricted to limitative constructions, but can also mark punctual past-time phrases: χι]μαίρας λ ἃς προσ[έλα]βον ἐν τῶι δ (ἔτει) ἀφόρους (*P. Mich.* 1.67.6–7, 243 BC).[237] While this example also shows that ἐν is at home in fairly staccato language, the plain dative seems to have an even greater affinity for formulaic phrasing. In the examples in *P. Mich.*, for instance, it tends to occur after the verb τελειόω[238] or in staccato language.[239] In the plural, most of the examples of the dative are prepositional phrases with ἐν, used in predictably limitative contexts.[240] But in some passages, an extended use of the simple dative comes to the fore, one also seen in post-Classical literary texts, in which the dative encroaches on a combination of the limitative ἐν and the durative accusative: (i) from an edict of Hadrian's (AD 136), pieced together from various papyri (*P. Heid.* 7.396, *P. Oslo* 3.78):

εἰ καὶ τοῖς προτέροις ἔτεσι ἑξῆς οὐ τελείαν μόνον, ἀλλὰ καὶ μείζω σχεδὸν ὅσην οὔπω πρότερον ἐποιήσατο τὴν ἀνάβασιν; (ii) from a tax exemption notice (*P. Berl. Leihg.* 2.35.6–7, AD 141): διὰ τὸ τοῖς προτέροις ἔτεσιν ἐν χερσείᾳ γεγο(νυῖαι) ὁρισθῆναι; (iii) from a land lease (*P. Oxy.* 1.101.24–5, AD 142; cf. *SB* 20.14338.3, AD 120; 20.14984.7, AD 140–210): ἐὰν δέ τις τοῖς ἑξῆς ἔτεσι ἄβροχος γένηται; (iv) from a letter (*P. Oxy.* 55.3810.20–1, 2C or 3C AD):

μεμισθωκέναι αὐτῷ Ὀννόφρι εἰς ἔτη δύο ἀπὸ τοῦ ἐνεστῶτος τ[ρει]σκαιδεκάτου ἔτους (*P. Mich.* 9.563.12–13, AD 128–9), but [συγκεχωρηκέναι αὐτὸν] ἐνοικῖν ἐφ᾿ ἔτη πέντε ἀπὸ τοῦ προκ(ειμένου) [ἐνάτου (ἔτους)] (*P. Mich.* 9.570.8–9, AD 105–6). Given the spelling mistakes in the second of each pair (μισθῶσαι for μισθώσασθαι, ἐνοικῖν for ἐνοικεῖν, the aspirated ἐφ᾿ before the smooth breathing at the start of ἔτος – a consistent rendering of the *Anlaut* of ἔτος in 3.185, which has καθ᾿ ἔτος later on in lines 15, 19, and 22, whereas 3.184 has κατ᾿ ἔτος in lines 9, 13, and 16), and recalling the tendency seen above for ἐπί to be somewhat more flexible in use, we may perhaps suppose that εἰς belonged to a slightly more formal register than ἐπί.

237 See also *P. Mich.* 1.30.E.3 (text obscure, but apparently the phrase modifies ἀπὸ τοῦ καταχθέντος οἴνου εἰς κερ(άμια(?)) ϙ, 256–245 BC), 5.337.13 (modifying ὁμολογεῖ … ἀπεσχηκέναι παρ᾿ αὐτοῦ τὴν τιμὴν καὶ τοὺς μισθούς, AD 26).
238 See *P. Mich.* 2.121.r.4.vii (AD 42), 5.232.8 (AD 36; line 16 of this papyrus offers, as a contrast, ἀφ᾿ ἧς ἐποιήσαντο ἐν τῶι κα (ἔτει) Τιβερίου Καίσαρος Σεβαστοῦ), 5.262.15 (AD 34–6), 5.340.r.24 (AD 45–6; to be sure, the plain dative is also found in this papyrus at v.9 modifying πεπραμένον), 5.341.3 (AD 47; once again, there is a second example, at line 6, modifying πεπραμένον). While with different verbs, the general form of *P. Mich.* 5.352.7 (AD 46) is similar. Contrast the examples given in the previous note.
239 See *P. Mich.* 5.346.3, 5 (AD 12–46).
240 Future-tense examples: *P. Eleph.* 24.11 (223–222 BC), *P. Oxy.* 75.5052.8 (AD 86–7); past-tense example, with limitative modifier: ἐν ὀλίγο<ι>ς ἔτεσι *SB* 20.14401.19 (AD 147).

243

ἐρρῶσθαί σε εὔχ<u>ο</u>(μαι), κυρία, πολλοῖς ἔτεσιν εὐτυχ(οῦσαν); (v) from official correspondence exempting a veteran from a tax (*SB* 16.12508.7–8, AD 149): [ἐ]δηλώθη ἐστρατεῦσθαι ἔτεσι πλείο<u>σ</u>[ι εἴκοσ]<u>ι</u> πέντε. Considering that these eight documents represent a full 18% of the forty-five hits for ἔτεσι(ν) up to AD 150 in the Duke Databank,[241] that the earliest of secure dating is from AD 120, and that at least two ((i), an imperial edict, and (v), with its military content) come from contexts where Latin influence may be suspected, it is reasonable to see here a cluster of examples that show the influence on the Greek dative of the Latin ablative of time within which.

---

[241] This percentage actually understates the prevalence of this construction, given that many of the other 37 hits are too lacunose for their syntax to be clear.

4

EXPRESSIONS OF TIME IN BIBLICAL GREEK

In studying Greek of the Hellenistic and early Roman period, the Septuagint and New Testament are crucial but problematic texts.[1] They are crucial, because they represent a corpus that is less influenced by Classical Attic models than are other texts, but problematic because their language has been influenced to an uncertain and uneven degree by the Semitic languages of the regions where they originated: Hebrew, the language, by this point primarily liturgical, out of which most of the Septuagint was translated, and Aramaic, the spoken language of most native inhabitants of first-century AD Palestine. As a result, in using these texts as evidence for the history of Greek, one must always compare the relevant constructions both with those found in the Semitic languages and with those found in Greek unlikely to have been influenced by Semitic in order to work out which developments are more probably due to language contact, and which are characteristic of all varieties of Greek.

In the last sections of Chapter 3, various diachronic trends in Greek came to the fore, notably a resurgence of the temporal dative in Roman times. In what follows, the Septuagint and New Testament will be scrutinized to determine the extent to which they also participate in these developments.

The Septuagint

In this section, we will focus on three constructions in turn. (i) With the accusative of time, we will see usage extended to the punctual event-type, almost certainly under the influence of the Hebrew original. (ii) The preposition ἐν is also used more than in

---

[1] For an introduction to some of the issues involved, see Voelz 1984, de Lange 2007, Drettas 2007, Janse 2007, and George 2010.

Classical Greek, again because of interference from Hebrew, but in this case remaining within the bounds of what would have been grammatical in Attic. (iii) The dative of time is still alive and well, despite not having a close counterpart in Hebrew that would regularly trigger its use; it does occasionally give up some ground to ἐν. For the most part, examples have been drawn from the Pentateuch, in the interests of having a uniform corpus that is not too unwieldy.[2]

The accusative of time in the Septuagint

The most striking new construction to occur in the Septuagint is the frequent use of the accusative in punctual constructions that would call for either a dative or genitive in Classical prose. This is clearest in constructions with νύξ, such as:

(1) καὶ ἐπέπεσεν ἐπ᾽ αὐτοὺς **τὴν νύκτα**

And he attacked them at night (Gen. 14:15)

Here, with an expression that simply denotes when the event described by the aorist verb takes place, early prose authors would simply have used the genitive (τῆς) νυκτός. But there are examples with other time nouns as well:

(2) διὰ τί οὐ συνετελέσατε τὰς συντάξεις ὑμῶν τῆς πλινθείας, καθάπερ ἐχθὲς καὶ **τρίτην ἡμέραν**, καὶ τὸ τῆς σήμερον;

Why did you not complete your brick quotas – as you did yesterday and the day before – so too today? (Ex. 5:14)

(3) καὶ σπερεῖτε **τὸ ἔτος τὸ ὄγδοον** καὶ φάγεσθε[3] ἀπὸ τῶν γενημάτων παλαιά· ἕως τοῦ ἔτους τοῦ ἐνάτου, ἕως ἂν ἔλθῃ τὸ γένημα αὐτῆς, φάγεσθε παλαιὰ παλαιῶν

And you will sow in the eighth year and eat from your old crops; until the ninth year, when the land's crop comes, you will eat of the old (Lev. 25:22)

That said, these examples are clearly more marginal than those with νύκτα. First, they are much rarer: whereas there are six examples in the Pentateuch of punctual νύκτα, all of which are at least as

---

[2] For the advantages of working from the Pentateuch, see Evans 2001: 3.
[3] In the Hellenistic period, φάγομαι starts to compete with ἔδομαι as the future of ἐσθίω; both forms are found in the LXX (BDR §74.2).

prototypically punctual as (1), sentence (3) is the only good example with ἔτος, and, while there are three other passages similar to (2), all of these are still in the phrase καθάπερ ἐχθὲς καὶ τρίτην ἡμέραν. Second, the contexts of these passages are more conducive to a durative accusative than those in which punctual νύκτα occurs.

In example (2), while the coordination with ἐχθές does suggest a precision in the statement of the time associated with punctual expressions, the emphasis is in fact not so much on those two days in particular, but on the extended period of time leading up to the present moment: ἐχθὲς καὶ τρίτην ἡμέραν is more idiomatically rendered 'previously', which would in fact call for a durative accusative.[4] What is more, because Attic prose too can view an event that occurred at a distance from the reference time not as an isolated point, but in terms of the period of time that extends from the event time to the reference time, the accusative of time with ordinals is found even in Classical Greek in contexts where, based on English translations, a punctual dative might be expected instead. Indeed, as much as this phrase might seem like translation language at first glance, there is in fact an exact parallel in Xenophon:[5]

(4) Νῦν δ', ἔφη ὁ Κῦρος, τί ποιοῦσιν; Ἐκτάττονται, ἔφασαν· καὶ ἐχθὲς δὲ καὶ **τρίτην ἡμέραν** τὸ αὐτὸ τοῦτο ἔπραττον

"And now," said Cyrus, "what are they doing?" "They're drawing out in battle formation," they said, "and both yesterday and the day before they were doing this same thing" (X. *Cyr.* 6.3.11)

Here, in contrast to example (2), where the impression given is that the activity in question was being carried out for an indefinite period of time even before the previous two days, the phrase

---

[4] Xenophon, for example, uses τὸν πρόσθεν χρόνον in this sense at *HG* 5.1.1, 7.4.30, *Cyr.* 2.1.16, and 6.1.27. That what this phrase really means in context is 'previously' is suggested by the Hebrew, which reads *ki-tmôl šilšōm gam-təmôl gam-hayyôm* 'as yesterday (and) the day before, also yesterday, also today': the second instance of *təmôl* needs to be understood to refer specifically to the previous day, which means that the first instance must refer more generally to past time. The NRSV translates the phrase with this more open-ended meaning both here and in its other eight occurrences: "as (he did *or* they were) before"; "as always"; or "previously" (Gen. 31:5, Ex. 5:7, 14; Jos. 4:18, 1 Sam. 14:21, 19:7, 21:6(5), 1 Macc. 9:44). Verse numbers in brackets refer to the NRSV where the numbering differs from that of the LXX.

[5] See also οὓς ὑμεῖς ἡμέραν πέμπτην τρεψάμενοι ἐδιώξατε 'whom you routed and pursued four days ago' (X. *HG* 2.4.13).

seems to convey its literal meaning – and even so, Xenophon uses the durative accusative.[6] This is rendered easier by the general tendency of accusatives of time to occur in μέν-clauses that look forward to δέ-clauses. While this exact syntactic environment is not the case in either (2) or (4), the idea is still the same: a contrast between a lasting state of affairs in the past and the present moment. (Or, to be more precise, in (4) the contrast is between what they are doing now and the expectation set up by νῦν δέ that they would have been doing something different before now, even though they were in fact doing exactly the same thing.) Finally, we can also expect this accusative to be motivated by reasons internal to Greek because an exact equivalent of ἡμέρα is not found in the Hebrew text, and so the phrasing here is not simply the result of slavish imitation.[7] So too in example (3), while a dative τῷ ἔτει τῷ ὀγδόῳ might be expected, there is again a scenario in which the actions in the first clause (σπερεῖτε, φάγεσθε) continue until the change marked by the second clause (ἕως τοῦ ἔτους τοῦ ἐνάτου). In this example, however, one cannot exclude the possibility of interference from the Hebrew, as the word for year is accompanied by the ordinal and preceded, rather unusually, by a particle that marks definite direct objects, which would have encouraged translation with a Greek accusative.[8]

The examples with νύξ, however, are different. In Genesis, for instance, there are twelve examples of the accusative singular νύκτα used adverbially, five examples of ἐν (...) νυκτί, and at most two examples of the genitive νυκτός – a particularly common construction with this particular noun in Classical Greek. Given that, in Attic, the genitive is as common as or more common than

---

[6] For another example, see τρίτην ἡμέραν in Th. 8.23.1–2 (= ex. (10) in Ch. 2).

[7] In the Hebrew *ki-tmôl šilšôm* ('as-yesterday (and) on.the.third'), the second word is essentially a one-off adverbial formation built to the triliteral root *šlš* 'three'. In Joüon–Muraoka it is thought to be a borrowing from Akkadian *ina šalši ūme* 'in three days' (§102b).

[8] In Hebrew:

û-zəra'tem	'ēt	haš-šānāh	haš-šəmînit
and-you.will.sow	D.O.	the-year	the-eighth

In BDB it is stated that the use of 'ēt with this temporal sense is rare (s.v. I.2.b) and only two other occurrences are given (Ex. 13:7, Deut. 9:25); see also Waltke & O'Connor 1990: 181. Note that the Greek word order (article–noun article–numeral) also matches the Hebrew.

the accusative, these figures already suggest that the accusative of time has grown beyond its Classical range. Such is indeed the case, as not only example (1) shows, but also five others like it, including two with demonstratives, which are frequently associated with punctual constructions.[9] (The other six adverbial expressions with νύκτα are durative, occasionally with an additional modal nuance, and would be unremarkable in Attic.[10]) Moreover, while one of the two examples with νυκτός is a legitimate modal genitive and not a by-product of the translation, the second is probably better understood as adnominal, if not on the basis of the Greek in its own right, then at least in light of the Hebrew *Vorlage*:

(5) ἐγινόμην τῆς ἡμέρας συγκαιόμενος τῷ καύματι καὶ παγετῷ **τῆς νυκτός**

By day I burned with heat and with frost by night (Gen. 31:40)

(6) εἶπεν δὲ ὁ θεὸς Ἰσραὴλ ἐν ὁράματι τῆς νυκτός

And God said to Israel in a dream at night (Gen. 46:2)

way-yômer	'ĕlōhîm	lə-yiśrā'ēl	bə-mar'ōt	hal-laylāh
and-said	God	to-Israel	in-dreams	the-night

In both passages, there are nouns that could potentially serve as heads for the genitives in question: παγετῷ in (5) and ὁράματι in (6). In (5), however, the adverbial reading is easier, insofar as there is a certain parallelism with the first half of the verse, and the hyperbaton separating τῆς ἡμέρας from τῷ καύματι makes the adnominal reading harder there. Furthermore, in the Hebrew, the nouns for both day and night are each governed by the preposition *bə* ('in'), so there is even less reason to take τῆς νυκτός as dependent on παγετῷ. As for (6), a Hebrew-less reader might not expect a definite noun phrase τῆς νυκτός to be dependent on an indefinite ὁράματι.[11] But in this passage, the Hebrew does in fact suggest that the translator had an adnominal reading in mind, for the word for dream is in the construct state, which indicates that there is another

---

[9] The other examples are found at Gen. 19:5, 20:3, 31:24, 32:23 (with ἐκείνην), and 19:34 (with ταύτην). The verb phrases they modify are all telic: εἰσελθόντες πρὸς σέ, εἰσῆλθεν πρὸς Ἀβιμέλεχ, ἦλθεν πρὸς Λαβάν, ἀναστὰς δὲ ... ἔλαβεν τὰς δύο γυναῖκας, ποτίσωμεν αὐτὸν οἶνον.

[10] These are found at 8:22 (modal: ἡμέραν καὶ νύκτα οὐ καταπαύσουσιν), and (all with ἐκείνην or ταύτην and with the aorist of κοιμάομαι) 19:33, 30:15, 30:16, 32:14, 32:22.

[11] In my corpus of Attic prose, when adnominal genitives of time nouns have the definite article, they are nearly always dependent on definite heads.

noun dependent on it.[12] Finally, there are the five examples of ἐν (...) νυκτί, of which two are limitative and three are punctual.[13] These, again, are not at odds with Attic expression, but the criterion that distinguishes the punctual uses with the accusative and those with ἐν is unclear from the Greek. Potentially, one could see some slight difference in the verbal semantics: the three constructions with ἐν have ὤφθη once and ποτίζω twice, whereas those with accusative are, primarily, verbs of motion.[14] But ποτίζω is also found with the accusative, and this distribution does not correspond to any familiar semantic dichotomy; furthermore, the verbs of motion that take the accusative occur three times in the phrase 'came in a dream', making them quite close to ὤφθη in sense. Far more instructive, in this case, is a glance at the Hebrew *Vorlage*. All three times that ἐν is used in Greek, the Hebrew has the preposition *bə*; in five of the six punctual examples with the accusative, the noun is simply used adverbially, with or without the article. In the sixth accusative (32:23), the Hebrew text does have the preposition, so we might expect the Greek here to have had ἐν as well. The discrepancy here is probably to be explained by the preceding context: in both 32:14 and 32:22, the simple accusative is called for because the construction is durative (the verb modified is κοιμάομαι), and the translator opts for this construction on semantic grounds even though the Hebrew has *bə* in both verses. This preference for the accusative may have carried over to 32:23, in which the *bə* is omitted from the translation, even though in this context ἐν would in fact have been grammatical Greek. In any case, it is clear that the use of the accusative and ἐν in punctual

---

[12] With the reading above, as printed in the *BHS*, the construct state (for which see n. 79) is morphologically the same as the absolute state, so one cannot be absolutely sure that *hallaylāh* is dependent on it. But (i) BDB takes it as such, (ii) *hal-laylāh* taken on its own as an adverb in the Pentateuch elsewhere means 'tonight' (BDB s.v.), and (iii) *BHS* notes that *mar'at*, in the singular, is a possible alternate reading (the singular and plural would be indistinguishable in a consonantal text, and the singular would match the number in the Greek better) – and this form is unambiguously the construct state; see Wevers (1993: 771). The NRSV translates the Hebrew "in visions of the night."

[13] Both limitative examples are modified by μιᾷ and refer to the fact that the Pharaoh's butler and baker both saw a dream on the same night (40:5, 41:11); of the three punctual examples, one, modified by ἐκείνῃ, is used of the verb ὤφθη (26:24), and the other two, both modified by ταύτῃ, are found with ἐπότισαν (19:33, 35).

[14] See n. 9.

constructions of νύξ matches the Hebrew more closely than any patterns seen in untranslated texts. Moreover, since the punctual accusative is not a usage that has much of a presence in the New Testament, let alone other texts of the first century AD, there is all the more reason to see it as conditioned by direct translation, rather than by any broader diachronic change.

What is more, one must also be wary of characterizing the entirety of the Septuagint based on a single book.[15] Even staying within the Pentateuch, we find a very different picture regarding punctual νύκτα. In the other four books, there is not a single other example of this usage, although there is one modal construction where it is parallel with ἡμέραν (Num. 14:14) and two more where it is parallel with ἡμέρας (Ex. 13:21, Num. 9:16), which is difficult to pin down as either genitive singular (with a discrepancy of case with respect to νύκτα) or accusative plural (with a discrepancy of number).[16] In all of these passages, the reference is to God's leading the people of Israel as a pillar of cloud by day, and of fire by night; the continuous duration of the event thereby comes into play, so the accusative would be natural in Attic as well. The other examples of temporal νύκτα in these four books are clearly durative, as signaled either by a modifier (6× ὅλην)[17] or the verb (καταλύσατε in the sense 'spend the night' (Num. 22:8), ὑπομείνατε (Num. 22:19)). In these books, the genitive of time reclaims its place as the favored construction for νύξ, with five punctual examples, five modal examples, and two habitual examples.[18] There is also one example of punctual ἐν τῇ νυκτὶ ταύτῃ (Ex. 12:12).

---

[15] Literature on the translation technique of the Septuagint is voluminous. For brief surveys, see Tov 1999b (as well as several of the other chs. in Tov 1999a), Fernández Marcos 2001: 22–31, as well as the essays in Aejmelaeus 1993.

[16] All in all, the genitive singular seems more likely, given the parallels elsewhere for mismatch of case, notably in the pairing of νυκτός with μεθ' ἡμέραν. The Hebrew does not help very much, as the word translated by ἡμέρας in Ex. 13:21 is *yômām*, which, whatever its diachronic origin, in synchronic terms is formed from the noun *yôm* by a derivational rather than an inflectional process – like νύκτωρ in Greek – and so has no number (Joüon–Muraoka §102b). In Num. 9:16, the MT does not even contain a word for day (though the apparatus criticus in the *BHS* notes the possibility of inserting *yômām* on the basis of the Greek, Syriac, and Vulgate texts).

[17] Ex. 10:13, 14:20, 21, Lev. 6:2, Num. 11:32, 14:1

[18] Punctual: Ex. 12:30, 31, 42, Num. 22:20, Deut. 16:1; modal: Ex. 13:22, 40:38, Num. 9:21, Deut. 1:33, 28:66; habitual: Num. 11:9, Deut. 23:11. All twelve are simply νυκτός, with no article or other modifier.

In short, the accusative of time is used in the Septuagint by and large in the same way it is used in Attic prose, as a marker of the durative event-type, as well as modal expressions in which the idea of continued activity comes to the fore. The chief exception, the use of νύκτα in punctual expresions, at least to judge from a survey of the Pentateuch, is limited to Genesis, where the choice of the accusative over ἐν^{+D} is motivated by the absence of a preposition in Hebrew.

Temporal expressions with ἐν^{+D} in the Septuagint

In the previous section, ἡμέρα more or less followed the Attic standard, and it was the anomalous behavior of νύξ that needed explanation. In considering the use of ἐν, by contrast, it is ἡμέρα which proves more problematic. As we saw, the use of ἐν with νυκτί is motivated by the presence of the preposition bə in Hebrew. With ἡμέρα, however, the alternation between ἐν and the *dative* of time, which one might also expect to be linked to the presence or absence of bə, in fact bears no relation thereto. Again, starting with Genesis, the dative occurs eleven times, ἐν fourteen times. All but twice, bə occurs in Hebrew, so the general pattern is that the translators keep ἐν in the translation 57% of the time, but 43% of the time get rid of it and opt for the simple dative instead. But before turning to these more common examples, consider first one of the two passages where bə does not occur in the Hebrew (the other will be dealt with below as example (8)):

(7) μήποτε ἀτεκνωθῶ ἀπὸ τῶν δύο ὑμῶν **ἐν ἡμέρᾳ μιᾷ**

Lest I be bereft of the two of you on one day (Gen. 27:45)

Here the Hebrew simply has *yôm 'eḥād*, the same phrase that is translated literally as ἡμέραν μίαν in a durative construction in Gen. 33:13. The choice of ἐν here is a good sign that the translators were alert to the fact that the assignment of more than one event (ἀτεκνωθῶ ἀπὸ τῶν δύο ὑμῶν) to bounded time period (note μιᾷ) calls for the limitative type, frequently marked by ἐν.

If we turn to the more numerous examples where bə does occur in the Hebrew, it helps to sort the data according to the modifiers of ἡμέρα, because some gravitate more towards the dative, others towards ἐν. With relative pronouns, the dative is preferred: ᾗ ἡμέρᾳ occurs five times, ἐν ᾗ ἡμέρᾳ only once.[19] (Incidentally, none of these are relative clauses in Hebrew, which, unlike Greek, does not have the syntactic flexibility of an inflecting relative pronoun; instead, these constructions are all of the type 'on the day of' with the infinitive.) With demonstratives, the translators preferred to retain the preposition: ἐν is used six times (seven if we may also count ἐν τῇ ἡμέρᾳ τῇ αὔριον in this category), whereas the simple dative is only used once.[20] The preposition is also retained in the one construction that has a substantive modifier, ἐν ἡμέρᾳ θλίψεως (35:3). The greatest variation occurs in the rendering of the constructions with the ordinal: five with the dative, four with ἐν.[21] In addition to the slight numerical preference for the dative, there are two additional reasons for thinking that the dative is the default choice, the use of ἐν somewhat marked.

The first is seen in example (8), along with (7) the other construction in this set where the underlying Hebrew does not have the preposition bə:

(8) περιέτεμεν δὲ Ἀβραὰμ τὸν Ἰσαὰκ **τῇ ὀγδόῃ ἡμέρᾳ**

And Abraham circumcised Isaac on the eighth day (Gen. 21:4)

way-yāmol	'Abrāhām 'et-Yiṣḥāq bənô	ben-šəmōnat yāmîm
and-he.circumcised	Abraham D.O.-Isaac his.son	son.of-eight days

Had the translators wanted the Greek to be closer to the underlying Hebrew, they could have done so with an adnominal genitive: υἱὸν ὀκτὼ ἡμερῶν or the like. Indeed, this option is chosen earlier in the text; see example (9):

(9) καὶ παιδίον **ὀκτὼ ἡμερῶν** περιτμηθήσεται ὑμῖν πᾶν ἀρσενικόν

And every eight-day-old male child of yours will be circumcised (Gen. 17:12)

---

[19] The five with the dative: Gen. 2:4, 17, 5:1, 2, and 21:8; the one with ἐν: 3:5.

[20] The seven with ἐν: 15:18, 26:32, 30:35, 33:16, 48:20 (all ἐκείνῃ), 7:13 (ταύτῃ), 30:33 (αὔριον); the one with the dative: 7:11.

[21] The five with the dative: 17:14, 21:4, 22:4, 31:22, 42:18; the four with ἐν: 2:2 (bis), 34:25, 40:20. In Rahlfs's text, one of the two instances of ἐν in 2:2 is omitted. For more details, see example (12) below.

Translation with the genitive is particularly easy in (9) because the verb is in the future tense: although the Hebrew here is unambiguously 'a child of eight days', the Greek could potentially be given a limitative reading: 'every child will be circumcised within eight days'. This cannot be done with the aorist in (8), where the adverbial temporal expression is chosen independently of the Hebrew, and it is the simple dative that is used.[22]

The second reason for believing that the dative was the unmarked way to render 'on the *n*th day' has to do with the passages where ἐν is used instead. Two of the four occur after the introductory verb ἐγένετο. See example (10):[23]

(10) ἐγένετο δὲ **ἐν τῇ ἡμέρᾳ τῇ τρίτῃ**, ὅτε ἦσαν ἐν τῷ πόνῳ, ἔλαβον ... ἕκαστος τὴν μάχαιραν αὐτοῦ

And it happened on the third day, when they were in pain, each ... took his sword (Gen. 34:25)

There is quite possibly double motivation for the use of ἐν rather than the dative here. First, the use of ἐγένετο as a placeholder verb with an expression giving the temporal setting for the subsequent clause is a noted Hebraism in the language of the Septuagint: Classical Greek prefers to work such expressions into the sentence with participles or subordinate clauses rather than with a paratactic construction with a verb like ἐγένετο.[24] As the temporal phrase is thus located in a Hebraizing construction to begin with, there is somewhat less reason to move away from the more literal translation (with ἐν) to a more idiomatic translation (with the dative). But there is another possible motivation as well: even in Thucydides, temporal phrases modifying ἐγένετο fall into a class of their own. Granted, they look rather different from the ἐγένετο δέ expressions in the Septuagint, but they are distinguished by

---

[22] In passing, we may also wonder whether this might be a passage where the Hebrew *Vorlage* for the LXX was simply different from the Masoretic Text that we have: not only the temporal expression is altered, but also Hebrew *bᵊnô* has dropped out. Wevers notes that the Hexapla added υἱὸν αὐτοῦ to match the MT (1993: 300).

[23] See also 40:20.

[24] See Beyer 1968: 29–62, Maloney 1981: 81–6, Voelz 1984: 959–60, George 2010: 268–70.

preferring the use of ἐν to other constructions. Passage (11) is typical:[25]

(11) τοσαῦτα μὲν ἐν τῷ θέρει ἐγένετο

All this happened during the summer (Th. 2.68.9)

Insofar as these expressions note that a number of discrete actions all took place within a given period of time, they fall into the limitative, rather than the punctual, category, which, with θέρος and χειμών, elicits the construction with ἐν in Thucydides.

If we view the Septuagintal use of ἐν in (10) as due to the limitative nature of statements like this that sum up various events that have taken place over a stretch of time, then we can perhaps also explain the third and fourth uses of ἐν with an ordinal number. These are both found in passage (12):

(12) καὶ συνετέλεσεν ὁ θεὸς ἐν τῇ ἡμέρᾳ τῇ ἕκτῃ τὰ ἔργα αὐτοῦ, ἃ ἐποίησεν, καὶ κατέπαυσεν ἐν τῇ ἡμέρᾳ τῇ ἑβδόμῃ ἀπὸ πάντων τῶν ἔργων αὐτοῦ, ὧν ἐποίησεν

- ἐν¹ om. 72–135 128-cII 76' 121 59 (= 4 out of 10 groups in Wevers (1974: 56–9))
- ἐν² om. 15' 25–408–646 d 56–129 75 121 120–122 509 Rahlfs (= 7 out of 10 groups)

And God finished his works, which he had done, on the sixth day, and on the seventh he rested from all his works, which he had done (Gen. 2:2)

Consider first just the first prepositional phrase. Although the construction is not quite parallel to that of (11) in that the works in question only *finished* on the sixth day, after being underway for the previous five, the same principle may well be at work: the clause that sums up the completion of multiple events is more likely to contain an expression with ἐν than one with the simple dative. The second phrase is admittedly more difficult to explain along these lines, as the act of resting does not represent the

---

[25] This construction is discussed in Ch. 2 as ex. (72). For other examples, see also 2.32.1, 4.88.2, in both of which the verb is ἐγένετο, and its subject ταῦτα. A clearer example of a limitative construction (but with a plural time noun, so less directly comparable) occurs at 1.118.2: ταῦτα δὲ ξύμπαντα … ἐγένετο ἐν ἔτεσι πεντήκοντα μάλιστα. There is a particularly close parallel to the LXX use at 1.87.6: ἡ δὲ διαγνώμη αὕτη τῆς ἐκκλησίας … ἐγένετο ἐν τῷ τετάρτῳ καὶ δεκάτῳ ἔτει τῶν τριακοντουτίδων σπονδῶν.

summing-up of multiple activities in the same way that συνετέλεσεν does. Perhaps the translators were here aiming for parallelism with the preceding phrase – or, perhaps, with Rahlfs, we should follow the reading without the preposition offered by seven of the major minuscule families (though Wevers reasonably suggests that its loss there can be explained by haplology).

To sum up, then, we see the following overall pattern with the rendering of Hebrew *bay-yôm* ('on the day') in the Greek of the Septuagint translation of Genesis: when the word for day is modified by a demonstrative, $ἐν^{+D}$ is preferred; when it is modified by a relative pronoun, the dative is preferred; so too the dative is preferred when it is modified by an ordinal number – although ἐν can be used instead in the ἐγένετο constructions and the συνετέλεσεν construction of passage (12). Why, then, do demonstratives on the one hand, and ordinals and relatives on the other, get different treatment? To begin with, any answer to this question should take into account the general diachronic trend: ἐν becomes extremely common in the New Testament (about 125×, compared to only fifty instances of the dative of time; by contrast, in Thucydides and Xenophon they occur equally frequently, with 116 examples of ἐν, and 114 of the dative), but the dative of time loses little ground to ἐν in the papyri and becomes even more widespread in Plutarch. Given that this is the case, the frequency of ἐν in the Pentateuch appears to be a Semitism, but the question remains: why does the dative of time in punctual constructions give way to ἐν, formerly a marker of limitative constructions, first in phrases where the noun is modified by a demonstrative, and only later in phrases with the relative or an ordinal? It is difficult to be completely sure, but one may first observe that, already in Thucydides and Xenophon, with certain nouns like θέρος and χειμών, the construction with ἐν was available to mark the punctual event-type. This state of affairs will have resulted from the inherent difficulty of distinguishing between the two types in certain phrases like *They planned to leave that winter*, where the ambiguity of placing an event in future time favors the limitative expression, with its designation of a broader time frame for an event, but the indication of a specific unit of time – 'that winter' – favors the punctual. But in certain environments, the dative of time was more likely to be fossilized in its

Table 22. *Modifiers of* ἡμέρα *in punctual constructions in the Pentateuch*

modifier	ἐν	dative of time
demonstrative[a]	38×	4×
ordinal[b]	10×	92×
relative	6×	28×

Note:
[a] This includes not only ἐκείνη and ταύτη, but also the phrase αὐτῇ τῇ ἡμέρᾳ

[b] This includes 5 examples, all with the dative, of τῇ ἡμέρᾳ τῶν σαββάτων.

earlier function: constructions with ordinal numbers are a good candidate for such fossilization, insofar as the enumeration of specific dates is the sort of temporal expression that can recur with regularity in, say, bureaucratic registers.

But before checking the preceding account of the dative and ἐν against the details of the papyri, one must also consider the extent to which the findings based on Genesis form part of a larger pattern in the Pentateuch: that the evidence of punctual νύκτα was limited to Genesis shows the danger of relying on a single book. Here, however, the pattern whereby demonstratives prefer ἐν, ordinals and relative pronouns, the simple dative, does extend to the rest of the Pentateuch. Combining all five books, the figures are as shown in Table 22.

Furthermore, the examples where ἐν occurs with the ordinal all show some sign of belonging to the limitative type: either they occur in the future (Lev. 23: 5, 6, 39, Num. 9:11, 19:19 (*bis*)) or they occur after ἐγένετο (Ex. 16:27). On the whole, this distribution matches the papyri well, with the proviso that, with these modifiers, the dative of time is always preferred in the papyri, and the demonstratives only favor ἐν in the sense that this is a more common minority expression with them than it is with the ordinals and relatives.[26]

---

[26] See nn. 200 and 201 in Ch. 3. Statistics are messy with the papyri because they are often lacunose, and they do not form a uniform corpus. But I count the number of papyri up to AD 150 attesting the dative and ἐν as follows: with demonstratives, 2× ἐν (*P. Muench.*

But despite the clarity of the pattern with ἡμέρα, it must be conceded that the same cannot be said of the use of the temporal dative and ἐν with ἔτος. With this time noun, the Pentateuch offers five instances of the dative of time, and thirteen with ἐν. All five of the datives of time are modified by ordinal numbers, as are all but two of the constructions with ἐν.[27] Nor is the preference for ἐν here due to a predominance of the limitative type: true, five of the constructions with ἐν occur with future-tense verbs, but so too do three of the five with the simple dative, an even greater proportion. The Hebrew text does not do much to elucidate the variation either: all but one of the eighteen passages have the preposition *bə*.[28] Given, then, that the Greek text primarily shows the occasional omission of the preposition from the translation, perhaps the best explanation is simply that some of the translators felt themselves at greater liberty to alter a literal translation with the preposition to the simple dative of time on the grounds that the latter was somehow more stylistically appropriate. This view gains some support from the textual variation seen in the manuscripts of the Septuagint. In particular, in several of the passages which Rahlfs and Wevers print with the preposition, some witnesses to the text omit it. Most striking in this respect is the evidence from quotations: John Chrysostom (twice) and Philo (once) omit the ἐν when citing these phrases from the Pentateuch.[29] And while a couple of the minority readings do involve the addition of the preposition, more of them involve its omission.[30] If one then tries to work out what circumstances will have favored the omission of the preposition, the picture is one of miscellaneous one-off factors. (i) Gen. 14:4 is

---

3.1.66, *P. Thomas* 9.13) vs 4× dative (*P. Hamb.* 1.27, *P. Koeln* 6.258, *P. Petr.* 2.17, 3.28, but these last two are lacunose); with ordinals, 1× ἐν (*O. Wilck.* 1170) vs 7× dative (*BGU* 2.647, 7.1549, 16.2626, *P. Giss. Apoll.* 8, *P. Mert.* 2.66, *P. Oxy.* 1.119, *P. Stras.* 4.227); with relatives, 1 × ἐν (*SB* 12.11016) vs 7 × dative (*Chr. Wilck.* 331, *P. Cair. Zen.* 3.59491, *P. Frankf.* 6, *P. Hib.* 1.29, *P. Lond.* 7.2028, 2036, *P. Oxy.* 14.1672).

[27] The exception is ἐν τῷ ἔτει τῆς ἀφέσεως (Lev. 25:13, 54); insofar as the modifier acts like an ordinal in singling out a particular year, these two examples will be included with the ordinal constructions in the following figures.

[28] The one exception is Gen. 14:4, but even here the form with the preposition is a variant reading.

[29] John Chrysostom *In Genesim* 53.235 (Gen. 8:13) and 54.563 (Gen. 47:18); Philo *De plantatione* 95 (Lev. 19:25).

[30] Addition of the preposition: Ex. 40:17 and Lev. 25:4; omission of the preposition: Gen. 14:5, Lev. 25:20 and 25:54, Num. 33:38 (in addition to the quotations from Chrysostom and Philo).

the one place where the Hebrew quite probably did not have the preposition, so its omission here is understandable. (ii) At Ex. 40:17, the phrase with ἔτει follows ἐν τῷ μηνὶ τῷ πρώτῳ: doubling of the preposition could have been seen as repetitive. (iii) Something similar may be at work in Lev. 19:24, which is followed in the next verse by a construction with the preposition. (iv) Apart from Ex. 40:17, the other four examples where ἐν is omitted all occur as the first constituent of the sentence, either directly after καί or incorporating δέ. While phrases with ἐν certainly also occur clause-initially (5×), they are found more often after the verb (8×), suggesting that a translator would be quicker to omit the preposition in comparatively routine temporal expressions in clause-initial setting phrases than in more pragmatically variable positions later on.[31]

All in all, it is clear that the distinction between ἐν and the simple dative in temporal expressions was a fine one: both with ἡμέρα and with ἔτος, it was affected by factors other than the nature of the expression found in the Hebrew *Vorlage*, and both the modifier of the expression and consideration of word order apparently played a role in selecting for one construction over the other. Moreover, while the phrases with ἐν are not ungrammatical Greek, their extremely high frequency in the Septuagint relative to the papyri should be understood as a Semitism.

The dative of time in the Septuagint

Conversely, the spread of the dative of time into limitative and even durative expressions, already seen in the post-Classical authors of Chapter 3, had only just begun in the Septuagint. This is easiest to observe when the time noun is in the plural. The Septuagint, for instance, has no durative expressions with χρόνοις, to match examples (38) and (42) from the New Testament.[32] Of the 228 instances of ἡμέραις in the whole of the Septuagint, 220 are governed by ἐν,[33]

---

[31] Post-verbal examples: Gen. 47:18, Lev. 25:20, 25:21, 25:54, Num. 9:1, 33:38, Deut. 1:3, 26:12.

[32] All five examples of χρόνοις in the LXX are governed by ἐν.

[33] When we turn to similar expressions in the New Testament, this figure will indicate well just how pronounced a Septuagintalism this construction is.

another five are datives of respect, all used in reference to people's ages (e.g. προβεβηκώς ταῖς ἡμέραις, Jos. 23:1), and at most three show an extended use of the dative of time:

(13) καὶ ἐποίησεν Σαλωμὼν τὴν ἑορτὴν ἐν τῷ καιρῷ ἐκείνῳ **ἑπτὰ ἡμέραις** (*šib'at yāmîm*) καὶ πᾶς Ἰσραὴλ μετ᾽ αὐτοῦ

And Solomon celebrated the festival at that time for seven days, as did all of Israel with him (2 Chron. 7:8)

(14) νῦν γίνεται καὶ οὐ πάλαι, καὶ οὐ **προτέραις ἡμέραις** (*lipnê-yôm*) ἤκουσας αὐτά

These things are coming into being now, and not long ago, and you did not hear these things during earlier days (Is. 48:7)

(15) συνίστανται δὲ αὐτῶν τὴν ἀπώλειαν ἀπὸ πέμπτης τοῦ Ἐπιφὶ ἕως ἑβδόμης **ἡμέραις τρισίν**

And they arranged their destruction from the fifth until the seventh of Epeiph, for three days (3 Macc. 6:38)

Of these examples, the first two are fairly clear durative expressions (although one could also have a limitative expression in (14) after the negative), and one would expect the accusative, not the dative. In neither of the two is the Greek construction motivated by the Hebrew: in the first, the Hebrew simply reads 'seven days', and in the second 'before today'.[34] As for (15), this could be another durative phrase, although a reading as some sort of goal expression is also possible, in which case the dative would be less unusual.[35]

Finally, there are eleven examples of ἔτεσι(ν) in the Septuagint, of which one is a dative of degree of difference, nine are governed by ἐν, and only one – in a textually corrupt passage – shows a limitative dative:

(16) καὶ τὸν οἶκον αὐτοῦ ᾠκοδόμησεν Σαλωμὼν **τρισκαίδεκα ἔτεσιν**

Some manuscripts offer ἔτη or τῷ τρισκαιδεκάτῳ ἔτει.

And Solomon built his house over thirteen years (3 Kings 7:38 (LXX), transposed from 1 Kings 7:1 (MT))

[34] For the translation of the Hebrew phrase in (14), see BDB s.v. *yôm* 7.i.
[35] As 3 Maccabees is agreed to have been written in Greek, there is again no reason to assume Semitic influence.

Again, the Hebrew is not responsible for the dative, as it reads simply *šəlōš 'eśrēh šānāh* ('thirteen years'),[36] so the motivation for the phrase lay within Greek itself, although it was unusual enough, if it is indeed the correct reading, to warrant spurious correction by later copyists.

The New Testament

Before discussing individual passages, a word about the textual tradition of the New Testament is in order, as it is vastly richer than that of the other texts in the study. This wealth of manuscripts poses problems because the number of variant readings in passages with unusual temporal constructions is also correspondingly higher. To a large extent, the discussion that follows can sidestep this issue by simply taking all the variants in the older manuscripts as evidence of genuine variation of expression in Greek of the first few centuries AD.[37] This is all the more reasonable a procedure in that most of the relevant passages have multiple manuscripts lining up on one or the other side of a textual uncertainty, making it less likely that a variant is due merely to a mistake by a single copyist. Furthermore, in such situations, it is usually easy to determine which reading is *difficilior*, and one can therefore be relatively confident in choosing which was original.

The accusative of time in the New Testament

Of the 103 accusatives of time in the New Testament,[38] most (87×) are clearly durative and thus require little comment. They are generally plural, often modified by a cardinal number, or, if singular, either modified by εἷς or ὅλος or modifying a typically durative

---

[36] The singular *šānāh* is common after the numerals eleven through nineteen (Waltke & O'Connor 1990: 279).

[37] I limit the readings cited to those found in the papyri and the major early uncial MSS, as reported in Nestle–Aland. These are **p**[4] (3C), **p**[46] (*c*.200), **p**[66] (*c*.200), **p**[75] (3C), ℵ (Codex Sinaiticus, 4C), A (Codex Alexandrinus, 5C), B (Codex Vaticanus, 4C), C (5C), D (5C Gospels and Acts, 6C Pauline letters).

[38] For the New Testament, the database consists of temporal expressions with ἡμέρα, νύξ, μήν, θέρος, χειμών, ἔτος, ἐνιαυτός, ὥρα, and χρόνος. Following BDAG s.v. κρίνω I take both examples of ἡμέρα in Rom. 14:5 as direct objects: ὃς μὲν [γὰρ] κρίνει ἡμέραν παρ' ἡμέραν, ὃς δὲ κρίνει πᾶσαν ἡμέραν.

verb (e.g. καὶ παρ' αὐτῷ ἔμειναν τὴν ἡμέραν ἐκείνην, Jn. 1:39). A further eight examples (νύκτα καὶ ἡμέραν, 4×) are modal, with the accusative still lending a durative overtone, insofar as the action is portrayed as lasting continuously through both day and night, the verbs in question being καθεύδῃ καὶ ἐγείρηται (Mk. 4:27), οὐκ ἀφίστατο ... λατρεύουσα (Lk. 2:37) and λατρεῦον (Acts 26:7), and οὐκ ἐπαυσάμην ... νουθετῶν (Acts 20:31). Another two, again a pair with ἡμέρα and νύξ, lie at the border of the modal type (because of the night–day contrast) and the habitual (because the time nouns are plural): ἦν δὲ τὰς ἡμέρας ἐν τῷ ἱερῷ διδάσκων, τὰς δὲ νύκτας ἐξερχόμενος ηὐλίζετο εἰς τὸ ὄρος τὸ καλούμενον Ἐλαιῶν (Lk. 21:37). In three further constructions, the accusative comes closer to the distributive type, as the event in question is said to occur every day. This can be made explicit by a modifier of the time noun (πᾶσάν τε ἡμέραν ἐν τῷ ἱερῷ καὶ κατ' οἶκον οὐκ ἐπαύοντο διδάσκοντες καὶ εὐαγγελιζόμενοι τὸν Χριστόν, Acts 5:42), by a construction in which ἡμέραν is reinforced by ἐξ ἡμέρας (ὁ δίκαιος ἐγκατοικῶν ἐν αὐτοῖς ἡμέραν ἐξ ἡμέρας ψυχὴν δικαίαν ἀνόμοις ἔργοις ἐβασάνιζεν, 2 Pet. 2:8), or by a monetary context (συμφωνήσας δὲ μετὰ τῶν ἐργατῶν ἐκ δηναρίου τὴν ἡμέραν ἀπέστειλεν αὐτοὺς εἰς τὸν ἀμπελῶνα αὐτοῦ, Mt. 20:2). Finally, in three examples the accusative is used in apparent punctual constructions:

(17) καὶ οὐ μὴ γνῷς **ποίαν ὥραν** ἥξω ἐπὶ σέ

And you will not know the hour when I will come to you (Rev. 3:3)

(18) ἔσπευδεν γὰρ εἰ δυνατὸν εἴη αὐτῷ **τὴν**[39] **ἡμέραν** τῆς πεντηκοστῆς γενέσθαι εἰς Ἱεροσόλυμα

For he was eager, if possible, to be in Jerusalem on the day of Pentecost (Acts 20:16)

(19) ἐπύθετο οὖν τὴν ὥραν παρ' αὐτῶν ἐν ᾗ κομψότερον ἔσχεν· εἶπαν οὖν αὐτῷ ὅτι Ἐχθὲς **ὥραν ἑβδόμην**[40] ἀφῆκεν αὐτὸν ὁ πυρετός

Then he asked them the hour at which he had begun to do better; then they told him, "Yesterday at the seventh hour the fever left him" (Jn. 4:52)

---

[39] Codex D adds εἰς before τὴν, but the reading of the other MSS is to be preferred as the *lectio difficilior*.
[40] Some Old Latin and Syriac versions offer differing ordinals.

In example (17), the accusative could perhaps be explained away as raising, with ποίαν ὥραν syntactically the object of γνῷς rather than an adverbial temporal expression modifying ἥξω. Still, the dative was potentially an option here, as shown by a thematically parallel passage in Matthew:

(20) γρηγορεῖτε οὖν, ὅτι οὐκ οἴδατε **ποίᾳ ἡμέρᾳ**⁴¹ ὁ κύριος ὑμῶν ἔρχεται

So stay awake, because you do not know on what day your lord is coming
(Mt. 24:42)

The accusative of example (18) could also be justified if the expression were understood as a durative expression, with the sense 'to spend the day of Pentecost in Jerusalem'. But the context – the preceding clause refers to Paul's passing by Ephesus without stopping so that he can get back to Jerusalem in time – suggests that the emphasis lies on the timely arrival in Jerusalem⁴² rather than on spending the whole of the day there.⁴³ With example (19), we have the most non-Classical accusative of time in the New Testament, in that the verbal event is telic and instantaneous and the time noun is modified by an ordinal number. Here, if anywhere, one expects a dative of time, as seen in the following section.⁴⁴

The dative of time in the New Testament

Considering the general decline of the dative, its temporal use is surprisingly common, but as this is also true of the post-Classical literature surveyed in Chapter 3,⁴⁵ there is no reason to see any particular Semitic motivation for its frequency in the New Testament.⁴⁶ There are fifty-seven examples, mostly with ἡμέρα

---

⁴¹ The reading ὥρᾳ is also found (and is implied by Latin, Syriac, Coptic versions), but the early uncial MSS have ἡμέρᾳ.

⁴² The scribe who added εἰς to codex D (see n. 39) will have understood the phrase in the same way.

⁴³ The preposition εἰς cannot be adduced as support for either view, as it can be used as a purely stationary local preposition in Acts: ἐγὼ γὰρ οὐ μόνον δεθῆναι ἀλλὰ καὶ ἀποθανεῖν εἰς Ἰερουσαλὴμ ἑτοίμως ἔχω (21:13).

⁴⁴ In the only other New Testament example of ὥρα modified by an ordinal number in a punctual construction, Mark uses the dative: τῇ ἐνάτῃ ὥρᾳ (15:34).

⁴⁵ See esp. n. 147 in Ch. 3.

⁴⁶ To be sure, the preposition *la*, the closest Hebrew counter part to the dative, is occasionally used in temporal constructions, but the two examples of punctual constructions given in Waltke & O'Connor did not result in temporal datives in Greek (1990: 206): (i) *lə-rûᵃh*

(31×), but also with ὥρα (13×), νύξ (6×), χρόνος (5×), and ἔτος (2×).
If anything, they attest to a broadening of the range of the construction, perhaps, as with the other post-Classical examples, under
the influence of Latin.[47] Consider first the expressions with ἡμέρα.
Many of these would be quite at home in Classical texts: twelve of them occur with
ordinal numbers, fifteen more with other ordinal-like modifiers that
specify the day in question (ποίᾳ, ἑξῆς, ἐκείνῃ, ἐπιούσῃ, ἐχομένῃ,
τάκτῃ, τοῦ σαββάτου (2×), τῶν σαββάτων (2×), the relative pronoun (2×), τῇ ἐσχάτῃ (3×)[48]). But the remaining four diverge from
the Classical standard:

(21) ἀλλ᾽ εἰ καὶ ὁ ἔξω ἡμῶν ἄνθρωπος διαφθείρεται, ἀλλ᾽ ὁ ἔσω ἡμῶν ἀνακαινοῦται
ἡμέρᾳ καὶ ἡμέρᾳ

But even if our outer self perishes, still the one within us is renewed every
day (2 Cor. 4:16)

(22) λατρεύειν αὐτῷ ἐν ὁσιότητι καὶ δικαιοσύνῃ ἐνώπιον αὐτοῦ **πάσαις ταῖς**
ἡμέραις ἡμῶν
dative of time p[4vid] B | πάσας τὰς ἡμέρας ℵ A C D

To serve him in holiness and righteousness before him all our days (Lk.
1:74–5)

(23) μηδὲ πορνεύωμεν, καθώς τινες αὐτῶν ἐπόρνευσαν, καὶ ἔπεσαν **μιᾷ ἡμέρᾳ** εἴκοσι
τρεῖς χιλιάδες
dative of time p[46] ℵ* B D* | ἐν add. ℵ² A C D[I]

Let us not practice immoral sex, just as some of them did, and 23,000 fell on
one day (1 Cor. 10:8)

---

hay-yôm 'at the cool of the day' becomes τὸ δειλινόν (Gen. 3:8); (ii) *la-'ēt 'ereb* 'at the
time of evening' becomes τὸ πρὸς ἑσπέραν (Gen. 8:11). The supposed durative example
they cite, *la-yāmîm 'ôd šib'āh* (Gen. 7:4), is in fact limitative 'in seven more days', and is
rendered ἔτι ἡμερῶν ἑπτά in the LXX. Still, the flexibility of the Aramaic preposition *la*
(see e.g. Rosenthal 1963: 34–5, Muraoka & Porten 2003: 262–3) might have further
encouraged confusion of the dative and accusative. That said, it is not one of the
prepositions that Segert notes as esp. important in temporal expressions, except to
introduce the name of the king by whose rule an event is dated or to give the month
during which a particular day is indicated (1986: 410).

[47] While NT Greek has not been greatly affected by Latin, it does show some traces of its
influence (Voelz 1984: 964–5); and if one is speaking of a change in Greek that is
widespread enough to be found in Polybius, Plutarch, Diodorus, and Epictetus, it is not
surprising to see the NT marked by the same development.

[48] This includes the two constructions in Jn. 6:39 and 6:40, where Nestle–Aland prints [ἐν]
τῇ ἐσχάτῃ ἡμέρᾳ; see (24a and 24b) below.

In (21), as Paul's use of ἡμέρᾳ has no earlier parallels, this passage is good evidence of an extension of the dative of time (with the time noun doubled and conjoined with καί) to express the distributive event type. With the other two passages, textual problems complicate the interpretation, but one may still reasonably conclude that they too attest to a widening use of the dative. First, πάσαις ταῖς ἡμέραις in (22) is a decidedly non-Classical durative construction; one very much expects the accusative found in most of the major uncials. As a result, it is much easier to imagine a scribe changing the dative found in $\mathbf{p}^4$ (if it does indeed read the dative) and Vaticanus to the accusative than vice versa. But, whether these two witnesses maintain the original reading or introduce the dative mistakenly, the fact remains that someone in the imperial period was using the dative of time beyond its Attic range. Roughly the same is true of (23), though here the construction is limitative, so the "correction" from a non-standard dative in this case requires only the addition of ἐν – an addition found in the original text of Alexandrinus and C, but not in $\mathbf{p}^{46}$ or Vaticanus, and only added into Sinaiticus and D by late correctors (c. 7C and 9C respectively). The dative thus appears to be original and, while not completely foreign to Attic usage,[49] certainly at the edges of what it allowed.

In the examples seen so far, the evidence upon which the Nestle–Aland text has to base its reading is relatively easy to interpret, and what the committee has chosen to print stands a reasonable chance of being the original Greek. In the following passages, however, they are forced to resort to brackets because there is greater uncertainty:

(24a) ἀλλὰ ἀναστήσω αὐτὸ [ἐν] τῇ ἐσχάτῃ ἡμέρᾳ
    dative of time $\mathbf{p}^{66}$ $\mathbf{p}^{75}$ B C | ἐν add. ℵ A D
    But I will raise it up on the last day (Jn. 6:39)

(24b) καὶ ἀναστήσω αὐτὸν ἐγὼ [ἐν] τῇ ἐσχάτῃ ἡμέρᾳ
    dative of time $\mathbf{p}^{75}$ B C | ἐν add. $\mathbf{p}^{66}$ ℵ A D
    And I will raise him up on the last day (Jn. 6:40)

---

[49] When the limitative type is called for because multiple events took place within a single time frame in the past, the boundary between it and the punctual is not watertight. Still, in Attic, one would expect ἐν here, as occurrences of the simple dative of time nouns modified by εἰς are extremely rare; see the discussion of Th. 6.27.1 (= ex. (48)) in Ch. 2.

Again, Vaticanus and, three out of four times, the papyri favor the simple dative, but, especially considering the variation in **p**⁶⁶ in quick succession, it is harder to be optimistic about recovering the original text here. But, if one combines the limitative example (23) (and to a lesser extent the durative dative in (22)) with the fact that the construction with ἐν is what is expected in Attic, it looks very much as if the papyri and Vaticanus show an original text that has extended the temporal dative beyond what Classical practice warrants, while the other major uncials are "correcting" this to the standard usage with ἐν (and, in (22), the accusative).

This interpretation is borne out by the temporal datives with other time nouns as well. It is not a usage that was common in Attic with νύξ, the genitive having been preferred instead. But temporal νυκτί occurs six times in the New Testament. Two of these are in past-time punctual constructions where the dative is comparatively good Attic:⁵⁰

(25) τῇ δὲ ἐπιούσῃ νυκτὶ ἐπιστὰς αὐτῷ ὁ κύριος εἶπεν

And on the following night, the Lord stood next to him and said (Acts 23:11)

(26) παρέστη γάρ μοι ταύτῃ τῇ νυκτὶ τοῦ θεοῦ, οὗ εἰμι [ἐγώ] ᾧ καὶ λατρεύω, ἄγγελος

For there stood by me on this night an angel of the God to whom I belong and whom I worship (Acts 27:23)

In a third, however, as in (22), a durative accusative of time would probably be more natural, given that verbs of sleeping are generally viewed as unbounded states, setting the stage for a punctual event that follows;⁵¹ that said, the demonstrative certainly makes the dative easier, as does the fact that the temporal unit signaled by τῇ νυκτὶ ἐκείνῃ includes not only the background event (the sleep), but also the foregrounded, telic rescue of Peter, which is described in the next verses:

---

⁵⁰ While the genitive was preferred, the dative was not uncommon as an alternative, esp. with demonstratives; see e.g. Th. 4.103.4 and 7.6.4 (examples (46) and (47) in Ch. 2).

⁵¹ Compare Th. 3.74.3, where the μέν-clause contains the phrase ἡσυχάσαντες τὴν νύκτα ἐν φυλακῇ ἦσαν, which is then followed in 75.1 with τῇ δὲ ἐπιγιγνομένῃ ἡμέρᾳ.

(27) ὅτε δὲ ἤμελλεν προαγαγεῖν αὐτὸν ὁ Ἡρώδης, **τῇ νυκτὶ ἐκείνῃ** ἦν ὁ Πέτρος κοιμώμενος μεταξὺ δύο στρατιωτῶν δεδεμένος ἁλύσεσιν δυσὶν φύλακές τε πρὸ τῆς θύρας ἐτήρουν τὴν φυλακήν

But when Herod was going to bring him forth, that night Peter was sleeping between two soldiers, bound by two chains, and guards in front of the door were watching over the prison (Acts 12:6)

The remaining three stretch the dative of time further; all are limitative constructions where one would expect ἐν; not surprisingly, with one of the three, textual variation enters the picture again:

(28) ἀμὴν λέγω σοι ὅτι σὺ σήμερον **ταύτη τῇ νυκτὶ** πρὶν ἢ δὶς ἀλέκτορα φωνῆσαι τρίς με ἀπαρνήσῃ

dative of time ℵ B C D | ἐν τῇ νυκτὶ ταύτη A

Truly I tell you that today, on this night, before the cock crows twice, you will deny me three times (Mk. 14:30)

(29) ἄφρων, **ταύτη τῇ νυκτὶ** τὴν ψυχήν σου ἀπαιτοῦσιν ἀπὸ σοῦ

Fool, on this night, they are demanding your soul from you (Lk. 12:20)

(30) λέγω ὑμῖν, **ταύτη τῇ νυκτὶ** ἔσονται δύο ἐπὶ κλίνης μιᾶς

I tell you, on that night there will be two on one bed (Lk. 17:34)

In all three, the event in question will take place on a particular night in the future (even if the future is not morphologically explicit in (29)), and, especially with the time noun νύξ, of which the temporal dative is rare, a construction with ἐν would conform more with Attic practice. Indeed, as we will see shortly, even in the New Testament itself, ἐν is the more common limitative marker.

So too with ὥρα, the dative of time appears to have spread past its Classical range. Of the thirteen examples, seven are good past-tense punctual constructions:[52]

(31) καὶ **τῇ ἐνάτη ὥρᾳ**[53] ἐβόησεν ὁ Ἰησοῦς φωνῇ μεγάλη

And at the ninth hour, Jesus cried out in a loud voice (Mk. 15:34)

---

[52] The other examples are αὐτῇ τῇ ὥρᾳ (Lk. 2:38 and 24:33, Acts 16:18 and 22:13), τῇ ὥρᾳ τοῦ θυμιάματος (Lk. 1:10), and τῇ ὥρᾳ τοῦ δείπνου (Lk. 14:17). In all of these passages, the older MSS are unanimous in having a dative of time, apart from Acts 16:18, where D has εὐθέως instead of αὐτῇ τῇ ὥρᾳ.

[53] In A and C, the word order is ὥρᾳ τῇ ἐνάτη, but none of the MSS cited in Nestle–Aland have anything other than a dative of time.

Another three are semantically, if not morphologically, future; still, a punctual, rather than a limitative construction, is comparatively natural because the time noun is modified by a relative or indirect interrogative pronoun that specifies a particular time:[54]

(32) διὰ τοῦτο καὶ ὑμεῖς γίνεσθε ἕτοιμοι, ὅτι ᾗ οὐ δοκεῖτε ὥρᾳ ὁ υἱὸς τοῦ ἀνθρώπου ἔρχεται

Therefore, you too should be ready, because it is at an hour you do not expect that the Son of Man is coming (Mt. 24:44)

In the last three, however, the modifier, μιᾷ, leads one to expect a limitative construction with ἐν, although it must be conceded that, as all three occur within a single chapter of Revelation, they provide little more weight than a single token would:

(33) οὐαὶ οὐαί, ἡ πόλις ἡ μεγάλη, Βαβυλὼν ἡ πόλις ἡ ἰσχυρά, ὅτι **μιᾷ ὥρᾳ** ἦλθεν ἡ κρίσις σου

dative of time ℵ C | μίαν ὥραν A[55]

Woe, woe, the great city, Babylon, the strong city, for in one hour your judgment has come (Rev. 18:10)

(34) οὐαὶ οὐαί, ἡ πόλις ἡ μεγάλη ... ὅτι **μιᾷ ὥρᾳ** ἠρημώθη ὁ τοσοῦτος πλοῦτος[56]

Woe, woe, the great city ... for in one hour, so much wealth has been devastated (Rev. 18:16–17)

In the first example, only the modifier, to be sure, signals the limitative context (a single event in past time could otherwise easily be punctual), but, taken together with what follows, that still seems the best reading. Both the dative of time of Sinaiticus and C and the odd accusative of Alexandrinus represent a movement away from Attic. Such a deviation is not surprising in this context: Revelation has long been recognized to be particularly non-Classical in its language, and these examples, with their poetic allusions to Babylon, would be especially subject to interference

---

[54] The other two examples both occur in the parallel passage in Luke: εἰ ᾔδει ὁ οἰκοδεσπότης ποίᾳ ὥρᾳ ὁ κλέπτης ἔρχεται (12:39), ὅτι ᾗ ὥρᾳ οὐ δοκεῖτε ... ἔρχεται (12:40). In the verse of Matthew corresponding to the first of these (24:43), there is again a dative of time, but with a different time noun: ποίᾳ φυλακῇ.

[55] Revelation is not found in B or D; the 10C MS 2329 offers ἐν μιᾷ ὥρᾳ.

[56] The construction in 18:19 is almost identical. In neither of these two is there any textual variation in the temporal phrase.

from Semitic models.[57] In (34), one could almost take the temporal phrase as an instrumental dative,[58] but the combination of τοσοῦτος and μιᾷ, together with the preceding context of (33), makes a limitative reading more likely. In any case, the overall impression is one of an extended use of the dative. Further evidence of the extension of the temporal dative is found with χρόνος. All five examples look strange by Attic standards. The first three are all in the singular, and in all one would expect a durative accusative; only the first, though, is textually sound:

(35) προσεῖχον δὲ αὐτῷ διὰ τὸ **ἱκανῷ χρόνῳ** ταῖς μαγείαις ἐξεστακέναι αὐτούς

And they paid attention to him because they had been amazed by his acts of magic for a long time (Acts 8:11)

The evidence from Acts, together with the papyrus and uncial support, is enough to make the dative also likely in the Lucan example, even if there is confusion as to both the temporal construction and whether it modifies the preceding or following verb:

(36) ἐξελθόντι δὲ αὐτῷ ἐπὶ τὴν γῆν ὑπήντησεν ἀνήρ τις ἐκ τῆς πόλεως ἔχων δαιμόνια καὶ **χρόνῳ ἱκανῷ** οὐκ ἐνεδύσατο ἱμάτιον

dative of time p^{75vid} ℵ*.c B | ἐκ χρόνων ἱκανῶν (with καί placed *after*) ℵ² A | ἀπὸ χρόνων ἱκανῶν (with ὅς, instead of καί, placed after) D

And when he went out on land, he was met by a man from the city who had demons, and for a long time he had not put on a garment (Lk. 8:27)

More uncertain is the passage in John, where there is a reasonable argument for taking the accusative as the original reading; but even

---

[57] While there are no exact Septuagintal models for these constructions, the language, along with general thematic similarities, is enough for Beale to see in this passage a conscious echo of Daniel 4 (1999: 907–8): (a) The accusative of ὥρα only occurs twice with μία in a temporal expression, both in alternate versions of Daniel 4:19 where a durative accusative is expected: (LXX) κινήσας τὴν κεφαλὴν ὥραν μίαν ἀποθαυμάσας ἀπεκρίθη μοι and (Theodotion) τότε ... ἀπηνεώθη ὡσεὶ ὥραν μίαν. (For the two versions of Daniel, see Fernández Marcos 2001: 88–92.) (b) The temporal dative of ὥρα never occurs with μία, whereas the Classical ἐν *does* occur once, again in Daniel: ἐνώπιόν μου ἐξεκόπη ἐν ἡμέρᾳ μιᾷ, καὶ ἡ καταφθορὰ αὐτοῦ ἐν ὥρᾳ μιᾷ τῆς ἡμέρας (4:17a (LXX)). For the unusually high number of Semiticisms and Septuagintalisms in the Greek of Revelation – esp. in passages with Old Testament resonances – see Charles 1920: cxlii–clii, Thompson 1985, Beale 1999: 100–7.

[58] Cf. the discussion of examples (169) through (173), from Plutarch, in Ch. 3.

if the dative is a corruption, it still shows an early extension of its use:[59]

(37) τοσούτῳ χρόνῳ μεθ᾽ ὑμῶν εἰμι καὶ οὐκ ἔγνωκάς με, Φίλιππε;
dative of time א*·² D | accusative of time p⁶⁶·⁷⁵ א¹ A B

I've been with you for this long a time, and you've not recognized me, Philip? (Jn. 14:9)

In short, while the dative of time, χρόνῳ, is not completely foreign to Attic,[60] when χρόνος is modified by adjectives denoting length of time and modifies a durative verb, as in (35) through (37), it is particularly striking not to have the accusative.

Also strange are the two examples with the plural of χρόνος:

(38) πολλοῖς γὰρ χρόνοις συνηρπάκει αὐτὸν καὶ ἐδεσμεύετο ἁλύσεσιν καὶ πέδαις φυλασσόμενος καὶ διαρρήσσων τὰ δεσμὰ ἠλαύνετο ὑπὸ τοῦ δαιμονίου εἰς τὰς ἐρήμους

For many times it had seized him, and, kept under guard, he was bound by chains and fetters, and breaking the bonds, he would be driven by the demon into the wilderness (Lk. 8:29)

In (38), it is unusual for χρόνος to be used in the sense of French *fois* or German *Mal*;[61] indeed, it here seems to anticipate the later development of the meaning 'year'.[62] But whatever its meaning here, it probably shows an extension of the dative of time beyond its Classical range; still, one cannot be entirely certain, because, somewhat surprisingly, there are no particularly good parallels in Attic for precisely this configuration of variables: a given event occurring on multiple occasions, with those occasions indicated as discrete entities by the presence of a modifier like πολλοί. This should in theory fall into the distributive or, better, habitual type, but the distributive type emphasizes the regular co-occurrence of the time noun and the event, which does not hold here, and most

---

[59] The 25th edn. of Nestle in fact printed the accusative rather than the dative.

[60] Leaving aside the fairly common usage where χρόνῳ is really a dative of degree of difference and means 'after some time', i.e. 'in time', the phrase that comes closest to a durative dative of time with χρόνῳ is X. *HG* 2.3.15 (= ex. (49) in Ch. 3): τῷ μὲν οὖν πρώτῳ χρόνῳ ὁ Κριτίας τῷ Θηραμένει ὁμογνώμων τε καὶ φίλος ἦν. But here the ordinal modifier makes the dative far easier than in the New Testament passages.

[61] Classical Greek has no real equivalent, preferring adverbial constructions like πολλάκις 'many times' or τὸ τρίτον 'for the third time'.

[62] See the examples cited as parallels to Lk. 8:29 s.v. χρόνος 1 in BDAG.

habitual constructions to some extent treat the time noun as an indistinct singular mass noun. In such habitual expressions, the time noun is either explicitly singular (e.g. τὸ γὰρ θηρίον συνδυάζεται μὲν ἀεί, μάλιστα δὲ ταύτην τὴν ὥραν, X. *Cyn.* 5.6) or, if plural, not given a modifier that draws attention to the individual instances of the time noun:

(39) τοὺς μὲν γὰρ κύνας τοὺς χαλεποὺς **τὰς μὲν ἡμέρας** διδέασι, **τὰς δὲ νύκτας** ἀφιᾶσι

For during the days, they tie up mean dogs, but during the nights they let them loose (X. *An.* 5.8.24)

As a result, the contrast between night and day is more prominent than the idea of repetition conveyed by the plural, and such constructions bleed over into the modal type. Nevertheless, there are a few reasonably close parallels to (38), which, in combination with weaker support from examples like (39), suggest that Attic would have chosen the accusative:

(40) καὶ εὐξάμενον τῷ Ἀπόλλωνι καὶ τῇ Ἀρτέμιδι τῇ Ἀγροτέρᾳ μεταδοῦναι τῆς θήρας λῦσαι μίαν κύνα . . . ἐὰν μὲν ᾖ χειμών, ἅμ' ἡλίῳ ἀνίσχοντι, ἐὰν δὲ θέρος, πρὸ ἡμέρας, **τὰς δὲ ἄλλας ὥρας** μεταξὺ τούτου

And, after vowing to give to Apollo and Artemis the Huntress a share of the catch, to let loose one dog . . . if it's winter, at the rising of the sun, if summer, before daylight, in the other seasons, in between these two times (X. *Cyn.* 6.13)

(41) ἀεὶ γὰρ δὴ **καὶ τὰς πρόσθεν ἡμέρας** εἰώθεμεν φοιτᾶν καὶ ἐγὼ καὶ οἱ ἄλλοι παρὰ τὸν Σωκράτη

For always, also on the previous days, we, both myself and others, were accustomed to visit Socrates (Pl. *Phd.* 59d1)

The accusative τὰς ἄλλας ὥρας in (40) specifies that, regularly, when it is one of the seasons that is neither winter nor summer, one should let one's hunting dogs loose at an intermediate time. Even though that release is a comparatively instantaneous activity (and so here, if anywhere, one might expect a punctual dative), the habitual accusative is used instead. Example (41) is even closer to the construction in (38), in that the verbal event is a past-time repeated action (rather than a general present). But again, although a one-time event would elicit a punctual dative (e.g. τῇ πρόσθεν ἡμέρᾳ at X. *An.* 2.3.1), in a repetitive habitual

271

context the accusative is found instead. The only potential counter-examples are ταῖς πρώταις ἡμέραις φοβερώτατα ἔχουσιν (X. Eq.Mag. 8.20) and ταῖς μὲν πρώταις ἡμέραις τε καὶ χρόνῳ προσγελᾷ τε καὶ ἀσπάζεται πάντας (Pl. R. 566d8) (= examples (7) and (78) in Chapter 3).[63] Here, though, the presence of the ordinal number as a modifier makes the dative far easier than it would be in (38).

In the second New Testament example of temporal χρόνοις, the dative of time as such is textually secure, but the passage as a whole is not:

(42) τῷ δὲ δυναμένῳ ὑμᾶς στηρίξαι ... κατὰ ἀποκάλυψιν μυστηρίου **χρόνοις αἰωνίοις** σεσιγημένου

But to the one who is able to strengthen you ... according to the revelation of the mystery that has been kept secret since time immemorial (Rom. 16:25)

The benediction that forms the last three verses of Romans (16:25–27) is in square brackets in Nestle–Aland on the grounds of both the content[64] and the textual tradition.[65] But even if it did not originally belong here, it does occur somewhere in the papyri and the main uncials and thus attests a dative of time not paralleled in Attic.

That the plural datives of time in (38) and (42) are not entirely isolated within New Testament idiom can be seen by comparing the two examples with ἔτος, both anomalous in their own way:

(43) εἶπαν οὖν οἱ Ἰουδαῖοι, **Τεσσεράκοντα καὶ ἓξ ἔτεσιν** οἰκοδομήθη ὁ ναὸς οὗτος, καὶ σὺ ἐν τρισὶν ἡμέραις ἐγερεῖς αὐτόν;

Then the Jews said, "This temple was built in forty-six years, and you will raise it up in three days?" (Jn. 2:20)

(44) καὶ καθελὼν ἔθνη ἑπτὰ ἐν γῇ Χανάαν κατεκληρονόμησεν τὴν γῆν αὐτῶν **ὡς ἔτεσιν τετρακοσίοις καὶ πεντήκοντα**[66]

And after destroying the seven tribes in the land of Canaan, he distributed their land to be their possession for about 450 years (Acts 13:19–20)

---

[63] In addition to the Attic examples, there is also τὸν χῶρον κεινὸν ἐν τῷ ἐτετάχατο οἱ Ἕλληνες τῇσι προτέρῃσι ἡμέρῃσι (Hdt. 9.57.3) (= ex. (130) in Ch. 3).

[64] Metzger 1971: 533–6, Käsemann 1980: 421–8.

[65] To record only the papyri and older uncials: p⁴⁶ has it, but after 15:33; A has it both at the end of the book and after 14:23; p⁶¹ ℵ B C D have it at the end of the book.

[66] This passage is confused in D (placing the temporal phrase with the following verse and, in the original hand, later corrected, reading ἕως instead of ὡς), but p⁷⁴ ℵ A B C all have the text as printed here.

In (43), one expects either a telic aorist modified by a limitative expression ('this temple was built in 46 years') or an atelic present with the durative event type ('this temple has been under construction for forty-six years').[67] In favor of the latter interpretation, found in the NRSV, is the historical context: the temple was not in fact complete at any point in Jesus' lifetime.[68] But the Greek speaks against this: it would require that the aorist be understood abnormally as an attempt to render the past-tense quality of what in English would be expressed by a present perfect progressive (in the active, 'they have been building'; the passive 'has been being built' is scarcely grammatical).[69] Furthermore, example (16) offers an excellent Septuagintal parallel for the use of the dative ἔτεσιν in a limitative phrase: the verb is the same, and the passage refers to the building of the first temple. The historical problem can presumably be resolved by understanding ὁ ναὸς οὗτος to mean not 'this completely finished temple' but rather 'this temple, which, though not completely finished, is still finished enough to merit being called a temple'.[70] This interpretation is consistent with the previous verse, where the temple is treated as finished enough for Jesus to refer to the possibility of destroying it: λύσατε τὸν ναὸν τοῦτον καὶ ἐν τρισὶν ἡμέραις ἐγερῶ αὐτόν.

As for (44), it is tempting to view this dative as somehow influenced by goal expressions, with the dative trumping the usual durative accusative because of the future-time reference. But one must not be misled by the fact that English uses _for_ to denote both goal and extent of time: these semantic roles do not overlap in Greek, and the accusative of time is still preferred even

---

[67] A typical example of Attic tense usage in the latter scenario: καίτοι πολλά γε ἔτη ἤδη εἰμὶ ἐν τῇ τέχνῃ (Pl. _Prt._ 317c1).

[68] It was begun by Herod the Great in 20/19 BC and not finished until AD 63. Barrett (1978: 200) translates "This sanctuary was built in forty-six years" and assumes that the evangelist was misinformed about when the temple was finished. Bultmann (1971: 127 n. 3) remains silent on this point, but refers to BDR §201, which treats the durative sense of the dative – even though the paragraph where they actually cite this passage is §200 n. 9, where they take it as limitative.

[69] Porter, citing Stagg (1972: 228), simply notes that this sentence is clear evidence that the aorist is not necessarily punctiliar in nature (1989: 183). Fanning describes the temporal phrase in conjunction with the aorist as showing an action 'leading up to its termination' (1990: 88).

[70] Cf. the second Death Star, in _The Return of the Jedi._

273

when the temporal duration is anticipated in the future.[71] Once again, the writers of the New Testament have gone further than Classical Greek in their use of the dative of time.

The genitive of time in the New Testament

By contrast, the temporal genitive is remarkably unproductive, only occurring forty-two times, and largely restricted to a few set constructions. Most prominent are the thirteen modal pairs of νυκτὸς καὶ ἡμέρας (sometimes with the terms reversed) that make up twenty-six of the examples. Five further examples also belong under this heading: one where ἡμέρας is contrasted with νύξ as a clause subject in what follows (Rev. 21:25), two habitual examples where νυκτός is used on its own (both in 1 Thes. 5:7), and two constructions with χειμῶνος where the event type lies in a grey area:[72]

(45) προσεύχεσθε δὲ ἵνα μὴ γένηται ἡ φυγὴ ὑμῶν **χειμῶνος** μηδὲ σαββάτῳ[73]

And pray that your flight does not take place during winter or on the Sabbath

(Mt. 24:20)

If, as seems likely, we can trust the textual tradition here, this passage offers a valuable minimal pair, with a genitive and dative of time in parallel. But to what event type should they be assigned? That σαββάτῳ is in the dative suggests the punctual type, considering how restricted in range this construction generally is; furthermore, the time nouns do indicate specific times. But the verb modified by the constructions is negated and refers to a future time event, thus suggesting the limitative type. What is more, the lack of reference to a particular winter or Sabbath lends a modal air to the context. Given this indeterminacy, it is no surprise that Matthew should pick different temporal expressions for the two

---

[71] See e.g. ὅσον κατ' ἀρχὰς τοῦ πολέμου οἱ μὲν ἐνιαυτόν, οἱ δὲ δύο, οἱ δὲ τριῶν γε ἐτῶν οὐδεὶς πλείω χρόνον ἐνόμιζον περιοίσειν αὐτούς (Th. 7.28.3). The accusative is also the standard construction in stating the length that treaties are to last, e.g. Hdt. 7.148.4, Th. 4.118.10.
[72] The other is found in the parallel passage in Mark (13:18), in which none of the older MSS add the reference to the Sabbath.
[73] While the MSS are uniform in reading χειμῶνος, D reads σαββάτου and some later MSS have σαββάτων or ἐν σαββάτῳ.

274

time nouns: with σάββατον, as the name of a specific day, the punctual element is highlighted with the dative; with χειμών, a more general reference to a season, the genitive brings the limitative-modal element to the fore.

Thus, in light of the pragmatic difference between what a speaker is likely to be communicating in a temporal construction with a season and one with a particular day, the transition from a modal to a punctual genitive of time with a noun like χειμών comes across as particularly easy.

And, as in other authors, this transition has been made most clearly with νυκτός, which, in addition to the modal examples noted above, occurs in five punctual expressions on its own and in one additionally modified by μέσης.[74] Less expected is a punctual genitive with ἡμέρα:

(46) **ἡμέρας μέσης** κατὰ τὴν ὁδὸν εἶδον, βασιλεῦ, οὐρανόθεν ὑπὲρ τὴν λαμπρότητα τοῦ ἡλίου περιλάμψαν με φῶς καὶ τοὺς σὺν ἐμοὶ πορευομένους

In the middle of the day while on the road, O king, I saw a light from heaven brighter than the sun, which shone all about me and those who were traveling with me (Acts 26:13)

Still, the genitive is not unmotivated: the timing of Paul's vision is important not in a strictly chronological way (this sentence does not form part of a linear narrative of what he was doing over the course of the different hours of the day), but rather because the blinding light is all the more impressive when recounted against the background of what would already have been a bright time of the day. There is thus a modal element to the context that helps trigger the genitive.

Of the remaining four genitives of time, three are unremarkable distributive examples,[75] leaving only one uncertain passage:

---

[74] On its own: Mt. 2:14, 28:13, Jn. 3:2, 19:39, Acts 9:25; with μέσης: Mt. 25:6.

[75] These are ἐὰν ἑπτάκις τῆς ἡμέρας ἁμαρτήσῃ εἰς σέ (Lk. 17:4), εἰς δὲ τὴν δευτέραν (sc. σκηνὴν εἴσεισιν) ἅπαξ τοῦ ἐνιαυτοῦ μόνος ὁ ἀρχιερεύς (Heb. 9:7), and οὐχὶ δώδεκα ὥραί εἰσιν τῆς ἡμέρας; (Jn. 11:9). In the last example, the genitive may be adnominal (NRSV: "Are there not twelve hours of daylight?") or predicative ("Does not a day have twelve hours?"; cf. the reading of D: οὐχὶ δώδεκα ὥρας ἔχει ἡ ἡμέρα;), but it also translates perfectly as a distributive ("Are there not twelve hours each day?"). In effect, the open-ended semantics of εἶναι mean that none of these readings can be excluded; in any case, the clause is a useful example of the easy transition from adnominal to distributive genitive.

(47) εἰσὶν γὰρ πνεύματα δαιμονίων ποιοῦντα σημεῖα, ἃ ἐκπορεύεται ἐπὶ τοὺς βασιλεῖς τῆς οἰκουμένης ὅλης συναγαγεῖν αὐτοὺς εἰς τὸν πόλεμον **τῆς ἡμέρας τῆς μεγάλης**[76] τοῦ θεοῦ τοῦ παντοκράτορος

For they are spirits of demons that perform signs, which go out to the kings of the whole world to bring them together to the war of *or* on the great day of God the almighty (Rev. 16:14)

Two interpretations are possible: one can take τῆς ἡμέρας τῆς μεγάλης as an adnominal genitive dependent on τὸν πόλεμον, specifying which war is meant; or one can read it as a limitative genitive elicited by the future time reference.[77] The NRSV translates "on," implying the latter reading, but the former is better because there are not in fact any good New Testament parallels for such a limitative genitive of time,[78] and a chain of dependent genitives is perfectly in keeping with the Semitic style of Revelation.[79]

Temporal ἐν *in the New Testament*

The comparative rarity of the genitive of time is largely explained by a considerable increase in the use of ἐν[+D], which, with the time nouns in my corpus, is not only the most common marker of the limitative event type (56×), but also the most common temporal expression altogether (127×). While some of the remaining examples belong to the modal-habitual nexus (5×), a common function

---

[76] The reading in **p**[47] and A is τῆς μεγάλης ἡμέρας, and ἐκείνης is added in some late MSS, but the phrase is always in the genitive.
[77] Beale translates "to gather them together for the war of the great day of God Almighty" (1999: 834–5).
[78] The regular construction for this is ἐν; see below.
[79] While a chain of genitives is certainly possible in indigenous Greek as well, they are particularly common in texts with Semitic influence, where they reflect the so-called construct chain, in which what another language might for example render as an adjective-noun combination is instead expressed through the combination of a phonologically weakened (i.e. no longer independent) head noun (the construct state) and a following dependent noun (in the absolute state); for similar patterns in Revelation, cf. ἡ ἀρχὴ τῆς κτίσεως τοῦ θεοῦ (3:14), ἡ κλεὶς τοῦ φρέατος τῆς ἀβύσσου (9:1). (For a brief explanation of the construct chain, see e.g. Lambdin 1971: 67–70, McCarter 2004: 338–9.) The Vulgate takes this line, reading: *congregare illos in proelium diei magni Dei omnipotentis.* One might also expect that the article in front of πόλεμον would also favor this view, esp. given anarthrous εἰς πόλεμον at Rev. 9:7 and 9:9. But the author of Revelation was apparently content to write εἰς τὸν πόλεμον even without a dependent genitive (20:8). Presumably war has been present enough as a discourse topic since 12:7 (καὶ ἐγένετο πόλεμος ἐν τῷ οὐρανῷ) that it can acquire the definite article relatively easily. For the unusually high number of Semitisms in Revelation, see n. 57.

of ἐν in other texts as well, most are simply punctual (66×). These categories should not, however, be taken too rigidly. As will become clear, many of the punctual examples, in particular, are borderline limitative constructions.

The fifty-six constructions which I have counted as limitative are overwhelmingly with ἡμέρα (51×), and all but three of these derive their limitative status from using a phrase with the plural of ἡμέρα (thus offering a time frame) to modify a discrete event. Particularly common are expressions with ἐν ἐκείναις ταῖς ἡμέραις (8×), ἐν ταῖς ἡμέραις ἐκείναις (7×), ἐν ταῖς ἡμέραις ταύταις (5×), and ἐν τρισὶν ἡμέραις (4×), as is the pattern where (ταῖς) ἡμέραις is followed with a personal name in the genitive (2× Νῶε, 2× Ἡρῴδου, 1× Ἡλίου, 1× Λώτ, 1× Ἀντιπᾶς). While ἐν would be the appropriate preposition to use in such a context in Attic as well, it should also be stressed that the overall idiom in many of these examples does diverge from the Classical standard: taking Herodotus, Thucydides, Xenophon, Plato, and Demosthenes together, there are only forty-two examples of limitative or punctual phrases where ἐν governs ἡμέρα; of these, only *six* combine the plural ἡμέραις with a demonstrative.[80] Nor does the usage with the demonstrative and plural occur at all in the data gathered from Polybius, Diodorus, Plutarch, and Epictetus. Given that the New Testament here matches Septuagintal idiom,[81] we thus have a textbook example of the scenario in which a construction that is perfectly grammatical Attic is nevertheless best considered a Semiticism because of the vastly greater frequency with which it

[80] What is more, a glance at these six shows that the communicative goal is usually different from that of the New Testament examples, which most often act simply to give the setting for the verbal event. The closest are Th. 4.91.1 (ἐν ταῖς ἡμέραις ταύταις ξυνελέγοντο ἐς τὴν Τάναγραν) and X. *HG* 7.1.42 (ἐν δὲ ταύταις ταῖς ἡμέραις ἐλθόντες ... ὑπερβαίνουσι τὸ Ὄνειον). In Pl. *Cri.* 49a9 (ἢ πᾶσαι ἡμῖν ἐκεῖναι αἱ πρόσθεν ὁμολογίαι ἐν ταῖσδε ταῖς ὀλίγαις ἡμέραις ἐκκεχυμέναι εἰσίν ... ;), the contrast of πᾶσαι and ὀλίγαις makes this more like other Classical limitative phrases which stress the unexpectedness of the event's having taken place within so short a time. The other three occur in a sequence in Demosthenes' *Against Meidias*; of these, 21.10 does not really count, as it is in a Νόμος; 21.11 (τὸ σῶμ' ὑβρίζεσθαί τινος ἐν ταύταις ταῖς ἡμέραις) and 21.12 (Μειδίας δ' ἐν αὐταῖς ταύταις ταῖς ἡμέραις ἄξια τοῦ δοῦναι τὴν ἐσχάτην δίκην ποιῶν δειχθήσεται) do count, but the temporal phrases refer to a more specific period of time (a religious festival, which is important for Demosthenes' legal argument) than is the case in the common New Testament type.

[81] As noted in the discussion preceding example (13), there are no fewer than 220 examples in the Septuagint of ἐν governing ἡμέραις.

occurs in the Septuagint and New Testament than in Attic or other Koine texts. Of the three remaining limitative examples with ἡμέρα, in one (Rev. 18:8), the time noun is modified by μιᾷ, and the event takes place in the future, so its limitative status is secure; in the other two (Mt. 24:50, Lk. 12:46), also with a future-tense verb, there is no single-word modifier, but the day in question is further specified by a relative clause, bringing it closer to the punctual constructions to be discussed next. As for the five examples with other time nouns, three are with νύξ and, insofar as the time noun is in the singular and modified with a demonstrative, they too start to look like the punctual type; still, they have other features that make the limitative a better category for them (and so cannot be used as evidence of the spread of ἐν into the punctual domain).[82] The other two, with χρόνος, are unremarkable.[83]

Of the sixty-six punctual constructions, more than half might also reasonably be considered limitative because the verbal event takes place in the future. Of the forty-seven examples with ἡμέρα, for instance, eighteen modify a future-tense verb, and another ten modify aorists and presents (mostly subjunctives) that refer to future time, leaving only nineteen examples that refer to past or, in one case, present time. In considering the extent to which the New Testament shows an increase in the use of ἐν at the expense of the dative of time, then, we should focus on the last group, as these are the constructions in which ἐν would be least expected in Classical texts.[84] Leaving aside the one example with textual

---

[82] Two occur in quick succession in Mt. 26:31 (πάντες ὑμεῖς σκανδαλισθήσεσθε ἐν ἐμοὶ ἐν τῇ νυκτὶ ταύτῃ) and 34 (ἐν ταύτῃ τῇ νυκτὶ πρὶν ἀλέκτορα φωνῆσαι τρὶς ἀπαρνήσῃ με). Both of these have two signs of the limitative type: multiple events will take place within the time period (note πάντες and τρίς respectively), and the verbs modified are future. The latter is textually uncertain: p³⁷ and D omit the preposition, showing the extended use of the dative of time. Closer to the punctual type is καὶ ἐν ἐκείνῃ τῇ νυκτὶ ἐπίασαν οὐδέν (Jn. 21:3) as the only thing to make it limitative is the negative οὐδέν.

[83] Both are singular; one has the demonstrative and is limitative by virtue of modifying a future verb (Acts 1:6); the other, τῶν συνελθόντων ἡμῖν ἀνδρῶν ἐν παντὶ χρόνῳ ᾧ εἰσῆλθεν καὶ ἐξῆλθεν ἐφ' ἡμᾶς ὁ κύριος Ἰησοῦς (Acts 1:21), is limitative in assigning multiple events (the winning over of several men) to a time span whose extent is brought out by παντί.

[84] The constructions I include in this category are Mt. 13:1, 22:23, Mk. 4:35, Lk. 1:59, 4:16, 19:42, 23:12, 24:13, Jn. 5:9, 7:37, 9:14, Acts 2:41, 8:1, 20:26, 2 Cor. 6:2, Heb 4:4, 8:9, Jas. 5:5, Rev. 1:10. While there are some minor differences in word order in the older MSS of a couple of these passages (and the phrase ἐν ᾗ ἡμέρᾳ at Jn. 9:14 only occurs in p⁶⁶, p⁷⁵, ℵ, and B; A and D have ὅτε), nowhere is the preposition omitted so as to yield a simple dative of time. Note also that they are spread evenly across a wide range of books.

THE NEW TESTAMENT

problems and one which might be considered limitative on grounds that it refers to a multiplicity of events (Acts 2:41), they can be sorted according to the modifiers of the time noun. Six occur with demonstratives:[85]

(48) ἐν ἐκείνῃ τῇ ἡμέρᾳ προσῆλθον αὐτῷ Σαδδουκαῖοι

On that day, some Sadducees came to him (Mt. 22:23)

Four have dependent genitives – three, like the following, in quotations of the Septuagint:[86]

(49) ἐθρέψατε τὰς καρδίας ὑμῶν ἐν ἡμέρᾳ σφαγῆς

You nourished your hearts on a day of slaughter (Jas. 5:5)

In three, a preceding adjective acts like a demonstrative in specifying the day; in one of these, further modifiers follow:[87]

(50) ἐν δὲ τῇ ἐσχάτῃ ἡμέρᾳ τῇ μεγάλῃ τῆς ἑορτῆς εἱστήκει ὁ Ἰησοῦς καὶ ἔκραξεν λέγων . . .

And on the last, great day of the festival, Jesus stood and shouted, saying . . . (Jn. 7:37)

Ordinals follow in two more examples:[88]

(51) καὶ ἐγένετο ἐν τῇ ἡμέρᾳ τῇ ὀγδόῃ[89] ἦλθον περιτεμεῖν τὸ παιδίον

And it happened on the eighth day that they came to circumcise the child (Lk. 1:59)

And two have intensive αὐτῇ:[90]

[85] See also Mt. 13:1, Mk. 4:35, Lk. 19:42, Jn. 5:9, Acts 8:1.
[86] See also Lk. 4:16 (the only one of the four where the genitive, τῶν σαββάτων, is a standard word for marking time), 2 Cor. 6:2 (ἐν ἡμέρᾳ σωτηρίας, in a quotation from the Septuagint (Is. 49:8)), and Heb. 8:9 (ἐν ἡμέρᾳ ἐπιλαβομένου μου τῆς χειρὸς αὐτῶν ἐξαγαγεῖν αὐτοὺς ἐκ γῆς Αἰγύπτου, also quoting the Septuagint (Jer. 38:32 = MT 31:32)). In (49), the Septuagint, to be sure, does *not* have ἐν[+D] (except as a very minor variant (Ziegler 1976: 209)): ἄγνισον αὐτοὺς εἰς ἡμέραν σφαγῆς αὐτῶν (Jer. 12:3).
[87] See also Acts 20:26 (ἐν τῇ σήμερον ἡμέρᾳ) and Rev. 1:10 (ἐν τῇ κυριακῇ ἡμέρᾳ).
[88] See also Heb. 4:4 (ἐν τῇ ἡμέρᾳ τῇ ἑβδόμῃ), in a quotation of Gen. 2:2.
[89] Alexandrinus moves the ordinal in front: τῇ ὀγδόῃ ἡμέρᾳ; the other main uncials have it after the noun.
[90] It is possible that these passages show the later, demonstrative use of αὐτός in the predicative position (p[75] even substitutes ἐκείνῃ for αὐτῇ), but the intensive reading is plausible in both passages, so we cannot use the pronoun as evidence of non-Classical language in these passages; cf. also BDR §288.2. The other passage is Lk. 24:13. For the development of demonstrative αὐτός, see Horrocks 2010: 128–9.

279

(52) ἐγένοντο δὲ φίλοι ὅ τε Ἡρῴδης καὶ ὁ Πιλᾶτος **ἐν αὐτῇ τῇ ἡμέρᾳ** μετ᾽ ἀλλήλων

And Herod and Pilate on that very day became friends with each other

(Lk. 23:12)

Turning now to Classical texts, how close do they come to this free use of ἡμέρα in the singular in punctual constructions with ἐν? Plato offers no similar examples at all. In Thucydides there is the set phrase ἐν ἡμέρᾳ ῥητῇ, which occurs three times, but in only one of these (ex. (38) in Ch. 2) has the event in question already come to pass. Apart from these, one finds only the isolated ἐν ᾗ μόνον ἡμέρᾳ οὐχ ὕποπτον ἐγίγνετο of 6.56.2 (ex. (39) in Ch. 2), where the use of ἐν could reflect a habitual nuance in the phrase. The same is true of the only punctual example of ἐν ἡμέρῃ in Herodotus (9.110.2). The closest that Xenophon comes are passages (10) and (11) in Chapter 3, where ἐν ἐκείνῃ/ταύτῃ τῇ ἡμέρᾳ modifies a past-tense verb. In both of these, however, multiple events are subsumed under the one temporal phrase, and these are thus closer to the limitative type than the New Testament examples just cited. It is in Demosthenes, where examples of ἐν τῇ ἡμέρᾳ with a demonstrative are more numerous than in the other authors, that one comes closest to finding ἐν in simple punctual constructions with ἡμέρα. But even here – see the discussion of examples (94) through (98) in Chapter 3, especially the last three – Demosthenes is exploiting the expectation that ἐν will mark a limitative construction when he uses it in punctual contexts. It is never an unmarked way of saying that an event happened on a particular day, as it is in the New Testament. Nor is punctual ἐν with ἡμέρα a combination that saw much growth in the post-Classical texts in my corpus: there are no examples in Polybius 1–5 (where ἐν is quite common in true limitative constructions), Diodorus 11–15, the first fourteen *Lives* of Plutarch, or Epictetus.

What the preponderance of punctual ἐν in the New Testament does resemble, however, is the Septuagint, where ἡμέρα and ἔτος, the nouns where the punctual dative would be most expected, are more often governed by ἐν. This similarity is reinforced by the particularities of the New Testament examples, four of which even occur in direct quotations from the Septuagint.[91] Several more passages have other signs of Septuagintal language. The most obvious example is (51), in which καὶ ἐγένετο is paratactically juxtaposed with the main verb ἦλθον in an imitation of the Hebrew *wayhî* construction,[92] and the ordinal number is placed after, rather than before, the noun, with doubling of the article.[93] Much the same can be said of the nineteen examples of punctual ἐν with other time nouns too. (a) Closest to Septuagintal models is the one example with μηνί, which again has the ordinal placed after the noun, with doubling of the article (ἐν δὲ τῷ μηνὶ τῷ ἕκτῳ ἀπεστάλη ὁ ἄγγελος Γαβριὴλ ἀπὸ τοῦ θεοῦ, Lk. 1:26); it also occurs in one of the most Septuagintalizing passages of the New Testament, the birth narrative in Luke. (b) The one example with ἔτει recalls the Septuagint in that the year is followed by a defining genitive (ἐν ἔτει δὲ πεντεκαιδεκάτῳ τῆς ἡγεμονίας Τιβερίου Καίσαρος ... ἐγένετο ῥῆμα θεοῦ ἐπὶ Ἰωάννην, Lk. 3:1), but it differs from it in that the genitive in question, ἡγεμονίας, does not occur often in the Septuagint (only 7×, of which 4× in 4 Macc. and Sir.). Still, it remains a clear punctual construction, and, in the rest of my literary corpus (Classical and non-Classical), only Th. 1.87.6 offers a parallel of a ἐν + ordinal + ἔτει (curiously, here too with a defining genitive, τῶν ... σπονδῶν, and again modifying ἐγένετο), so the numerous Septuagintal examples remain closer in feel. In this example, however, the presence of numerous genitive absolutes of dating in the verse and the existence of punctual constructions with ἐν + ἔτει in the papyri (see Ch. 3 n. 237) mean that the model for the preposition here may instead be bureaucratic language. (c) Of the two examples with νύξ, one might reasonably be considered modal, as it is followed by δι᾿ ὁράματος, thus placing emphasis on

[91] These are 2 Cor. 6:2, Heb. 4:4, 8:9, Jas. 5:5. The high frequency of ἐν as opposed to the dative extends to the instrumental and comitative dative as well: for Mark, see Maloney (1981: 179–82).

[92] For further explanation of this, see George 2010: 268–70 and 274–5.

[93] To be sure, ordinals frequently come after the noun in Classical Attic as well: in datives of time with ἡμέρα in Thucydides, for example, one has this order at 2.19.1, 6.8.3, 8.107.1, and, with hyperbaton, at 4.90.3. But none of these examples have the definite article, let alone a repeated article; by contrast, the ordinal comes before the noun in such constructions 4× with πρώτη (all with the article) and 6× with other ordinals (none with the article).

281

night, as opposed to day, as the time of dreams (Acts 18:9), but the other is a past-time punctual phrase (1 Cor. 11:23). (d) The remaining fifteen examples are all with ὥρα. Of these, six lie at the boundary with the limitative type, five because of future-time reference, one because it refers to a multiplicity of events,[94] but the other nine are all past-time constructions, six with ἐκείνῃ, three with intensive (or demonstrative?) αὐτῇ, which has a Septuagintal antecedent at Dan. 5:5.[95] In short, as with limitative ἐν, so too the high frequency of punctual ἐν in the New Testament represents an extension of Attic usage under the influence of the Septuagint.

Conclusion

The temporal expressions of the Septuagint and New Testament show small, but significant, differences from those of Attic Greek, of which the two most noticeable are the increased use of ἐν in limitative and punctual constructions, and the spread of the dative into limitative and durative expressions. The latter development is paralleled by evidence from the wide range of post-Classical authors surveyed in Chapter 3, and therefore need not be attributed to any interference from Semitic languages. But the expressions with ἐν (especially those of the general shape ἐν ταῖς ἡμέραις ἐκείναις), although not un-Attic if taken individually, occur with a frequency not seen elsewhere outside Judeo-Christian Greek. Given the stylistic similarities between such phrases in the New Testament and their Septuagintal counterparts, their proliferation should be regarded as ultimately originating in translation from Hebrew.

---

[94] Future-time reference: Mt. 10:19, 24:50, Mk. 13:11, Lk. 12:12, 12:46; multiplicity of events: Lk. 7:21.
[95] With ἐκείνῃ: Mt. 8:13, 18:1, 26:55, Jn. 4:53, Acts 16:33, Rev. 11:13; with αὐτῇ: Lk. 10:21, 13:31, 20:19.

5

A RETROSPECTIVE: GOING BACK IN TIME

Given the expansiveness of the concept of time, it is inevitable that much has been left undiscussed in this book. There is no space, for example, to consider the interface between the linguistic expression of time and the cultural views held by the ancients on the nature of time and how it is reckoned.[1] And while the corpus has included a wide enough range of prose texts to show that temporal expressions are, by and large, uniform from genre to genre, poetic usage is too complicated a question to be included in any real detail.[2] But one topic that should not be left unexamined is the diachronic origin of the patterns seen in Classical and post-Classical prose. While the evidence left to us from pre-Classical texts is scanty indeed – and here we cannot avoid poetry – it does offer some hints about how the Greek system of temporal expressions developed. The obvious text to examine is Homer.[3] Because epic poetry does not offer as high a density of temporal phrases as prose history, the data do not suffice to answer the same questions as in previous chapters with the same sort of rigor; accordingly, the following chapter is structured as a survey of the relevant time

[1] For the latter, see Nilsson 1920, Fränkel 1960: 1–22, and now Hannah 2009.
[2] For the difference between poetic and prose constructions in the sphere of case assignment and prepositions, see Bers 1984: 62–101. For Sophocles in particular, expressions of time are covered in Moorhouse 1982. (i) The accusative is found in durative constructions, with some possible extension (44–5). (ii) The genitive generally matches the evidence from prose, with the possible exception of *El.* 698, where the dative would be more natural (58–9); (iii) It is with the dative of time that Sophocles appears to diverge most from prose usage, as some of the examples (*Ant.* 14, *Ph.* 715) suggest that the simple dative could be used in limitative expressions which would require the addition of ἐν in prose (87–8). It is perhaps telling that Moorhouse's discussion also includes one example with ἐν (*Tr.* 149), which is otherwise covered on p. 107. None of the other prepositional usages catalogued are particularly surprising, apart, perhaps, from the use of κατά$^{+A}$ in a few constructions (*Aj.* 801, *OC* 1079, *Ant.* 55) that span a range from punctual to limitative, all of which Moorhouse lumps together as meaning 'during the course of' (1982: 116).
[3] For a basic survey of temporal constructions in Homer, see Chantraine 1953: 45 (accusative), 59 (genitive), 81 (dative), 91 (ἀνά$^{+A}$), 96 (διά$^{+A}$), 102 (ἐν^{+D}), 104 (εἰς^{+A}), 107 (ἐπί$^{+G}$), 109 (ἐπί$^{+D}$), 111 (ἐπί$^{+A}$), 119 (μετά$^{+A}$), 131 (πρό$^{+G}$), 133 (πρός^{+A}), 144 (ὑπό$^{+A}$).

nouns in order to highlight those areas where some satisfactory conclusions can be reached.

Day and night in Homer

Did ἡμέρα and νύξ behave as differently in Homer as they did in later Greek? The evidence is not conclusive, but what little there is points to rather less divergence, with the temporal dative of νύξ far more frequent than in later Greek relative to the genitive of time. Not only does the genitive νυκτός only occur ten times in Homer, but five of these are found in the phrase (ἐν) νυκτὸς ἀμολγῷ, another is a genitive of comparison, and another is adnominal.[4] Two more examples, while closer to being adverbial temporal genitives, must instead be seen as partitive, and dependent on τρίχα, rather than as directly dependent on the verb of their clause:[5]

(1) ἦμος δὲ τρίχα **νυκτὸς** ἔην, μετὰ δ' ἄστρα βεβήκει

> And when it was the third watch of the night, and the stars had passed their zenith (*Od.* 12.312)

Only one true genitive of time remains, and it looks very much like the punctual genitives seen in later Greek, indicating that an event occurred at night, but not specifying *which* night:

(2) κεῖθεν δὲ πλαγχθέντες ἱκάνομεν ἐνθάδε **νυκτός**

> And drifting away from there, we arrived here at night (*Od.* 13.278)

By contrast, the dative νυκτί is more common (21× in Homer), but, once again, few of these are datives of time. It is often the object of πείθεσθαι (5×: *Il.* 7.282, 293, 8.502, 9.65, *Od.* 12.291) or an adjective or verb of comparison (4×: *Il.* 1.47, 12.463, *Od.* 11.606,

---

[4] The phrase νυκτὸς ἀμολγῷ is found at *Il.* 15.324 (κλονέωσι), 22.28 (φαίνονται), 22.317 (εἶσι), and *Od.* 4.841 (ἐπέσσυτο); it is headed by the preposition ἐν at *Il.* 11.173 (ἐφόβησε μολών), which shows no obvious semantic or syntactic difference from the constructions with the simple dative; all five examples occur in similes in which the verbs describe a stereotypically night-time occurrence, such as the appearance of a star. The genitive of comparison occurs at *Il.* 3.10–11, again a simile: εὖτ' ... κατέχευεν ὀμίχλην | ποιμέσιν οὔ τι φίλην, κλέπτῃ δέ τε νυκτὸς ἀμείνω. The adnominal genitive: ἐγγὺς γὰρ νυκτός τε καὶ ἤματός εἰσι κέλευθοι (*Od.* 10.86).

[5] The other example, also sandwiched between τρίχα and ἔην, occurs at *Od.* 14.483.

20.362). More interesting as a bridge between temporal and non-temporal uses is the instrumental dative (4×):[6]

(3) ἀλλ' Ἥφαιστος ἔρυτο, σάωσε δὲ **νυκτὶ** καλύψας

But Hephaestus pulled him away, and he saved him by wrapping him in night

(*Il.* 5.23)

The temporal dative, not unreasonably given its easy translation in English with prepositions like *in* and *at*, is generally classified as a locative dative.[7] But the potential for functional overlap between the Indo-European locative and instrumental was considerable,[8] as can be seen from their syncretism in Greek and Germanic (with the dative) and in Latin (with the ablative) – not to mention the ambiguity present in the translation above: in English, to locate an event as taking place at night, we use *at*, while the preposition *in*, potentially just as locatival, takes on an instrumental force when it has anarthrous *night* as its object. That said, while a temporal reading is not possible with the English, one could picture this as a spatial expression, with Hephaestus portrayed as wrapping Idaeus up inside the physical envelope of darkness. This example thus recalls Thucydidean ὑπὸ νύκτα, which is found disproportionately frequently with verbs of sailing, suggesting navigation under the night-time sky, as well as Homeric διὰ νύκτα, used of motion not just *at* night, but *through* the almost tangible darkness of night.[9] That this is so for the instrumental datives is further indicated by the presence of the visual epithet ἐρεβεννῇ in the example at *Il.* 13.425.

Furthermore, the personification of night extends the syntactic range of the dative of νύξ past that of other time nouns, as seen clearly in the following passage, spoken by Sleep:

(4)   καί κέ μ' ἄϊστον ἀπ' αἰθέρος ἔμβαλε πόντῳ,
εἰ μὴ **Νὺξ** δμήτειρα θεῶν ἐσάωσε καὶ ἀνδρῶν·
τὴν ἱκόμην φεύγων, ὃ δ' ἐπαύσατο χωόμενός περ.
ἅζετο γὰρ μὴ **Νυκτὶ** θοῇ ἀποθύμια ἔρδοι

---

[6] See also *Il.* 13.425, *Od.* 20.351 ('engulfed in darkness'; Rutherford 1992: 233), 23.372.
[7] Delbrück 1893: 224–5, Kühner–Gerth: 445–6, Smyth 1920: 352, Schwyzer–Debrunner: 158–9.
[8] See Delbrück 1893: 246 (he mentions example (7)), Kühner–Gerth: 446 Anm. 5, Lass 1994: 232, Luraghi 2003: 52, Langslow 2009: 381, Weiss 2009: 213.
[9] For ὑπὸ and διὰ νύκτα, see Dyer (1974) and the discussion of examples (97) through (101) in Ch. 2.

And he would have cast me from the sky into the sea, not to be seen, if Night, who subdues gods and men, had not saved me. I came to her in flight, and he held back despite his anger. For he shrank from doing anything hateful to swift Night (*Il.* 14.258–61)

Because of this personification, the dative can assume its usual role with animate participants of marking the person affected; it also makes easier the constructions with πείθεσθαι, noted above, whose dative object is often personal. There are, however, three constructions with ordinals that give solid evidence of the punctual use of the dative. That said, in all of these, the ordinal is δεκάτη, and it is Odysseus' wanderings that are described, thereby providing a salutary reminder that, in using the Homeric poems as a corpus, we cannot simply use the raw numbers as a guide to real productivity of a construction:

(5) ἐννῆμαρ φερόμην· **δεκάτῃ** δέ με **νυκτὶ μελαίνῃ**
νῆσον ἐς Ὠγυγίην πέλασαν θεοί

I was carried for nine days, and on the tenth, black night, the gods brought me to the island Ogygia (*Od.* 7.253–4)[10]

Similar to this is the one construction with a demonstrative:

(6) **τῇδε** γὰρ αὖ μοι **νυκτὶ** παρέδραθεν εἴκελος αὐτῷ

For on this night, [a dream-image] resembling Odysseus slept beside me
(*Od.* 20.88)

Most remarkable, however, is an example without a modifier, in which the construction is probably modal (although there is no explicit constrast with 'by day'). Classical prose would have used νυκτός, ἐν νυκτί, or νύκτωρ here, a clear sign that the domain of the temporal dative shrank in the centuries following Homer:[11]

---

[10] See also *Od.* 12.447 (ἔνθεν δ' ἐννῆμαρ φερόμην, δεκάτῃ δέ με νυκτί), 14.314 (= 7.253).

[11] Pindar was still able to use the dative, as seen in the opening of *Olympian* 1: ὁ δὲ χρυσὸς αἰθόμενον πῦρ | ἅτε διαπρέπει νυκτί ("but gold, like fire burning in the night, stands out"), but also has the genitive in a comparatively punctual construction: αἰτέων λαοτρόφον τιμάν τιν' ἑᾷ κεφαλᾷ, νυκτός ὑπαίθριος (*O.* 6.60–1) ("asking at night under the open sky for an honor for his person that would help his people"). The combination of νυκτός with ὑπαίθριος here again highlights the association of night-time events with the sky overhead.

(7) ἀλλὰ ἑκὰς νήσων ἀπέχειν εὐεργέα νῆα,
νυκτὶ δ' ὁμῶς πλείειν

But keep your well-built ship far away from islands, and sail equally by night

(*Od.* 15.33–4)

Finally, there are two prepositional constructions; first, one with ἐπί^{+D}:

(8) ἀλλ' ἤτοι **ἐπὶ νυκτὶ** φυλάξομεν ἡμέας αὐτούς

But during the night we will stand guard over ourselves (*Il.* 8.529)

In Attic Greek, this preposition is not found in temporal expressions with the dative. That it could be so used in Homer in a durative construction shows that the dative, as other evidence amply indicates, participated more vigorously in prepositional constructions in Homer than later on.[12] By contrast, the other example, with ἐν, would be right at home in Attic prose:

(9) Ἕκτορι δ' ἦεν ἑταῖρος, **ἰῇ δ' ἐν νυκτὶ** γένοντο,
ἀλλ' ὃ μὲν ἂρ μύθοισιν, ὃ δ' ἔγχεϊ πολλὸν ἐνίκα

[Polydamas] was Hector's companion, and they were born on a single night, but the one was far superior with words, the other with the spear (*Il.* 18.251–2)

This is a prototypical limitative construction, with two events – the births of Polydamas and Hector – assigned to a single time frame, marked out as such with the modifier ἰῇ; as such, the use of ἐν^{+D} is entirely expected.

All in all, there is little that can be proven from these data. On the one hand, there are tantalizing hints that the rules governing temporal expressions with νύξ are slightly different from those of Classical Attic: the punctual dative is found four times, the genitive only once, and ἐπί^{+D} occurs in a durative construction. On the other, those four punctual dative tokens only include two distinct types, so it is not statistically valid to conclude that the dative is significantly more common at this stage. Moreover, the distribution of the punctual genitive without a modifier, the punctual datives with demonstratives and ordinal numbers, is typical of Classical prose, as is the use of ἐν to

---

[12] See Luraghi 2003: 330, Bortone 2010: 154–5. The spatial metaphor that underlies this usage (presumably that of close contact (Luraghi 2003: 298)) does not seem to be as vivid as in the examples of διὰ νύκτα and ὑπὸ νύκτα.

mark the one clear limitative construction. In short, the evidence is consistent with the scenario that the dative is gradually on the retreat, with the preponderance of the genitive of time νυκτός in Attic a later development, but it by no means conclusively proves it. This is hardly surprising given not only the overall rarity of the forms νυκτός and νυκτί in Homer (10× and 21×, respectively, compared to 50× and 12× in Thucydides), but also, more importantly, the low percentage of these forms that are actually adverbial expressions of time (7× out of 31×, or 23%, for Homer, as opposed to 57× out of 62×, or 92%, for Thucydides).

With ἡμέρα, the situation is even less conclusive than with νύξ, as it is still used frequently enough with the dative in Classical Greek that we would hardly expect to be able to track a decline from Homeric levels in the best of circumstances. Furthermore, a simple comparison of Homeric and later data is complicated by the near absence of ἡμέρα itself from epic poetry, as it can only fit into dactylic hexameter if the final syllable scans short by cor-reption. In practice, this only occurs six times, always in the nominative.[13] Instead, Homer prefers the neuter ἦμαρ, both in that form (82×), which can also occur as the second element of compounds (ἐννῆμαρ 12×, ἑξῆμαρ 4×, αὐτῆμαρ 3×, πανῆμαρ and ποσσῆμαρ 1× each), and with the oblique stem ἠματ- (ἤματ(α) 57×, ἤματ(ι) 49×, ἤματος 1×), which is never compounded; the derivative adjective ἠματίη, -αι is also found four times.[14] This collection of forms raises the following questions: Is it significant that the genitive is so rare? What is the relationship between the compounds with -ῆμαρ and the constructions with the simplex ἤματα? Why is the form ἦμαρ ambiguous with respect to number? Synchronically, it looks singular, but its sense is plural not only in compounds like ἐννῆμαρ (where it is natural enough for number to be neutralized; compare English a nine-day [not nine-days] event), but also in the formula νύκτας τε καὶ ἦμαρ (8×).[15]

---

[13] The singular ἡμέρη (Il. 8.541, 13.828, Od. 24.514) and the plural ἡμέραι (Od. 11.294, 14.93, 14.293) occur 3× each.

[14] For the replacement of ἡμέρα by ἦμαρ, see Wachter 2012: 70. To his reasoning that ἡμέρα (or rather ἡμέρη) was the standard Ionic form by this point can be added the fact, noted below, that ἦμαρ is picked up by the feminine article in examples like (14).

[15] This phrase is found after the hephthemimeral caesura at Il. 5.490, 22.432, 24.73, Od. 2.345, 10.28, 10.80, 15.476, 24.63.

That the genitive only occurs once – and, even then, is adnominal rather than adverbial[16] – is partly explained by the use of the adjective ἡματίη (4×):

(10) ἔνθα καὶ ἡματίη μὲν ὑφαίνεσκεν μέγαν ἱστόν,
νύκτας δ' ἀλλύεσκεν

There, by day, she kept weaving a great web and during the nights she would undo it (*Od.* 2.104–5 = 24.139–40, ≈ 19.149–50)

(11) πλεῖαί τοι οἴνου κλισίαι, τὸν νῆες Ἀχαιῶν
ἡμάτιαι Θρήκηθεν ἐπ' εὐρέα πόντον ἄγουσι

Your huts are full of wine, which the ships of the Achaeans bring daily from Thrace over the broad sea (*Il.* 9.71–2)

In both passages, a repeated activity is described, marked clearly as such in (10) by the iterative -σκ- forms, where the μὲν ... δέ contrast with νύκτας additionally indicates that this is a modal construction. The second example, in which the emphasis lies on the regular delivery of the wine, rather than its occurrence by day rather than by night, counts as distributive. As Classical Greek could use the temporal genitive in both of these contexts, we see here one reason for the construction's lower frequency in Homer.[17]

Now, given that the temporal genitive of ἡμέρα is distributed unevenly in Classical authors, the above observation is probably sufficient to account for the discrepancy between Homer and Thucydides – the latter only has nine examples of temporal ἡμέρας, of which four are distributive constructions used in financial transactions of a sort not typical of Homer, and three of the remaining five are modal constructions that resemble example (10) above. Xenophon, however, is fonder of ἡμέρας, which occurs thirty-one times as a temporal genitive. Of these, eleven are distributive expressions, primarily relating to money, and may be disregarded in a comparison with Homer. The remaining twenty,

---

[16] The line is cited at the end of n. 4.
[17] To cite Herodotus (whose Ionic we might expect to be closer than Attic to Homeric usage), with the first example, compare ἀμφίβληστρον ... τῷ τῆς μὲν ἡμέρης ἰχθῦς ἀγρεύει, τὴν δὲ νύκτα τάδε αὐτῷ χρᾶται (2.95.2); with the second, εἰ χοίνικα πυρῶν ἕκαστος τῆς ἡμέρης ἐλάμβανε (7.187.2). In the first of these, note also the shift from the genitive of time in the μέν clause to the accusative in the δέ clause as evidence that the accusative νύκτας in the second line of (10) could potentially be compatible with a genitive in the first line.

however, include seventeen where ἡμέρας is explicitly coordinated with νυκτός, five times in negative constructions (οὔτε νυκτὸς οὔτε ἡμέρας), but mostly in positive ones (καὶ ἡμέρας καὶ νυκτός). As such, these expressions occur in contexts very similar to those in which Homer deploys νύκτας τε καὶ ἦμαρ:

(12)   ἐν δὲ γυνὴ ταμίη **νύκτας τε καὶ ἦμαρ**
ἔσχ᾽, ἢ πάντ᾽ ἐφύλασσε νόου πολυϊδρείῃσιν

And a woman housekeeper, who guarded everything with experienced skill, stayed inside by night and by day (*Od.* 2.345–6)

(13)   δορυφόρους, οἳ κύκλῳ μὲν **νυκτὸς καὶ ἡμέρας** ἐφύλαττον περὶ τὰ βασίλεια

Bodyguards, who kept watch around the palace by night and by day (X. *Cyr.* 7.5.68)

Now Classical prose authors can certainly use the accusative in such phrases, but it is not very common. For instance, Xenophon, in contrast to his seventeen examples of the genitive in 'by night and by day' constructions, uses the accusative only in τὸν δεινὸν χειμῶνα στρατευόμενοι καὶ νύκτα καὶ ἡμέραν οὐδὲν πεπαύμεθα (*An.* 7.6.9) and οὕτως ... καὶ νύκτα καὶ ἡμέραν διάγει (*Hier.* 7.10).[18] But even the second of these is not really a good parallel, for the verb modified by the phrase is διάγει, which regularly takes an accusative that lies at the border between the temporal accusative and a direct object. Herodotus, to be sure, has three examples of the modal accusative plural, but all of these involve two separate clauses (e.g. τὰς μὲν ἡμέρας ... τὰς δὲ νύκτας), and the three examples which, like Homeric νύκτας τε καὶ ἦμαρ, occur within a clause all have the genitive instead.[19] In short, one may reasonably give as an additional reason for the low frequency of the Homeric genitive of time the preference for this accusative construction instead.

But how exactly does this construction work? If ἦμαρ is singular, why is it in parallel with plural νύκτας? While it is true that the

---

[18] We cannot count *An.* 6.1.14 (ἔπλεον ἡμέραν καὶ νύκτα πνεύματι καλῷ) as a parallel, as the start of the next clause (τῇ δ᾽ ἄλλῃ [*sc.* ἡμέρᾳ]) makes clear that this accusative means 'for one day and night', not 'by day and by night'.

[19] The accusatives: 3.18.1, 9.37.3, 9.93.1; the genitives: 2.133.4, 5.23.2, 8.71.2; at 2.95.2 the use of the genitive extends to a passage where the expressions are split over two clauses (i.e. where one otherwise finds the accusative).

plural would not fit metrically into this particular formula, ἦμστ(α) is quite common (57× in total) in other contexts, mostly ἤματα πάντα (30×, of which 26× are line-end), but also, once, in a pairing with νύκτας at *Il.* 23.185–6 (ἀλλὰ κύνας μὲν ἄλαλκε Διὸς θυγάτηρ Ἀφροδίτη | ἤματα καὶ νύκτας). Existing explanations of the construction are twofold. First, there is the widespread view that -αρ represents a collective ending inherited from a stage of Proto-Indo-European in which the morphological expression of number had not yet been regularized in neuter nouns to the Classical opposition of singular, dual, and plural.[20] Leumann, however, suggested that the plural use of ἦμαρ is a comparatively recent development resulting from the extension of -ημαρ, which is found as a second element in compounds with numerals as their first element (1950: 100).[21]

While a syntactic study is unlikely to settle the matter – either starting point could easily lead to the use of ἦμαρ in a modal expression – it is still worth considering the competition between compound adjectives and the simplex nouns in durative expressions with cardinal numerals. On the one hand, we find some accusatives of time that exactly match later usage, as they are situated in a μέν-clause that sets up a δέ-clause with the punctual dative of an ordinal numeral:[22]

(14) ἕνδεκα δ' ἤματα θυμὸν ἐτέρπετο οἷσι φίλοισιν
ἐλθὼν ἐκ Λήμνοιο· δυωδεκάτῃ δέ μιν αὖτις
χερσὶν Ἀχιλλῆος θεὸς ἔμβαλεν

---

[20] With respect to this particular problem, Wackernagel compares the lack of differentiation between singular and plural in a Vedic syntagm (RV 1.64.5) where neuter plural *divyāni* ('heavenly') modifies neuter singular *ūdhar* ('udder') (1909: 3); he is followed by Benveniste (1935: 95) and Chantraine (1958: 212–13), who also see in ἦμαρ an old plural. More generally, the problem of number in the neuter noun has been surveyed by Clackson (2007: 100–4); he also discusses ἦμαρ in particular at 1994: 97.

[21] Leumann's position was supported, with much discussion of the phonological history of the form ἐννῆμαρ, by Timothy Barnes in a talk at the 14th Fachtagung of the Indogermanische Gesellschaft (Sep. 2012); the handout and a video of the talk are available at fachtagung.dk.

[22] A similar example occurs at *Od.* 5.278–9 (= 7.267–8): ἑπτὰ δὲ καὶ δέκα μὲν πλέεν ἤματα ποντοπορεύων, | ὀκτωκαιδεκάτῃ δ' ἐφάνη ὄρεα σκιόεντα, in which the first clause has both a δέ, marking it as a new unit, and a μέν, to set up the contrast with the following dative of time. Note also the slightly more complicated passages at *Od.* 5.388, 9.74, 10.142, where the following ordinal modifies the subject of a full temporal clause. A final example is found at *Od.* 19.199.

And for eleven days, after he had returned from Lemnos, his heart took pleasure in his friends' company, but on the twelfth a god cast him back into the hands of Achilles (*Il.* 21.45–7)

On the other, there are functionally equivalent constructions which deploy a compound adjective instead:[23]

(15) ἐννῆμαρ μὲν ἀνὰ στρατὸν ᾤχετο κῆλα θεοῖο,
     τῇ δεκάτῃ δ' ἀγορήνδε καλέσσατο λαὸν Ἀχιλλεύς

For nine days the god's arrows ranged through the army, but on the tenth Achilles called the people to an assembly (*Il.* 1.53–4)

In both types, it is at first glance surprising to find the feminine τῇ δεκάτῃ in place of τῷ δεκάτῳ given that the days are neuter (explicitly in the first example, by morphological implication in the second), but this apparent mismatch may presumably be explained as an intrusion of the gender of the more common Greek word for day.[24] Finally, there is one line in which a compound adjective in fact co-occurs with simplex ἦμαρ:

(16) ἐννῆμαρ μὲν ὁμῶς πλέομεν νύκτας τε καὶ ἦμαρ

For nine days we sailed on equally, both nights and days (*Od.* 10.28)

Taken together, such close parallels between the use of the compound and that of both expected ἤματα and unexpected ἦμαρ at least make Leumann's proposal of an extension of a modal use of ἦμαρ from the compounds syntactically plausible. That said, this extension would certainly be easier if epic had inherited the formula νύκτας τε καὶ ἦμαρ from an earlier stage of the language in which ἦμαρ was not specifically singular – and the limitation of this use to this phrase could suggest a fossilized inheritance rather than a creative extension of a collective ἦμαρ on the part of the poet.[25]

---

[23] Of the twelve occurrences of ἐννῆμαρ (7× *Il.*, 5× *Od.*), δεκάτῃ follows in the next clause in all five of the Odyssean examples and in three of the Iliadic ones; in another two passages, δεκάτη follows as a nominative (modifying ἠώς both times); twice, there is no corresponding use of the ordinal.

[24] Cf. n. 14. The use of the *to- demonstrative as an article in any case suggests a younger layer of epic language here (Leumann 1950: 12 n. 2, Chantraine 1953: 165).

[25] Barnes (see n. 21) nicely explains the limitation of collective ἦμαρ to this phrase by assuming an earlier formula with *āmōr (here following Leukart 1987: 358–61), with the anomalous -ōr ending (seen also in νύκτωρ) replaced with -αρ on the model of the 2nd element of the compound.

It remains to consider briefly the expressions with the dative ἤματι (49×). For the most part, these are unremarkable punctual constructions: thirty-five times with demonstratives, four times with ordinals.²⁶ It occurs twice more in similes where a habitual nuance may be detected;²⁷ the final example with the dative on its own is the clearest indication that the range of the temporal dative is wider than in Attic, as it is used in a limitative phrase marked by ἰῷ:

(17) οἳ μὲν πάντες ἰῷ κίον ἤματι Ἄϊδος εἴσω

(of Andromache's brothers) who all went to Hades on one day (*Il.* 6.422)

In the remaining seven passages, the dative is strengthened by ἐπί (cf. (8) above). As none of these are straightforward punctual examples, it is reasonable to posit a real functional difference here, with ἐπί used when the construction is closer to the limitative or distributive type. The best limitative examples are found at *Il.* 10.48 (ἄνδρ' ἕνα τοσσάδε μέρμερ' ἐπ' ἤματι μητίσασθαι) and *Od.* 2.284 (ὡς δὴ σφιν σχεδόν ἐστιν ἐπ' ἤματι πάντας ὀλέσθαι), where multiple events, signaled as such by the verbal subject (τοσσάδε and πάντας respectively), are confined to a single day; also tending in this direction are two examples in general relative clauses that look forward to the future, *Il.* 13.234 (ὅς τις ἐπ' ἤματι τῷδε ἑκὼν μεθίῃσι μάχεσθαι) and 19.110. The distributive sense is clearest in the famous description of the whirlpool Charybdis:

(18) τρὶς μὲν γάρ τ' ἀνίησιν ἐπ' ἤματι, τρὶς δ' ἀναροιβδεῖ

Three times a day it spouts forth water, three times it sucks it back up

(*Od.* 12.105)

It is also present in *Od.* 14.105 (τῶν αἰεί σφιν ἕκαστος ἐπ' ἤματι μῆλον ἀγινεῖ, with ἕκαστος as a typical indication of the distributive type) and probably also in *Il.* 19.228–9, in which Odysseus urges Achilles to limit his lamentation to a single day for each fallen man

---

²⁶ This includes 26 examples of ἤματι τῷ (of which 25 occur at the start of the line, and 17 continue by explaining the demonstrative with a ὅτε-clause), five of line-end ἤματι κείνῳ, and four with τῷδε. The four examples with ordinals, all quite different from one another, occur at *Il.* 9.363, 11.707, *Od.* 5.34, 6.170.

²⁷ These are found at *Il.* 12.278–9 (ὥς τε νιφάδες χιόνος πίπτωσι θαμειαί | ἤματι χειμερίῳ) and 16.384–5, the one example where the -ι is elided (ὡς δ' ὑπὸ λαίλαπι πᾶσα κελαινὴ βέβριθε χθὼν | ἤματ' ὀπωρινῷ).

(ἀλλὰ χρὴ τὸν μὲν καταθάπτειν ὅς κε θάνῃσι | νηλέα θυμὸν ἔχοντας ἐπ᾽ ἤματι δακρύσαντας).

In short, the Homeric usage of the dative ἤματι is largely in line with that of Attic, as it occurs by far the most often in punctual expressions. But it was also flexible enough to be used once in a clear limitative phrase; moreover, it was strengthened with ἐπί, rather than ἐν or κατά⁺ᴬ, to mark both limitative and distributive constructions.

The year in Homer

While night and day are the most common time nouns in Homer, we can also glean some information from other nouns as well. Both of the primary nouns for year, ἔτος and ἐνιαυτός, are common. The latter, as one would expect given its later usage, is particularly common in references to the year as a repeating cycle.[28] This is especially evident in passages where both nouns are found together:

(19) ἀλλ᾽ ὅτε δὴ **ἔτος** ἦλθε **περιπλομένων ἐνιαυτῶν**
τῷ οἱ ἐπεκλώσαντο θεοὶ οἶκόνδε νέεσθαι

But, once the year-cycles had revolved, when the year came in which the gods had ordained for him to return home (*Od.* 1.16–17)

Here, ἔτος is used of the year as a temporal signpost locating the one-time event of Odysseus' return, while ἐνιαυτός, with περιπλομένων, describes the year as a recurring phenomenon.[29]

[28] Of the 27 examples of ἐνιαυτός, it occurs 7× with a verb indicating the revolution of the year (περιτροπέων at *Il.* 2.295, περιτελλόμενοι/περιπλόμενοι at *Il.* 2.551, 8.404, 418, 23.833, *Od.* 1.16, 11.248) and 5× with the epithet τελεσφόρον, which highlights the role of the year in bringing to a close a repeating cycle (*Il.* 19.32, *Od.* 4.86, 10.467, 14.212, 15.230). One may also note the close juxtaposition of the seasons in *Od.* 10.469: ἀλλ᾽ ὅτε δή ῥ᾽ ἐνιαυτὸς ἔην, περὶ δ᾽ ἔτραπον ὧραι. Incidentally, the distinction between the two words for year in Greek does not match that between *an* and *année* in modern French. While *an* is found in simple expressions of time, often modified by a cardinal number, *année* highlights the passage of time and often occurs with ordinal numbers (L'Huillier 1999: 611–12); Greek ἔτος may be used in both of these contexts.

[29] In this connection, it is perhaps also significant that, in the nominative, Homer shows a strong preference for ἔτος (11×, all singular) over ἐνιαυτός (2× singular, 1× plural). Of the examples with ἔτος, nine have an ordinal modifier, one has πόστος ('which-th?'), and the last is ex. (19), with the τῷ clause fulfilling a comparable function: that is, in all of these the emphasis lies on the simple reckoning of linear time. In other words, if reduced from a

That said, while we find from later Greek that ἔτος is preferred in durative expressions covering many years (kings in Herodotus, for example, reign for a particular number of ἔτη, not ἐνιαυτούς), this accusative of time is not so common in Homer, where ἔτεα is metrically awkward, though not impossible, and only found once: at *Il.* 2.328 it precedes πτολέμιξομεν, which eliminates the tribrach.[30] Moreover, the two examples of the genitive ἔτεος are also with περιτέλλομαι, suggesting that, whatever semantic difference between the two words may have been present, it was weak enough that it could be blurred for metrical convenience:

(20) ἀλλ' ὅτε δὴ μῆνές τε καὶ ἡμέραι ἐξετελεῦντο
ἂψ **περιτελλομένου ἔτεος** καὶ ἐπήλυθον ὧραι

But when the months and days were drawing to an end, as the year cycled round, and the seasons approached (*Od.* 11.294–5 = 14.293–4)

One must also be wary of assigning too much weight to the idea that ἔτεα was avoided for metrical reasons: ἔτει/ἔτεϊ is found seven times, the former (1× only) with correption before ἦλθον (where ἔτε' could also have stood), the latter with a long final syllable in the formula ἤλυθον εἰκοστῷ (4×) / ἔλθοι ἐεικοστῷ (2×) ἔτεϊ ἐς πατρίδα γαῖαν. Given the semantic improbability that this formula is direct evidence of the older dative ending *-ei (superseded by the locative ending *-i when the two cases syncretized), this formula must instead show the metrical flexibility with which the long ending, originally functionally distinct, came to be simply a convenient alternative.[31] In any case, this use of a temporal dative in a punctual

---

full clause to an adverbial, they would be natural datives of time. By contrast, of the two examples of ἐνιαυτός, one does not have any such modifier, and the emphasis on cyclical time is brought out in a following clause (ἀλλ' ὅτε δὴ ῥ' ἐνιαυτὸς ἔην, περὶ δ' ἔτραπον ὧραι, *Od.* 10.495); the other, to be sure, does have an ordinal modifier, but occurs in a very different context, namely the speech in which Odysseus expresses the men's frustration at having been away at Troy for so long: ἡμῖν δ' εἴνατός ἐστι περιτροπέων ἐνιαυτός | ἐνθάδε μιμνόντεσσι (*Il.* 2.294). Here it makes excellent sense for the poet to use not the word that emphasizes the year as a linear calendrical measurement, but rather one that brings to the fore the endless cycling of the seasons without any progress in the war. As for the plural ἐνιαυτοί, it occurs in the same book for the same reasons (ἐννέα δὴ βεβάασι Διὸς μεγάλου ἐνιαυτοί, 2.134).

[30] Neither elided ἔτε' nor contracted ἔτη ever occurs.

[31] Cf. the treatment of δέπαϊ in the lines cited by Hoekstra (1965: 116–17); earlier in the book, he suggests that the formula with ἔτεϊ may have originally been followed by e.g. πτολίπορθος Ὀδυσσεύς (52 n. 2). In any case, that such arbitrariness should attend the

construction with ἔτος and an ordinal number would also be perfectly at home in Classical prose.[32]

In a further sign that not too great a distinction should be made between the two words for 'year', we also find that ἐνιαυτός is just as at home as ἔτος in this construction, marking a specific year:[33]

(21) πέρθετο[34] δὲ Πριάμοιο πόλις **δεκάτῳ ἐνιαυτῷ**

And the city of Priam was sacked in the tenth year (*Il.* 12.15)

Nor does one word look more deeply embedded in formulaic language than the other: ἔτει is, to be sure, more closely associated with one particular formula, and each of the five datives of ἐνιαυτῷ occurs in a different line (with three different ordinals among them) – but all five of these also occur at line-end, so, in the end, this word's metrical flexibility is not very great either.

In another example of the impasses one reaches in attempting to do syntactic work on Homer, we may consider the use of the accusative of ἐνιαυτός in what are primarily durative constructions: the singular occurs thirteen times in the two poems, ten times preceded by εἰς and three times used absolutely; the plural occurs three times, twice preceded by ἐς and once used absolutely. When we look for characteristics that might distinguish the two constructions, we find tantalizing glimpses of possible distinctions, but nothing that can be securely proven. Take the three plural examples. Right from the start, we are actually reduced to working with only two examples because two are the same line, leaving only one prepositional and one absolute example:

(22) οὐδέ κεν **ἐς δεκάτους περιτελλομένους ἐνιαυτοὺς**
  ἕλκε᾽ ἀπαλθήσεσθον, ἅ κεν μάρπτῃσι κεραυνός

extension of a recently-lost case ending is hardly surprising given the similar fate of -φι (Thompson 1998). That one would originally have expected the short *i* of the Indo-European locative is supported by the occurrence of *we-te-i* in Mycenaean (not *we-te-e* for /wetehei/, the Mycenaean *s*-stems having avoided this dative-locative ending (Ventris & Chadwick 1973: 86; Hajnal 1995: 227)). It occurs doubled, like Skt. *varṣe-varṣe*, in the sense 'every year' (PY Es 644; Ventris & Chadwick 1973: 278–9, *DMic.* s.v., Hajnal 1995: 229).

[32] The one example of disyllabic ἔτει, with correption before ἦλθον, also occurs with an ordinal (*Od.* 4.82).

[33] See also *Od.* 2.175, 3.391, 16.18, 17.327.

[34] The imperfect here comes in a sequence of aorists and may hide an original zero-grade thematic aorist *πάρθετο (Chantraine 1958: 389–90).

Not even in ten revolving years would they heal from whichever wounds the thunderbolt wreaks upon them (*Il.* 8.404–5 = 418–9)

(23) εἴ οἱ καὶ μάλα πολλὸν ἀπόπροθι πίονες ἀγροί,
    ἕξει μιν καὶ **πέντε περιπλομένους ἐνιαυτούς**
    χρεώμενος

    Even if his rich fields are very far away, he will have it, in his use, for five years in succession (*Il.* 23.832–4)

Based on these two passages, it is tempting to see ἐς as introducing a limitative construction (with telic ἀπαλθήσεσθον), with the plain accusative used for the durative (with atelic ἕξει). Still, it seems unwise to extrapolate so much out of just two examples, especially given the anomalous use of the ordinal δεκάτους in (22) when the context seems to demand the cardinal. The easiest explanation is to see this as a conflation of the ordinal construction with the singular (δεκάτῳ ἐνιαυτῷ) and the cardinal construction with the plural (ἐς δέκα ἐνιαυτούς).[35] While this is fairly unproblematic, it remains odd enough that one is reluctant to argue for a limitative reading of ἐς on this basis alone.

Moving on to the singular, one can see some possible nuances distinguishing the examples without εἰς from those with it, but there is also clear overlap between the two, and, in the end, not enough evidence to reach a firm conclusion. Start with the three examples of the plain accusative. In two of these, the accusative might instead be read as a direct object of τλῆναι (which can be used either transitively or absolutely):

(24) ἤ τ' ἂν τρυχόμενός περ ἔτι τλαίης **ἐνιαυτόν**

    Though being impoverished, you could endure (for) one more year
    (*Od.* 1.288 ≈ 2.219 (τλαίην))

The third forms a bridge to the examples with εἰς:

(25) οἱ δ' **ἐνιαυτὸν ἅπαντα** παρ' ἡμῖν αὖθι μένοντες
    ἐν νηΐ γλαφυρῇ βίοτον πολὺν ἐμπολόωντο

---

[35] Thus Sommer, who points to the regularity with which ἐνιαυτός occurs with ordinal numbers (1950: 8); so too Kirk, who curiously suggests a feminine δεκάτῃ ἐνιαυτῇ (1990: 330). For discussion of another example of an ordinal used as a cardinal, see Hutchinson (1985) ad A. *Th.* 125.

And they, staying with us here for a whole year, through trade acquired considerable goods in their hollow ship (*Od.* 15.455–6)

Here it is less likely that ἐνιαυτόν can be explained away as an object of μένοντες. While μένω certainly can take a direct object of the awaited endpoint,[36] such a reading is difficult with ἐνιαυτόν modified by ἅπαντα in such a way as to emphasize the duration of the event, rather than its termination. What is more, example (25) has the same verbal root as a couple of the examples with εἰς:

(26) ἔνθα παρ' αὐτῷ μεῖνα **τελεσφόρον εἰς ἐνιαυτόν**

> I stayed there with him for a year, with the completion it brings (*Od.* 14.292)

Now, one could argue that a rather different reading is necessary here, with ἐνιαυτός meaning something more like 'anniversary', and μένω construed with an adverbial marking the endpoint of the waiting ('until the day that marked a year's worth of waiting').[37] But while the presence of τελεσφόρον as an epithet might be thought to support this interpretation, it remains difficult given an example that occurs a hundred lines earlier:

(27) ῥηϊδίως κεν ἔπειτα καὶ **εἰς ἐνιαυτὸν ἅπαντα**
οὔ τι διαπρήξαιμι λέγων ἐμὰ κήδεα θυμοῦ,
ὅσσα γε δὴ ξύμπαντα θεῶν ἰότητι μόγησα

> Easily, then, even over the course of a full year, I would not finish telling the sorrows of my heart, all the things that, in total, I struggled through by the will of the gods (*Od.* 14.196–8)

Here, ἐνιαυτόν is modified by ἅπαντα, which makes a durative interpretation more plausible for the temporal expression – or, even better, given the negated verb and the future time reference, a limitative one. We had already seen in example (22) some grounds for assuming that εἰς could mark this event-type in Homer; between that example, (27), and the following, it seems all but certain:

(28) τρὶς γὰρ τίκτει μῆλα **τελεσφόρον εἰς ἐνιαυτόν**

> For the sheep give birth three times in a full year (*Od.* 4.86)

---

[36] See e.g. μείναμεν Ἠῶ δῖαν (*Il.* 11.723, *Od.* 9.151, etc.), where dawn marks the endpoint of the men's waiting, not the period during which they wait.
[37] Indeed, this is the position that Chantraine takes: "[*Il.* 19.32, *Od.* 4.456] εἰς ἐνιαυτόν 'dans un an' (ἐνιαυτός exprimant l'achèvement du cycle de l'année)" (1953: 104).

Once again, it is difficult to suggest that ἐνιαυτόν marks the anniversary rather than the whole period of the year, with εἰς used in the sense 'until, by': Menelaus here is describing the ewes of Libya as part of a mini-travelogue, and the emphasis lies not on a single deadline before which the verbal event takes place, but rather a repeated occurrence that is regularly bounded by the time frame of a year.

There remain seven other examples of εἰς ἐνιαυτόν, all of which could potentially be viewed in one of two ways: either with εἰς as 'until, by', followed by the anniversary sense of ἐνιαυτόν, or with the noun indicating a period of a year, thereby requiring εἰς to be understood as marking a durative expression.[38] Now, there of course remains a good reason to try to maintain the 'until, by' reading of εἰς (which is, after all, the temporal meaning one would expect given its place-to-which spatial sense):[39] in several other expressions, it does mark an endpoint. Such is its force with ἠῶ, ἠέλιον καταδύντα, and γῆρας, and, even more regularly, in the phrase εἰς ὅ κεν 'until', as noted by Chantraine (1953: 104). But, as Chantraine is also aware, there are other expressions too where it is easier to assume a broadening of the usage of εἰς: at *Od.* 3.138, where ἐς ἠέλιον καταδύντα means 'at sunset', or *Od.* 14.384, where he translates the prepositional phrases in καὶ φάτ' ἐλεύσεσθαι ἢ ἐς θέρος ἢ ἐς ὀπώρην as "ou au cours de l'été ou au cours de l'automne."[40] The best way to reconcile this is presumably to recognize the constructions with ἐνιαυτός as a sort of pivot: in the first instance, they will have meant 'until the anniversary', but as ἐνιαυτός became reanalyzed as referring to the period of time leading up to the anniversary, so too the preposition will have been reanalyzed as marking a durative construction.

---

[38] The examples in question modify the following verbs: κεῖται (*Il.* 19.32), θητεύσαμεν (*Il.* 21.444), φύλασσε (*Od.* 4.526), παρὰ σοί γ' ἀνεχοίμην (*Od.* 4.595), ἥμεθα (*Od.* 10.467), μίμνειν (*Od.* 11.356), χρήματα ... εἶχε (*Od.* 15.230). In all of these, the semantic context is amenable to either interpretation: the verbal events in question lead up to a clear definite endpoint (this is esp. clear in *Il.* 21.444, where the servitude of Poseidon and Apollo to Laomedon is a punishment limited at the start to a year's duration), but these are also the sorts of verbs that are particularly prone to occur in ordinary durative constructions in later prose.

[39] See Luraghi 2003: 109–10.

[40] In fact, I find the 'by' reading of ἐς fairly easy here: 'and he said that he would come either by summer or by autumn'.

The sheer number of examples with ἐνιαυτός will have abetted this reinterpretation, and the general potential for confusion between 'while' and 'until' is also demonstrated by the use of the same subordinating conjunction to express both ideas (admittedly with different constructions) in both Classical Greek (ἕως) and Latin (*dum*). Only three examples of ἔτος and ἐνιαυτός remain. Two are genitive absolutes with περιτελλομένων / περιπλομένων ἐνιαυτῶν (*Il.* 2.551, *Od.* 1.16 = ex. (19)), which match the genitive absolutes of Thucydides and Xenophon discussed in Chapter 1; both authors use ἐτῶν with participles of verbs like παρελθεῖν that mark the passage of time. The final example is a limitative genitive of a sort that one expects to find more often in Classical prose, but is in fact rather rare:

(29) ἐλθὼν γάρ ῥ᾽ ἐκάκωσε βίη Ἡρακληείη
τῶν προτέρων ἐτέων, κατὰ δ᾽ ἔκταθεν ὅσσοι ἄριστοι

For the mighty Heracles had wreaked destruction when he came in earlier years, and all the best men had been killed (*Il.* 11.690–1)

This should certainly count as limitative: the noun in the temporal phrase is plural, and the verb refers to repeated, telic acts of destruction. But while the genitive of time is thus a natural choice, it is in fact fairly uncommon in Classical prose for the noun to be plural: of the 91 genitives of time in Herodotus, only four are plural; of the 145 in Thucydides, only six; of the 188 in Xenophon, only four. What is more, only one of these fourteen plural examples refers to a past-time event – and even this example is negated, making it more markedly limitative than (29).[41] All in all, this suggests that not only the dative of time, but also the genitive of time, underwent some narrowing of function between Homer and the fifth century, with ἐν becoming the preferred marker of past-time limitative expressions with plural time nouns.[42]

---

[41] See Hdt. 2.115.6, 4.151.1 (the sole example with past-time reference), 6.58.3, 9.26.4; Th. 2.97.2, 4.26.2, 4.105.2, 5.14.3, 6.21.2, 7.3.1, X. *HG* 7.5.18, *An.* 1.7.18, 4.7.20, *Cyr.* 6.2.38.

[42] See e.g. Hdt. 2.142.3 (ἐν μυρίοισί τε ἔτεσι), 8.66.1 (ἐν ἑτέρησι τρισὶ ἡμέρησι), Th. 1.118.2 (ἐν ἔτεσι πεντήκοντα), 3.51.4 (ἐν ἡμέραις ὀλίγαις), X. *HG* 2.4.21 (ἐν ὀκτὼ μησίν), 4.4.18 (ἐν ὀλίγαις ἡμέραις).

Other time nouns in Homer

Other time nouns, notably the seasons, only offer further isolated scraps of information, although these again all suggest that the dative was of wider use in Homer than later on, especially considering the strong tendency for the seasons to construe with the genitive in Classical prose. The noun θέρος occurs five times in Homer, each time in a different syntactic construction. Leaving aside the nominative (*Od.* 11.192) and a phrase with ἐς that marks the time by which something will happen (*Od.* 14.384),[43] we are left with three adverbial usages marking events taking place during the summer. Two of these match later usage: both are negated modal constructions, one with the genitive (*Od.* 7.118), one with ἐν (*Od.* 12.76):

(30) τάων οὔ ποτε καρπὸς ἀπόλλυται οὐδ᾽ ἀπολείπει
      χείματος οὐδὲ θέρευς, ἐπετήσιος[44]

      And their fruit never perishes nor fails during winter or summer, lasting throughout the year (*Od.* 7.118)

(31)   οὐδέ ποτ᾽ αἴθρη
      κείνου ἔχει κορυφὴν **οὔτ᾽ ἐν θέρει οὔτ᾽ ἐν ὀπώρῃ**

      Nor does clear sky ever surround its peak, either in summer or in autumn
                                          (*Od.* 12.75–6)

The third, however, is a dative in a habitual construction, where later Greek would also use the genitive or ἐν:

(32) ἡ δ᾽ ἑτέρη **θέρεϊ** προρέει ἐϊκυῖα χαλάζῃ

      But the other spring flows forth in summer like hail (*Il.* 22.151)

The situation is similar with χειμών and χεῖμα, which together furnish only three adverbial temporal expressions.[45] As seen above in example (30), one finds the expected genitive in a

---

[43] Or possibly 'during which', as Chantraine suggests (1953: 104); see n. 40 of this chapter.

[44] As with ἠματίη, here too we see Homeric Greek using an adjective modifying the subject in place of an adverbial expression.

[45] The other constructions are χεῖμα as a nominative at *Od.* 14.487, and χειμών as a nominative at *Od.* 4.566 and 14.522, as a direct object at *Il.* 3.4, and as an adnominal genitive at *Il.* 17.549.

modal construction, but a second modal expression with χεῖμα offers the accusative instead:

(33) ἀλλ' ὅ γε **χεῖμα μὲν** εὕδει ὅθι δμῶες ἐνὶ οἴκῳ,
ἐν κόνι ἄγχι πυρός, κακὰ δὲ χροΐ εἵματα εἷται·
αὐτὰρ ἐπὴν ἔλθησι θέρος τεθαλυῖά τ' ὀπώρη

But during the winter he sleeps where his slaves do in the house, in the ashes by the fire, and he wears poor clothes about his body; but when summer comes and flourishing autumn (*Od.* 11.190–2)

Here the accusative, in place of the genitive, makes good sense: χεῖμα occurs in a μέν-clause that sets up a punctual expression in the following αὐτάρ-clause. Such contexts have repeatedly favored the durative accusative. The one adverbial construction with χειμών, however, is a dative:

(34) ἐρχθέντ' ἐν μεγάλῳ ποταμῷ ὡς παῖδα συφορβόν,
ὅν ῥά τ' ἔναυλος ἀποέρσῃ **χειμῶνι** περῶντα

Caught up in a great river, like a boy swineherd, whom a mountain-stream sweeps off as he is crossing it in a storm (*Il.* 21.282–3)

The event-type of this construction lies at the intersection of the punctual and the modal types. On the one hand, χειμῶνι simply indicates the time at which the crossing took place, and there is no explicit contrast with another time noun – as is perhaps only to be expected given that χειμών here means 'storm', not 'winter' (with which 'summer' is so readily juxtaposed). On the other, χειμῶνι lacks the modifiers, like demonstratives, that typically characterize the prototypical punctual construction, and it occurs in a simile, which suggests a recurring timelessness that fits the modal type better. In either case – but especially if the construction counts as modal – such a dative would not be expected in later prose. Finally, the situation is similar with ὀπώρη[46] and ἔαρ,[47] although neither of these nouns shows any unexpected datives.

---

[46] It occurs 4 × in Homer, 1 × in the nominative (ex. (33)), 1 × after ἐς, in parallel with θέρος (*Od.* 14.384), 1 × in a modal construction with ἐν (ex. (31)), and 1 × in a modal genitive referring to the regular rising of Sirius in late summer (ὅς ῥά τ' ὀπώρης εἷσιν, *Il.* 22.27).
[47] It occurs only 2 × in Homer, 1 × as an adnominal genitive (*Il.* 6.148), 1 × in a genitive absolute – which, like so many of the temporal genitive absolutes of Classical prose,

Conclusion

The data from Homer do not allow the same level of certainty about the conditions governing the choice of temporal construction as we can achieve with later prose texts, where temporal phrases are not only much more common, but less subject to skewing of the evidence because of the formulaic nature of composition in the epic tradition. Still, we do see convincing signs that certainly the dative of time and possibly the genitive were used more freely than in Classical prose. This renders likely the account proposed in Chapter 2: the standard position of the handbooks, that the genitive, as an old partitive, denoted time within which, the dative, as an old locative, time when, makes sense from an Indo-European, and even Homeric perspective. That it works less well in Thucydides or Xenophon is due to diachronic change within Greek, in particular the long-term decline of the dative.

would remain grammatical, as a modal genitive of time, if the participle were omitted: ὡς δ' ὅτε Πανδαρέου κούρη, χλωρηῒς ἀηδών, | καλὸν ἀείδησιν ἔαρος νέον ἱσταμένοιο ("... when spring has just begun") (*Od.* 19.518–19).

6

SUMMARY

Most of the material presented in this work is aimed primarily at classicists who wish to know more about the nuances that distinguish the various temporal expressions in Ancient Greek – nuances that often can only be detected through careful attention to the philological context of the passages in question. As the proper evaluation of that context requires considerable familiarity with Greek, I have made no attempt to gloss the examples for a wider linguistic audience. But since some of the findings will be of interest to linguists more generally, this final chapter offers a summary aimed at those who do not know Greek, structured in accordance with the general types of constructions discussed, followed by an account of the main diachronic trends.

Durative expressions

The standard way of marking duration of time in Greek is to put the time noun in question into the accusative case. This has long been recognized as the temporal equivalent of the spatial use of the Indo-European accusative to express an extent of space:

(1) *kaì*   **hēmérās**   *mèn*   **pénte**   *hēsúkhazon*
    and   days.ACC.PL   PCL   five   they.stayed.quiet.IMPF

And they stayed quiet for five days (Thucydides 3.107.3 = Ch. 2 ex. (1))

Now the word *mén*,[1] which I have glossed simply as a particle, sets up the expectation of a second clause to follow, typically marked by *dé*; this pair may sometimes be translated as 'on the one hand . . . on

---

[1] Cited in isolation, *mén* carries an acute accent; when an accented word follows, as in the example, that accent changes to a grave (as happens regularly in any word whose final syllable would otherwise have the acute).

the other hand', although in this example that would lead to a gross over-translation. Here, as often elsewhere, a durative expression in a *mén*-clause leads up to a punctual (Time When) expression in the subsequent *dé*- clause:

(2) *têi   dè   héktēi   etássonto   amphóteroi   hōs es mákhēn*
    the.DAT PCL sixth.DAT drew.up.IMPF both.sides   as for battle

But on the sixth, both sides drew up as if for battle (3.107.3, ctd.)[2]

In (2), which follows directly after (1), the day on which a punctual event interrupts the preceding static period is signaled with the dative of time, again unproblematically seen as continuing an Indo-European locative of time when (Greek having syncretized the locative together with the dative). Note that the verb tense in both (1) and (2) is the imperfect, formed from the imperfective present stem of the verb. The other main narrative past tense of Greek, the aorist, which has perfective aspect, would also have been grammatical in both examples, as the choice of the imperfective or perfective past tense is determined more by the large-scale structure of the narrative than by any strong correlation between accusatives of time and the imperfect or datives of time and the aorist.[3]

In addition to the accusative, Greek can also mark durative constructions with the preposition *epí* (with the accusative) or *diá* (with the genitive); in the corresponding spatial uses, these prepositions indicate extent of space and path respectively. Typical examples:

(3) *tò   gàr   Rhḗgion   epì polùn   khrónon   estasíaze*
    the   PCL Rhegium   for much.ACC time.ACC was.in.turmoil.IMPF

For Rhegium had been torn by faction for a long time (4.1.3 = Ch. 2 ex. (26))

(4) *hūetoû   háma   dià nuktòs   polloû*
    rain   at.the.same.time through the.night.GEN much
    epigenoménou
    having.taken.place.AOR

At the same time, much rain having fallen throughout the night (2.4.2 = Ch. 2 ex. (21))

---

[2] This and all further examples in this chapter are taken from Thucydides unless otherwise indicated.
[3] For a good recent study of this, see Allan 2007.

Example (3) is typical of constructions in which the accusative is reinforced by *epí* in that the time noun is modified by *polús* 'much', which, because it comes before the noun, is marked as particularly salient.[4] Other modifiers common in *epí*-phrases include *pleîstos* 'most' and cardinal numbers. Constructions with *diá* and the genitive usually emphasize that an event took place continuously throughout the period in question, as is here suggested by the modifier *polloû* 'much' (in agreement with *hūetoû* 'rain'); this nuance comes even more to the fore when, as often, the time noun is modified by *hólos* 'entire'.[5] There are also one-off lexical effects associated with individual time nouns. When used with *khrónos*, the local sense of *diá* to indicate path follows a different semantic development: rather than shifting from 'through' to 'throughout', it shifts to 'over the course of', emphasizing the transition that has taken place between the starting point and the end point rather than the continuity throughout. Thus, *dià khrónou* comes to mean 'after (a period of) time'.

Punctual expressions

Traditionally, Greek grammars have taught that Time When phrases – in this work labeled punctual because they specify the point in time at which they occurred[6] – place the time noun in the dative case. By and large, this is an accurate description of the dative of time, as seen in example (2) above, or the following:

(5) **héktōi**   *dè*   **étei** ...   *pólemos*   *egéneto*   *perì Priénēs*
    sixth.DAT   PCL   year.DAT   war   took.place.AOR   over Priene

And in the sixth year, there was a war over Priene (1.115.2)

Typically, the time noun in such expressions is modified by an ordinal number, a demonstrative, or other adjectives (e.g. *ho autós* 'the same', *ho epigignómenos* 'the next') that single out one instance of the time noun in question.

What has not been well understood, however, is the extent to which the dative is only used as the default marker of punctual

---

[4] See Dik 1997, Bakker 2007 and 2009.   [5] See the discussion on p. 124 in Chapter 3.

[6] Note that, in this study, 'punctual' does not mean 'objectively instantaneous in a Vendlerian sense'; see n. 10 in Ch. 1.

expressions with certain time nouns, namely those for day (*hēmérā*), month (*mén*), and year (*étos*). The nouns for night (*núx*) and the seasons (*théros* 'summer', *kheimṓn* 'winter'), by contrast, regularly occur with the genitive:

(6) **toû**   *d'*   **autoû**   **kheimônos**   *kai Dêlon*   *ekáthēran*
    the.GEN   PCL   same.GEN   winter.GEN   also Delos   they.purified.AOR

And in the same winter they also purified Delos (3.104.1 = Ch. 2 ex. (62))

Examples like (6), where the modifier is particularly likely to indicate a punctual construction, are common enough that the genitive can be seen to be the default case with these nouns; more typical, however, are expressions that lie further away from the prototypical center of the punctual type:

(7) *hoì*   *tèn*   *phulakèn*   *diexêlthon*   **tês**   **nuktós**
    Who   the   guard   passed.through.AOR   the.GEN   night.GEN

(The three hundred men,) who slipped through the guard at night (7.85.2 = Ch. 2 ex. (51))

While the temporal phrase here indicates the time when the event took place, the time noun in question is not singled out by a modifier to set it apart from other instances of that same noun: here, there is a definite article, but *nuktós* can also occur completely on its own. Because of the lack of modifier, such constructions come closer to another type, the modal-habitual construction, to be discussed below.

A second construction can also mark punctual expressions with this latter class of nouns (night and the seasons), the preposition *en* ('in') with the dative:

(8) **en** *dè*   **tôi**   **autôi**   **thérei** ...   *estráteusan*
    in PCL   the.DAT   same.DAT   summer.DAT   they.campaigned.AOR
    epì Minôian
    against Minoa

And in the same summer ... they attacked Minoa (3.51.1 = Ch. 2 ex. (76))

Such phrases are often indistinguishable in use from those with the genitive, but, at least with this class of time nouns, punctual constructions do not make up as great a proportion of the phrases with *en* as they do of those with the genitive.

307

Limitative expressions

While the genitive of time, as has just been seen, can be used in punctual expressions, it has in the past been characterized most often as marking Time Within Which. This functional category has not been subject to much careful description in the past, especially regarding the boundary between it and the Time When expressions associated with the dative. That there is potential for confusion is clear: punctual expressions like (2) and (5), with the dative, could be understood as indicating that the event modified by them took place at some point within the given day or year. As a result, a phrase like that in (6) could be described as a Time Within Which genitive, that in (5) as a Time When dative, and left at that, even though they both assign an event to a particular instance of a time noun, and so both fall into my punctual category. Far better, then, to restrict the Time Within Which category, which I rechristen the limitative, to a more specific set of circumstances: phrases which refer to the sort of period of time characteristic of the durative (prototypically plural nouns modified by cardinal numbers), but rather than using that period to indicate how long an unbounded, atelic event went on for (as in (1) or (3)),[7] instead limit a bounded, telic event to some point or points within that period:

(9) *hoùs*   *ṓionto*   **hēmerôn olígōn**   *ekpoliorkḗsein*
    Whom   they.thought.IMPF   days.GEN few.GEN   make.surrender.FUT

Whom they thought they would force to surrender in a few days (4.26.4 = Ch. 2 ex. (29))

Here, the time noun is plural and modified by *olígos*, and so is the sort of configuration one would also meet in the accusative case as a durative expression – but not in the dative as a punctual one. But it differs from the durative type in that it modifies a telic verb, *ekpoliorkḗsein*, referring to an event that will not take place continuously during those days (as in the durative type), but only on one of

---

[7] Example (4), which I have also classified as durative, is not obviously atelic, given its aorist verb *epigenoménou*. In this instance, however, the verbal event does last for the entirety of the night, and the fact that the verb is less compatible than usual with a durative expression gives added reason to strengthen the temporal phrase by using *diá* with the genitive rather than just the accusative.

them, as yet unspecified. That the verb in question is future-tense, as here, is also common in the limitative type: in general, a speaker is less likely to be able to pin down to one particular day an event that has not yet taken place than one that already has. Another feature conducive to limitative expressions is the presence of a negative:

(10) *oúte tis xénos*   *aphîktai*   **khrónou**   **sukhnoû**   *ekeîthen*
nor any visitor   has.arrived.PF   time.GEN   long.GEN   from.there

Nor has any visitor arrived from there in a long time (Plato *Phaedo* 57a)

As with future-time events, so too with those that do not happen at all, the limitative construction – which must ultimately have developed from the Indo-European partitive genitive – is appropriate because the speaker is indicating that the event did not take place at any point in the given period of time, rather than assigning it affirmatively to one particular point in time.

All the limitative examples so far have the genitive of time, but, as already seen in the examples of nouns that take a punctual genitive of time, there is overlap between the genitive and the preposition *en* with the dative, and this extends into the limitative constructions as well. In particular, *en* is often used instead of the dative in yet another common context for the limitative: when multiple discrete events are said to have taken place over a period. Typical examples:

(11) **en miâi hēmérāi**   *Lárīsan kaì Hamaxitòn kaì Kolōnàs . . .*
in one.DAT day.DAT   Larisa and Hamaxitus and Colonae
parélabe
he.won.over.AOR

In one day he took control of Larisa, Hamaxitus, and Colonae
(Xenophon *Hellenica* 3.1.16)

(12) *taûta*   *dè xúmpanta . . .*   *egéneto*   **en étesi pentḗkonta** **málista**
these.things PCL all   happened.AOR in years.DAT fifty   about

And all these things happened in about fifty years (1.118.2 = Ch. 2 ex. (44))

In the first of these, the modifier *miâi* 'one' is a good sign of the limitative construction: one does not usually say that something happened on a single day unless it is an event one would not expect to fit into so short a period – often, as here, because it is a composite event of the sort that typifies the limitative event-type. The second shows a common subtype, in which, at the end of an extended narrative, an anaphoric pronoun (often *taûta* 'these things' or *tosaûta* 'this many things'), which sums up all the events that have taken place in that stretch of narrative (often, in histories, a season or a year), is the subject of a semantically light verb like *egéneto* 'took place, happened'.

In keeping with their compatibility with future-time events, limitative constructions are also at home in the protases of conditionals:

(13) *ouk ára éti*   *makheîtai*   *ei **en taútais** ou*   *makheîtai*
     not then any.more   he.will.fight   if in these.DAT not   he.will.fight
     taîs   ***hēmérais***
     the.DAT   days.DAT

> Then he will not fight any more if he doesn't fight during these days
> (Xenophon *Anabasis* 1.7.18)

Such conditionals, it will be seen, form a bridge between the limitative type and the next three types, which are closely related to each other.

Habitual, distributive, and modal expressions

All of the event types seen so far have, as their prototypical function, the assignment of (i) a single event, (ii) a composite, but bounded event, or (iii) the non-occurrence of that event to a particular point in time or stretch of time. But languages also need to deal with events that occur repeatedly, be it on a regular cycle or not. Consider the following two examples:

(14) **nuktòs**   **kaì hēmérās**   *ephúlatton*   *perì tà basíleia*
     night.GEN   and day.GEN   they.stood.guard.IMPF   around the palace

> Night and day they stood guard around the palace (Xenophon *Cyropaedia*
> 7.5.68 = Ch. 1 ex. (15))

(15) *drakhmḕn gàr*   ***tês hēmérās***   *hékastos elámbanen*
     a.drachma PCL   the.GEN day.GEN   each received.IMPF

> For each received a drachma per day (7.27.2 = Ch. 2 ex. (32))

In both passages, the imperfect is a sign (though not conclusive evidence) that the events described recur day after day. In (14), which I call habitual, the temporal expression simply describes an event as occurring regularly during the time in question: that is, *hēmérās* means approximately 'repeatedly during the day'. The same is also true of the expression in (15): once again, an event occurs repeatedly during the stated time. The difference is that (15), classified as a distributive expression, also conveys the idea that there is a one-to-one correspondence between the occurrence of the time noun and the action of the verb. The genitive case is frequently used for both types, but the distributive is often marked more strongly, with either *katá* with the accusative case,[8] the word *hékastos* 'each', or both:

(16) *hoùs*   **katà étos**   **hékaston**   *Korínthioi*   *épempon*
     whom   in year.ACC   each.ACC   the.Corinthians   sent.IMPF

those whom the Corinthians sent every year (1.56.2)

Another important feature of (14) is that *hēmérās* 'by day' is in parallel with *nuktós* 'by night'. When these two time nouns occur together, the emphasis on the whole lies not on fitting the event into a particular chronological framework, but rather on the more general circumstances under which the event is carried out – circumstances that could equally well be spatial ('by land or by sea') or instrumental ('by hook or by crook'). The genitive is also common when phrases with time nouns take on this modal nuance. But, as always, there is scope for individual nouns to take unusual constructions: *metá* with the accusative, which usually means 'after', with *hēmérā* as its object means 'by day'; and the morphological isolate *núktōr* frequently has the modal sense 'by night'.

Diachronic issues

One of the advantages of taking Ancient Greek as one's corpus is the ability to track the historical development of a construction over

---

[8] The original spatial sense of *katá* with the accusative was probably 'down(stream), with the flow, following', but it had early acquired a distributive sense (*hízonto katà stíkhas* "they sat down rank by rank" *Iliad* 3.326) that was easily transferred to the temporal sphere.

a considerable stretch of time. As it happens, in the period studied (*c*.8C BC–2C AD), the distribution of the various temporal expressions remains remarkably stable. Still, it is not completely static, and two main questions arise: (a) How does the split marking of the punctual construction arise, with some nouns taking the genitive, others the dative? (b) It has long been known that the dative case was undergoing a gradual decline in this period:[9] how did this affect its use in punctual constructions?

To answer the first question, it is useful to set Homer (*c*.8C BC) against Classical Attic of the 5–4C BC: in Homer, the division of time nouns into two categories (those, like day, month, and year, that take a punctual dative, and those, like night and the seasons, that take a genitive) has not yet been established, as all nouns can take a temporal dative; by the time of Thucydides, it is clearly in play. In other words, with the second group of nouns, contexts that had previously elicited the dative, come to require the genitive instead, as is well in keeping with the general retreat of the dative. But why does this happen only to certain time nouns, rather than to all of them? The answer lies in the nature of the constructions in which the two groups of nouns occur. Whereas the first group, which we may call calendrical time nouns, are frequently used to pinpoint when a particular event took place and so occur in prototypical punctual constructions, nouns of the latter, non-calendrical group, are more often used not to indicate, for example, which night an event took place, but simply to contrast its occurrence at night-time with other, daytime events (as in (7)). Because they lack the specificity of expressions in which a particular instance of the time noun is singled out, they lie on the border between the punctual and the modal-habitual type, and were thus prone to influence from the modal-habitual genitive. This was not only the natural choice in examples like (7), but also crept into what might reasonably be considered prototypical punctual constructions, like (6), which *do* specify a particular instance of the time noun. The genitive did not, however, wholly supplant the dative, which continued to be used occasionally with non-calendrical time nouns: see examples (46) and (47) in Chapter 2. That the dative was most likely

---

[9] See Bortone 2010: 154–5 (the decline of the local dative between Homer and Attic serving as an esp. close parallel to that of the temporal dative), 181–2; Horrocks 2010: 91, 107–8, 116–17, as well as Jannaris 1897: 341–2, and Luraghi 2003: 330–1.

to be maintained in the narrow confines of dating formulae is confirmed by the Ptolemaic papyri, where it continues to be used in this way with *núx* ('night'; see example (185) in Chapter 3). The second issue is more complicated. Given what has just been described, one might expect a continued decline of the dative, with the genitive replacing it even in the calendrical time nouns. But in fact it enjoys something of a renaissance, even spreading into limitative constructions where previously one would have expected the genitive or *en* with the dative. At the same time, *en* is also becoming more common. Understanding why both of these developments take place requires looking not only to the distribution of these developments in different types of texts, but also beyond Greek, to external factors. First, consider the increase of the dative in limitative constructions. A typical example:

(17) **dusìn hēmérais**   *katanúsās*   *eis tòn ... aigialón*
     two.DAT days.DAT   having.made.it   to the ... shore

Having made it to the shore in two days (Diodorus Siculus 14.61.4 = Ch. 3 ex. (159))

This innovation is widely attested: there are good examples in Polybius (2C BC), Diodorus (1C BC), Plutarch (late 1C–early 2C AD), Epictetus (early 2C AD), as well as in papyri (though only securely from the 2C AD; see the final section in Chapter 3); it is not especially common in the Pentateuch (3C BC), but it does occur in the New Testament (1C AD). The explanation usually given for this unexpected rise in the dative is that it was caused by the influence of Latin, whose ablative of time is used in limitative expressions. The above distribution confirms this suspicion: it is not yet there in the comparatively early Pentateuch, occurs early in Polybius and Diodorus, who are both working in a Roman environment, but not in Ptolemaic papyri, where Latin will not have exercised nearly as much influence. But as Latin becomes more prominent in Egypt, it even starts to occur there in the imperial period.

The rise of *en* can also be attributed to outside influence, but here the pattern is different. In Polybius, it is apparently replacing the genitive as the preferred limitative marker, but it is not especially common in Diodorus or Plutarch, where it continues to be used primarily in limitative constructions generally and in punctual ones with non-calendrical time nouns: while there is a very slight growth of punctual *en* (Chapter 3, exx. 179 and 180), it is not as pronounced as that of the limitative dative. Where *en* really does come to the fore is in the papyri (where with *étos* 'year' in particular it is a common alternative to the simple punctual dative) and, even more so, in the Septuagint and New Testament, where its rise must be due to contact with the Semitic languages. This is particularly easy to show for Biblical Greek: the presence of *en* in the Septuagint corresponds to that of *bə* in the Hebrew, and many of the examples in the New Testament have clear Septuagintal antecedents. A couple of examples show the wide use of *en* in contexts for which there are only a very few Attic parallels:

(18) *egéneto dè*   ***en têi hēmérāi***   ***têi trítēi***
      it.happened PCL   in the.DAT day.DAT   the.DAT third.DAT

      And it happened on the third day (Gen. 34:25 = Ch. 4 ex. (10))

(19) ***en ekeínēi***   ***têi hēmérāi***   *prosêlthon autôi Saddoukaîoi*
      on that.DAT   the.DAT day.DAT   came   to.him Sadducees

      On that day, some Sadducees came to him (Mt. 22:23 = Ch. 4 ex. (48))

In the first example, a punctual construction in which *hēmérā* is modified by an ordinal number would typically have the dative of time in Attic. Still, this example is the best Attic of the three, for with this particular verb, *egéneto* ('it happened'), constructions with *en* are unusually common, as the general situation is often that of summing up multiple events that took place in the period in question:[10]

(20) *tosaûta*   *mèn*   ***en tôi thérei***   *egéneto*
      this.many.things   PCL   in the.DAT summer.DAT   happened

      All this happened during the summer (2.68.9 = Ch. 2 ex. (72))

In the second example, the use of *en* is again grammatical Attic, although one has to move forward to Demosthenes to find a good parallel; he can use *en* to mark punctual constructions with the calendrical time nouns, but only in certain emphatic contexts, as if to zoom in on the point at which the event took place in the wider

---

[10] Cf. also Th. 1.87.6 (= Ch. 2 ex. (45)), which has an *en* phrase with *étos* 'year' modified by an ordinal, with *egéneto* as the main verb.

frame of the day, in effect treating the punctual construction as if it were limitative. The following example, for instance, comes from one of the most dramatic moments in any of Demosthenes' speeches, when he highlights his role (in his eyes at least) as the savior of Athens:

(21) *ephánēn toínun hoûtos*   **en ekeínēi têi hēmérāi**   *egṓ*
    I.appeared then that.man   in that.DAT the.DAT day.DAT   I

So I appeared as that man on that day, I did (Demosthenes *On the crown* 173 = Ch. 3 ex. (97))

As in punctual constructions, so too the limitative use of *en* is particularly widespread in Judeo-Christian language, as can be seen from its frequency with the plural of *hēmérā*. In the New Testament, for instance, there are twenty-two examples of *en* with the dative plural *hēmérais* modified by a demonstrative; but, taking Herodotus, Thucydides, Xenophon, Plato, and Demosthenes all together, there are only six such examples.[11] That this feature of the New Testament shows the stylistic influence of the Septuagint is shown not only by the Septuagintalizing context of many of the New Testamental constructions, but also by the sheer number of such constructions in the Septuagint: 220 examples of *en* with the plural *hēmérais*, with over sixty of these occurring with the demonstrative. The same pattern holds true when a personal name in the genitive takes the place of the demonstrative; thus, an expression like the following, while perfectly grammatical Attic (*en* with the dative is exactly the construction one would expect in a past-time limitative phrase), is still very stylistically characteristic of Biblical Greek:

(22) *egéneto*   **en taîs hēmérais**   **Hērṓidou basiléōs** ...   *hiereús tis*
    there.was   in the.DAT days.DAT   of.Herod king   priest a.certain

There was in the days of king Herod a certain priest (Lk. 1:5)

In the end, then, what happens to the dative and *en* cannot be reduced to a scenario in which one expression simply gives way to the other: both come to be used more broadly than in Attic, the former because of Latin, the latter because of the Semitic languages.

---

[11] And even these six examples look very different from the New Testament examples: see Ch. 4 n. 80.

BIBLIOGRAPHY

Adams, J. N. (2003) *Bilingualism and the Latin Language*. Cambridge.

Aejmelaeus, A. (1993) *On the Trail of the Septuagint Translators*. Kampen, Netherlands.

Allan, R. J. (2003) *The Middle Voice in Ancient Greek*. Amsterdam.

(2007) "Sense and sentence complexity: Sentence structure, sentence connection, and tense-aspect as indicators of narrative mode in Thucydides' *Histories*," in Allan and Buijs: 93–121.

and M. Buijs (eds.) (2007) *The Language of Literature: Linguistic Approaches to Classical Texts*. Leiden.

Asheri, D. (ed.) (1988) *Erodoto: Le Storie*, Vol. 1, Book 1. Milan.

Bakker, E. J. (1993) "Boundaries, topics and the structure of discourse: An investigation of the Greek particle δέ," *Studies in Language* 17 (2): 275–311.

(ed.) (1997a) *Grammar as Interpretation: Greek Literature in its Linguistic Contexts*. Leiden.

(1997b) *Poetry in Speech: Orality and Homeric Discourse*. Ithaca, NY.

(ed.) (2010) *A Companion to the Ancient Greek Language*. Malden, MA.

Bakker, S. J. (2007) "Adjective ordering in Herodotus: A pragmatic explanation," in Allan and Buijs: 188–210.

(2009) *The Noun Phrase in Ancient Greek: A Functional Analysis of the Order and Articulation of NP Constituents in Herodotus*. Leiden.

and G. C. Wakker (2009) *Discourse Cohesion in Ancient Greek*. Leiden.

Barrett, C. K. (1978) *The Gospel According to St. John: An Introduction with Commentary and Notes on the Greek Text*, 2nd edn. Philadelphia, PA.

Basset, L. (1994) "Structure des syntagmes prépositionnels en grec ancien," in Jacquinod: 151–64.

(2009) "The use of the imperfect to express completed states of affairs: The imperfect as a marker of narrative cohesion," in Bakker and Wakker: 205–19.

Beale, G. K. (1999) *The Book of Revelation: A Commentary on the Greek Text*. Grand Rapids, MI.

Benveniste, E. (1935) *Origines de la formation des noms en indo-européen*. Paris.

Bers, V. (1984) *Greek Poetic Syntax in the Classical Age*. New Haven, CT.

Beyer, K. (1968) *Semitische Syntax im Neuen Testament*, Vol. 1. *Satzlehre* Part I, 2nd edn. Göttingen.

Bhat, D. N. S. (1999) *The Prominence of Tense, Aspect and Mood*. Amsterdam.

Binnick, R. I. (1991) *Time and the Verb: A Guide to Tense and Aspect*. New York.

Biraud, M. (1994) "L'Expression de la périodicité en attique classique et chez Hérodote: Cas, prépositions, déterminants," in Jacquinod: 165–80.

Bortone, P. (2010) *Greek Prepositions: From Antiquity to Present*. Oxford.

Breitenbach, H. R. (1967) "Xenophon," *RE* 9A Part 2: 1569–2052.

Breitenbach, L. (1878) *Xenophons Memorabilien*. Berlin.

Brixhe, C. (1994) "Autour de l' 'OBJET'," in Jacquinod: 21–44.

Buijs, M. (2005) *Clause Combining in Ancient Greek Narrative Discourse*. Leiden.

(2007) "Aspectual differences and narrative technique: Xenophon's *Hellenica* and *Agesilaus*," in Allan and Buijs: 122–53.

Bultmann, R. (1971) *The Gospel of John: A Commentary* (tr. G. R. Beasley-Murray). Philadelphia, PA.

Burnet, J. (1924) *Plato's Euthyphro, Apology of Socrates, and Crito*. Oxford.

Chanet, A.-M. (1994) "Sème négatif et génitif grec," in Jacquinod: 45–62.

Chantraine, P. (1953) *Grammaire homérique*, Vol. 2. Paris.

(1958) *Grammaire homérique*, Vol. 1. Paris.

(1999) *Dictionnaire étymologique de la langue grecque*, w. supplement. Paris.

Charles, R. H. (1920) *A Critical and Exegetical Commentary on the Revelation of St. John*, Vol. 1. New York.

Christidis, A.-F. (ed.) (2007) *A History of Ancient Greek: From the Beginnings to Late Antiquity*. Cambridge.

Clackson, J. (1994) *The Linguistic Relationship between Armenian and Greek*. Oxford.

(2007) *Indo-European Linguistics*. Cambridge.

Comrie, B. (1976) *Aspect*. Cambridge.

Cornford, F. M. (1937) *Plato's Cosmology*. London.

Crespo, E., J. de la Villa, and A. R. Revuelta (eds.) (2006) *Word Classes and Related Topics in Ancient Greek*. Louvain-la-Neuve.

Delbrück, B. (1893) *Vergleichende Syntax der indogermanischen Sprachen*, Vol. 1. Strasbourg.

De Rosalia, A. (1991) "Il latino di plutarco," in G. D'Ippolito and I. Gallo (eds.), *Strutture formali dei "Moralia" di Plutarco: Atti del III Convegno plutarcheo Palermo, 3–5 maggio 1989*. Naples: 445–59.

Devine, A. M. and L. D. Stephens (2006) *Latin Word Order: Structured Meaning and Information*. Oxford.

(2013) *Semantics for Latin: An Introduction*. Oxford.

Dewald, C. J. (2005) *Thucydides' War Narrative: A Structural Study*. Berkeley, CA.

Dik, H. (1995) *Word Order in Ancient Greek: A Pragmatic Account of Word Order Variation in Herodotus*. Amsterdam.

(1997) "Interpreting adjective position in Herodotus," in Bakker (1997a): 55–76.

(2007) *Word Order in Greek Tragic Dialogue*. Oxford.

Dillery, J. (1995) *Xenophon and the History of His Times*. London.

Dindorf, L. (1862) *Xenophontis Memorabilia Socratis*. Oxford.

Dittenberger, W. (1881) "Sprachliche Kriterien für die Chronologie der platonischen Dialoge," *Hermes* 16 (3): 321–45.

Dover, K. J. (1955) "The Patmos scholia and the text of Thucydides," *Classical Review* 5: 134–7.

(1960) *Greek Word Order*. Cambridge.

Drettas, G. (2007) "The Translation (Targum) of the Septuagint" (tr. W. J. Lillie), in Christidis: 887–96.

Dubuisson, M. (1979) "Le Latin des historiens grecs," *Les Études classiques* 47: 89–106.

(1985) *Le Latin de Polybe: Les Implications historiques d'un cas de bilinguisme*. Paris.

Duhoux, Y. (1992) *Le Verbe grec ancien: Éléments de morphologie et de syntaxe historiques*. Louvain-la-Neuve.

Dyer, R. (1974) "The coming of night in Homer," *Glotta* 52: 31–6.

Edwards, M. W. (1997) "Homeric style and oral poetics," in Morris and Powell: 261–83.

Evans, T. V. (2001) *Verbal Syntax in the Greek Pentateuch: Natural Greek Usage and Hebrew Interference*. Oxford.

(2010) "Standard Koine Greek in Third Century BC Papyri," in T. Gagos, (ed.), *Proceedings of the 25th International Congress of Papyrology*. Ann Arbor, MI: 197–206.

and D. D. Obbink (eds.) (2010) *The Language of the Papyri*. Oxford.

Fanning, B. M. (1990) *Verbal Aspect in New Testament Greek*. Oxford.

Fernández Marcos, N. (2001) *The Septuagint in Context: Introduction to the Greek Versions of the Bible* (tr. W. G. E. Watson). Boston, MA.

Fillmore, C. J. (1969) "Types of lexical information," in F. Kiefer (ed.), *Studies in Syntax and Semantics*. Dordrecht: 109–37.

Fränkel, H. (1960) *Wege und Formen frühgriechischen Denkens*, 2nd edn. Munich.

García Domingo, E. (1979) *Latinismos en la koiné (en los documentos epigráficos desde el 212 a. J. C. hasta el 14 d. J. C.)*. Burgos.

Gautier, L. (1911) *La Langue de Xénophon*. Geneva.

George, C. H. (2005) *Expressions of Agency in Ancient Greek*. Cambridge.

(2006) "The spatial use of ἀνά and κατά with the accusative in Homer," *Glotta* 82: 70–95.

(2008) Review of Rijksbaron (2006a), *BMCR* 2008.02.24.

(2010) "Jewish and Christian Greek," in Bakker: 267–80.

(2011) "The temporal characteristics of the historical present in Thucydides," in Lallot et al.: 223–40.

Gildersleeve, B. L. (1903) "Temporal sentences of limit in Greek," *American Journal of Philology* 24: 388–407.

(1911) *Syntax of Classical Greek from Homer to Demosthenes*, Vol. 2. New York.

Givón, T. (1985) "Iconicity, isomorphism and non-arbitrary coding in syntax," in Haiman: 187–219.

BIBLIOGRAPHY

Gomme, A. W. (1956a) *A Historical Commentary on Thucydides*, Vol. 2, Books 2–3. Oxford.

(1956b) *A Historical Commentary on Thucydides*, Vol. 3, Books 4–5.24. Oxford.

Gomme, A. W., A. Andrewes, and K. J. Dover (1970) *A Historical Commentary on Thucydides*, Vol. 4, Books 5.25–7. Oxford.

Gomme, A. W., A. Andrewes, and K. J. Dover (1981) *A Historical Commentary on Thucydides*, Vol. 5, Book 8. Oxford.

Haiman, J. (ed.) (1985) *Iconicity in Syntax*. Amsterdam.

Hajnal, I. (1995) *Studien zum mykenischen Kasussystem*. Berlin.

Hannah, R. (2009) *Time in Antiquity*. London.

Hering, J. (1935) *Lateinisches bei Appian*. Leipzig.

Heubeck, A. and A. Hoekstra (1989) *A Commentary on Homer's Odyssey*, Vol. 2, Books 9–16. Oxford.

Hoekstra, A. (1965) *Homeric Modifications of Formulaic Prototypes: Studies in the Development of Greek Epic Diction*. Amsterdam.

(1989) "Books XIII–XVI," in Heubeck and Hoekstra: 145–287.

Hornblower, S. (1996) *A Commentary on Thucydides*, Vol. 2, Books 4–5.24. Oxford.

(2008) *A Commentary on Thucydides*, Vol. 3, Books 5.25–8.109. Oxford.

Horrocks, G. C. (1981) *Space and Time in Homer: Prepositional and Adverbial Particles in the Greek Epic*. New York.

(2010) *Greek: A History of the Language and its Speakers*, 2nd edn. Malden, MA.

Hude, K. (1927) *Scholia in Thucydidem ad optimos codices collata*. Leipzig.

Hutchinson, G. O. (1985) *Aeschylus: Septem Contra Thebas*. Oxford.

Jacquinod, B. (ed.) (1994) *Cas et prépositions en grec ancien*. Saint-Étienne.

(ed.) (2000) *Études sur l'aspect verbal chez Platon*. Saint-Étienne.

Jannaris, A. N. (1897) *An Historical Greek Grammar, Chiefly of the Attic Dialect*. London.

Janse, M. (2007) "The Greek of the New Testament," in Christidis: 646–53.

Jiménez, M. D. (1998) "La expresión de relaciones temporales en ático clásico," in M. E. Torrego (ed.), *Nombres y funciones: Estudios de sintaxis griega y latina*. Madrid: 65–110.

Jong, I. J. F. de, and R. Nünlist (eds.) (2007) *Time in Ancient Greek Literature*. Leiden.

Käsemann, E. (1980) *Commentary on Romans* (tr. G. W. Bromiley). Grand Rapids, MI.

Kennedy, G. A. (1963) *The Art of Persuasion in Greece*. Princeton, NJ.

Kirk, G. S. (1990) *The Iliad: A Commentary*, Vol. 2, Books 5–8. Cambridge.

Klein, W. (1994) *Time in Language*. London.

Kölligan, D. (2007) *Suppletion und Defektivität im griechischen Verbum*. Bremen.

Lallot, J. (2007) "L'Opposition aspectuelle 'Présent' – Aoriste dans la Grande Loi de Gortyne," in Allan and Buijs: 154–67.

Lallot, J., A. Rijksbaron, B. Jacquinod, and M. Buijs (eds.) (2011) *The Historical Present in Thucydides: Semantics and Narrative Function*. Leiden.

Lambdin, T. O. (1971) *Introduction to Biblical Hebrew*. New York.

Lange, N. de (2007) "Jewish Greek," in Christidis: 638–45.

Langslow, D. (2002) "Approaching bilingualism in corpus languages," in J. N. Adams, M. Janse, and S. Swain (eds.), *Bilingualism in Ancient Society*. Oxford: 23–51.

(tr. and ed.) (2009) *Jacob Wackernagel: Lectures on Syntax with special reference to Greek, Latin, and Germanic*. Oxford.

(2012) "The language of Polybius since Foucault and Dubuisson," in C. Smith and L. M. Yarrow (eds.), *Imperialism, Cultural Politics, and Polybius*. Oxford: 85–110.

Lass, R. (1994) *Old English: A Historical Linguistic Companion*. Cambridge.

Leukart, A. (1987) "*Po-ro-qa-ta-jo, to-sa-pe-mo, a-mo-ra-ma* and others: Further evidence for Proto-Greek collective formations in Mycenaean and early alphabetic Greek," *Minos* 20–22: 343–65.

Leumann, M. (1950) *Homerische Wörter*. Basel.

L'Huillier, M. (1999) *Advanced French Grammar*. Cambridge.

Lorente Fernández, P. (2003) *L'Aspect verbal en grec ancien: Le Choix des thèmes verbaux chez Isocrate*. Louvain-la-Neuve.

Luraghi, S. (2003) *On the Meaning of Prepositions and Cases: The Expression of Semantic Roles in Ancient Greek*. Amsterdam.

MacDowell, D. M. (1990) *Demosthenes: Against Meidias*. Oxford.

Maloney, E. C. (1981) *Semitic Interference in Marcan Syntax*. Chico, CA.

Masqueray, P. (1954) *Xénophon: Anabase*, Vol. 2, Books 4–7. Paris.

Mastronarde, D. J. (1993) *Introduction to Attic Greek*. Berkeley, CA.

Matić, D. (2003) "Topic, focus, and discourse structure: Ancient Greek Word Order," *Studies in Language* 27 (3): 573–633.

Mayser, E. (1934) *Grammatik der griechischen Papyri aus der Ptolemäerzeit*, Vol. 2.2.: *Satzlehre: Analytischer Teil, zweite Hälfte*. Berlin.

McCarter, P. K., Jr. (2004) "Hebrew," in R. D. Woodard (ed.), *The Cambridge Encyclopedia of the World's Ancient Languages*. Cambridge: 319–64.

Metzger, B. M. (1971) *A Textual Commentary on the Greek New Testament*. London.

Mommsen, T. (1895) *Beiträge zu der Lehre von den griechischen Präpositionen*. Berlin.

Moorhouse, A. C. (1982) *The Syntax of Sophocles*. Leiden.

Morris, I. and B. Powell (eds.) (1997) *A New Companion to Homer*. Leiden.

Muchnová, D. (2011) *Entre conjonction, connecteur et particule: Le Cas de ἐπεί en grec ancien*. Prague.

Muraoka, T. and B. Porten (2003) *A Grammar of Egyptian Aramaic*, 2nd edn. Leiden.

Napoli, M. (2006) *Aspect and Actionality in Homeric Greek: A Contrastive Analysis*. Pisa.

Nilsson, M. P. (1920) *Primitive Time-Reckoning*. Lund.

Palm, J. (1955) *Über Sprache und Stil des Diodoros von Sizilien*. Lund.

Palmer, L. R. (1962) "The language of Homer," in Wace and Stubbings: 75–178.

Pestman, P. W. (1990) *The New Papyrological Primer*, 5th edn. of M. David and B. A. van Groningen, *Papyrological Primer*. Leiden.

Porter, S. (1989) *Verbal Aspect in the Greek of the New Testament with Reference to Tense and Mood*. New York.

Rijksbaron, A. (2006a) *The Syntax and Semantics of the Verb in Classical Greek*, 3rd (US) edn. Chicago.

(2006b) "The meaning and word class of πρότερον and τὸ πρότερον," in Crespo, de la Villa, and Revuelta: 441–53.

Rochette, B. (2010) "Greek and Latin bilingualism," in Bakker (2010): 281–93.

Rood, T. (2007) "Thucydides," in De Jong and Nünlist: 131–46.

Rosenthal, F. (1963) *A Grammar of Biblical Aramaic*. Wiesbaden.

Ruijgh, C. J. (1971) *Autour de "τε épique": Études sur la syntaxe grecque*. Amsterdam.

(1994) "La Préposition ἐπί: Valeurs sémantiques et choix des cas," in Jacquinod: 133–48.

Ruipérez, M. S. (1982) *Structure du système des aspects et des temps du verbe en grec ancien* (tr. M. Plénat and P. Serça). Paris.

Rusten, J. S. (1989) *Thucydides: The Peloponnesian War Book II*. Cambridge.

Rutherford, R. B. (1992) *Homer: Odyssey Books XIX and XX*. Cambridge.

Segert, S. (1986) *Altaramäische Grammatik mit Bibliographie, Chrestomathie und Glossar*. Leipzig.

Slings, S. R. (1997) "Figures of speech and their lookalikes: Two further exercises in the pragmatics of the Greek sentence," in Bakker (1997a): 169–214.

Smith, C. S. (1997) *The Parameter of Aspect*, 2nd edn. Dordrecht.

Smith, J. R. (1903) *Xenophon: Memorabilia*. Boston, MA.

Smyth, H. W. (1920) *Greek Grammar*. Cambridge, MA.

Sommer, F. (1950) "Zum Zahlwort," *Sitzungsberichte der Bayerischen Akademie der Wissenschaften, Philosophisch-historische Klasse:* Heft 7.

Stadter, P. A. (1989) *A Commentary on Plutarch's Pericles*. Chapel Hill, NC.

Stagg, F. (1972) "The abused aorist," *Journal of Biblical Literature* 91: 222–31.

Stallbaum, G. (1846) *Platonis Apologia et Crito*. Gotha and London.

Stein, H. (1901) *Herodotos*, Vol. 1, Book 1, 6th edn. Berlin.

(1908) *Herodotos*, Vol. 4, Book 7, 6th edn. Berlin.

Tarbell, F. B. (1880) *The Philippics of Demosthenes*. Boston, MA.

Taylor, A. E. (1929) *Plato: Timaeus and Critias*. London.

Thompson, R. (1998) "Instrumentals, datives, locatives and ablatives: The -φι case form in Mycenaean and Homer," *PCPS* 44: 219–50.

Thompson, S. (1985) *The Apocalypse and Semitic Syntax*. Cambridge.

Tov, E. (1999a) *The Greek and Hebrew Bible: Collected Essays on the Septuagint* (= *Vetus Testamentum* suppl. 72). Leiden.

(1999b) "The nature and study of the translation technique of the Septuagint," in Tov: 239–46.

Trédé, M. (1992) *Kairos: L'À-propos et l'occasion*. Paris.

Trevett, J. (1992) *Apollodoros the Son of Pasion*. Oxford.

Usher, S. (1999) *Greek Oratory: Tradition and Originality*. Oxford.

Vendler, Z. (1957) "Verbs and times," *Philosophical Review* 66: 143–60.

Ventris, M. and J. Chadwick (1973) *Documents in Mycenaean Greek*, 2nd edn. Cambridge.

Verkuyl, H. J. (1972) *On the Compositional Nature of the Aspects*. Dordrecht.

H. de Swart, and A. van Hout (eds.) (2005) *Perspectives on Aspect*. Dordrecht.

Villa, J. de la (1994a) "The relevance of nominal semantics for the syntax of Greek prepositionnal [sic] phrases," in Jacquinod: 193–209.

(1994b) "El léxico como determinante de la función: Los sintagmas preposicionales que expresan tiempo en Homero," in *Actas del VIII Congreso Español de Estudios Clásicos*, Vol. 1. Madrid: 331–8.

Voelz, J. W. (1984) "The Language of the New Testament," *ANRW* II.25 (2): 893–977.

Wace, A. J. B. and F. H. Stubbings (eds.) (1962) *A Companion to Homer*. London.

Wachter, R. (2012) "The other view: Focus on linguistic innovations in the Homeric epics," in Ø. Andersen and D. T. T. Haug (eds.), *Relative Chronology in Early Epic Greek Poetry*. Cambridge: 65–79.

Wackernagel, J. (1909) "Zur griechischen Wortlehre," *Glotta* 2: 1–8.

(1920) *Vorlesungen über Syntax*, Vol. 1. Basel.

Waltke, B. K. and M. O'Connor (1990) *An Introduction to Biblical Hebrew Syntax*. Winona Lake, IN.

Ward, J. S. (2007) "Roman Greek: Latinisms in the Greek of Flavius Josephus," *CQ* 57: 632–49.

Watkins, C. (1965) "Latin *nox* 'by night': A problem in syntactic reconstruction," in A. Heinz, M. Karaś, T. Milewski, J. Safarewicz and W. Taszycki (eds.), *Symbolae linguisticae in honorem Georgii Kuryłowicz*. Wrocław: 351–8. Repr. in *Selected Writings*. Innsbruck, 1994: Vol. 1: 97–104.

Weiss, M. (2009) *Outline of the Historical and Comparative Grammar of Latin*. Ann Arbor, MI.

Wevers, J. W. (ed.) (1974) *Septuaginta*, Vol. 1: *Genesis*. Göttingen.

(1993) *Notes on the Greek Text of Genesis*. Atlanta.

Wierzbicka, A. (1993) "Why do we say *in* April, *on* Thursday, *at* 10 o'clock? In search of an explanation," *Studies in Language* 17 (2): 437–54.

Wilamowitz-Moellendorff, U. von (1880) "Exkurse zu Euripides Medea," *Hermes* 15: 481–523 (= *Kleine Schriften* 1.17–59).

Yunis, H. (2001) *Demosthenes: On the Crown*. Cambridge.

Zeyl, D. J. (tr.) (1997) *Timaeus*, in J. M. Cooper (ed.), *Plato: Complete Works*. Indianapolis: 1224–91.

Ziegler, J. (ed.) (1976) *Septuaginta*, Vol. 15: *Jeremias, Baruch, Threni, Epistula Jeremiae*. Göttingen.

GENERAL INDEX

accusative of time, 304–6
    distinguished from other accusatives, 56–9
    in Demosthenes, 170–3; in punctual
        expressions, 182–5
    in Epictetus, 228–9
    in Herodotus, 185–93; in punctual
        expressions, 185–7
    in Homer, 290–2, 296–300
    in papyri, 235
    in the New Testament, 261–3
    in the Septuagint, 246–52; in punctual
        expressions, 248–52
    in Thucydides, 60–76
    in Xenophon, 119–24
adjectives of posteriority in temporal
    expressions, 31–3
adnominal genitive, 44–5
Apollodorus, 181
approximative expressions, 107–16, 147–52
aspect, 25–7

Biblical Greek, 245–82
bilingualism, 5

calendrical time nouns, 101–3, 174, 202,
    203, 212
cardinal numbers in temporal expressions,
    29–30

dative of degree of difference, 52–5
dative of possession, 52
dative of reference, 51–2
dative of respect, 51
dative of time, 1, 306–7
    distinguished from other datives, 50–5
    durative, 228
    in Demosthenes, 173–4

in Diodorus, 211–12
in Herodotus, 193–204
in Homer, 284–8, 293, 301
in papyri, 231, 234, 237
in Plato, 159–66
in Plutarch, 217–19
in Polybius, 204–5
in the New Testament, 263–74
in the Septuagint, 252–61
in Thucydides, 77–103
in Xenophon, 125–30, 145–7
limitative, 204–5, 217–19, 228
replaced by genitive of time, 312–13
Demosthenes, 169–85
Diodorus Siculus, 211–17
distributive expressions, 10, 15–17, 310–11
    in Herodotus, 196
    in Thucydides, 107–8
    in Xenophon, 122–3, 126–7, 129–30
durative expressions, 8–12, 304–6
    in Demosthenes, 170–3
    in Epictetus, 228–9
    in Herodotus, 187–93
    in Homer, 296–300
    in Plato, 156–9; with χρόνος, 166–9
    in Thucydides, 60–76
    in Xenophon, 119–24, 153–4
    negative, 21–4

Epictetus, 228–30
event type, 7–25

genitive absolute, 36–44, 300
    common in Diodorus, 212–13
genitive as verbal object, 35–6
genitive of comparison, 35
genitive of measure, 35–6

genitive of time, 1, 306–7, 308–10, 310–11
  distinguished from other genitives, 34–50
  in Demosthenes, 174–81
  in Diodorus, 212
  in Epictetus, 229
  in Herodotus, 193–204
  in Homer, 284, 300
  in papyri, 232–3, 234, 236, 240
  in Plato, 159–66
  in Plutarch, 219–21
  in Polybius, 206
  in the New Testament, 276
  in Thucydides, 77–103
  in Xenophon, 119–22, 125–30, 144–5
  less common in Homer, 289–90
  replacing dative of time, 312–13

habitual expressions, 10, 15–17, 310–11
  in Xenophon, 119–22, 129–30, 130–43
  negative, 17–18
Herodotus, 185–204
historical present in punctual expressions, 27
Homer, 283–303

instrumental dative, 50

Jiménez, M. D., 28–34

Latin influence on Greek temporal
  expressions, 5, 205, 212, 232, 244,
  264, 313
limitative expressions, 10, 12–15, 308–10
  and multiplicity of events, 13
  in Demosthenes, 173–85
  in Herodotus, 193–204
  in papyri, 232–3, 238
  in Plato, 159–66; with χρόνος, 166–9
  in Thucydides: day, month, year, 89; night,
    seasons, 77–103; χρόνος, 103–6
  in Xenophon: day, month, year, 125–30;
    night, seasons, 130–43; χρόνος,
    144–54
  negative, 19–21
  telicity of, 12–14

modal expressions, 10, 16, 76–101, 310–11
  in Demosthenes, 180–1
  in Herodotus, 197–9
  in Xenophon, 119–22, 126–7, 129–30

modifiers role in determining temporal
  expressions, 27–34, 252–7
Mons Claudianus, 232

negatives in temporal expressions, 17–24, 309
New Testament, 261–82

ordinal numbers in temporal expressions,
  33–4

papyri, 169–244
partitive genitive, 45–50
phonotactics, 209
Plato, 156–69
Plutarch, 217–27
poetry, low frequency of temporal
  expressions in, 4–5
Polybius, 204–11
punctual expressions, 8–12, 306–7
  in Demosthenes, 173–85
  in Herodotus, 185–7, 193–204
  in papyri, 237
  in Plato, 159–66
  in Thucydides: day, month, year, 89;
    night, seasons, 77–103
  in Xenophon: day, month, year,
    125–30
    night, seasons, 130–43; χρόνος, 144–54
  negative, 18–19

quantifying adjectives in temporal
  expressions, 29–30

Semitic influence on Greek temporal
  expressions, 5, 245–82, 315
Septuagint, 245–61
syntactic ambiguities, 34–59

Thucydides, 60–117
  compared with Xenophon, 154–6

Vendler, Z., 8
verbs of motion, 226–7
verbs of ruling, 189–93

word order, 74, 189–93

Xenophon, 118–56
  compared with Thucydides, 154–6

INDEX OF GREEK WORDS

ἅμα, 43
ἀνά + accusative, 209–10
ἀναπίπτω, 229
ἄρχω, 189–93
αὐτός ("the same"), 30–1
βασιλεύω, 189–93
γίγνομαι, 185–7
ἐγένετο in Biblical Greek, 254–5
διά + genitive, 70–3, 76, 122–4, 155, 156–9,
    172–3, 188, 305
    punctual in Diodorus, 216–17
    punctual in Plutarch, 227
διάγω, 56–7
ἔαρ
    accusative of time, 121–2
    genitive of time, 100
εἰς, 296–300
εἷς, 13
ἕκαστος, 16, 311
ἐν, 2–4, 14, 30, 82–4, 87–9, 103–6, 130–43,
    144–54, 155, 156, 159–65, 177–80,
    203–4, 206–8, 212, 222–4, 229,
    237–8, 252–9, 276–82, 287, 307,
    309, 315
    with ἡμέρα, 126–8, 276–82
    with μήν, 129
    with νύξ, 92–4
ἐνιαυτός
    accusative of time, 68–9,
        296–300
    dative of time, 196
    distinguished from ἔτος, 294–6
    genitive of time, 86, 174–5
    in papyri, 240–1
    with διά + genitive, 172–3
    with εἰς, 296–300
    with ἐπί + accusative, 123
ἐπέχω, 58

ἐπί + accusative, 70, 73–6, 122–4, 154, 155,
    156–9, 170–2, 189–93, 305
ἐπί + dative, 287, 293–4
ἐπί + genitive, 233–4, 237
ἐπιγιγνόμενος, 30, 32
ἔτος
    accusative of time, 68, 182–3, 246
    dative of time, 86, 243–4, 258–9, 260–1,
        272–4
    distinguished from ἐνιαυτός, 294–6
    genitive of time, 86, 162–5, 179–80,
        202, 300
    in papyri, 241–4
    with διά + genitive, 159
    with ἐν, 86–7, 162–5, 179–80, 258–9
    with ἐπί + accusative, 189–93
    ἐτῶν in expressions of age, 35–6
ἦμαρ, 288–94
    accusative of time, 289–92
    dative of time, 293
    with ἐπί + dative, 293–4
    νύκτας τε καὶ ἦμαρ, 289–92
ἡμάτιος, 288–9
ἡμέρα
    accusative of time, 61–6, 119–21, 183–5,
        246–8, 262
    with πᾶσαν, 188
    dative of time, 77–8, 102–3, 125–8, 165,
        173–4, 195–6, 211–12, 219, 231–2,
        252–9, 259–60, 264–6
    genitive of time, 16, 17, 78–82, 119–21,
        125–8, 177, 196–8, 220–1, 275–6
    with τῆς αὐτῆς, 206
    in papyri, 234
    rare in epic poetry, 288
    with διά + genitive, 157
    with ἐν, 97–100, 131–5, 142–3
    with ἐπί + accusative, 122, 158, 170–2

ἡμέρα (cont.)
with ἐπί + genitive, 233–4, 237
with μετά + accusative, 6–7
with ὑπό + accusative, 109–12, 235–6
θέρος, 100–1
accusative of time, 67–8
dative of time, 97, 206, 301
genitive of time, 95–7, 121–2, 131–5,
142–3
in genitive absolutes, 37–43
in Homer, 301
in papyri, 239
with ἐν, 84–5, 129–30, 177, 180, 237–8
τοῦ αὐτοῦ θέρους, 27
τοῦ ἐπιγιγνομένου θέρους, 27
καιρός, 106, 150
κατά + accusative, 10, 16, 147–52, 155, 311
common in Diodorus, 213–16
common in Polybius, 210–11
in approximative expressions, 107–16
in distributive expressions, 107–9
κατόπιν, 223
λοιπός, 30, 105
μὲν ... δέ, 9, 18, 199, 239, 304
μένω, 58–9, 61
μετά + accusative, 6–7, 311
μετόπωρον
genitive of time, 121–2
μήν
accusative of time, 67
dative of time, 84–5, 129–30, 237
genitive of time, 84–5, 129–30, 175–7,
180, 236–7
in papyri, 236–8
with ἐν, 82–4, 125–8, 177–9, 252–9, 276–82
with ἐπί + accusative, 158
with ἐπί + genitive, 237
νύκτωρ, 311
νύξ, 100–1
accusative of time, 66–7, 119–21, 208–9,
235, 246
punctual, 248–52
dative of time, 89–90, 95, 102–3, 135–7,
142–3, 201–2, 234, 266–7, 288
genitive of time, 1–4, 17, 91–2, 95,
102–3, 119–21, 130–1, 135–43,
159–61, 180–1, 201, 205, 212,
224–7, 229–30, 234, 248–52, 284
in genitive absolutes, 37–43

in papyri, 234–6
with διά + accusative, 112
with ἐν, 2–4, 92–4, 95, 137–43, 248–52,
287
with ὑπό + accusative, 112–13
νύκτας τε καὶ ἦμαρ, 289–92
νυκτὸς ἀμολγῷ, 5, 284
νύκτωρ, 6–7, 141–3, 156, 161, 180–1,
208, 224–7, 229–30, 235–6
frequency in different authors, 166
ὅλος, 22–4, 172–3
περί + accusative, 155
in approximative expressions, 107–16
ῥητός
as modifier of ἡμέρα, 83
σάββατον, 275
τυραννεύω, 189–93
ὑπό + accusative, 156, 235–6
in approximative expressions, 107–16
ὑστεραῖος
τῇ ὑστεραίᾳ, 1, 18
φθινόπωρον, 114–15
χεῖμα, 302
χειμών, 100–1
accusative of time, 67–8
dative of time, 202, 302
genitive of time, 95–7, 121–2, 131–5,
142–3, 206, 274
in genitive absolutes, 37–43
in papyri, 239–40
with ἐν, 100, 131–5, 142–3
τοῦ αὐτοῦ χειμῶνος, 27
τοῦ ἐπιγιγνομένου χειμῶνος, 27
χρόνος, 306
accusative of time, 69–70, 166–9
dative of time, 145–7, 269–72
genitive of time, 103–6, 144–5
in approximative expressions, 115–16,
147–52
Thucydides vs. Xenophon, 155–6
with διά + genitive, 55, 70–1, 123, 158–9
with ἐν, 103–6, 144–54, 169
with ἐπί + accusative, 75–6
with κατά + accusative, 147–52
χρόνῳ distinguished from dative of time,
52–5
ὥρα
accusative of time, 262–3
dative of time, 267–9

INDEX OF PASSAGES DISCUSSED

DEMOSTHENES
3.5: 176
6.35: 178
7.36: 176
18.35: 177
18.173: 178, 315
18.215: 178
21.16: 181
21.31: 183
21.34: 173
21.41: 171
21.56: 183
24.40: 175
24.113: 181
24.197: 173
25.11: 184
30.15: 176
33.5: 182
42.7: 172
42.26: 176
47.42: 171
47.65: 184
49.60: 175
50.10: 180
50.61: 224
53.15: 181
54.3: 182
57.10: 177
59.99: 181
59.116: 177

DIODORUS SICULUS
11.21.5: 213
11.81.5: 215
13.56.1: 217
13.86.3: 216
13.91.4: 215
13.108.4: 215

14.46.6: 214
14.61.2: 313
14.61.4: 211
15.1.6: 214
15.18.2: 215

EPICTETUS
2.6.19: 228
2.18.3: 228
Fr. 23: 228

HERODOTUS
1.14.4: 190
1.102.1: 192
1.111.1: 188
1.130.1: 191
1.163.2: 192
1.166.1: 192
2.22.4: 188
2.42.6: 195
2.93.6: 202
2.121α.3: 198
2.137.2: 191
2.161.2: 192
3.55.1: 186
3.57.2: 196
3.85.2: 197
3.86.1: 200
4.140.4: 198
4.159.1: 193
4.172.2: 201
5.65.3: 191
5.92η.1: 195
5.112.1: 185
5.116.1: 186
5.121.1: 199
6.42.1: 210
6.69.1: 201

6.107.1: 200
7.12.1: 201
7.195.1: 202
7.203.1: 189
8.78.1: 197
8.107.1: 199
9.57.3: 195
9.101.2: 197
9.121.1: 210

HOMER
Il. 1.53–4: 292
Il. 5.23: 285
Il. 6.422: 293
Il. 8.404–5: 297
Il. 8.418–9: 297
Il. 8.529: 287
Il. 9.71–2: 289
Il. 9.362: 102
Il. 10.385–6: 111
Il. 11.690–1: 300
Il. 12.15: 296
Il. 14.258–61: 286
Il. 18.251–2: 287
Il. 21.45–7: 292
Il. 21.282–3: 302
Il. 22.151: 301
Il. 23.832–4: 297
Od. 1.16–17: 294
Od. 1.288: 297
Od. 2.104–5: 289
Od. 2.219: 297
Od. 2.345–6: 290
Od. 4.86: 298
Od. 7.118: 301
Od. 7.253–4: 102, 286
Od. 10.28: 292
Od. 11.190–2: 302
Od. 11.294–5: 295
Od. 12.75–6: 301
Od. 12.105: 293
Od. 12.312: 284
Od. 13.278: 103, 284
Od. 14.196–8: 298
Od. 14.292: 298
Od. 14.293–4: 295
Od. 15.33–4: 287
Od. 15.455–6: 298
Od. 19.149–50: 289

Od. 20.88: 286
Od. 24.139–40: 289

NEW TESTAMENT
1 Cor. 10:8: 264
2 Cor. 4:16: 264
Acts 8:11: 269
Acts 12:6: 267
Acts 13:19–20: 272
Acts 20:16: 262
Acts 23:11: 266
Acts 26:13: 275
Acts 27:23: 266
Jas. 5:5: 279
Jn. 2:20: 272
Jn. 4:52: 262
Jn. 6:39: 265
Jn. 6:40: 265
Jn. 7:37: 279
Jn. 14:9: 270
Lk. 1:5: 315
Lk. 1:59: 279
Lk. 1:74–5: 264
Lk. 8:27: 269
Lk. 8:29: 270
Lk. 12:20: 267
Lk. 17:34: 267
Lk. 23:12: 280
Mk. 14:30: 267
Mk. 15:34: 267
Mt. 22:23: 279, 314
Mt. 24:20: 274
Mt. 24:42: 263
Mt. 24:44: 268
Rev. 3:3: 262
Rev. 16:14: 276
Rev. 18:10: 268
Rev. 18:16–17: 268
Rom. 16:25: 272

PLATO
Cri. 44a7: 160
Grg. 471b5: 161
Lg. 656e5: 183
Lg. 758a8: 157
Lg. 758b7: 158
Lg. 810b4: 163
Lg. 954d5: 164
Mx. 237d3: 167

Mx. 243a8: 165
Phd. 57a8: 309
Phd. 59d1: 271
Plt. 307e10: 163
Prt. 310a8: 160
Prt. 328e2: 169
R. 566d8: 165
Sph. 236e3: 168
Ti. 22d2: 158
Ti. 23a7: 159
Ti. 26a1: 158

PLUTARCH
Aem. 33.1: 221
Alc. 18.6: 219
Alc. 37.2: 218
Cam. 23.7: 220
Cam. 26.2: 227
Cam. 35.3: 220
Cam. 39.4: 218
Cam. 43.1: 223
Fab. 13.7: 218
Per. 28.7: 218
Rom. 12.5: 222
Them. 10.1: 218

POLYBIUS
1.1.5: 205
1.24.8: 210
1.74.9: 206
2.27.6: 208
3.50.9: 209
3.51.6: 209
4.80.16: 206
5.105.3: 211
5.107.4: 207

SEPTUAGINT
2 Chron. 7:8: 260
3 Kings 7:38: 260
3 Macc. 6:38: 260
Ex. 5:14: 246
Gen. 2:2: 255
Gen. 14:15: 246
Gen. 17:12: 253
Gen. 21:4: 253
Gen. 27:45: 252
Gen. 31:40: 249
Gen. 34:25: 254, 314

Gen. 46:2: 249
Is. 48:7: 260
Lev. 25:22: 246

THUCYDIDES
1.2.2: 108
1.3.2: 104
1.6.3: 183
1.18.3: 69
1.20.3: 55
1.30.3: 97
1.30.4: 97
1.33.2: 106
1.56.2: 311
1.87.6: 86
1.93.1: 105
1.93.3: 109
1.98.3: 52
1.100.2: 52
1.103.1: 53
1.115.2: 306
1.117.1: 114
1.118.2: 86, 309
2.3.4: 93
2.4.2: 55, 71, 305
2.13.3: 107
2.15.4: 85
2.18.4: 106
2.27.1: 97
2.31.1: 46, 114
2.57.2: 57
2.58.1: 99
2.58.2: 105
2.68.9: 98, 255, 314
2.73.1: 61
2.86.5: 73
2.92.6: 110
2.94.3: 55, 71
3.1.1: 46
3.7.1: 96
3.13.4: 98
3.17.3: 98
3.26.1: 95, 307
3.30.3: 92
3.51.1: 99, 307
3.51.4: 82
3.52.1: 48
3.68.3: 74
3.75.1: 78

329

3.86.1: 36
3.87.2: 35
3.88.1: 96
3.91.1: 36
3.94.1: 47
3.104.1: 95
3.107.3: 61, 304, 305
3.116.3: 109
4.1.3: 75, 305
4.2.1: 48
4.5.2: 30
4.6.2: 61
4.7.1: 107
4.23.2: 80
4.26.4: 30, 79, 308
4.27.1: 97
4.38.4: 32, 62
4.39.2: 113
4.44.1: 75
4.67.2–3: 67
4.68.2: 94
4.78.1: 48
4.85.4: 44
4.101.5: 112
4.103.4: 89
4.110.1: 92
4.118.12: 64
4.122.6: 52
4.130.1: 32, 91
4.131.3: 91
4.135.1: 56
5.3.5: 107
5.19.1: 45
5.20.3: 108
5.24.2: 46
5.25.3: 74
5.26.1: 108
5.32.1: 115
5.34.2: 54
5.35.7: 98
5.49.1: 96
5.59.1: 80
5.74.1: 104
5.79.1: 68
6.3.2: 86
6.4.4: 52
6.5.3: 54
6.8.1: 47
6.21.2: 85

6.27.1: 90
6.30.1: 83
6.56.2: 83
6.64.1: 110
6.65.1: 56
6.65.2–3: 110
6.88.5: 68
6.94.1: 48
6.97.1: 46
7.3.1: 30
7.6.4: 32, 89
7.19.3: 107
7.27.2: 79, 310
7.28.2: 97
7.28.3: 69
7.33.1: 113
7.40.2: 79
7.43.2: 80
7.43.6: 94
7.44.1: 84
7.51.2: 62
7.73.2: 62
7.73.3: 80, 94
7.74.1: 58
7.75.1: 78
7.77.6: 63
7.80.3: 93
7.81.1: 114
7.82.1: 55, 71
7.85.2: 91, 307
8.2.2: 67
8.7.1: 48
8.23.1–2: 64
8.29.1: 104
8.35.4: 110
8.71.3: 79
8.76.1: 69
8.97.2: 69
8.99.1: 98
8.102.1: 91

XENOPHON
Ages. 2.1: 129
Ages. 5.3: 133
An. 1.2.6: 26
An. 1.7.18: 19, 310
An. 1.8.22: 146
An. 2.3.22: 154
An. 2.4.1: 59

An. 2.6.20: 35
An. 3.1.3: 21
An. 3.3.20: 136
An. 3.4.16: 46
An. 3.4.18: 12, 51
An. 3.4.31: 12
An. 3.4.35: 4, 140, 141
An. 4.2.4: 23
An. 4.2.16–17: 151
An. 4.2.17: 145
An. 4.6.12: 141
An. 5.6.1: 51
An. 5.8.14: 132
An. 5.8.24: 271
An. 6.4.25: 18
An. 7.1.40: 18
An. 7.2.21: 12
An. 7.6.1: 45
An. 7.6.7: 45
Cyn. 4.11: 122
Cyn. 6.13: 271
Cyr. 1.4.14: 57
Cyr. 1.6.25: 133
Cyr. 3.1.17: 13
Cyr. 3.3.26: 140
Cyr. 3.3.29: 20
Cyr. 5.3.28: 13
Cyr. 5.3.43: 4, 127, 139
Cyr. 5.3.44: 140
Cyr. 6.1.1: 56
Cyr. 6.2.34: 122
Cyr. 6.3.11: 183, 247
Cyr. 7.5.16: 138
Cyr. 7.5.25: 136
Cyr. 7.5.68: 15, 290, 310
Cyr. 8.1.18: 21
Cyr. 8.1.23: 152
Cyr. 8.5.9: 35
Cyr. 8.8.17: 133
Eq.Mag. 8.20: 125
HG 1.1.11: 142
HG 1.1.13: 136
HG 1.1.14: 1
HG 1.2.7: 11
HG 1.2.17: 131
HG 1.2.18: 147
HG 1.4.12: 20
HG 1.6.27: 2

HG 2.1.5: 45
HG 2.1.22: 135
HG 2.1.23: 50
HG 2.2.3: 136
HG 2.3.4–5: 150
HG 2.3.15: 146
HG 2.4.13: 183
HG 2.4.43: 147
HG 3.1.16: 309
HG 3.2.1: 12
HG 3.2.6: 43
HG 3.2.13: 152
HG 3.2.21–3: 149
HG 3.2.30: 131
HG 3.5.21: 26
HG 4.1.29: 147
HG 4.5.4: 136
HG 4.5.5: 14, 128
HG 4.6.5: 16
HG 4.6.11: 128
HG 5.1.19: 138
HG 5.3.1: 43
HG 5.3.24: 142
HG 5.4.58: 64, 119
HG 6.2.15: 152
HG 6.4.10: 148
HG 6.4.13: 148
HG 6.4.26: 140
HG 6.5.51: 145
HG 7.1.25: 145
HG 7.4.32: 23
Hier. 6.7: 148
Hier. 6.11: 153
Mem. 1.6.2: 134
Mem. 2.2.5: 11
Mem. 2.2.8: 119, 139
Mem. 3.11.16: 17
Mem. 4.2.12: 16
Mem. 4.3.4: 3, 137
Mem. 4.3.8: 132
Mem. 4.8.2: 129
Oec. 5.4: 134
Oec. 9.4: 135
Oec. 9.10: 123
Oec. 11.19: 150
Oec. 16.14: 127, 133
Vect. 1.4: 123
Vect. 4.23: 17

CPSIA information can be obtained
at www.ICGtesting.com
Printed in the USA
LVHW011933220520
656326LV00014B/264

9 781108 820257